Persecution a..d

Studies in the History of Religious and Political Pluralism

Volume 2

Edited by Richard Bonney

PETER LANG

Oxford · Bern · Berlin · Bruxelles · Frankfurt am Main · New York · Wien

Persecution and Pluralism

Calvinists and Religious Minorities
in Early Modern Europe 1550–1700

Richard Bonney
and D.J.B. Trim
(eds)

PETER LANG

Oxford · Bern · Berlin · Bruxelles · Frankfurt am Main · New York · Wien

Bibliographic information published by Die Deutsche Bibliothek
Die Deutsche Bibliothek lists this publication in the Deutsche
Nationalbibliografie; detailed bibliographic data is available on
the Internet at ‹http://dnb.ddb.de›.

British Library and Library of Congress Cataloguing-in-Publication Data:
A catalogue record for this book is available from *The British Library*,
Great Britain, and from *The Library of Congress*, USA

ISSN 1661-1985
ISBN 3-03910-570-1
US-ISBN 0-8204-7597-1

© Peter Lang AG, International Academic Publishers, Bern 2006
Hochfeldstrasse 32, Postfach 746, CH-3000 Bern 9, Switzerland
info@peterlang.com, www.peterlang.com, www.peterlang.net

Printed in Germany

Contents

Abbreviations

Add. MS(S)	Additional Manuscript(s)
Bod. Lib	Bodleian Library, Oxford
BL	British Library, London
BN	Bibliothèque Nationale, Paris
BSHPF	*Bulletin de la Société de l'Histoire du Protestantisme Français*
DNB	*Dictionary of National Biography*
HMC	Historical Manuscripts Commission
HJ	*Historical Journal*
JEH	*Journal of Ecclesiastical History*
LSF	Library of the Society of Friends, London
n.d.	No date
P&P	*Past and Present*
PRO	The National Archives, U.K. (formerly Public Record Office)
RO	Record Office

Contributors

RICHARD BONNEY was Professor of Modern History at the University of Leicester from 1984 until his retirement in 2006. The Founding Editor of *French History*, he was President of the Society for the Study of French History in 2003–2005, Director of the European State Finance Project, and is also a non-stipendiary priest in the Church of England. He has published numerous books on European, political, financial and religious history. His latest book is *Jihad: From Qur'an to bin Laden* (Basingstoke, 2004).

JOHN COFFEY is Reader in Early Modern History at the University of Leicester. He has published numerous articles and book chapters, and is the author of *Politics, Religion and the British Revolutions: The Mind of Samuel Rutherford* (Cambridge, 1997) and *Persecution and Toleration in Protestant England, 1558–1689* (London, 2000). He has recently completed *John Goodwin and the Puritan Revolution: Religion and Intellectual Change in Seventeenth-Century England* (London, 2006).

CHRISTOPHER DURSTON (1951–2005) was Professor of History at St Mary's College, Twickenham and then Senior Lecturer at the University of Plymouth in 2004–2005. He published widely on seventeenth-century British history. His books included *The Family and the English Revolution* (Oxford, 1989), biographies of *James I* and *Charles I* (London, 1993, 1998), and, last to appear, *Cromwell's Major Generals: Godly Government during the English Revolution* (Manchester, 2001).

PAUL C.-H. LIM is Assistant Professor of Historical and Systematic Theology at Gordon-Conwell Theological Seminary, Massachusetts, USA. He is the author of *In Pursuit of Purity, Unity and Liberty:*

Richard Baxter's Puritan Ecclesiology in its Seventeenth-Century Context (Leiden, 2004).

JUDITH POLLMANN is Tutor in History at Somerville College and University Lecturer in Modern History, University of Oxford. She has published on early-modern European religious history in German, Dutch and English, including *Religious Choice in the Dutch Republic: The Reformation of Arnoldus Buchelius* (Manchester, 1999). She is currently working on a book on Catholic responses to religious change in the sixteenth-century Low Countries.

LUC RACAUT is Lecturer in Early Modern History at the University of Newcastle. In addition to publishing a number of scholarly papers, he is the author of *Hatred in Print: Catholic Propaganda and Protestant Identity during the French Wars of Religion* (Oxford, 2002). He is at present working on a book on the Catholic reformation in France.

BRIAN E. STRAYER, Professor of History at Andrews University, in Michigan, USA, is the author of *Lettres de cachet and Social Control in the Ancien Regime, 1659–1789* (Oxford, 1992), *Huguenots and Camisards as Aliens in France, 1589–1789* (Lampeter, 2001) and *Bellicose Dove: Claude Brousson and Huguenot Resistance to Louis XIV, 1647-1698* (Brighton, 2003).

D. J. B. TRIM is Lecturer in History at Newbold College, and Visiting Research Fellow, School of History, at the University of Reading. He has published numerous papers and edited *The Chivalric Ethos and the Development of Military Professionalism* (Leiden, 2003) and *Cross, Crown and Community: Religion, Government and Culture in Early-Modern England 1400–1800* (Oxford, 2004).

MARY TRIM was at the time of writing Senior Lecturer in Children's Literature at the University of Loughborough. She is the author of many scholarly articles and chapters and of *Growing and Knowing: A Selection Guide for Children's Literature* (München, 2004). Now retired, she is still actively researching: her current project is the role of children in early-modern English non-conformancy.

DAVID L. WYKES is Director of Dr Williams's Library, London, having been for many years on the staff at University of Leicester; he still teaches, as guest lecturer at Harris Manchester College, Oxford. His publications include many articles in scholarly journals on nonconformist history.

Preface

This volume is the ultimate outcome of a colloquium, held at Newbold College in September 1999 and supported by the British Academy, on religious minorities and the enforcement of conformity in Europe since the Reformation. Lasting four days and attended by over eighty delegates from eighteen countries, it was held to mark an anniversary: the 125th anniversary of the Seventh-day Adventist church in Britain and Europe; but it was not simply to *commemorate* a century and a quarter of one Protestant denomination's existence in Europe. Rather, the anniversary was the *occasion* to consider a significant problem: the extent to which different churches, even different faiths, can exist (and co-exist) in a pluralist, *secular* society.

Two volumes of essays have emerged from that conference, but neither are proceedings volumes.[1] In each volume, essays especially commissioned in order to ensure fuller treatment of the subject matter supplement papers delivered at the conference, the authors of which have in the interim made (often considerable) changes and additions in the light of the original vigorous discussions, of further research and, in some cases, of peer review.

The problem this volume considers has only become of greater importance since the conference. It is of great historical interest, but it is also of vital importance today. The challenges of multi-culturalism and increasingly diverse religious beliefs seem to threaten to fragment the unity of Western society. Even before '9/11' there were signs that the late twentieth-century pluralist consensus was breaking down; the apparent threat of Islamic extremism has induced even greater anxiety that this might be the case. Five centuries ago, Europe was one – but the spiritual unity of Christendom was ruptured by the Protestant Reformation, which led to intense intolerance and religious violence.

---

1   See also Richard Bonney and D. J. B. Trim (eds), *Religious Minorities and the Development of Pluralism in Modern Britain and France*, Studies in the History of Religious and Political Pluralism, II (Oxford and Bern, 2006).

The last half-century has seen the culmination of a gradual trend away from persecution, towards pluralism; but might that trend now be reversed? Fear of cults and of faiths or confessions perceived as alien has led several European states once more to seek to control the religious practices of their citizens. These papers are presented in the hope that a greater historical understanding may be gained from them and that they may provide some insight into current dilemmas.

The editors are deeply grateful to the British Academy for its award of a British Conference Grant. This funding enabled scholars from Eastern Europe and South Asia to attend, when they could not otherwise have done so, and allowed all costs to be covered. Smaller grants from the Royal Historical Society and the Newbold Alumni Association, making possible discounted attendance for postgraduate students, were much appreciated. At a later stage, subventions from the University of Leicester, Centre for the History of Religious and Political Pluralism (courtesy of the Sternberg Foundation) and the Newbold College Staff Development Committee helped to defray the expenses of publication.

Thanks also go to Andrew Willis and Nefisa Dizdarevic for their valuable assistance at the original conference; and to Jeremy Tidwell and Dr Gillian Hawkes for their invaluable work preparing camera-ready copy, without which the volume would not have made it to press.

Richard Bonney
D. J. B. Trim

RICHARD BONNEY AND D. J. B. TRIM

Introduction

The essays in this volume examine religious diversity in early modern Europe through a consideration of the experiences of Calvinists up to the early eighteenth century. Both courageous resisters of persecution and zealous oppressors of others, Calvinists provide an ideal lens to study the dialectic between persecution and pluralism. In the sixteenth century, Europe, having for a millennium constituted 'Christendom', suddenly became multi-confessional. Many statesmen, prelates and people in general preferred to try to recreate, by force if need be, the old confessionally unitary continent, rather than learning to get along. Understanding these responses is important historically, if we are to understand why European society developed as it did, but it is also potentially valuable as it struggles to reconcile individualism and sectarianism with continuity and stability. National communities are increasingly multi-ethnic and multi-faith, as well as multi-cultural, in character. They typically comprise a plurality of fundamental opinions and inherited cultures; can they relate to each other without involving either oppression or anarchy? Is it possible both to respect differences and to ensure the continuity and stability of the state?

This volume does not pretend to answer those questions – but it does provide some of the material on which answers will need to be based. To find solutions to the problems posed by pluralism, historical perspective is essential, because people frequently respond in similar ways to similar circumstances. Thus, the past often does have lessons to teach us about the present and insights to offer for the future. In addition, many issues that divide cultures reflect historic divergences between religions; if these are not properly understood, then attempts at interfaith and intercultural bridge-building are more likely to end in disaster.

I   Subject Matter, Purpose and Structure

The essays in this volume are historical, not sociological: they do not
attempt to apply historical 'lessons' directly to the present, nor do they
propose solutions to modern problems. Their collective purpose is to
increase awareness and understanding of the historical context of
persecution, and of the origins of pluralism in early modern Europe.
The historicised understanding of religious diversity that they provide
has, however, much to offer to debates over pluralism. This volume is
not only aimed at historians, but also at political and social scientists,
and scholars working across the humanities.

A work using the word 'pluralism' in its title needs to supply
some definitional framework, inasmuch as the term has a wide variety
of meanings. Philosophically, it is the recognition that there is more
than one ultimate principle or kind of being; and the principle that it is
the multiplicity and diversity of things, rather than their unity, that is
foundational to understanding the universe; but it is also the concept
that the plurality of different value systems is a positive. In political
science it is the ideal that power should be dispersed among functional
and cultural groups, such as religious sects, trade unions, professional
organizations and ethnic minorities, rather than concentrated in the
hands of a single elite or group of elites. It asserts that diversity is
beneficial to society and that minority cultural, ethnic and religious
groups should therefore maintain their distinctive cultural values and
practices, retaining their identity, rather than being subsumed within
one constructed national or communal identity.

Intrinsic to pluralism, then, is the contrast between a group, on
the one hand, and, on the other, a larger whole of which the group is a
part. Academic study of pluralism has mostly been in the disciplines
of political theory and the history of political ideas, and has focused
on the relations between associations – whether parties, churches or
voluntary groups – and the state and society of which they are a part,
and especially on the value that such associations can have for society
as a whole. But pluralism, of course, can also be understood in other
ways. As enhanced mobility of persons and of ideas has transformed

homogeneous societies into heterogeneous ones, so the relationships between individual groups and larger wholes have assumed crucial practical importance and become the subject of greater critical debate. Leaving aside the recent concept of 'comprehensive pluralism' advanced by Michael Rosenfeld,[1] the academic study of pluralism now takes a number of forms and considers a number of issues:

(i)   associational pluralism, which considers the importance of associations in sustaining democracy;

(ii)   questions about social identity, such as those connected with gender;

(iii)   the human race and its place within the world's eco-system;

(iv)   relationships between different religions and the different confessions or communions within the different faiths, whether at an institutional or personal level;

(v)   states and their role in international society;

(vi)   institutional relations between states and larger confederal or federal organizations.

Integral to all, however, is a concern for how the individual group and the larger whole can be related to each other without involving either oppression or anarchy, and how individuality can be harmonised with continuity and stability.

This latter problem was real and immediate in post-Reformation Europe, where religious unity had been fundamental for centuries, and where confessional plurality generally resulted in chaos. In religious terms, 'pluralism' has two different meanings. It can mean a system in which multiple faiths or confessions coexist within a single polity or community, all accepting that other religious groups have the right to practice their faith, even if one or more of these assert primacy or superiority (whether in national heritage, value-systems, theology, or

---

1   This is 'a conception of the good that holds that protecting and encouraging the greatest possible proliferation of conceptions of the good that might peacefully coexist together is the good': Michael Rosenfeld, *Just Interpretations: Law Between Ethics and Politics* (California, 1998), chs 7 and 8. The authors acknowledge the assistance of Dr Ian Harris (University of Leicester) in the formulation of their definitions of pluralism.

practice) over all or most of the others, and even where one or more actually are more important, politically or numerically. No attempt is made to *enforce* conformity, even where proselytising takes place. It can also, however, have another meaning which is a development of the first – a principle that all faiths or confessions are of equal value, and that all ought not only to accept the existence of other religious groups, but also not to ascribe pre-eminence to any characteristic belief, practice, or quality, to or of any of them.

Most Christian churches now accept pluralism in the first sense; in the second it is accepted by some, particularly in the West – yet it is anathema to many others. It is the first form of pluralism with which the essays in this volume are chiefly concerned.

There are many studies of dissent and religious toleration in late medieval and early modern Europe.[2] Philosophical or theoretical texts

2   On Europe, see Joseph Lecler, *Histoire de la tolérance au siecle de la Réforme* (Paris, 1955); and as *Toleration and the Reformation*, trans. T. L. Westow (New York and London, 1960); Perez Zagorin, *How the Idea of Religious Toleration Came to the West* (Princeton, 2003) and David Nirenberg, *Communities of Violence: Persecution of Minorities in the Middle Ages* (Princeton, 1996). For national or regional overviews see W. K. Jordan, *The Development of Religious Toleration in England from the Beginning of the English Reformation to the Death of Queen Elizabeth* (London, 1932); John Coffey, *Religious Toleration in Seventeenth-Century England* (London, 2000); Joachim Whaley, *Religious Toleration and Social Change in Hamburg, 1529–1819* (Cambridge, 1985); Brian E. Strayer, *Huguenots and Camisards as Aliens in France, 1598–1789: The Struggle for Religious Toleration* (Lewiston, 2001); and Andrew R. Murphy, *Conscience and Community: Revisiting Toleration and Religious Dissent in Early Modern England and America* (Philadelphia, 2001). More detailed studies are incorporated in collections of essays: e.g. Béla K. Király (ed.), *Tolerance and Movements of Religious Dissent in Eastern Europe* (Studies on Society in Change, 1/East European Monographs, 13, 1975); W. J. Sheils, (ed.), *Persecution and Toleration* (Studies in Church History, 21, 1984); Ole Peter Grell, Jonathan I. Israel and Nicholas Tyacke (eds), *From Persecution to Toleration: The Glorious Revolution and Religion in England* (Oxford, 1991); Ole Peter Grell and Bob Scribner (eds), *Tolerance and Intolerance in the European Reformation* (Cambridge, 1996). Scott L. Waugh and Peter D. Diehl (eds), *Christendom and its Discontents: Exclusion, Persecution and Rebellion, 1000–1500* (Cambridge, 1997); C. Berkvens-Stevelinck, J. Israel and G. H. M. Posthumus Meyjes (eds) *The Emergence of Tolerance in the Dutch Republic* (Leiden, 1997); John Christian Laursen (ed.), *Religious Toleration: 'The Variety*

on toleration and pluralism also consider this period, since historians of political ideas conventionally date their origins, at least in Western civilisation, to early modern Europe.[3] However, the stark alternatives of oppression or toleration are not the only choices prompted by the emergence of religious diversity; as we will see, persecution and pluralism are not so much polarities as different ends of a spectrum; and the story of the journey from one to other is rarely a linear narrative of progress. The essays in this volume seek to amplify the full range of responses to religious diversity – it is in this broad approach, as well as in the more detailed knowledge supplied, that they make a new contribution.

The focus on Calvinists is also valuable. They could not accept, as the Lutherans did, that princes or city fathers could decide their subjects' or citizens' faith by fiat, leaving the losers of this contest for confessional acceptance obliged to emigrate to a state that did adhere to their confession, conform, or face dire punishment. Such a scheme could not be countenanced because of the Calvinist doctrine of divine predestination; where there were members of God's elect (the church invisible) – individuals chosen for salvation by God in the dawn of time – there must also be the church visible, with all the organisational and liturgical manifestations characteristic of the 'Reformed Church'. Thus, Calvinists from the first were unwilling to accept the idea of a confessionally unitary state – unless it was a Calvinist one. Calvinists

---

of Rites' from Cyrus to Defoe (New York, 1999); Ole Peter Grell and Roy Porter (eds), *Toleration in Enlightenment Europe* (Cambridge, 2000); Keith Cameron, Mark Greengrass and Penny Roberts (eds), *The Adventure of Religious Pluralism in Early Modern France* (Oxford and Bern, 2000); Ronald Po-chia Hsia and Henk van Nierop (eds), *Calvinism and Religious Toleration in the Dutch Golden Age* (Cambridge, 2002). See also Gerrit Voogt, *Constraint on Trial: Dirk Volckertsz Coornhert and Religious Freedom* (Sixteenth Century Essays and Studies, 52, 2000); and Hans R. Guggisberg, *Sebastian Castellio, 1515–1563: Humanist and Defender of Religious Toleration in a Confessional Age* (Aldershot, 2003).

3   E.g. John Plamenatz, *Man and Society: Political and Social Theories from Machiavelli to Marx*, new edn, rev. M. E. Plamentaz and Robert Wokler, vol. 1, *From the Middle Ages to Locke* (London and New York, 1992), ch. 3, esp. 83–9, 114–41. David Runciman, *Pluralism and the Personality of the State* (Cambridge, 1997), esp. ch. 2.

were heroic resisters of religious persecution and doughty warriors in the holy wars that their resistance ignited; they produced some of the most important arguments for religious toleration; but they were also intolerant of other confessions, not only when in a majority in a state, but even when a minority. There are striking superficial similarities between late sixteenth- and seventeenth-century Calvinists, and late twentieth- and twenty-first-century Muslims.[4] A fuller exploration of Calvinists' experience of and responses to, religious diversity is thus of particular relevance to current debates about pluralism.

Of the nine chapters that follow, four are based primarily on analysis of published texts: sixteenth-century French Catholic polemic and seventeenth-century English religious literature and treatises on toleration.[5] One is a synthesis of existing historical work and modern editions of contemporary documents.[6] Each of the remaining essays is based on archival sources, albeit with an admixture of contemporary published literature. On the whole, however, the questions asked of these sources, and the methods used to analyse them, are those of historians although two chapters additionally reflect psychological and theological approaches.[7]

Most essays are case-studies, though one is a long-term overview of a particular national history of 'persecution and pluralism'.[8] Three are studies of important issues in particular national contexts, in the mid- to long-term; one examines a particular community's experience of religious diversity.[9] The final four case-studies are more narrowly

---

4   A point recognised by scholars, but not yet subjected to sustained investigation. See Fredric Jameson, 'Religion and Ideology: A Political Reading of *Paradise Lost*', in Francis Barker, *et al* (eds), *Literature, Politics and Theory: Papers from the Essex Conference, 1976–94* (London and New York, 1986), 35–56, for a reading of Milton in light of the Iranian Revolution; and Daniel Benjamin and Steven Simon, *The Age of Sacred Terror* (New York, 2002), 81, who compare the causes and goals of latter-day Islamic extremists with those of early-modern Calvinists.

5   Chapters by Luc Racaut, John Coffey, Mary Trim and Paul C.-H. Lim.

6   Chapter by Richard Bonney.

7   Chapters by Mary Trim and Paul Lim, respectively.

8   Chapter by Richard Bonney.

9   Chapters by Luc Racaut, Judith Pollman and John Coffey, and chapter by Mary Trim, respectively.

focused, thematically and chronologically, but cast light on important subjects.[10] The essays do collectively reflect the full geographic and chronological range of the Calvinist experience in early modern Europe. However, they are not evenly distributed across the continent or period and thus there are some gaps in the volume's coverage.

Furthermore, although the case-study approach means that issues are covered in depth, rather than superficially, there is a greater need for the main themes to be extrapolated. Thus, while this introduction begins with a précis of the essays, it goes on to address wider issues and in doing so partially fills some of the gaps in the essays' coverage, drawing on evidence from those areas and eras not addressed by any of the chapters.

The most unfortunate of these gaps are the lack of considerations of Calvinism in Scotland, which strongly influenced both the English and Dutch Reformed Churches; and in Germany, Transylvania and Poland – not the heartlands of the Reformed Church, but all countries in which Calvinists were minorities. Another apparent lacuna is that there are no studies of the Huguenots *per se*. As there is a wealth of scholarship on the subject, however, we include essays that important and innovative in the issues they explore or their treatment of them, rather than simple overviews of existing scholarship – we have drawn on this in any case, in sketching out themes, issues, and conclusions.[11] A reconsideration of the process by which Calvin and his lieutenants achieved a monopoly of French Protestantism in the 1550s–60s would have been valuable, but this ultimately proved impossible.[12]

---

10 Chapters by Christopher Durston, Paul Lim, Brian E. Strayer and David L. Wykes.

11 Important works in English are Nicola Sutherland, *The Huguenot Struggle for Recognition* (New Haven and London, 1980); Philip Benedict, *Rouen during the Wars of Religion* (Cambridge, 1981); idem, *The Huguenot Population of France, 1600–1685: The Demographic Fate and Customs of a Religious Minority* (Transactions of the American Philosophical Society, 81:5, 1991); idem, *The Faith and Fortunes of France's Huguenots, 1600–1685* (Aldershot, 2000); Barbara B. Diefendorf, *Beneath the Cross: Catholics and Huguenots in Sixteenth-Century Paris* (New York and Oxford, 1991).

12 Robert M. Kingdon, *Geneva and the Consolidation of the French Protestant Movement 1564–1572: A Contribution to the History of Congregationalism, Presbyterianism, and Calvinist Resistance Theory* (Travaux d'Humanisme et

There are no studies of Calvinists in Switzerland – the heartland of the movement, of course. But, again, Swiss Calvinism is well documented in modern scholarship.[13] And Calvinists were neither in a minority, nor tolerated other minorities, in those cantons where they dominated, so this is not as serious a gap as it may seem.

There are no studies of *sixteenth*-century English Calvinism. This means nothing on the origins of Puritanism, or the relationship of Calvinists to the national church created by the Elizabethan settlement, often said (by Anglican historians) to have been a conscious *via media* (middle way) between Rome and Geneva. There is also nothing on the persecution of Presbyterians in the 1580s–90s or the persecution of Puritans by the Caroline regime in the 1620s–30s. There is a vast bibliography of work on these subjects, though, so that there is no need for another potted history; and, again, we draw on this wealth of scholarship later in the introduction.[14]

Renaissance 112, 1967). There are now important studies by Denis Crouzet and Thierry Wanegffelen. Crouzet, *La genèse de la Réforme française, 1520–1562* (Paris, 1996); idem, *Jean Calvin* (Paris, 2000). Wanegffelen, *Ni Rome ni Genève. Des fidèles entre deux chaires en France au xvie siècle* (Paris, 1997); idem, *Une difficile fidélité: Catholiques malgré le concile en France, XVIe–XVIIe siècles* (Paris, 1999); idem (ed.), *De Michel de l'Hospital á l'édit de Nantes. Politique et religion face aux Eglises* (Clermont Ferrand, 2002).

13   E.g. in English by Robert M. Kingdon, *Geneva and the Coming of the Wars of Religion in France 1555–1563* (Travaux d'humanisme et renaissance, 22; 1956); E. W. Monter, *Calvin's Geneva* (New York: 1967); William G. Naphy, *Calvin and the Consolidation of the Genevan Reformation* (Manchester, 1994, with a new preface, Louisville and London, 2003).

14   Key works are Patrick Collinson, *The Elizabethan Puritan Movement* (London, 1967); idem, *Godly People: Essays on English Protestantism and Puritanism* (London, 1983); Peter Lake, *Moderate Puritans and the Elizabethan Church* (Cambridge, 1982); idem, *Anglicans and Puritans? Presbyterianism and English Conformist Thought from Whitgift to Hooker* (London and Boston, 1988); idem, *The Boxmaker's Revenge: 'Orthodoxy', 'Heterodoxy' and the Politics of the Parish in Early Stuart London* (Manchester, 2001); Nicholas Tyacke, *Anti-Calvinists: The Rise of English Arminianism c.1590–1640* (Oxford, 1987); Michael Walzer, *The Revolution of the Saints* (London, 1966); Paul S. Seaver, *The Puritan Lectureships: The Politics of Religious Dissent, 1560–1662* (Stanford, 1970); J. S. McGee, *The Godly Man in Stuart England: Anglicans, Puritans, and the Two Tables, 1620–1670* (New

There are also no studies of the Calvinist refugee communities in England, made up of émigrés from France, the Low Countries, Spain and Italy. These are, however, another much-studied phenomenon and have been considered from many perspectives, including as religious minorities; again, rather than commissioning a brief overview we have preferred to utilise existing scholarship in the introduction.[15] Finally, there is nothing on the interactions of Calvinists and Jews. For all the intolerance of Calvinist regimes, they had a strong affinity with the Old Testament and with the messianic prophecy that if the ten lost tribes of Israel were once more gathered together then the second coming of Christ was at hand:[16] these motives led them to grant

Haven and London, 1976); R. J. Acheson, *Radical Puritans in England, 1550–1660* (London, 1990); Peter White, *Predestination, Policy and Polemic: Conflict and Consensus in the English Church from the Reformation to the Civil War* (Cambridge, 1992); Kenneth Fincham (ed.), *The Early Stuart Church, 1603–1642* (Basingstoke, 1993); Anthony Milton, *Catholic and Reformed: The Roman and Protestant Churches in English Protestant Thought, 1600–1640* (Cambridge, 1995); Judith D. Maltby, *Prayer Book and People in Elizabethan and Early Stuart England* (Cambridge, 1998); Peter Lake and Michael Questier (eds), *Conformity and Orthodoxy in the English Church, c.1560–1660* (Woodbridge, 2000).

15 Notably Andrew Pettegree, *Foreign Protestant Communities in Sixteenth-Century London* (Oxford, 1986); Ole Peter Grell, *Dutch Calvinists in Early Stuart London: The Dutch Church at Austin Friars 1603–1642* (Leiden, 1989); idem, *Calvinist Exiles in Tudor and Stuart England* (Aldershot, 1996); Charles Littleton, '"Geneva on Threadneedle Street": The French Church of London and its Congregations, 1560–1625' (Unpubl. Ph.D. thesis, University of Michigan, 1996); Andrew Spicer, *The French-Speaking Reformed Community and their Church in Southampton, 1567–c.1620* (Huguenot Society, n.s. 3/Southampton Records Series, 39, 1997); Nigel Goose and Lien Luu (eds), *Immigrants in Tudor and early Stuart England* (Brighton, forthcoming).

16 In 1644 Menasseh met Antonio de Montesinos, who persuaded him that some at least of the North American Indians were the descendants of the lost ten tribes of Israel and that one of these tribes was living in the Ecuadorean jungle. This supposed discovery gave a new impulse to Menasseh's Messianic hopes. But he was convinced that the Messianic age needed as its precursor the settlement of Jews in all parts of the known world. Filled with this idea, he turned his attention to England, whence the Jews had been expelled since 1290. Menasseh published *The Hope of Israel* in an English edition in 1650. The great artist Rembrandt was associated with Menasseh's movement. In 1655 Rembrandt

toleration to Jewish minorities. This was particularly true of the Dutch Republic. It was from Holland that Cromwell summoned Rabbi Menasseh ben Israel after receiving his seven-point plan for the readmission of the Jews in November 1655. On 18 December, Cromwell dismissed an advisory conference which had failed to reach a decision, letting the members know that he intended to admit the Jews unofficially if necessary. It is significant that the only time that Jewish scholars and adventurers, poets and writers, lived freely and could practise their religion in Portuguese-controlled Brazil was during the twenty-four years of Dutch occupation of the northeast (1630–54).

The following summary of the essays' contents situates each in contemporary developments, so that their significance is plain. This presages a discussion of issues fundamental to several chapters and themes that collectively emerge. The fundamental issues are amplified drawing on the wider scholarship on Calvinism and on religious toleration in this period. Finally, conclusions are drawn – both about the experience of different Calvinist communities as religious minorities, or interacting with religious minorities in early modern Europe; and wider conclusions about persecution, pluralism and religious diversity. These last are tentative – not so much conclusions, as hypotheses or questions that can be applied by students of pluralism and religious diversity in other places and at other times to their own areas or periods. By such generalizing the experiences of the first generations of Calvinists can hopefully be more readily integrated into the more general history of religious and political pluralism, envisaged by the series this volume inaugurates.

illustrated the rabbi's messianic treatise, *Piedra Gloriosa*, a book which emerged from, and was fashioned to appeal directly to, the movement within Dutch Protestantism known as 'philosemitism': Michael Zell, *Reframing Rembrandt. Jews and the Christian Image in Seventeenth-Century Amsterdam* (Los Angeles and Berkeley, 2002).

II National Contexts

Two chapters focus on France. France was pivotal for Calvinists – had the Huguenots, as they were called in France, been successful in propagating their faith, they would have brought one of the two great centralised monarchies of Europe under the sway of the Reformed Churches. Also, Calvinism in France was remarkably cohesive – the fruit partly of conscious efforts by Calvin and his lieutenants to ensure that Protestantism in France equated to Calvinism. The resoluteness and organization of Calvinists in France provoked a similarly resolute response from Catholics. The result was eight civil wars in thirty-six years – or, according to a recent history, about a dozen in sixty-seven years – of civil wars; even when the monarchy was nominally at peace with the Reformed Church and its aristocratic leaders, confessionally motivated communal violence between citizens was commonplace.[17]

The first chapter, by Luc Racaut, is a study of the discourse of persecution. He shows the importance of propaganda in producing the white-hot confessional environment that resulted in the notorious St Bartholomew's Massacre (24 September 1572) and a myriad of other, smaller riots, affrays and massacres. Popular opinion was probably already polarised over Protestantism, but Catholic polemicists made concentrated efforts to ensure that such initiatives as there were for tolerance and co-existence failed. France is also important because, thanks partly to the Huguenots' tenacity and organization, nearly forty years of civil wars (the *guerres de religion*) throughout the 1560s through to the 1590s, resulted in stalemate and the cession of religious toleration, granted by the crown in the Edict of Nantes, in 1598. France thereby became the first officially pluralist state in Europe.[18]

---

17   Cf. Mack P. Holt, *The French Wars of Religion, 1562–1629* (Cambridge, 1995); and Natalie Zemon Davis, 'The Rites of Violence: Religious Riot in Sixteenth-Century France', *P&P*, no. 59 (1973): 51–91; Denis Crouzet, *Les guerriers de Dieu. La violence au temps des troubles de religion, vers 1525–vers 1610* (2 vols, Paris, 1990).

18   See Cameron, Greengrass and Roberts (eds), *Adventure of Religious Pluralism in Early Modern France.*

But the Edict of Nantes was predicated on the presumptions that evangelism was a more effective way of dealing with Protestants than war or persecution – and that, in consequence, France would not be pluralist for long. When it became clear that not all Huguenots would convert the reaction was, ultimately, persecution, in an attempt to recreate the confessionally unitary state. This process is examined by Brian E. Strayer in his chapter. Over the seventeenth century, a discourse of religious toleration had developed (the British dimensions of which are analysed by John Coffey in his chapter), partly in response to the horrors engendered by the Europe-wide wars of religion of *c.*1560–1650. Whereas voices pleading for acceptance of religious diversity in the 1560s had been easily drowned out, a hundred years and more after, there was a much wider willingness to consider a persecutory response to pluralism objectionable. It was only after a sustained campaign by the clergy of the Catholic Church in France that Louis XIV gave way to his instincts, despite contrary counsels from some of his ministers, and went ahead with the revocation of the Edict of Nantes.

The Netherlands, like France, was a stronghold of Calvinism. But in the seventeenth-century Dutch Republic, unlike France, other forms of Protestantism flourished and there was no Reformed hegemony. To achieve victory over Spain in the Dutch Revolt it had been necessary to secure the active support of, or at least not to alienate, a wide cross-section of society and as a result Roman Catholics and Jews were effectively tolerated.[19] The Reformed Church had a pre-eminent status in society and in the Dutch polity, but it was never the state church. Thus the United Provinces, like France, became a pluralist state, if not exactly a tolerant one. Only Calvinists had the right to public worship and this monopoly was maintained against minority agitation, but all persons had freedom of conscience. All religious groups in the Dutch Republic were thus in the unusual position (for early modern Europe) of existing in an open religious economy. However, this did not result

---

19   J. L. Motley, *History of the United Netherlands: From the Death of William the Silent to the Twelve Years Truce 1609* (4 vols, New York, 1879–80), 3: 264–5; Jonathan I. Israel, *The Dutch Republic: Its Rise, Greatness, and Fall 1477–1806* (pb. edn, Oxford, 1998), 162, 164, 194–5, 215, 362–6.

in the tacit acceptance of the existence of multiple faith communities, but rather in a competitive confessional market for followers, the ramifications of which Judith Pollmann examines in her chapter. Multi-confessionalism resulted in what Dr Pollmann terms 'confessional segregation', and the strengthening of confessional identity, defined in opposition to rivals. The pluralist religious economy did not result in any lessening of hostility between the rival confessions, even if inter-confessional tension did not break out into actual hostilities.

Calvinism's association with Switzerland, France, Scotland and New England is very widely known; its importance in England, the Netherlands and parts of Germany is certainly familiar to historians. Less well-known is that Calvinism was an important minority faith in Eastern Europe.[20] In medieval Hungary, the Roman Catholic Church had been so closely bound to the king and his estates that it has been described as a 'state church' rather than an independent institution.[21] But this was to change. The chapter by Richard Bonney is an overview of the experience of religious diversity in Hungary, from the point of view of its Calvinist community, between the national disaster at Mohács in 1526 and the Peace of Szatmár in 1711. Hungary in this period was divided not just confessionally, between Catholic, Protestant and Muslim, but also politically, between the Habsburgs and the Ottomans. Therefore, as Professor Bonney identifies, it was 'a testing ground [...] of religious and political pluralism over almost two centuries'. He concludes that

> from being in the *avant-garde* of political and religious pluralism in the era of partition and rebellion between 1526 and 1711, Hungary in the era of the strict application of the *decretalis* oath had fallen very much into the European rearguard. It was not until Joseph II's reign that nearly a century of persecution was halted with the Patent of Toleration of 1781.

20 Graeme Murdock, *Calvinism on the Frontier, 1600–1660: International Calvinism and the Reformed Church in Hungary and Transylvania* (Oxford, 2000) is a recent valuable study of the latter two countries.
21 János M. Bak, 'Politics, Society and Defense in Medieval and Early Modern Hungary', in idem and Béla K. Király (eds), *From Hunyadi to Rákóczi: War and Society in Late Medieval and Early Modern Hungary* (Studies on Society in Change, 12/East European Monographs, 104; 1982), 1.

The remaining chapters are all on seventeenth-century England. Calvinism was of course important in sixteenth-century England and its history involved some persecution – of the movement generally, but briefly, by the regime of 'Bloody' Mary; and of those zealous presbyterians who doggedly defied Elizabeth I's preference for episcopal ecclesiastical government. But the Elizabethan Church of England was essentially Calvinist, in theology if not ecclesiology. Convicted Calvinists ('Puritans') were almost certainly a plurality, if not a majority, of English Protestants; only an extreme Calvinist sect, not Calvinists, was persecuted by an Anglican hierarchy which mostly subscribed to Calvinist doctrine while rejecting Reformed church government. Persecution of Roman Catholics, anti-Trinitarians and radical Protestant sects such as the Anabaptists and Family of Love, meanwhile, was carried out partly for political reasons and was not the fruit of a strictly Calvinist point of view, since Lutherans (and Catholics) also persecuted Anabaptists and anti-Trinitarians. Thus, the focus is not here on the English and Welsh Calvinist experience in the sixteenth century.

In the seventeenth century, English Calvinists passed through a unique trajectory. This might be described as the evolution from a marginalised minority under Charles I and Archbishop Laud to a group which gained political power at the centre in the 1640–2 and then won the civil war. Thereafter the group fragmented into Presbyterians, Independents and other sectaries. Cromwell tried to rally all the 'godly' into his cause (see Christopher Durston's chapter), but increasingly this was perceived as an attempt by a minority to impose a particular form of conformity on the majority. Following the restoration of Charles II, the Calvinists once more became a minority. Along the way, some of the most important early proponents of religious toleration emerged in England and New England. However, they had little success in England until the Interregnum brought Oliver Cromwell to power as Lord Protector, while in New England, the tolerationist colony of Rhode Island owed its location to fact that its celebrated founder, Roger Williams, was expelled from Massachusetts so obnoxious were his views on toleration to its Calvinist population. However, Parliamentary victory in the Civil Wars owed much to members of Protestant minorities – mobilised by Parliament due to the exigencies of war and unwilling, having helped achieve victory, to give up the effective liberty of conscience of wartime. Cromwell was disinclined to persecute other Protestants (especially former comrades in arms) over 'matters indifferent', or *adiaphora* – that is, those things 'neither commanded nor proscribed' clearly by scripture.[22] Indeed, in practice Cromwell was not even enthusiastic about persecuting Roman Catholics. The freedom of religion granted, in practical terms, to Congregationalists, various kinds of Baptists, Muggletonians, Quakers (examined by Mary Trim in her chapter), Ranters and others during the Interregnum effectively let out of the bottle the genie of confessional multiplicity that generations of ecclesiastical and political leaders had worked to keep confined.[23] Attempts by the restored Stuart monarchy and Anglican hierarchy to re-establish a confessionally unitary state foundered on the determined resistance of both mainstream and Independent Calvinists, who had now to learn to live as a permanent minority.

The arguments for and against religious toleration and reasons an unwilling government and church hierarchy eventually adopted it, are the subject of chapter 5, by John Coffey. Along with the emergence of multiple confessions came the emergence of scepticism – disbelief in any revealed religion, though at this stage tending more towards deism than atheism. In the story of the emergence of toleration, as usually told, these sceptics and their arguments are given a starring role. But Dr Coffey shows that radical sceptics did not always favour toleration, which was more commonly argued for by devout Christians. More, it was the dogged (and dogmatic!) refusal of Calvinist minorities to conform, obliging the state and state church to grant a modicum of toleration, which was ultimately responsible for toleration passing from the texts of political theorists to a legal enactment. Thus, Coffey argues, the emergence of religious pluralism in early modern England owed more to militants than it did to moderates. Yet, even as many Calvinists were refusing to compromise with any other confession,

---

22 Quoted by Paul Lim in his chapter.
23 D. J. B. Trim and P. J. Balderstone (eds), 'Introduction', to *Cross, Crown and Community: Religion, Government and Culture in Early Modern England, 1400–1800* (Oxford, Bern, New York and Frankfurt am Main, 2004).

others were moving towards accepting confessional pluralism – a process examined by Paul Lim in his chapter.

It was the culmination of developments during the Interregnum. The Protectoral government sought to build mobilise Calvinists of all sects in order to impose the 'reformation of manners' that 'the Godly' hoped would follow the Reformation of the Church – Christopher Durston examines these coalitions of the Godly and their efforts in his chapter. As a result, even though Puritanism had been fissured by the disputes between Presbyterians and Independents after the First Civil War, the different Calvinist factions (later to become different denominations) began to identify each other again as brethren. The actions of what Professor Durston regards as 'deeply unpopular local cliques of Puritans', ignoring their position as a minority in an attempt to impose their value system on the majority by force, was, he contends, a primary reason 'for the emphatic national repudiation of Puritanism which followed the return of Charles II in 1660'. The extraordinary transformation of English Calvinism from a pre-eminent theological force in the 1590s and a triumphant political force with widespread support in the 1640s, into a marginal movement by the 1690s, thus owes much to a Calvinist persecuting mentality – it is an exquisite irony that the Calvinist would-be enforcers of conformity of the 1650s became the heroic non-conformists of the late seventeenth and early eighteenth centuries. The persecution they endured (illuminated in the chapters by Mary Trim and David L. Wykes) was harsher and lasted longer than historiographical orthodoxy admits, as Dr Wykes points out. In enduring this persecution, Calvinists had in their favour the resolution and cohesion referred to already, but an additional important factor in their survival in late Stuart England was that they were finally able to develop an ecclesiology of 'Protestant diversity', as Dr Lim terms it, based on the principle of *adiaphora*. It was partly because Dissenters (a variety of Calvinists, as well as non-Calvinists) were able to act collectively that they survived persecution. Calvinists finally gave up the dream of a confessionally unitary, Calvinist, state and by doing so secured their own future within an England which had a new religious economy – one which, like the Netherlands, was in spite a monopolistic church, pluralist and would remain so.

III Fundamental Issues

Thus far we have been considering the theme of each chapter and how it fits into early modern European history. But what issues are basic to our understanding of all the chapters? What common themes emerge? One fundamental issue is the importance of early modern, rather than modern, concepts of persecution, toleration, church and state, and religious diversity. Sixteenth- and seventeenth-century writers often use similar terms to those we use today but often mean rather different things by them. Also, as might be expected, attitudes to these issues varied over Europe and over time and were frequently shaped by local exigencies, not theoretical ideals. We therefore undertake here a closer examination of post-Reformation understandings of, and attitudes to, religious diversity (or pluralism), persecution, toleration, ecumenism, and the appropriate relationship between the church and the state. We also consider what underpinned these attitudes. By pluralism here we do not mean a concept of all world-views or ideologies as being equal in value. Rather, we mean confessional pluralism: essentially religious diversity.

Sixteenth-Century Views of Persecution

Given the attitudes towards religious diversity, the ruling elites of early modern Christendom were naturally predisposed towards persecution of heretics and schismatics. Of course, the development of Protestantism led to a redefining, for some people at least, of what 'heretical' meant. There was also the fact that Protestanism was much stronger than any previous heretical movement, so that many more people now faced the sanctions of imprisonment or execution. The huge increase in numbers of people suffering horrible deaths helped to undermine the consensus that persecution was natural, indeed the only, response to religious plurality. It took time, however, for that standard position to fall. This was partly due to conservatism, but it was partly because of the early modern understanding of persecution.

One of the least helpful stereotypes of religious persecution is that seen in the latter parts of the movie adaptation of Umberto Eco's novel, *The Name of the Rose*, in which a harsh and hypocritical inquisitor, given the name of a real Dominican inquisitor, Bernardo Gui (d. 1331), burns three innocents at the stake, motivated by envy, sexual frustration and an unthinking intolerance of any opinions contrary to his own. Persecution is thus the fruit of bigotry and prejudice. The actual reasons for persecution are usually more complex. It may of course arise from simple intolerance, but may also arise from a general love of the sinner, whose sin is hated: if one wished to save people's eternal souls, then one must, if possible, compel them to see their errors. If punitive measures could achieve this, then persecution was still in everyone's best interests.

Execution was the ultimate sanction, but because it was imposed only on a heretic who refused to be corrected, by definition it could not help him or her to realise their errors. Yet even execution could still be imposed from the best intentions, rather than out of simple cruelty. For not only the soul of the heretic was at stake. Heresy was generally seen as insidious – it was characterised constantly as pollution, as an infectious disease such as leprosy, as a cancer.[24] It could not be localised. So even if Christian charity would provide the answer: that he or she must die, lest their infection spread, lest they taint or contaminate their entire community. Just as cutting out a cancer was harmful for the area of the body involved, but saved the body as a whole, so the Christian must steadfastly, unwaveringly cut out the cancer of heresy out of a body politic, so that the nation might be saved. Thus, even execution could be an act of love, to correct and save souls, for even though heretics, presumably, were damned, one would be saving the souls of all those around them.

Such a view of persecution and execution for religious reasons is probably repellent to most people today – covering acts of brutality under the shield of piety and charity will probably seem obnoxiously hypocritical. But simply to excoriate those who held such attitudes is the easy answer. To understand why early modern people acted as they did is a necessary precondition to understanding why they moved

24   Davis, 'Rites of Violence'; chapter by Luc Racaut, below.

away from such notions. This in turn may be helpful as we confront the classical liberal dilemma – of whether people who are inherently tolerant, open-minded Westerners propose imprisoning Muslims for expressing views with which they disagree not out of simple irritation at having to hear a contrary viewpoint, but out of sincere concern for the future of the liberal democratic state. There is little difference, in many respects, to the motivation of many (though clearly not all) early modern persecutors.

The ultimate extension of 'persecution as act of Christian love' was holy war. In the fifteenth century the Lollards, a heterodox movement in England, had condemned recourse to the Old Testament to justify use of violence against religious opponents, or conversion by force,[25] but this was very much a minority point of view and certainly had no impact on elites who of course actually conducted persecution and crusades. From the Catholic point of view, where heretics were in such numbers that they were a threat to an orthodox Christian society, as in France or the Netherlands, or had actually hijacked a state and so were a danger to their neighbours, as in England (or, earlier, Germany, as Charles V would have seen things), then it was not only legitimate, but necessary, for Catholic princes to wage war against them. Even the official backing given to the St Bartholomew Massacres by the Catholic ruler Charles IX might be viewed by the deluded king himself, and some of his entourage, as an act of Christian love.[26] Such attitudes could be held by otherwise liberal men. As Robert Stradling points out, Diego de Saavedra y Fajardo (1584–1648), a kinsman of Cervantes and, like him, a writer who had some scepticism about traditional values and was a proponent of peace, nevertheless had no doubt that 'war was often necessary in defence of true religion' and that 'the cross of crusade sanctioned all'.[27] And such attitudes could in turn lead to atrocities: the fifteenth-century wars against the Hussites

25   André Corvisier, *La guerre: Essais historiques* (Paris, 1995), 322.
26   Denis Crouzet, *La nuit de la Saint-Barthélemy: un rêve perdu de la Renaissance* (Paris, 1994). The interpretation, however, remains contentious.
27   R. A. Stradling, *Spain's Struggle for Europe, 1598–1668* (London, 1994), xv–xvi, citing Saavedra Fajardo, *Idea de un príncipe político-christiano* (Madrid, 1949), 70–1.

have been characterised as the cruellest wars of the Middle Ages in western Europe; massacres of wounded and prisoners were common in the French Wars of Religion and the Dutch Revolt. Religious war was notably harsh.[28]

Both Protestants and Catholics persecuted, and it may be that the 'Radical Reformation' only did not become persecutory because its protagonists never achieved political power, remaining a persecuted minority. Catholics and Protestants alike used the rhetoric of holy war in polemic and supported wars of religion in practice. Both sides even quoted the same Biblical texts to support intolerance. Thus, Edward VI was hailed by English Protestants as a 'new Josiah' – the original Josiah was a youthful king who came to the throne of Judah by providence and proceeded to attempt to purge idolatrous and impure religion from the Israelites. Edward VI seemed a perfect match, since during his minority (alas! he never lived to full maturity) the remnants of 'idolatrous' Catholic religion seemed to be being purged from Israel for good.[29] Such Old Testament referencing is often regarded as typically Calvinist, but it was also Catholic: the injunction that 'the Lord your God is a jealous God'[30] motivated both Calvinists to attack 'idolatrous' Roman practices and Catholics to extirpate heretics. In 1573, for example, the Cardinal de Lorraine also cited the example of Josiah in an address to Charles IX, who, like Josiah (and Edward) had come to the throne as a minor. Josiah had gathered the priests, lords and people of Judah to destroy the idols of Baal, *and* the actual unfaithful themselves – 'heretiques' as the Cardinal pointedly (and unscripturally) calls them – thereby destroying 'all other Religions

---

28   Corvisier, *La guerre*, 54–6, 328; Crouzet, *Les guerriers de Dieu*, i. 387–9; D. J. B. Trim, 'Fighting "Jacob's Wars". The Employment of English and Welsh Mercenaries in the European Wars of Religion: France and the Netherlands, 1562–1610 (unpubl. Ph.D thesis, University of London, 2002), 75–6. There is no overview of religious war in the period covered by this volume, though for a valuable treatment of the subject in a slightly earlier period see Norman Housley, *Religious Warfare in Europe, 1400–1536* (Oxford, 2002).

29   For Josiah see 2 Ki. Chs. 22–3 and 2 Ch. Chs. 34–5. On Edward VI see Diarmaid MacCulloch, *Tudor Church Militant: Edward VI and the Protestant Reformation* (London, 2000).

30   Ex. 20:5.

than the true one'. Charles was then urged to be the Josiah of France and so achieve a 'rebirth' of 'the faith and Catholic Religion'.[31]

Meanwhile, other attitudes towards persecution existed, ones that helped to reinforce minorities in their 'deviancy' rather than majorities in their persecutory resolution. The French theologian Augustin Marlorat, himself later martyred, declared that it is in being overcome themselves that the saints, in turn, overcome.[32] English Protestants believed that 'the true church of Christ [is] knowen in this, that it suffereth persecution, and doeth not persecute agayne'; indeed, one of the distinguishing characteristics of the 'whorish church of Antichriste [was] her bluddy persecutions'.[33] In other words, persecution was a sign of true religion and was for this reason to be embraced by true followers of Christ. Nobody in the sixteenth century seems to have declared that 'the blood of the martyrs is the seed of the church', but this concept was certainly alive – among both Protestants, and Catholics, a royal minister in France declaring, for example, that though zealous Catholics might 'slaughter a few [Huguenots], but the earth, fertilised by such calamities and drenched with their blood' would yield a rich harvest of many more.[34] As we will see, a concern that persecuted 'heretics' might in fact be Christian martyrs motivated the late sixteenth and the seventeenth centuries.

31 Fontainebleau, 28 May 1573, Bibliothèque Sainte-Geneviève MS 188, fos 348–50; and see Crouzet, *Les guerriers de Dieu*, i. 270, ii. 197.
32 Augustin Marlorat, *A Catholike exposition upon the Revelation of Sainct John*, English edn (London, 1574), fo.157r.
33 John Daus, intro. to English trans. Of Heinrich Bullinger, *A Hundred Sermons upon the Apocalips of Jesu Christe* (London, 1561), sig. Aiiir, in R. Bauckham, *Tudor Apocalypse* (Courtenay Library of Reformation Classics 8, 1979), 62, 66.
34 Loris Petris, 'Faith and Religious Policy in Michel de L'Hospital's Civic Evangelism', in Cameron, Greengrass and Roberts, *Adventure of Religious Pluralism in Early Modern France*, 136. See idem, 'Guerre et paix dans les *Carmina* de Michel de L'Hospital', *Bibliothèque d'Humanisme et Renaissance*, 61 (1999), 95–108; idem, *La Plume et la tribune. Michel de L'Hospital et ses discourse (1559–62). Suivi de l'édition du De sacra Francisci II. Galliarum regis initiatione, regnique ipsius administrandi providential, Mich.Hosp. Sermo (1559) et des discourse de Michel de L'Hospital (1560–1562)* (Geneva, 2002).

The Trend Towards Toleration (Sixteenth and Seventeenth Centuries)

Medieval attitudes towards religious diversity derived from St Augustine and were hostile to the concept. For Augustine, intolerance in pursuit of the unity of the Christian Church is a virtue, and tolerance only defensible when, due to political weakness, the presservation of the Church requires accommodation rather than confrontation with its enemies. This is purely prudential justification of tolerance, born out of weakness. The classic expression of the standard attitude in Christendom towards the relationship of church to state *and* towards religious uniformity is a French re-formulation of Ephesians 4:5, dating back at least to the ninth century and proverbial by the sixteenth century: 'un roi, une loi, une foi'– one king, one law, one faith.[35] This situation was only moderately altered by the Reformation. Luther placed great stress on the role of the magistrate or prince (i.e. the secular power) in reforming the church. A true division between the secular and ecclesiastical did not exist in his thinking. It is true that Calvin himself asserted what sounds like a concept of a division between church and state. He wrote:

> There is a twofold government of man; one aspect is spiritual [...] the second is political [...] There are in man, so to speak, two worlds, over which different kings and different laws have authority.

If this distinction were not borne in mind, the resultant mingling of the two, 'which have a completely different nature', would be at the least 'unwise'.[36] In practice, however, because of the way that ecclesiastical organization and government administration developed in Geneva, such a division was largely nominal. The church and state in Geneva – the Calvinist archetypical polity – were in effect different arms of the same body, not distinct at all.

---

35   Lecler, *Toleration and the Reformation*, i.68, 71; Richard Bonney, 'The Obstacles to Pluralism in Early Modern France', in Cameron, Roberts and Greengrass, *Adventure of Religious Pluralism in Early Modern France*, 209.

36   *Institutes of the Christian Religion* [1536], trans. and ed. Ford Lewis Battles, rev. edn (London/Grand Rapids, 1986), 184, 207.

Stereotypical older views of the Puritans (especially those in New England) and Huguenots as fighting, *inter alia*, for tolerance, are very far from the mark, although, in the case of France, still accepted by a surprising number of historians.[37] This is not to say that the issue of confessional co-existence was not even on the horizon of the Reformers. Indeed, the first translation of Calvin into English is of 'a letter on the question of coexistence with the Papists' first published in Antwerp in 1544.[38] But the weight of opinion was overwhelmingly against it.

The actual horrors of immolation alive, breaking at the wheel, and torture, were such that the idealised view of persecution as an act of Christian love was increasingly untenable, especially as the numbers of people potentially subject to such horrors greatly increased, making it less likely that persecution *could* purge the body politic of heresy, or restore the unity of Christendom. The fact of confessional division, palpable by mid century in several countries, demanded an alternative response politically, too, for otherwise the outcome might, as some statesmen presciently foresaw, be political partition as well as religious division. From the 1550s onwards, then, while the traditional attitudes towards religious diversity continued to predominate, new approaches began to be espoused, by theologians and philosophers, but also by politicians.

The concept of pluralism, even in the sense of multiple co-existence confessions, was initially still well beyond early modern thinkers. The initial discourses on religious liberty and toleration are not so very libertarian or tolerationist by modern standards; the later developments of these limited beginnings into something approaching pluralism was probably not inevitable and certainly took a long time, passing through several intermediate stages.

---

37   Mario Turchetti, 'Middle Parties in France during the Wars of Religion', in Philip Benedict, *et al* (eds), *Reformation, Revolt and Civil War in France and the Netherlands 1555–1585* (Koninklijke Nederlandse Akademie van Wetenschappen, Verhandelingen, Afdeling Letterkunde, n.s. 176; 1999), 171.

38   Francis Higman, 'Calvin's Works in Translation', in Andrew Pettegree, Alasatair Duke and Gillian Lewis (eds), *Calvinism in Europe, 1540–1620* (Cambridge, 1994), 87.

In the early years of the Reformation Philip of Hesse had allowed limited toleration of Anabaptists and other minorities. He would not execute them solely on the grounds of their beliefs, but he did not permit sedition, and those who actively shared their faiths *did* face the sanction of the law, including ultimately execution.[39]

Coming from a Calvinist context, Sebastian Castellio produced in 1554 what has been called the 'first manifesto in favour of toleration', though such a characterization of his views is premature, as is the characterization of him as 'the apostle of tolerance'.[40] His views were to mature and in the mid-1550s he argued not *for* religious liberty but rather *against* persecution. He condemned only persecution of beliefs on issues God had not made plain (what would come to be called *adiaphora*) rather than persecution of all heterodox beliefs.[41] Initially at least, Castellio 'did not did not say, any more than Calvin did, that every man has the right to believe what he chooses and to assert his belief'.[42] Castellio's theme was that most religious differences were so minor that they did not deserve the ultimate sanction; fellow Christians, whose only fault was sincerely to differ from the majority view on issues where scripture itself was often unclear, should not be punished more severely than thieves.[43] Castellio was also concerned that those who were being punished might actually be martyrs – a similar concern was voiced by the Italian Jacopo Aconcio, from his religious exile in London: churchmen were very willing to condemn, but too reluctant to show the humility

39   N. M. Sutherland, 'Persecution and Toleration in Reformation Europe', in Sheils, *Persecution and Toleration*, 155.

40   Guggisberg, *Sebastian Castellio*, 55, 81. Marian Hillar, 'Sebastian Castellio and the Struggle for Freedom of Conscience', *Essays in the Philosophy of Humanism*, 10 (2002), 31–56 (also available to download at URL <http://www.socinian.org/castellio.html>); André Dufau, 'Sébastien Castellion: Défenseur de la liberté religieuse au XVIe siècle', *Conscience et Liberté*, no. 21 (1981), 13.

41   Plamenatz, *Man and Society*, i. 124.

42   Ibid. i. 125.

43   Guggisberg, *Sebastian Castellio*, 86. 'Who', exclaims Castellio, 'would today wish to become a Christian when those who confess themselves Christians are slain by other Christians without mercy by fire and water and the sword and are treated more cruelly than murderers or robbers?'

demonstrated by Christ, and their condemnations produced only discord, rather than the unity that Christ had prayed for.[44] Castillio's theories on toleration did evolve. But in 1562 he was arguing on principle that it was wrong to force people to violate their consciences.[45]

At approximately the same time, the Roman Catholic Chancellor of France, Michel de L'Hospital, became convinced that 'it is stupid to think that this division of minds can be settled by the power of the sword and with gleaming armour'.[46] At the colloquy of Poissy (1561), a rare example of sixteenth-century 'ecumenical' dialogue, he stressed to the assembled Catholic and Calvinist delegates that force had failed to resolve the problem of religious diversity, and called on the former to be slow to condemn those 'of the new religion, who are baptised Christians like they are'.[47] L'Hospital's preference was for all to follow the example of Christ, who 'loved peace, and orderes us to abstain from armed violence [...] He did not want to compel and terrorise anybody through threats, nor to strike with a sword'.[48] But L'Hospital was not an advocate of pluralism either. He still believed in a Catholic nation of France, but distinguished 'between eternal laws and temporary remedies', regarding edicts of toleration as provisional measures to deal with a religious diversity which would, in the end, disappear – but through peaceful dialogue, rather than war or persecution.[49]

---

44   Ibid. (Christ has been killed as a heretic); Aart de Groot, 'Acontius's Plea for Tolerance', in Randolph Vigne and Charles Littleton (eds), *From Strangers to Citizens: The Integration of Immigrant Communities in Britain, Ireland and Colonial America, 1550–1750* (London/Brighton, 2001), 48–54.

45   Turchetti, 'Middle Parties in France during the Wars of Religion', 171.

46   Quoted in Petris, 'Faith and Religious Policy in Michel de L'Hospital's Civic Evangelism', 137.

47   Donald Nugent, *Ecumenism in the Age of the Reformation: The Colloquy of Poissy* (Cambridge, 1974), 95; Turchetti, 'Middle Parties in France during the Wars of Religion', 170.

48   Quoted in Petris, 'Faith and Religious Policy in Michel de L'Hospital's Civic Evangelism', 137.

49   Turchetti, 'Middle Parties in France during the Wars of Religion', 171–2; Petris, 'Faith and Religious Policy in Michel de L'Hospital's Civic Evangelism', 140–1.

Just as Protestant and Catholic used the same texts to justify persecution, so they used the same texts to justify a shift away from it and towards toleration or, more accurately in the language of the times, the public 'acceptance', or permitting, of religious diversity.[50] Tolerationists consistently took inspiration from the parable of the wheat and the tares, the message of which is unusually precise, since it is one of the few parables explained by Christ at the time; the fact that He took the time to expound a message of toleration for those of divergent views lent it strength.[51] Castellio, in the preface to his French translation of the Bible (published 1555), dedicated (optimistically!) to Henri II, declared that there were now so many contrary opinions, while true and false doctrine were now so confused that, if men sought to disentangle them, 'there is danger lest the wheat be rooted out with the tares'.[52] De L'Hospital likewise, when arguing that only a general council of the church could resolve the religious differences between Catholic and Protestant then cited the wheat and chaff as grounds for not persecuting Protestants until such a council could meet.[53]

By the mid-1570s, L'Hospital was proved to have been prescient. As he foresaw, force had proved utterly ineffective in reuniting the people of France in confessional concord. Five civil wars and one

---

50   '*Tolérer* and *tolérance* seem ill-suited to express what would become a universal moral principle of the Enlightenment. In 1562 the words *permettre* and *permission* seem to be better suited for the task, as *tolérance* is used much more frequently by those opposed to toleration, *permission* by those in favour of it'. William H. Huseman, 'The Expression of the Idea of Toleration in French during the Sixteenth Century', *Sixteenth-Century Journal*, 15 (1984), 293–310 at 306.

51   Matt. 13:24–30 (parable), 36–43 (explanation).

52   Guggisberg, *Sebastian Castellio*, 62. Roland H Bainton (ed.), *Concerning Heretics; Whether they are to be Persecuted and How they are to be Treated; A Collection of the Opinions of Learned Men, Both Ancient and Modern; An Anonymous Work Attributed to Sebastian Castellio Together with Excerpts from Other Works of Sebastian Castellio and David Joris on Religious Liberty* (New York, 1935), 257–8. Hillar, 'Sebastian Castellio and the Struggle for Freedom of Conscience'.

53   Petris, 'Faith and Religious Policy in Michel de L'Hospital's Civic Evangelism', 140.

massacre on the scale of the attack on New York in September 2001 had not done the trick. Even arch-Catholics were beginning to come around to L'Hospital's way of thinking. At the meeting of the Estates-General of France in 1577, at which each of the three Estates resolved that there should be uniformity of religion, the duc de Montpensier, one of Henri III's 'most influential counsellors' and known for his Catholic zeal, shocked the deputies with a speech arguing for limited toleration.[54] Although making it clear that he did not 'favour any other but the Roman Catholic religion', nevertheless, in light of 'the evils which the recent wars have brought us, and how much this division is leading to the ruin [...] of this poor kingdom', he felt 'constrained to advise [...] the tolerance and sufferance of those of the new opinion'. It would only be:

> For a short time [...] until by means of a council [... or] other means, their Majesties having thus reconciled and united their subjects, God can bless us with only one religion, the Roman Catholic faith held and followed by all previous kings, and in which I protest to live and die.[55]

Nevertheless, coming from an intimate of a king who had been deeply complicit in the Saint Bartholomew's Massacre, it was a remarkable concession.

Among the nobility, too, there was willingness to suffer the Huguenots to live. One remonstrance presented at the Estates-General stressed that, 'although it was 'highly desirable for all the people [...] to live in one Roman Catholic and apostolic religion' and though it was of course 'true that when people have only one religion, a king is better obeyed and served', nevertheless civil conflict was one of the 'greatest afflictions' that a people or king had to endure. Believing that 'violence eventually leads to self-destruction', they pleaded with the king, albeit 'by no means approv[ing] of the so-called reformed religion', to reject further persecution and religious war.[56]

---

54 See Mack P. Holt, *The Duke of Anjou and the Politique Struggle during the Wars of Religion* (Cambridge, 1986), 81–6 (at 85).
55 Quoted in ibid. 84–5.
56 Quoted in ibid. 85.

These examples reveal how a willingness to 'suffer' (the choice of word is striking) religious minorities was not an ethical but rather a practical decision. There was no concept of pluralism – only a lack of enthusiasm for persecution as a way of ending religious diversity. But it is also striking that, despite the expression of these sentiments, the Estates-General in 1577 pushed Henri III into repealing the edicts of pacification of 1576, which had ended the fifth civil war by granting the Huguenots liberty of public worship as well as of conscience – in fact, something approximating to full toleration. Had this edict lasted, France *would* have been pluralist. It is a telling fact that instead the edicts excited such a strong Catholic reaction that France was plunged in the short term into another civil war, and in the long term to another twenty-two years of religious war.[57] Civil war might provoke limited sufferance of heterodoxy; but real toleration would only provoke more civil war.

The concept of complete religious liberty granted on moral and humanitarian principles was as yet too radical, however, to have a widespread appeal, and it remained very much a minority position.[58] Plamenatz observes:

> Though the 'free church' principle, once firmly established, leads inevitably to toleration, it took the Calvinists a long time to accept its implications. Belief in toleration among the religious comes more easily to groups which either, like the Anabaptists in Germany and Holland and their Baptist and other successors in England and America, from the first conceive of the Church as merely a voluntary association of believers, or which, like the Socinians, though they think a Universal Church desirable, do not require uniformity of belief.[59]

As late as the 1620s the States of Holland not only placed restrictions on the province's Jewish community (interfaith, rather than confessional, toleration was always a more radical step), but also refused requests from Lutherans for toleration, closed existing

---

57   Mark Greengrass, 'Pluralism and Equality: The Peace of Monsieur, May 1576', in Cameron, Greengrass and Roberts, *Adventure of Religious Pluralism in Early Modern France*, 45–63; Holt, *The Duke of Anjou*, 66–9, 86–7.

58   One of the rare sympathisers, at least in publication, was Dirk Coornhert: see the biography by Voogt, *Constraint on Trial*.

59   Plamenatz, *Man and Society*, i. 115.

Lutheran churches in Rotterdam and Leiden.[60] The Amsterdam consistory in 1657 directed the attention of the magistrates to the actions of the émigré English Quakers, who, in turn, 'were shocked by what they considered the persecuting spirit in the "official" church'. But they also severely criticised the Remonstrants, or Arminian opponents of the mainstream Calvinist church in the Netherlands.[61] All in all, the experience of the Quaker leader William Ames in the Dutch Republic moved him to write that a 'congregation which persecutes' was 'not the congregation of Christ but the synagogue of Satan. Oh, how appears the devouring wolf under the sheep's clothing'.[62]

As Christian thinkers and rulers began to grapple, then, with the problem of entrenched, sizeable minorities, diversity or pluralism was still unthinkable; but persecution was seen as an inappropriate way of assuring confessional unity. Toleration was thus something into which one was forced by the present circumstances of the world. It was not an ideal, and there was no reason to grant it in countries where the heterodox were a small enough minority that they *could* be constrained or out-muscled in the traditional way. Toleration was granted, in Poland and Transylvania, with figurative gnashing of teeth, because a government was weak; or, as in France, or the Netherlands in 1567, because a government that was strong in most ways, was confronted by an unusually strong and well-organised heterodox movement.[63]

Toleration was also a tactical ploy – the idea that, in the words of Michel de L'Hospital, 'charity, prayers, persuasions, the Word of God', rather than arms were appropriate 'weapons' for the struggle between confessions. The early church had sought to convert only by persuasion, never by compulsion, and yet had spread throughout the Roman Empire. Even the challenge of heresy and dissension had been

---

60 Israel, *Dutch Republic*, 476.
61 J. van den Berg, 'Quaker and Chiliast: The "contrary thoughts" of William Ames and Petrus Serrarius', in R. Buick Knox (ed.), *Reformation Conformity and Dissent: Essays in Honour of Geoffrey Nuttall* (London, 1977), 183.
62 Ibid. quoting William Ames and John Higgins, *De valsche propheten bekent aen haere vrughten* (1659), 26.
63 Sutherland, 'Persecution and Toleration in Reformation Europe', 155.

met successfully, but not by force of arms, guile or deceit, but 'by an exemplary life of prayers [and] by genuine dialogue'.[64] In the words of Richard Hooker, a champion of Anglicanism, facing the divisions in the Church of England: 'There will come a time when three words uttered with charity and meekness shall receive a far more blessed reward than three thousand volumes written with disdainful sharpness of wit', or of course than open repression.[65] In short, one tolerated minorities not so much because of ethical or moral considerations stemming from one's Christianity, but because *this* was the best means of re-converting them and so ending the confessional multiplicity that early modern people found almost impossible to accept. Thus, if war *had* worked as a means of ending religious diversity, toleration would not have been an issue. Toleration was not so much a principled position, as a missiological methodology.

When toleration *was* granted, it was usually regarded as a short-term measure. In France for example, it was assumed that Protestants would be converted, thus ending the undesirable pluralist state brought about by the Edict of Nantes, which was characterised by seventeenth-century royal officials as 'a shadow, forced by the necessity of the times'.[66] Such attitudes were also common for the seventeenth-century English advocates for toleration – most were millenarians in world view: a characteristic of the millennium, it as thought, would be a coming together of different Christian opinions. So any grant of toleration was bound to be short term, since shortly those who were currently foolish enough to maintain incorrect doctrine would have their eyes opened by the Holy Spirit.[67] For those whose apocalyptic framework did not incorporate a millennium of peace *before* the second coming of Christ, since the end of the world was still nigh, toleration was still inherently short-term.

---

64   Petris, 'Faith and Religious Policy in Michel de L'Hospital's Civic Evangelism', 138–9.
65   Quoted in Nugent, *Ecumenism in the Age of the Reformation: The Colloquy of Poissy*, 1.
66   Quoted in Richard Bonney, *Political Change in France under Richelieu and Mazarin, 1624–1661* (Oxford, 1978), 384.
67   We are indebted to John Coffey for a discussion of these points.

And even when toleration was granted, it was usually limited. Liberty of conscience was all that could be conceded at first – the right not to make windows into men's souls! As we have seen, exceptions in France during the era of the *guerres de religion*, only provoked further hostilities. James VI of Scotland (the most resolutely Calvinist state in existence outside Geneva), on acceding to the throne of England as James I, wrote to the archbishops and bishops of the Church of England, reassuring them that, 'although the King thought the shedding of blood [...] should not be exacted for diversity of opinion', in all other respects 'they may uphold the laws for preservation of religion'.[68] The strict Elizabethan laws against religious diversity were maintained and if execution was not imposed on Protestant dissidents, under Charles I they faced branding and the loss of their ears. Removing the sanction of the death penalty was thus only a limited concession. As time went on, by a natural evolution, more liberties might be granted, but there was always great reluctance to make not only the first concession, but any concession thereafter. Thus, toleration was rarely or never, at least until the very end of the period, liberty as it has come to be understood by modern political theorists. Even opponents of arbitrary, absolutist civil government, might envisage religious toleration as fairly circumscribed. A recent study of Milton's writings and speeches argues that he:

> favours what Isaiah Berlin calls 'negative' liberty, the absence of external constraints, for the sake of Berlin's 'positive' liberty, which consists in spiritual fulfilment or self-realization. Not only the events of the Interregnum but also his humanism and his historiography showed him that 'positive' liberty, though attractive as a spiritual freedom [...] destroys both liberties for those who do not agree with the believers.[69]

This concept of a religious liberty that was no more than absence of constraints seems about as far as early modern society could go.

---

68 *Calendar of State Papers, Domestic Series, 1603–10*, Sept. (?) 1603, 40.
69 John K. Hale, 'England as Israel in Milton's Writings', *Early Modern Literary Studies*, 2:2 (1996), 1–54, <http://www.shu.ac.uk/emls/02-2/halemil2.html>, conclusion no. 18.

Changing Views of Church and State

The theory that there was, or ought to be, a division between church
and state was given renewed impetus by the Reformation, since it
provided ammunition for minorities. In 1559, for example, the
Calvinist 'professouris of Christis ewangell' in Scotland wrote to the
(French) Catholic regent, Mary of Guise, asserting that, because there
was a 'kingdome temporall' parallel to and separate from 'Christis
kingdome' which ought to be ruled by Christ alone, she, as a human,
had no 'preheminent nor authoritie above the kyrk'.[70]

A contrary trend also developed as the fruit of the Reformation,
however, inspired by the chaotic religious wars which it spawned.
This was what one might term the Divine Right of Kings Discourse,
which posited that obedience was close to godliness. This trend was
evident in the early seventeenth-century English church. The arch-
Anglican Richard Hooker devoted the eighth book of his
Ecclesiasticall Politie to arguing that 'in a Christian Kingdom, he
whose power is greatest over the Common-wealth' *could* in fact
'lawfully have supremacy of power also over the Church', at least 'so
far as to order thereby and to dispose of spirituall affaires'.[71] And a
1642 pamphlet, directed against the Catholic Irish rebels unusually
from a royalist rather than Puritan perspective, advises the Irish

> Yes love your king, feare heavens tribunall seat;
> So shall your soules without disturbance rest,
> Till Christ shall come to make you fully blest.

---

70   Alan R. MacDonald, 'Ecclesiastical Representation in Parliament in Post-
     Reformation Scotland: The Two Kingdoms Theory in Practice', *JEH* 50 (1999),
     39.
71   Richard Hooker, *Of the Lawes of Ecclesiasticall Politie; The Sixth and Eighth
     Books* (London, 1648), at 144. *Hooker's Ecclesiasticall Politie: Book VIII*,
     Raymond Aron Houk (ed.) (New York, 1931), 166.

As Ethan Shagan observes, to English Calvinists, 'this implication that Catholics could be saved if only they obeyed their king must have resonated harshly indeed.'[72]

There was also an increasing trend towards accepting that other confessions and those who held them might include some truth as well as views regard The Calvinist poet and minister, John Donne, famous in his own time for his sermons,

> saw that were most men held their convictions as absolutes and thought of them as 'true', others as 'false', in fact 'men are moulded in their religious beliefe rather more by the accidents of birth, education and fate' than by intellectual processes.[73]

King James VI and I, as Brown Patterson shows, was able to combine sincere Calvinism with an ecumenical desire to reunify Christendom.[74] But when the Anglican Richard Hooker, in a sermon at the Temple, suggested

> that Rome might still have 'the foundation of faith' of a Christian church' it caused outrage among many English Calvinists. He did not withdraw from his position; he substantiated it by a course of argument, concluding that 'the best-learned in our profession are of this judgment, that all the heresies and corruptions of the Church of Rome do not prove her to deny the foundation directly'.[75]

Donne's and James's irenic/ecumenical attitudes were unusual. To be sure, later in the century the non-conformist churchman Richard

72   Ethan Howard Shagan, 'Constructing Discord: Ideology, Propaganda, and English Responses to the Irish Rebellion of 1641', *Journal of British Studies*, 36 (Jan. 1997), 19, quoting from T*he Just Reward of Rebels, the Life and Death of Jack Straw and Wat Tyler* (London, 1642).

73   A. L. Rowse, *The Elizabethan Renaissance: The Cultural Achievement* (Basingstoke, 1972), 333; Jordan, *The Development of Religious Toleration in England*, 39.

74   W. B. Patterson, *King James VI and I and the Reunion of Christendom* (Cambridge, 1997).

75   Rowse, *The Elizabethan Renaissance*, 333, citing *The Works [...] of Richard Hooker*, J. Keble (ed.), 7th edn, rev. R. W. Church and F. Paget (Oxford, 1888), 3: 483–547.

Baxter was, at least in theory, also unusually ready (for a Calvinist) to accept theological and/or ecclesiological tenets in order to achieve union with other Christians; but in practice Baxter was notable for helping to found a distinct Presbyterian denomination and was often hostile to the Congregationalist Calvinists; his anti-Catholicism was in any case vitriolic and would always have prevented anything other than pan-Protestant ecumenism, rather than pan-Christian union.[76] In short, while both had some points in common, both also had distinctive viewpoints – and both were uncommon. Early modern Calvinism generally was inimical to ecumenism – and to pluralism. The belief in an 'elect' allowed room for certain kinds of ecumenism, but *not* for inter-*faith* as opposed to inter-denominational or inter-confessional dialogue.

The main exception in the early modern period, and a vital figure in Europe's radical Enlightenment,[77] was thus not a Calvinist but a Jew. Baruch Spinoza was not an advocate of pluralism, yet he remained firm in his advocacy of tolerance. Tolerance was useful in combating intolerant, autocratic, governments and repressive power-driven theologians who spread false religion. For Spinoza, the state should institute religion to the extent that it commands obedience to God, justice and charity. Spinoza referred to this as the 'outward observance of piety', which would conform with 'the public peace and well-being'. In contrast, Spinoza emphasised that the 'inward worship of God and piety in itself are within the sphere of everyone's private rights and cannot be alienated'. No matter how powerful the state, it could not force a person to abandon his or her own beliefs. Therefore, a state bent on stamping out views it abhorred would be bound to achieve 'disastrous results'. By insisting that all religions that were practised during his lifetime in the Netherlands shared a common core, Spinoza managed to make a compelling case for complete

---

76   See William Lamont, 'False Witnesses? The English Civil War and English Ecumenism', in Bonney and Trim, *Development of Pluralism in Modern Britain and France*.

77   Spinoza's seminal importance for the Radical Enlightenment emerges clearly from J. I. Israel, *Radical Enlightenment. Philosophy and the Making of Modernity, 1650–1750* (Oxford, 2001).

religious tolerance. In particular, though a minority religion, Judaism ought to be tolerated because it shared a common core with Christianity. Similarly, Spinoza himself, a Jewish renegade, ought to be tolerated because of his unbinding commitment to the core teaching of Judaism, notwithstanding his rejection of particular glosses imposed by Jewish theologians. Spinoza was personally affected by religious intolerance both as a Jew in a Christian world, and as an outcast from the Amsterdam Jewish community that excommunicated him in 1656. Thus, the ardent proponent of tolerance on prudential grounds and as a private and public virtue was well acquainted with the effects of both inter- and intra-communal intolerance.[78] J. I. Israel contends that Spinoza's views on toleration were forged in opposition to partisan Calvinist feuding:[79]

> In Spinoza, the rule that the individual must always submit to the law and the state as regards his actions but is free in thought and speech to express his own judgments emphatically applies to liberty to write and publish. All efforts, he warns, to restrict expression of views, and publicising one's views in print, not only unjustly curtails legitimate freedom but is palpably dangerous to the state. The struggle between the Remonstrants and the Counter-Remonstrants in the early seventeenth-century Dutch Republic, he maintains, proves with the utmost clarity that the 'real schismatics are those who condemn the writings of others and seditiously incite the quarrelsome multitude against the writers, and not the authors themselves who generally write only for scholars and appeal to reason alone; and that, finally, the real disturbers of peace are those who, in a free commonwealth, vainly seek to abolish freedom of judgment which cannot be suppressed'.
>
> Ultimately, what Spinoza means by 'libertas philosophandi', which is proclaimed in the very subtitle of his book, is the right of every individual to inwardly reject, outwardly argue against, and ultimately help to overthrow, all prevailing structures of theological and ecclesiastical tradition, hierarchy and authority [...] The shift from the quest for religious freedom to the quest for

---

78 Michael Rosenfeld, 'Spinoza's Dialectic and the Paradoxes of Tolerance: A Foundation for Pluralism?', Cardozo Law School, Public Law Research Paper 79 (2003). Downloadable from <http://papers.ssrn.com/sol3/papers.cfm?abstract _id=466360>

79 J. I. Israel, 'Locke, Spinoza and the Philosophical Debate Concerning Toleration in the Early Enlightenment (c. 1670–c. 1750)', Koninklijke Nederlandse Akademie van Wetenschappen, Amsterdam (1999), downloadable at <www. knaw.nl/publicaties/pdf/981137.pdf>

philosophical freedom which begins with Spinoza's critically important theory
of toleration is, in fact, one of the most characteristic features of the early
Enlightenment.

For Jonathan Israel, 'Spinoza's theory of toleration […] is worlds
away from Locke's, and is also a more modern conception of
toleration'. 'Spinoza's', he argues,

> is clearing a much wider space for liberty than do Locke or Bayle with their
> theologically-based theories of toleration. Nor is this a point of merely
> theoretical interest. For in early Enlightenment Europe and the middle decades
> of the eighteenth century […] there was a marked tendency for censorship of
> ideas to become secular rather than, as in the past, ecclesiastical, but this by no
> means implies that censorship became less forceful or less inclined to ban
> opinions and doctrines.[80]

IV Common Themes

So much for the issues that are fundamental across the essays. What of
the common themes that emerge? The first is the importance of
spiritual elitism if we are to understand Calvinists, who after all
believed themselves to be God's 'elect'. This highlights another
theme: the role of religion in both dividing minorities from and
integrating them into society. This is especially true of Calvinists,
arguably due to their conception of themselves as a divinely chosen
'elect'. Calvinists in England, Scotland, the Netherlands, Germany
and Eastern Europe matched Roman Catholics, Anglicans and
Lutherans in their intolerance of other Protestant minorities, such as
Anabaptists, Mennonites, Quakers, and of course Lutherans and
Arminian Anglicans – not to mentions Catholics. This was true even
in Hungary where the Ottoman regime tolerated all Christian
minorities as a way of undermining Catholic resistance. The example

80   Ibid.

of religious pluralism in wider society did not change basic Calvinist attitudes.

Another recurrent theme is the readiness of persecuted minorities to place limits on toleration, and even to persecute other minorities, if given the chance. Roger Williams, the most powerful and passionate writer on religious liberty of the seventeenth century, was nevertheless disinclined to grant religious toleration to Roman Catholics.[81] John Bunyan, a persecuted Baptist, nevertheless quarrelled vigorously with Quakers and other minorities, especially anti-Trinitarians, whose activities he wished to see constrained.[82] Members of minorities are also willing to marginalise others within their group. The fissuring of English Calvinism is an example of this. Quaker women, initially leaders, were forced to conform to a role expected of women. They tended to defer to male leaders, who were ready to condemn some women speakers, at any rate, as hysterical.[83] Other studies of women in religious minorities bear out this pattern of marginalisation.[84]

In Britain, the determined resistance to intolerance of Calvinists, together with Catholics and members of Protestant sects, resulted in the state granting reasonably full toleration, laying the foundation for an (eventually) pluralist society. In France and Hungary, however, the end result of Calvinist particularism was that, with the triumph of militant Catholicism, such toleration as had existed was extinguished and replaced by fierce persecution on a sixteenth-century scale. However, among the Calvinist governing class of the United Provinces, and in Oliver Cromwell, certitude of salvation produced Christian forbearance for those of other faiths, at least if they did not threaten

---

81 Williams and many other Protestants believed that Catholics could never be good citizens of the state because they owed their first allegiance to the Pope. The state could thus require Catholics to wear distinctive clothing and be prohibited from carrying arms, even while they were allowed to practise their religion freely in private.

82 David Walker, 'Bunyan and the Body and Kingdom of Christ, 1656–1663', *Bunyan Studies*, 8 (1998), 6–27.

83 Chapter by Mary Trim.

84 E.g. Penny Mahon, 'Domesticating Discourses: Woman as Writer in the Early Nineteenth-century Peace Society', in Bonney and Trim, *Development of Pluralism in Modern Britain and France*.

the state. The willingness of Puritans in the 1650s to enforce 'godly' conformity among the population at large (which produced an angry backlash) suggests, however, that toleration in the Dutch Republic may have been due to non-religious, cultural factors; and to individualism in the case of Cromwell.

Another theme is that persecution comprises more than killing or imprisoning. Indeed, such dramatic fates as public execution, or even imprisonment, can help spread heterodox opinion: proverbially, 'The blood of the martyrs is the seed of the church'. A dramatic end, with a guarantee (as it was assumed) of immediate transition to the heavenly kingdom – these could induce men and women to screw themselves up to face a torment-filled death. Less dramatic persecutory ploys may be more effective. In the ninety years after the Edict of Nantes, despite a strong programme of religious re-education, Protestantism in France was not eradicated – this was why the revocation of the Edict of Nantes by the Edict of Fontainebleau was necessary. However, Protestants' numbers had been drastically reduced. They were rarely in danger of life and limb before 1685, but life was constantly more difficult, in areas both great and small, because of their heterodox beliefs. The same was true in England for Catholics. Only priests faced death, but ordinary recusants faced higher tax bills and many civil penalties – their numbers, too, remained low. There must have been many early modern English people, nominally Protestant, who secretly preferred Catholicism; and many seventeenth-century French people, nominally Catholic, who preferred Calvinism. But while these 'Nicodemites' might have made the population of both countries more confessionally mixed than their church and state hierarchies wished, it is misleading to characterise the resultant blend as 'pluralist'.[85] The facts are that declared allegiance did matter – everyone thought so; and by conforming, such crypto-Catholics and crypto-Calvinists made their original movements more marginal. Sympathy is not the same as active support, as is clear from the fate of the Jacobites in Britain.

85   *Pace* Alexandra Walsham, 'England's Nicodemites: Crypto-Catholicism and Religious Pluralism in the Post-Reformation Context', in Cameron, Greengrass and Roberts, *Adventure of Religious Pluralism in Early Modern France*, 289–304.

Likewise, the non-conformist minorities in the aftermath of the Restoration (1660) also did not face death, but faced civil difficulties, higher taxes, and other forms of harassment. Children were taken away from their families and, in defiance of the law, imprisoned and sometimes badly beaten.[86] Legal cases brought into question the validity of Quaker marriages and this gave considerable anxiety to the members of at least one Quaker regional meeting.[87] Dissenters were denied burial, had dogs loosed on them, and were abused, threatened and roughed up in the streets. These sorts of harassing tactics – petty, mean-spirited, not always causing great immediate suffering, but potentially extremely wearing and disheartening – continued even after England had, officially, become a tolerant state.

This demonstrates another point. Persecution need not be state-directed repression. Cromwell met George Fox, the Quaker leader, three times. After the first meeting in 1653, Cromwell 'with tears in his eyes said, "Come again to my house; for thou and I were but an hour of a day together, we should be nearer one to the other"; adding the he wished [Fox] no more ill than he did his own soul'. Such sentiments did not prevent continuing persecution of both Fox and the Quakers at a local level. States can have 'religious liberty' in law but not in reality. Just as racism (and racial prejudice) cannot be legislated out of existence, so too religious prejudice and confessional intolerance can flourish even where toleration has been enacted by an enlightened, or browbeaten, central government. This emerged clearly from two papers at the original conference, one of which is published in each volume.[88] It is easier where toleration, rather than genuine pluralism, exists: thus, the fact that late seventeenth-century Dissenters had only limited rights gave their opponents in society room for manoeuvre. Their right to worship had been confirmed but only in limited places and circumstances, and they were not free to

86   Chapter by Mary Trim, '"Awe Upon My Heart": Children of Dissent, 1660–1688', in Trim and Balderstone, *Cross, Crown and Community*, 245–76.
87   Berkshire RO, D/F 2 A 3/26A.
88   David L. Wykes, below; James Deming, 'Martyrs for modernity: The three hundredth jubilee of the French Reformation and the Catholic/Protestant debate on the Huguenot martyrs', in Bonney and Trim, *Development of Pluralism in Modern Britain and France*.

conduct all ecclesiastical rites; this provided further scope for harassment. The right to worship, even when real, not nominal, is thus not necessarily the same thing as religious liberty, toleration, or pluralism.[89]

V   Conclusions

The experiences of Calvinists as religious minorities and interacting with religious minorities in early modern Europe yields some interesting conclusions, and poses some potentially uncomfortable questions. The theology of Calvinists was a major factor in their refusal to compromise, in the face of overwhelming odds, but also in spite of common ground with other Protestants. This was partly due to their belief of themselves as the elect, but it was also due to their 'remnant theology'. God had always, so Biblical history indicated, had a chosen people, set apart from the world by special divine calling. It was this 'remnant', who still obeyed God's commands and were true to His calling, that was called out of Babylon at the end of time.[90] Calvinists never worried, therefore, if they were a minority. As the confession of the Dutch Reformed Church 'declared the Church might appear to the world to be "very small", as in the time of Ahab, yet even then the Lord had reserved to Himself seven thousand, who had not bowed down to Baal.'[91] But the same sense of spiritual elitism that gave them their 'sense of being a chosen people' and which inspired them during persecutions, could also make them odious to their neighbours and, in fact, ensure that they *remained* a minority.[92]

89   And see Strayer, *Huguenots and Camisards*.
90   Rev. 12:17. Cf. Rom. 11:5.
91   Alastair Duke, 'The Ambivalent Face of Calvinism in the Netherlands, 1561–1618,' in Menna Prestwich (ed.), *International Calvinism, 1541–1715* (Oxford, 1985), 132.
92   H. Lüthy, 'Variations on a Theme by Max Weber', in Prestwich, *International Calvinism*, 379–80; Duke, ibid.

This conclusion prompts a question. John Coffey suggests that Christians, because they believed in the fallen nature of man had a natural tendency towards acceptance of others; dogmatists were well aware of their own fallen nature/shortcomings! But it is not clear that Calvinists would have been as likely to accept themselves as sinful. Obviously, some Calvinists did so – but from Castellio on, those who did so faced great attack. Castellio suggested that those Calvin was willing to persecute might actually be martyrs, and Calvin did not take kindly to the implication. Thus, theological, rather than sociological, factors are again probably critical in explaining their attitudes to other minorities and to persecution and pluralism. Are minorities more likely to be persecutors themselves? We often hold up suffering minorities as admirable *because* they suffer, but if they were given power might they often not act the same way?

British Calvinists' relatively enthusiastic espousal of religious toleration in the 1670s and after may be regarded as essentially a matter of convenience. Once *they* were the persecuted parties, with no longer any realistic chance of creating a Calvinist nation, arguments for toleration and confessional plurality suddenly became rather more attractive. This is too cynical a view, however. It disregards the genuine rethinking of traditional orthodoxies that almost invariably and very naturally accompanies any sudden revision in a movement's fortunes. In particular Calvinists, because of the extreme nature of their belief in divine foreknowledge, were obliged to rethink their entire worldview once it was clear that their efforts were not going to end in the establishment of a national church. Conviction as well as convenience was thus almost certainly involved in the shift towards a tolerationist stance. And this is made all the more likely because of existing trends in English Calvinism.

Radical English Calvinists held up the (regenerate) conscience as sovereign because it had been moved by God's spirit or grace and so could not 'be subordinated to any authority or authoritative external criteria'. This made conscience king – or Pope, as Catholic opponents charged. But conscience was individual, not communal. Radical Puritanism was thus subversive, because it 'undermined appeals to accepted authority, advanced a radical kind of subjectivity and legitimated the right of the people to speak and act for themselves'.[93] Individualistic concepts were already latent within Calvinism because of its emphasis on individual election. Calvinists were also suspicious of the study of 'cases of conscience' (or 'casuistry' as it became known), presumably because their Roman Catholic adversaries (not least the Jesuits) embraced it so enthusiastically. Puritans preferred instead to preach a 'rigorist morality as the best means of combating lay licentiousness'.[94] This only served to reinforce the trend towards individual autonomy already inherent in Calvinism. The product was, at more than one level, a 'conviction that when it came to moral and spiritual matters, people were served best by being left to direct themselves'.[95] The upshot of such attitudes naturally reinforced other trends towards religious toleration and a form of pluralism, with the state no longer being regarded as competent to determine individuals' confessional loyalties.

On the other hand, we must be wary of teleological readings of the history of pluralism. The essays gathered in this volume reinforce the conclusions of other scholars that liberty of conscience, toleration and pluralism are different. John Plamenatz argued: 'toleration and liberty of conscience are not [...] by any means the same; but they are intimately related'.[96] The reader of this volume will surely agree, but do they inevitably lead to each other? It is tempting to suggest that once liberty of conscience has been granted, toleration and then full religious liberty will follow, followed by pluralism. The British experience, as this volume shows, is that once liberty of conscience is granted, toleration is likely to follow, with the advent of pluralism a consequence, in turn. Political pluralism, 'coexistence of rival value systems in political thought and the existence of permanent competition between political parties' was a slower development. The religious language in which politics was described was remarkably

---

93   James Tully, 'Governing Conduct', in Edmund Leites (ed.), *Conscience and Casuistry in Early Modern Europe* (Cambridge/Paris, 1988), 19.
94   Margaret Sampson, 'Laxity and Liberty in Seventeenth-Century English Political Thought', in ibid. 117.
95   Edmund Leites, 'Introduction' and 'Casuistry and Character', in ibid. 4, 119.
96   Plamenatz, *Man and Society*, 115.

slow to be diluted by more secular conceptions, with 'freethinking' only by the 1730s being seen as one of the core principles underlying British liberty.[97]

The French and Hungarian experience, however, is the opposite to the British – persecution, once given up, is not given up for good, but remains an option that can be, and sometimes is, embraced again. Once a regime rejects persecution, a society is not suddenly on the road to pluralism. Subsequent developments are not 'bound to happen', especially since concession of some kind of liberty will often excite hostility that retards, or even makes impossible, the concession of further freedom. In any event, even when the repudiation of persecution and institution of limited sufferance of religious diversity *is* then subsequently followed by toleration, religious liberty and pluralism, the process has often been a slow one.

What are the differences between toleration and liberty? And is 'toleration' a good thing? A leading twentieth-century ecumenist and advocate of religious liberty has argued strongly that

> belief is not an intrinsic, fundamental right, but a favour granted in a spirit either of generosity or condescension. Tolerance suggests that those tolerating may be suffering (like a sick person 'tolerating' pain), but stoically put up with other religions and denominations. It is dangerous to base religious liberty on either human generosity or endurance.[98]

One is reminded of the duc de Montpensier's suggestion that France should 'suffer' the Huguenots. The words we use to define values are themselves important, and so perhaps the value of 'toleration' needs rethinking by those confronted today with religious diversity and especially unwelcome religious minorities.

As Professor Bonney and Dr Trim suggest, societies exist at different levels, and pluralism and toleration may be understood to

---

97 Pasi Ihalainen, *The Discourse of Political Pluralism in Early Eighteenth-Century England. A Conceptual study with special reference to terminology of religious origin* (Helsinki, 1999), 314–8. Definition of political pluralism: ibid. 319.

98 Bert B. Beach, 'The Intolerance of Toleration', *Liberty*, Jan.–Feb. 1999, 13. See Strayer, *Huguenots and Camisards as Aliens in France*, 505–12.

work at different levels.[99] There are also different levels of integration and assimilation. A pioneering study of these processes in early modern England concludes that that integration operates 'on many different levels' and characterises it as 'a multi-layered process, not monolithic and all-embracing'.[100] Possibly only a society at the highest level is able simply to accept the defiant, peculiar particularism of groups whose values are at odds with those of society in general. Early modern societies mostly fell short in this respect (the Dutch and British Republics and Ottoman Empire are only qualified exceptions), but awareness of the dynamics of early modern persecution should ensure there is no complacency as modern, western governments and societies grapple with issues such as whether to fund minorities' education of their children if it may perpetuate sectarianism (e.g. creationism); whether to protect ethnic and religious rights that appear to clash with gender rights (e.g. wearing of headscarves); and whether groups, seeking to restrict the free speech of others, have the protection of free speech laws (e.g. the *Satanic Verses* case).

Another conclusion is that the waning of religious zeal and discrediting of theological dogma are not necessary preconditions for the emergence of toleration and pluralism. There are two reasons for this. First, reliance on human reason and abilities, rather than simple (or indeed simplistic!) faith in a deity, is generally regarded as positive and it underpinned the Enlightenment and thus, eventually, modernity; yet it is not a panacea against either intolerance or repression. Second, the simple equation 'religion = dogmatism = repression' is fallacious.

Both intellectually sophisticated societies, and societies (and polities) that have avowedly embraced scepticism have been guilty of intolerance. In the sixteenth century, the court of François I of France was a centre of humanist learning, but despite the hopes of Calvinists, François and his son, Henri II, were both staunch persecutors. The radical tolerationism of Dutch thinkers such as Grotius was deeply unwelcome in their homeland, for all its sophisticated and sceptical

---

99   Appendix to Richard Bonney's chapter.
100 Nigel Goose, 'The Dutch in Colchester in the 16th and 17th Centuries: Opposition and Integration', in Vigne and Littleton, *From Strangers to Citizens*, 88–98 at 96.

intellectual culture – the people most persecuted in the 1620s Netherlands were those who argued for more religious liberty. Hobbes declared that a politician was preferable to a fanatic and made the distinction between public and private religion: outwardly, at least, the believer had to conform to the religion of the ruler.[101] The transformation of the new church Louis XVI was constructing to hold the relics of Ste Geneviève into the Panthéon, from a shrine of superstition to a temple of reason, may seem symbolic of a wider change brought about by the French Revolution – but the advent of

---

101 Justin Champion writes: 'at one level [...] it is apparent that Hobbes proposed a profoundly conformist model of public religion. Citing the licence of Naaman, all believers, whether Christian, Jewish, Mahometan or otherwise, were bound to obey publicly authorised religion. Importantly however Hobbes did not consider this unbending obligation as a type of intolerance. Crucial to his understanding was the distinction between public and private religion. Hobbes had no objection in theory to the principle of a diversity of religions within any particular state. Indeed in Chapter 12 [of *Leviathan*] he had applauded the model of the Romans who "made no scruple of tolerating any Religion whatsoever in the City of Rome itselfe; unless it had something in it, that could not subsist with their civil government". The citation of the precedent of the alternative Churches of "Paul, or Cephas, or Apollos" suggested that Hobbes ultimately approved of a system of public religion where worship was practised "every man as he liketh best". The unorthodoxy of this position was apparent to Hobbes: and he ensured that such passages, which were in clear contradiction to the established Church settlement, were excluded from later editions of the work [...] Hobbes made the distinction between internal and external worship transparent in Chapter 31, "The Kingdom of God by Nature": "Publique, is the worship that a commonwealth performeth, as one person. Private, is that which a Private Person exhibiteth. Publique, in respect of the whole commonwealth is free; but in respect of Particular men it is not so". To reinforce the point Hobbes continued "Private is in secret Free; but in the sight of the multitude, it is never without some restraint, either from the lawes, or from the opinion of men; which is contrary to the nature of Liberty". In private then Hobbes suggested that belief was unrestrained and more importantly unmonitored: as long as this internal understanding remained unpublished in the broadest sense it was acceptable. Once again the dynamic of restraint was not directed against the theoretical opposition to diversity but against the social effects of challenges to constituted doctrinal authority'. Champion, 'Private is in secret free. Hobbes and Locke on the Limits of Toleration, Atheism and Heterodoxy': <www.personal.rhul.ac.uk/uhra/026/tolerate.pdf>

educated scepticism in place of blind faith did not create a pluralist society. Even the celebrated 1787 Edict of Tolerance 'did not grant the Huguenots religious liberty'.[102] The revolutionary apostles of reason were soon demolishing not only the old shrine of Ste Geneviève but also sacking many of Paris's churches in an orgy of destruction as bad as any wrought by intolerant (and iconoclastic) Protestants in the Reformation. Faithful Catholics in the Vendée were slaughtered en masse; Huguenot pastors and Roman Catholic priests, monks and nuns were indifferently guillotined or imprisoned, with Catholic and Protestant sometimes sent to the same galley.[103] All were victims of a regime that, having literally elevated reason to the status of a deity, was as persecutory of its religious opponents as any historical church.

By contrast, official religious toleration emerged in the Dutch Republic and England – both Christian states. It was granted by Dutch Calvinists and to British ones because of arguments propounded by Christians. These Christian tolerationists were, however, dogmatists: they were trying to get toleration accepted as part of Christian dogma. It is notable that Seventh-day Adventists, members of an evangelical denomination with remarkably dogmatic attitudes on issues such as science and religion, are among the strongest proponents of religious liberty; their commitment to this has led to them working, even with Communists and atheists, against laws privileging particular faiths or religious practices, across Europe, North America and Australasia. Their commitment to religious liberty comes from their experience of being persecuted for their beliefs – thus, it is *because* of their dogmatism, not coincident with it or in spite of it. In sum, just as scepticism and pluralism are not necessarily linked, neither are dogmatism and intolerance. It is true that in Hungary and France the zeal with which Calvinists clung to their beliefs only excited an equal zeal amongst their confessional opponents to stamp them out. But in the Netherlands and England, the experience of Calvinists as and with religious minorities moved Christians of all sides, largely because of arguments rooted in the New Testament and a Christian sense of

102   Strayer, *Huguenots and Camisards*, 487.
103   Ibid. 501.

charity, finally to persecute no more. Here lie the roots of modern Western pluralism.

The idea that pluralism cannot flourish alongside widespread religious commitment is the fruit of a humanist/secularist mindset, not only sceptical about, but openly antagonistic towards religion, which is often expressed in polemical language, of a type used in the heyday of religious wars, rather than that characteristic of modern inter-church and inter-faith dialogue.[104] Most importantly, it is unsubstantiated by the evidence. Religious hatred it still all too common among religious people in general and Christians in particular, but the experience of Calvinists and religious diversity in early modern Europe suggests that in the original belief system lie not only the cause, but also the cure.

If this is to be true, however, then the papers gathered in this volume suggest that creeds and sects need a kind of internal pluralism. Dialogue needs to take place not only between different faiths and denominations but also *within* them. Sects and denominations are rarely monolithic; there will always be different traditions and points of view represented within them. When these fissures broaden into cracks, then often the movement itself will splinter, with the resultant new sects often openly hostile to each other. European Christianity thus split into Roman and Protestant and Protestant split into Lutheran and Calvinist. English Christianity split into Anglican and Calvinist, and Calvinist split further again. When members accept each other, it is frequently a first step to accepting people of other confessions or religions, or of none.

The dogmatism of Calvinists tended to produce intolerance of others and an ability to withstand external persecution; but it also may have induced persecution by confessional opponents. Their spiritual elitism gave them a potent sense of identity which in turn helped them to resist repression in the sixteenth century and then to defy extreme pressure to conform (especially in England and France) in the seventeenth century. But was this sense of identity actually enhanced

---

104 Cf. John Coffey, 'The Myth of Secular Tolerance', *Cambridge Papers*, 12:3 (Sept. 2003), 1 (also available to download at URL <http://www.jubilee-centre.org/cambridge_papers/index.php>).

by persecution? And was the persecution that provoked by Calvinists' 'sectarianism' actually beneficial to them? Certainly when the French revolutionary regime began to consider restoring religious liberty, one Huguenot pastor believed that persecution helped to concentrate the minds of his flock, and that, hence, 'persecution is less dangerous for the faith than tolerance'.[105] Michael Walzer points out that 'Jean-Paul Sartre's well-known argument that anti-Semitism is what sustains Jewish identity can be repeated for many other minority groups'.[106] Integrationist pressures from a majority population do not always 'succeed in obliterating cultural and religious differences'; sometimes they instead

> serve in fact to reinforce them. They mark off the members of the minority groups, discriminate against them because of their membership, compel them to rely on one another, forge intense solidarities.[107]

It is too facile, however, to suggest that Calvinists almost needed the persecutory, repressive strains they faced throughout most of early modern Europe. First, as Walzer also points out, 'neither the leaders of [...] minority groups nor their most committed members would choose a regime of intolerance'. Second, Jews and other minority groups 'attach real value to the group's history and culture and assume that this is what generates individual identification'.[108] And they may well be right. The distinctive ecclesiology of the Reformed Churches; their unusual emphasis on communal religion, with consistories empowered to investigate church members' affairs and interfere in them; and the distinctive liturgy, rejecting certain types of vestment, music and so forth that even other Protestants accepted – all these would have made Calvinists distinctive and 'alien' within communities in which another confessions was in a majority regardless of whether such communities were naturally inclined to be tolerant or intolerant. The distinctive cultures of English Dissenters in

---

105 Quoted in Jacques Poujol, 'Le changement d'image des protestants pendant la Révolution', *BSHPF*, 135 (1989), 503.
106 Michael Walzer, *On Toleration* (New Haven and London, 1997), 118.
107 Ibid. 83–4.
108 Ibid. 84, 118.

general and Quakers in particular far outlasted the seventeenth-century persecutions described in later chapters. Even more striking, Dutch Calvinists maintained their strong identity even when the majority confession, as the chapter by Dr Pollman makes clear. Although Calvinist confessional identity does seem to have been defined most powerfully in opposition to, and even in despite of, other confessional groups, the evidence thus suggests that persecution is not necessary for the formation of a strong confessional identity and culture.

This is not to say, too, that persecution was not without its effects on the victimised minority. Quakers became less radical over time, as Dr Trim shows. Thoroughgoing and persistent persecution over two hundred years reduced the Huguenots from 10% of France's population to less than 2%. Nevertheless, as the case of France indicates, brutal repression is unlikely entirely to destroy a minority with a strong identity and structure. The 'blood of the martyrs' is not always 'the seed of the church'. The experience of persecution may be one that a minority comes to value in some ways, but it is always a negative one. The irony is that pluralism may also often prove to be a negative experience for groups that hold strong, absolute beliefs, like Calvinists (or indeed many other Christians, and many Muslims and Jews). But since pluralism was a later development this is an issue best explored in another volume.

Luc Racaut

Persecution or Pluralism? Propaganda and Opinion-Forming during the French Wars of Religion

The French Wars of Religion are one of the most salient points in the history of persecution and pluralism. One event in the wars, the massacre of St Bartholomew's day, has captured the imagination of subsequent generations to become a symbol of persecution. Another, the promulgation of the Edict of Nantes, is on the contrary remembered in collective memory as the triumph of pluralism. Recent scholarship has shown that the two extremes were moderated by intermediate measures, agreements of religious co-existence, that pre-dated the Edict of Nantes and that many contemporaries refused to choose between either Rome or Geneva.[1] The choice was rendered all the more difficult by the fact that the second half of the sixteenth century saw an explosion of religious propaganda published in the vernacular, on both sides of the confessional divide.

The importance of print culture in the forming of opinions and patterns of behaviour, can no longer be set aside. Although the case for the importance of printing in the Protestant Reformation has been made over and over, the Catholic side of the story has been largely ignored. In the first decades of the French Wars of Religion a rhetoric of exclusion was spun by Catholic authors who concentrated on portraying the Protestants in the worst possible light. Catholic theologians were opposed to a royal policy, wavering between repression and pacification, that was unable to re-establish religious concord.[2] It

---

1   Olivier Christin, *La Paix de Religion: L'Autonomisation de la Raison Politique au XVIe siècle* (Paris, 1997); Thierry Wanegffelen, *Ni Rome ni Genève* (Paris, 1997), idem, *Une Difficile Fidélité: Catholiques malgré le Concile en France XVIe–XVIIe siècles* (Paris, 1999).

2   O. Christin, 'From Repression to Pacification: French Royal Policy in the Face of Protestantism', in P. Benedict, Ph. Marnef and others (eds), *Reformation,*

can be argued that Catholic propaganda was relatively successful in promulgating persecution in the short term. On the other hand it could do little to prevent the establishment of confessional pluralism in France, the one thing that its authors abhorred the most.

The violence of the French Wars of Religion, particularly the massacre of St Bartholomew's day, has always excited the imagination. The novel of Alexandre Dumas *La Reine Margot*, spectacularly adapted to the screen by Patrice Chereau in 1994, is only one of many fictional accounts inspired by this event.[3] What struck the imagination of Dumas and still fascinates the spectator of the film *La Reine Margot* is the seemingly unprovoked violence directed at French Protestants. The press of Huguenots in the entourage of Henri de Navarre being thrown on the spears of the Paris watch or the random killing of innocents in the streets, makes a vivid impression on the viewer. How could this ever happen? In trying to answer this question, the relationship between propaganda and the formation of public opinion needs to be taken into account.

Denis Crouzet, in his monumental *Les Guerriers de Dieu*, discusses print culture at length in arguing that it mirrored a 'civilisation of eschatological anguish' largely accountable for the violence of the French Wars of Religion.[4] Crouzet's stress on the eschatological undertones of certain works has been questioned by other historians, notably Larissa Taylor in the case of François Le Picart.[5] Other examples are Antoine de Mouchy, Robert Ceneau, Esprit Rotier, Jean de La Vacquerie and Antoine du Val, all mentioned

Revolt, and Civil War in France and the Netherlands, 1555–1585 (Amsterdam, 1999), 201–14.

3   Alexandre Dumas, *La Reine Margot* (Paris, 1845); Philippe Joutard, Janine Estèbe and others (eds), *La Saint-Barthélemy: Ou les Résonances d'un Massacre* (Neuchâtel, 1976), 116–17.

4   Denis Crouzet, *Les Guerriers de Dieu: La Violence au Temps des Troubles de Religion vers 1525–vers 1610* (Paris, 1990), 1: 131; Mark Greengrass, 'The Psychology of Religious Violence', *French History* 54 (1991), 467–74 at 473.

5   Larissa J. Taylor, *Heresy and Orthodoxy in Sixteenth-Century Paris: François Le Picart and the Beginnings of the Catholic Reformation* (Leiden, 1999), 190, 200–2, 205; Kathleen A. Parrow, 'From Defense to Resistance: Justification of Violence during the French Wars of Religion', *Transactions of the American Philosophical Society* 83 (1993), 12–3.

by Crouzet as members of an 'intelligentsia of prophets of violence'.[6] These authors, among others, collectively drew up a picture of the Huguenot heretic, drawn from the scriptures and Church Fathers, that had little to do with eschatology.[7] Crouzet was successful in inserting eschatological anguish into the historiography of the French Wars of Religion, but whether it was as central as he suggests is a matter for serious consideration. Our own fears of a global ecological or economic disaster on the dawn of a new millennium should convince us that no historical argument can be built on the specificity of any period of history in respects of millenarianism. One could argue that apocalypticism has been part of human culture ever since men realised they were mortal: it is a lot easier to contemplate the end of all things than it is to contemplate one's own.

The question of the use of the vernacular, usually seen to be the prerogative of the Reformed, is central to understanding the relationship between the printed media and the formation of public opinion. Catholics were equally concerned with the impact of propaganda on the 'unlearned' as were the Protestants, especially at a time where literacy rates were very low. By resorting to the vernacular, Catholics argued that the Protestants were catering to the unlearned and the *femmelettes* (silly women). The fear of social upheaval ('turning the world upside down') was consistently brandished by Catholics from the outset of the Reformation. After the conspiracy of Amboise (1560), numerous pamphlets argued that the Protestants wanted to abolish the monarchy and establish a commonwealth where everything was shared in common (and first of all women).[8] Unlike their German

6   Crouzet, *Guerriers de Dieu*, 1: 201–2.
7   Luc Racaut, *Hatred in Print: Catholic Propaganda and Protestant Identity during the French Wars of Religion* (Aldershot, 2002).
8   René Benoist, *Brieve Response a quelque remonstrance faicte a la roine mere du Roy, par ceux qui se disent persecutez pour la parolle de Dieu* (Paris, 1561), sig. A6v; Augustin Marlorat, *Remonstrance a la Royne Mere du Roy, par ceux qui sont persecutez pour la parole de DIEU. En laquelle ils rendent raison des principaux articles de la Religion, & qui sont aujourdhuy en dispute* (Paris, 1561), sig. B6v; Edmond Auger, *Sommaire des Heresies, abus, impietez et blasphemes qui sont en la Cene des Calvinistes, & nouvelle Religion pretendue reformee* (Paris, 1568), sigs. E4r–v.

counterparts, however, French Catholics were quick to respond in kind so that the 'simple', who were most at risk, would be instructed.[9] As the Catholic propagandist Artus Désiré wrote: 'Heresy needs to be destroyed in France by French books; a book in the French language will be more fruitful than thirty in Latin'.[10]

Early modern language in print is marked by the inter-connectedness between the written and the oral. Preaching constituted the greatest point of contact between clergy and laity and was probably the most influential means of conveying information during this period.[11] Celebrated preachers commanded large audiences, and theologians were better known for their ability to speak than for their writing. The predominance of the spoken word is illustrated by the following lines by René Benoist, who prefaced the 1566 edition of the sermons of Le Picart by Nicolas Chesneau: 'It should be noted here that the most learned and greatest men have written little or nothing [...] because to teach, engage and persuade men through the spoken word is much more difficult than writing at one's leisure'.[12] We

9   Antoine du Val, *Mirouer des Calvinistes et Armure des Chrestiens, pour rembarrer les Lutheriens & nouveaux Evangelistes de Genéve* (Paris, 1562), sig. A2v; René Benoist, *La Manière de cognoistre salutairement Jésus Christ* (Paris, 1561) sig. D1v; Francis Higman, '"Il eroit trop plus decent respondre en Latin": les Controversistes catholiques du XVIe siècle face aux écrits Réformés', *Travaux d'Humanisme et Renaissance* 326 (1998), 515–30; Larrissa Taylor, *Soldiers of Christ: Preaching in the late medieval and Reformation France* (Oxford, 1992); R. E. Hallmark, 'Defenders of the Faith: the Case of Nicole Grenier', *Renaissance Studies* 11/2 (1997), 123–40. Hallmark's opening remark is typical of the way Catholics are perceived in the historiography, at 123: 'In both France and Germany, Catholic apologists were slower – and obviously more reluctant – to respond in the same vein. French exponents of orthodoxy were even more leaden-footed than their German counterparts, though their response was not perhaps as tardy as has sometimes been suggested'.

10   Frank S. Giese, *Artus Désiré: Priest and Pamphleteer of the Sixteenth Century* (Chapel Hill, 1973), 125.

11   Alfred Soman, 'Press, Pulpit, and Censorship in France before Richelieu', *Proceedings of the American Philosophical Society* 120 (1976), 439–63, at 440.

12   Taylor, *Heresy and Orthodoxy*, 2–5; René Benoist, Preface to François Le Picart, *Les Sermons et Instructions Chrestiennes pour tous les jours de Caresme et Féries de Pasques* (Paris, 1566), sig. *5r.

should take these words seriously as they were written by someone who was himself a celebrated preacher and a prolific writer.[13] Nicolas Chesneau also published the sermons of Claude d'Espence who wrote in June 1562: 'of the five sermons that follow, the first three were preached in part, collected and transcribed by a man of great memory'.[14]

Reliance on memory is a predominant feature of oral cultures, and these lines indicate a changing relationship with the written text. Polemical authors valued the spoken word but reluctantly recognised the need to challenge the views of the Reformers in print. The overlap between the written and the oral is illustrated by the performance of Antoine de Mouchy at the Council of Trent. This formidable insight into the rhetorical conventions of the time is provided by the diary of an Italian cardinal who admired de Mouchy's ability to speak continuously for two hours 'as if he had learned by heart something that he had written'.[15] Antoine de Mouchy was a senior member of the Faculty of Theology as was Robert Ceneau, also prominent at Trent. Another orator noticed for his rhetorical excellence was Simon Vigor who ran into trouble with the Crown on several occasions for speaking his mind in public.[16] Simon Vigor published his sermons where the Crown was criticised for not taking a strong enough stance against

13   René Benoist, François le Picart and Nicolas Chesneau were friends as well as linked by the same voluntary zeal to defend the Catholic faith against heresy. Nicolas Chesneau was probably the most important printer in Paris, and from 1563 onwards he had the monopoly on the works of René Benoist, one of the most published vernacular authors of the sixteenth century. Benoist's notoriety was such that he benefited from a royal privilege that allowed him to nominate a printer who had the exclusive rights to print his works. A copy of this privilege dated 4 December 1563 names Chesneau as the beneficiary.

14   Claude d'Espence, *Cinq sermons ou traictez de maistre Claude d'Espence* (Paris, 1562), sig. *2r.

15   Alain Tallon, *La France et le Concile de Trente: 1518–1563* (Rome, 1997), 735, 741–2 (Demochares, Greek for 'pleasing to the people', was de Mouchy's pen name).

16   Barbara B. Diefendorf, *Beneath the Cross: Catholics and Huguenots in Sixteenth-Century Paris* (Oxford, 1991), 153, 157; Tallon, *La France et le Concile de Trente*, 735.

heresy.[17] Another preacher who published his sermons, Claude d'Espence, offers another insight into the relationship between writing and preaching: 'But I forget myself and instead of writing a preface I catch myself delivering a sermon'.[18]

What can be found in print was probably a pale reflection of what was heard in sermons. Although few printed sermons survive, we know that many preachers got into trouble for the views they expressed in public. A notorious example is provided by Jean de Hans whose sermon provoked the disturbance at the Church of St Médard in 1561, and who was subsequently arrested.[19] In 1564, Artus Désiré encouraged the population of Paris to resist the royal order to disarm from the pulpit and was banished for his pains.[20] Simon Vigor, another celebrated preacher, ran foul of the Crown on at least two occasions, in 1568 and 1571, for criticising the royal policy of conciliation.[21] René Benoist was also asked to withdraw one of his books which dealt with the incendiary topic of the Cross of Gastines in 1571.[22] Prophetically, Jean Bodin asserted in 1583: 'The eloquent tongue of a mutinous orator is like a dangerous knife in the hands of a madman.'[23] Nicolas Pasquier made a very similar point after the assassination of Henri IV:

> The ability of a preacher to speak well is an attractive and valuable gift. [...]
> But, if he decides to abuse the sweetness of his language, there is no more
> terrible plague on a Kingdom than this well-spoken preacher [...] his tongue

17   Simon Vigor, *Oraison Funebre prononcee aux Obseques, de treshaute, tres-
      puissante, & tres-Catholique Princesse, ma Dame Elizabeth de France, Royne
      des Espagnes, prononcee en l'Eglise nostre Dame de Paris, le XXV. du mois
      d'Octobre* 1568 (Paris, 1568), sig. H4r.
18   D'Espence, *Cinq sermons*, sig. **1r.
19   Baron de Ruble, 'L'Arrestation de Jean de Hans et le Tumulte de Saint-Médard:
      Decembre 1561', *Bulletin de la Société de l'Histoire de Paris et de l'Ile de
      France* 13 (1886), 85–96.
20   Giese, *Artus Désiré*, 30.
21   Diefendorf, *Beneath the Cross*, 147–58.
22   Edouard de Barthélemy (ed), *Journal d'un curé Ligueur de Paris sous les trois
      derniers Valois* (Paris, 1866), 134.
23   Jean Bodin, *Les six livres de la république* (Paris, 1583), 4: 661–2 quoted in
      Soman, 'Press, Pulpit, and Censorship', 441.

becomes a weapon of violence on which depends the life or death of those for whom and against whom he uses it.[24]

The aims of the authors of propaganda can be pieced together from the texts themselves. The avowed aim of Antoine du Val's *Mirouer des Calvinistes*, for example, is unambiguous:

> We have collected this little book, to guard and arm you against them [the Protestants]. By reading it, you will learn that their false doctrine, their life and diabolical jargon, is contrary to their pretence and false discourse.[25]

On the whole, pamphlets were designed to influence public opinion, to spread or deny rumours about the character of Protestants and defend the basic tenets of Catholic orthodoxy against the Calvinists' attacks.[26] With the politicisation of the conflict, in the 1560s, Catholic propaganda was increasingly aimed at the Crown for 'favouring the heretics', and unambiguously argued for continued persecution rather than toleration of religious pluralism.

How legitimate is it to speak of propaganda? Historians of early modern print have expressed differing views on the matter.[27] Peter Matheson argues that the polemic of the German Reformation hardened into propaganda by the mid-sixteenth century through a process of 'gradual declension of Reformation rhetoric' where 'opponents were bestialised, Jews transmuted into well-poisoners, the Papacy depicted as the gaping arse of Hell'.[28] In France the same phenomenon can be said to have taken place, except that it was predominantly targeted by Catholics against Protestants, rather than the reverse. The distinction between mere literature of persuasion and

---

24   Jeffrey K. Sawyer, *Printed Poison: Pamphlet Propaganda, Faction Politics, and the Public Sphere in Early Seventeenth-Century France* (Oxford, 1990), 18.

25   Du Val, *Mirouer des Calvinistes*, fol. 3r.

26   Maurice Prestat, 'De la Guerre Psychologique à la Guerre Médiatique', in Gérard Chaliand (ed.), *La Persuasion de Masse: Ses Origines Contemporaines* (Paris, 1992), 23–81, at 27.

27   Robert W. Scribner, *For the Sake of Simple Folk: Popular Propaganda for the German Reformation* (Cambridge, 1981), 8; Sawyer, *Printed Poison*, 9, 16; Peter Matheson, *The Rhetoric of the Reformation* (Edinburgh, 1998), 6.

28   Matheson, *Rhetoric of the Reformation*, 26, 44–5, 249.

propaganda is, so to speak, academic as the two are often indistin-guishable. Calling this material 'propaganda' points to specific techniques rather than passing judgement on the material itself. Propaganda was associated in the twentieth century with the willing manipulation of people's perceptions, by telling them lies.[29] It is clear, however, that the authors themselves were convinced that what they were putting forward was true. Without judging authors for what they did, it is none the less possible to discern some rules they used to do it:

1. The rule of 'simplification': reducing all data to a simple confrontation between 'Good and Bad', 'Friend and Foe'.
2. The rule of disfiguration: discrediting the opposition by crude smears and parodies.
3. The rule of transfusion: manipulating the consensus values of the target audience for one's own ends.
4. The rule of unanimity: presenting one's viewpoint as if it were the unanimous opinion of all right-thinking people: drawing the doubting individual into agreement by the appeal of star-performers, by social pressure, and by 'psychological contagion'.
5. The rule of orchestration: endlessly repeating the same messages in different variations and combinations.[30]

Although all these rules were not followed unanimously, a given pamphlet will at least conform to two or three of these principles.

Rule one, the polarisation and over-simplification of complex and ambiguous issues, pervades the material published by Catholic authors. Robert Ceneau, for instance, wrote that one should be 'either all Calvinist or totally faithful, in short either totally white or totally

---

29   Bertrand Taithe and Tim Thornton, 'Propaganda: a misnomer of rhetoric and persuasion?' in Bertrand Taithe and Tim Thornton (eds), *Propaganda: Political Rhetoric and Identity 1300–2000* (Stroud, 2000), 1–16, at 2: 'propaganda is a social phenomenon and therefore operates in several directions, that is not simply a message communicated from the powers to the public but also a reciprocal message, self-reinforcing and flexible, which must contain the logic and elements of truth, which must explain and make sense of political and social reality to the point that the propaganda message will become significant of a whole political cosmology'.
30   Norman Davies, *Europe: A History* (London, 1997), 500.

black'.[31] Inversion was used by Catholic polemicists who turned the table on the first generation of Reformers to show that the Reformation was a manifestation that 'time was out of joint'. The words of Isaiah 5:20: 'Ah, you who call evil good and good evil, who put darkness for light and light for darkness, who put bitter for sweet and sweet for bitter!'[32] were used often against Protestants, notably by Antoine de Mouchy, Claude d'Espence, and Artus Désiré.[33] It was also used by Protestants against their arch-enemy, the duc de Guise: 'This one has changed God into Satan: Christ into Belial, peace into war, the blessing into the wrath of God, a legitimate government into a tyranny'.[34]

The second rule, crude smears and parodies, was probably the most consistently observed and, in the most extreme cases, produced accusations of orgy, cannibalism and infanticide.[35] Penny Roberts uncovered the case of a city councillor of Troyes who escaped prosecution in 1562 by arguing that his only reason for attending a Protestant meeting was the hope of taking part in such an orgy.[36] Furthermore, the myth of the orgiastic Protestants was mixed with the poignant reality of the Parisian persecutions during which time

31 Robert Ceneau, *Response Catholique contre les Heretiques de ce temps* (Paris, 1562), sig. A7r.
32 New Revised Standard Version (1993).
33 Antoine de Mouchy, *Responce a Quelque Apologie que les heretiques ces jours passés ont mis en avant sous ce titre: Apologie ou deffence des bons Chrestiens contre les ennemis de l'Eglise catholique* (Paris, 1558), sig. A4v; d'Espence, *Cinq sermons*, sig. C8v; Artus Désiré, *L'Origine et Source de tous les maux de ce monde, par l'incorrection des peres & meres envers leurs enfans, & de l'inobedience d'iceux, Ensemble de la trop grande familiarité & liberté donnée aux servans & servantes* (Paris, 1571), sig. E4v.
34 Anon., *Advertissement a la Royne Mere du Roy, Touchant les miseres du Royaume au temps present, & de la conspiration des ennemis de sa Majesté* (Orleans, 1562), sig. b3v.
35 Luc Racaut, 'Accusations of Infanticide on the eve of the French Wars of Religion', in M. Jackson (ed.), *Infanticide: Historical Perspectives on Child Murder and Concealment, 1550–2000* (Aldershot, 2002), 18–34.
36 Penny Roberts, *A City in Conflict: Troyes during the French Wars of Religion* (Manchester, 1996), 84 note 64; BN, Dupuy MS 698 (Pithou), f. 243v (I owe thanks to Penny Roberts for the transcript of this document).

children were left abandoned on the streets of Paris. Lancelot du Voisin de la Popelinière's *Histoire de France* recounts how preachers on street corners added credit to the accusations of infanticide and cannibalism by pointing at these children as those the Protestants had intended to eat during their orgies.[37] Catholic polemicists, like du Val, Ceneau and others, resorted to this story because it had been used repeatedly against heretics for generations long before the advent of the Reformation, especially in the first Christian centuries and the central Middle Ages. The comparison with earlier heresies, whose precedents served to justify the accusations levelled at the Protestants, was the lynchpin of the Catholic argument against the Reformation.

The third rule is observed in many works that appealed to the consensus value of gender roles and the 'great chain of beings' to show that Protestants were turning 'the world upside down'. For example, Bosquet, a member of the *Parlement* of Toulouse, deplored the appeal of the Reformation to women and the perverse effect it had on husbands' natural authority:

> Having allowed their 'wifes' to go to the Minister, and to do all other damnable & apostastic exercises, they 'disaprove' of the husbands who forbid their wives from acting alike, having maintained that they should not be punished, nor coerced by their husbands to do their will; as if the husband was not the master of his wife: as if a Catholic wife had license to become a heretic without his consent and against his will.[38]

In appealing to the overwhelming patriarchal values of early modern society, Catholic authors were sure to have a captive audience. The supposed superiority of men over women transcended cultural barriers, and is found among the elite as well as in popular customs, such as the Charivari.

The fourth rule is illustrated by the Catholics' ability to argue that theirs was the view that was universally held before the advent of

---

37   Lancelot du Voisin de la Popelinière, *L'Histoire de France enrichie des plus notables occurances survenues ez Provinces de l'Europe & pays voisins* (La Rochelle, 1581), f. 148v.

38   M. G. Bosquet, *Sur les troubles advenus en la ville de Tolose l'an 1562* (Toulouse, 1595), 157.

the Reformation. Eucharistic symbolism permeates the discourse of Catholic polemicists, who pitched the unity of the Catholic Church against the multiplicity of the heresies. The Polish cardinal, Hozius, harked back to a time when Christendom was one as in Genesis 11:1, 6: 'now the whole earth had one language and the same [...] they are one people, and they have all one language', comparing the Reformation to the Tower of Babel. Catholicism was predominantly associated, in the minds of the illiterate majority, with unity and tradition summed up in the inscription found on the façade of the Hôtel de Ville: 'One king, one law, one faith'.[39] By resorting to the argument of tradition, these authors were hoping that their audience would stay in the bosom of the Roman and apostolic Church and close the dangerous debate initiated by the Reformers. This standpoint had the unfortunate consequence of cutting out completely those who had already been converted. To use Cold War rhetoric, the aim of the authors of Catholic propaganda was 'containment' rather than 'rollback'.

Finally, the fifth rule of orchestration is illustrated by the recurrence of the themes in many different media, through a process described by McLuhan as 'hybridisation'.[40] We have already discussed the importance of preaching and the interaction between written and oral. The language of propaganda is often marked by oral strategies: rhythm, repetition, alliteration, antithesis, and parallel. Poetry, in itself a hybrid of oral and written, is a privileged tool of propaganda, on both sides of the confessional divide.[41] Visual media are also present as the language of propaganda drew on popular imagery, familiar stories and fears. For example the representation of heresy as an hysterical woman turning scripture on its head can be found in print in the work of Robert Ceneau in 1562.[42] Pierre de l'Estoile reports that on 23 June 1588 (on St John's day) 'the representation of a great fury named heresy was burned on the fire of St

---

39   Diefendorf, *Beneath the Cross*, 159.
40   Marshall McLuhan, *Understanding Media: The Extensions of Man* (New York, 1964).
41   P. Tarbé (ed.), *Recueil de Poésies Calvinistes, 1550–1566* (Geneva, 1968).
42   Ceneau, *Response Catholique*, sig. D5r.

John'.[43] This representation was used on the title page of a German anti-Calvinist pamphlet at the turn of the seventeenth century and features in Cesare Ripa's *Iconologia* (1618).[44] This example gives us an insight into the power of symbolism and the cohesion between different media in representations of heresy.[45] The processions, show trials, executions (in effigy and in the flesh) and massacres that punctuated the French Wars of Religion should also be taken into account.[46]

An observation on the conspicuous absence of woodcuts in French printed books, by contrast to Lutheran Germany, is warranted at this point. Although it can be ascribed to Calvinist distrust of images, on the Protestant side, it does not account for their absence in Catholic material.[47] Robert Scribner indicated that in Germany, by the middle of the sixteenth century, woodcuts were gradually superseded by print owing to a change in tastes.[48] Andrew Pettegree suggested that the psalm replaced the woodcut in France as a way of conveying the Protestant message to the illiterate. Songs were expressions of

43   J-L. Flandrin (ed.), *Journal d'un Bourgeois de Paris sous Henri III par Pierre de l'Estoile* (Paris, 1966), 261–2.

44   Cesare Ripa, *Nova Iconologia* (Padua, 1618), 244; C. S. Clifton, *Encyclopedia of Heresies and Heretics* (Oxford, 1992), 123; Bodo Nischan, *Prince, People, and Confession: The Second Reformation in Brandeburg* (Philadelphia, 1994), 53 (the woodcut represents Calvinism as a medusa flailing Luther with snakes, preventing him from arguing with a Catholic bishop).

45   Matheson, *Rhetoric of the Reformation*, 37; Scribner, *For the Sake of Simple Folk*, 3.

46   Natalie Zemon Davis, 'The Rites of Violence: Religious Riot in Sixteenth-Century France', *P&P*, 59 (1973), 51–91; David Nicholls, 'The Theatre of Martyrdom in the French Reformation', *P&P*, 121 (1988), 49–73.

47   French exceptions include Luther and Melanchthon, *De Deux Monstres Prodigieux, a savoir, d'un Asne-Pape, qui fut trouvé à Rome en la riviere du Tibre, l'an 1496. Et d'un veau-moine nay à Friberg en Misne, l'an 1528*, (Geneva, 1557) printed in Gothic font which is extremely unusual in itself as the Garamond font was predominant during this period; other exceptions are reported by Philip Benedict, 'Of Marmites and Martyrs: Images and Polemics in the Wars of Religion', in *The French Renaissance in Prints from the Bibliothèque Nationale de France* (exhibition catalogue of the Grunwald Centre for the Graphic Arts, Los Angeles, 1995), 108–37.

48   Scribner, *For the Sake of Simple Folk*, 7, 249.

militancy, sung in defiance of the Catholic majority in cities, and later on the battlefield of the Wars of Religion.[49] Catholics also wrote many songs that were reported by Pierre de l'Estoile during the League and collected in modern editions.[50] This suggests that evolution of tastes and modes of expression directly affected printers' publishing strategy. This symbiotic and interactive relationship between consumers and producers of propaganda contributed to the creation of a recognisable 'public opinion'.[51]

The coherence of the Catholic response to the Reformation rested on a common repertory of images, borrowed from the history of the Church's many brushes with heresy, that could be usefully added to Natalie Davis' definition of the 'rites of violence'.[52] Examples of this imagery can be used to illustrate the second and third rule touched upon above: the widespread belief that Protestants were lecherous and the ability of Catholic propagandists to appeal to the consensus values of their audience. Drawing on the scriptural description of the Church as the bride of Christ, Catholics drew a parallel between heresy and adultery. This argument drawn from Ephesians chap. 5, v. 22–4 was used by John Eck and by Robert Ceneau:

> Wives, be subject to your husbands as you are to the Lord. For the husband is the head of the wife just as Christ is the head of the Church, the body of which he is the Saviour. Just as the Church is subject to Christ, so also wives ought to be, in everything, to their husbands.[53]

---

49   Andrew Pettegree, *Huguenot Voices: The Book and the Communication Process During the Protestant Reformation* (Greenville, 1999); H. L. Bordier (ed.), *Le Chansonnier Huguenot du XVIe siècle* (Geneva, 1969).

50   Flandrin (ed.), *Journal d'un bourgeois de Paris*.

51   Matheson, *Rhetoric of the Reformation*, 34.

52   Davis, 'The Rites of Violence': 'I would suggest that they can be reduced to a repertory of actions, derived from the Bible, from the liturgy, from the action of political authority, or from the traditions of popular folk justice, intended to purify the religious community and humiliate the enemy and thus make him less harmful'.

53   John Eck, *Les lieux communs de jean Ekius, contre Luther* (Lyon, 1551), sigs. a8r–b1r; Ceneau, *Response Catholique*, sig. E3r.

These authors implied that by breaking away from the Church, the Protestants were committing an act akin to adultery. John Eck first used the analogy to argue that just as men should not have more than one wife, they could belong to only one Church: 'Christ did not have two wives, the Church of the Apostles and ours is one, before Luther was born'. This argument was elaborated upon by René Benoist: 'friendship and sweetness cannot be as great between married men and women [...] as it is between Jesus Christ and his Church in general, but in particular to each true Christian'.[54] This was in turn reproduced by Jean Talpin in his *Remonstrance a Tous Chrestiens* arguing the analogy between fidelity in marriage and the unity of the Church very strongly:

> we know that in true and legitimate marriage, the man is joined to only one bride. [...] We see, that in man there is but one head, also that there is one body. [...] Understand this comparison of great conformity, perfect communion & convenience with the things above said, we declare the undivided link between Jesus Christ & his Church.[55]

The flip-side of the analogy between marriage and the Church, is the association between heresy and fornication. This explains why anti-Protestant propaganda often resorts to 2 Peter 2:14: 'They have eyes full of adultery, insatiable for sin. They entice unsteady souls. They have hearts trained in greed. Accursed children!'[56] Robert Ceneau asserted that 'Women abandon their husbands, & the husbands their wives to run to such people' and directly accused the Protestant heresy of breaking up marriages.[57] According to du Preau, Catholics were married to their Church and could not participate in the ceremonies of the Protestants without committing something akin to adultery:

54 René Benoist, *La Maniere de Cognoistre Salutairement Jésus-Christ* (Paris, 1564), sig. C1v.

55 Jean Talpin, *Remonstrance a Tous Chrestiens qui se sont separez de l'Eglise Romaine* (Paris, 1572) sigs. M2v, N8v.

56 De Mouchy, *Responce a Quelque Apologie*, sig. G5v; Gabriel du Preau, *Des Faux Prophetes, seducteurs, & hypocrites, qui viennent à nous en habit de brebis: mais au dedans sont loups ravissans* (Paris, 1563), sig. C1r.

57 Ceneau, *Response Catholique*, sig. B3r.

> just as it is forbidden for the children of God to take the daughters of men as their wives (as found in Genesis) [...] it is forbidden for Catholics to talk to heretics or to partake in their ceremonies without offending God.[58]

The numerous references to adultery in anti-Protestant propaganda can be explained by the theologians' conception of the Church as the bride of Christ, and of heresy as a whore. The description of Protestants as being 'soiled with all sorts of fornication and adultery',[59] accused of assembling in secret 'to conceive bastards, with poor, and well abused *femmelettes*',[60] and 'ravish & rape the sacred virgins of God, entertain & debauch the women from their husbands',[61] flows directly from this analogy. Although the majority would have been insensitive to the finer points of the analogies that were drawn by Catholic authors, all could understand their conclusions. The writings of these authors provide useful insights into the contemporary perceptions of the Protestants. The Reformed conventicles – which were held in secret – were thought to be the scene of sexual orgies and excuses for depravity, which contrasted with apparent virtue in daylight.

The distinction and parallel between the true Church as a lawful bride and heresy as a whore was not the prerogative of French Catholics. In one instance it was used by a Walloon Calvinist, Gui de Brès, who wrote against the Anabaptists: 'a whore will always defend her virtue more vigorously than an honest woman'.[62] The German Catholic George Witzel used a similar dichotomy to describe the Lutheran Church as a young girl: 'our Calvinists prefer to our

---

58 Du Preau, *Des Faux Prophetes*, sig. C1v.
59 Ceneau, *Response Catholique*, sig. D8r.
60 Gabriel de Saconay, *Discours Catholique, sur les causes & remedes des Malheurs intentés au Roy, & escheus à som peuple par les rebelles Calvinistes* (Lyon, 1568), sig. D7r.
61 Bontemps Legier, *Response aux Objections et poincts principaux de ceux qui se disent aujourd'huy vouloir reformer l'Eglise, & s'appellent fideles & croyans à l'Evangile* (Paris, 1562), sig. C4v.
62 Gui de Brès, *La Racine, Source et Fondement des Anabaptistes ou rebaptisez de nostre temps* (Rouen, 1565), 68.

[Church] a young girl who is only ten years old'.[63] The distinction is also found in England in the work of the Catholic John Proctor who depicted heresy as a 'wanton, sensual and deceitful woman'.[64] The same opposition was used in a Huguenot source against the duc de Guise: 'he has turned [...] from his legitimate wife [...] to chamber-maids and whores'.[65] Finally the Jesuit Martino del Rio, in his dis-course about magic published at the turn of the seventeenth century, spoke about heresy in these terms: 'Evil spirits are accustomed to use heretics as though they were beautiful prostitutes to draw people into error. For it is clear that in Scripture heresy is called a prostitute'.[66]

The uniformity with which these rhetorical conventions were used in France, England and the Empire, by Catholics as well as Protestants suggests that they were very versatile. The polemical use of inversion in the German Reformation has been well studied by Robert Scribner, who provides numerous examples of satirical wood-cuts depicting the overturning of the Papacy, the monastic orders and the ecclesiastical hierarchy.[67] Catholics soon turned the table on their adversary in describing Protestantism as a source of divisiveness and chaos, breaking up the body social and the body politic into as many parts as a body has limbs. Cardinal Hozius' *Des Sectes et Hérésies* re-produced the anthropomorphic symbolism expressed in the feast of Corpus Christi when describing Luther as 'tearing apart the body of Christ'.[68] This analogy was used by René Benoist in a treatise de-fending transsubstantiation against the Reformers:

63   George Witzel, *Discours des Moeurs, tant des anciens heretiques que nouveaux Lutheriens & Calvinistes, auquel leur resemblance est clerement demonstrée* (Paris, 1567), 9.

64   John Proctor, *The waie home to Christ and truth leadinge from Antichrist and errour* (1556) a translation of the fifth-century French Saint Vincent de Lérins cited by Tom Betteridge, '"Mete Covers for such Vessels": Sexual Deviancy and the English Reformation' (unpublished paper, read at the Reformation Studies Colloquium, Wadham College, Oxford, 1998), 16 pages, 4.

65   *Advertissement a la Royne Mere du Roy*, sig. b3v.

66   Peter G. Maxwell-Stuart, *The Occult in Early Modern Europe: A Documentary History* (London, 1999), 167.

67   Scribner, *For the Sake of Simple Folk*.

68   Stanislas Hozius *Des Sectes et Hérésies de nostre temps: traicte composé premierement en Latin, par reverend Pere en Dieu monseigneur Stanislas*

when he is eaten he is not divided into parts, and he is not torn in the sacrament in the way that meat is when sold in a butcher shop: he is received without wounds, and is eaten whole.[69]

The same imagery was used in Germany in a woodcut depicting Protestant Reformers (Melanchthon, Zwingli and Calvin among them) dissecting the body of Luther into as many pieces.[70]

Disease was also a common way of describing heresy from at least the Middle Ages onwards.[71] Cardinal Hozius followed in the steps of a long line of authors in referring to heresy as a 'spiritual leprosy':

a gangrenous limb is amputated for fear of infecting the rest of the body: the bodies of leprous men are segregated for fear of infecting the healthy with their leprosy: all the more reason for segregating those who are stained in their heart with the spiritual leprosy, for fear that they might infect the flock of Jesus Christ?[72]

Hozius also wrote: 'about one hundred and forty years ago, the Waldensian leprosy infected the kingdom of Bohemia'.[73] Antoine de Mouchy used a similar analogy: 'it is necessary to amputate gangrenous flesh [...] to prevent the house, the whole, the body and the flock from burning, being corrupted, rot and perish'.[74] For the same reason Gentian Hervet argued that Protestants should be segregated like Jews to avoid contagion: 'you are mixed in with everybody else [...] so that one is obliged whether he likes it or not to

Hozie, Evesque de Varme en Pouloigne, dedié au roy de Pouloigne, & nouvellement mis en François (Paris, 1561), 32.

69 René Benoist, *Claire Probation de la necessaire manducation de la substantielle & reale humanité de Jesus Christ, vray Dieu & vray homme, au S. Sacrement de l'autel* (Paris, 1561), sig. H3r.

70 Bodo Nischan, *Lutheran and Calvinists in the Age of Confessionalization* (Aldershot, 1999), 215.

71 R. I. Moore, 'Heresy as Disease', in D. W. Lourdeaux and D. Verhelst (eds), *The Concept of Heresy in the Middle Ages* (Louvain, 1976), 1–11.

72 Hozius, *Des Sectes et Hérésies*, 20, 78.

73 Ibid. 7.

74 De Mouchy, *Responce a Quelque Apologie*, sig. C8v.

speak with you, despite the fact that your conversation is no less contagious than the plague'.[75]

Gabriel de Saconay, writing in 1568, wrote that medieval kings had given a good example by 'purging their kingdom from this contagious vermin'.[76] If disease was caused by disharmony in the body, civil war was caused by disharmony in the body politic that only the King could cure. This was consistent with his role as physician expressed in the medieval custom of 'touching for the King's Evil'. Throughout the French Wars of Religion, Catholic authors appealed to the precedent of the Albigensian Crusade in the hopes that the Valois would call a Crusade against the Huguenots.[77] After successive pleas, the Catholic propaganda finally turned against the monarchs them-selves and the curative powers of Henri III were significantly questioned by Leaguer preachers because of his accommodating pos-ition towards Protestantism.[78] It could be argued that it was the failure of the Valois to acknowledge and harness the power of propaganda that led to their ultimate downfall; by contrast Henri IV, and the Bourbons generally, were much more successful in this respect.[79]

In so far as one can make out the aims and strategies of Catholic propaganda, to what extent was it successful in influencing the thoughts and actions of its audience? What did common perceptions of Protestants owe to the writings and sermons of Catholic authors? The interactivity between printed material and its readership suggests that it might be more productive to turn the question on its head: to what

75   Gentian Hervet, *Discours sur ce que les Pilleurs, Voleurs, & Brusleurs d'Eglises disent qu'ilz n'en veulent qu'aux prestres* (Reims, 1562), sig. F6v.

76   Gabriel de Saconay, *De la Providence de Dieu sur les Roys de France treschrestiens, par laquelle sa saincte religion Catholique ne defaudra en leur Royaume. Et comme les Gotz Arriens, & les Albigeois en ont esté par icelle dechassés* (Lyon, 1568), sig. Y4r.

77   Luc Racaut, 'The Polemical use of the Albigensian Crusade during the French Wars of Religion', *French History* 13 (1999), 1–19.

78   Mark Greengrass, *France in the Age of Henri IV: The struggle for stability* (London, 1995), 35.

79   Luc Racaut, 'The cultural obstacles to religious pluralism in the polemic of the French Wars of Religion' in K. Cameron, M. Greengrass, and P. Roberts (eds), *The Adventure of Religious Pluralism in Early-Modern France* (Oxford and Bern, 2000), 115–27.

extent did the perceptions and portrayal of Protestants found in printed propaganda reflect the concerns and fears of the public at large? Whether this material spread through the illiterate population 'orally' is difficult to determine, but this process was not one-sided. The ideas found in print owed as much to the welling-up of oral discourse into the literate world as the reverse.[80] Oral discourse, which, unless it leaves a written trace, is inaccessible to the historian, can thus be grasped through written material that had such an interactive relationship.

Matheson has argued that the success of pamphlets depended on how well they addressed the concerns of their audience and thus reflected their views:

> Perhaps the pamphlet, however, is the most reliable evidence, like a periscope sticking out of the ocean, of that vast, submarine force of discussion and dissent, which we call public opinion. [...] Successful pamphlets are those which reflect and at the same time spread and modify the 'pulsations' of oral discourse.[81]

Unfortunately the data for undertaking a systematic study of the relative success of certain books as opposed to others are still missing but some trends can already be discerned from a representative sample.[82] The violent propaganda which has been outlined here responded to a certain 'demand' and the recurrence of certain ideas suggests that they enjoyed a relative success. It this way, polemical pamphlets can be construed as a gauge of 'public opinion', a recipient of influences coming from below, rather than as a purely 'top-down' phenomenon.

---

80 Matheson, *Rhetoric of the Reformation*, 20–1, 37; Sawyer, *Printed Poison*, 69; Scribner, *For the Sake of Simple Folk*, 2–3, 8; Miriam Yardeni, *La Conscience Nationale en France pendant les Guerres de Religion 1559–1598* (Louvain, 1971), 5.

81 Matheson, *Rhetoric of the Reformation*, 27, 32.

82 This research will be facilitated by the completion of the French Vernacular Book Project (St Andrews Reformation Studies Institute, 69 South Street, St Andrews KY16 9AL, UK).

Furthermore, the material found in these pamphlets pervades the culture of sixteenth-century France.[83] For example, in the affair of the rue St Jacques, it is obvious that the idea that Protestants took part in orgies co-existed both in the oral and the written spheres. Feeding off each other, the rumours which spread by word of mouth in the streets of Paris were fuelled by written accounts disseminated by Catholic authors, and vice-versa. In France, in the second half of the sixteenth century, polemical authors were certainly aware of the impact of their opponents' writing and were themselves writing to credit or deny a given rumour. The allegation that it was the 'vulgar' whose opinion was being manipulated was made by the anonymous chronicler of the massacre of Cabrières and Mérindol, writing in 1555:

> they have had the reputation among common folk of practising incest, sorcery and enchantment and of being completely devoted to the Devil, meeting in conventicles as much to indulge in lewd behaviour and do other execrable things as to conduct their 'Sabbat' [I use their terminology] with the Devil who is present on that occasion.[84]

The concern of Protestant authors for the dissemination of rumours among 'common folk' is an interesting reversal of the situation in Germany. In France, it seems that it was the Catholics who had the ear of the common folk.

To use the analogy of disease, so prized among Catholic authors, ideas spread like viruses. The analogy is probably even more powerful today, deepened by our knowledge of how viruses actually work. A media analyst, Douglas Rushkoff, recently carried the analogy to its logical conclusion in *Media Virus!* Like viruses, ideas travel in the information network replicating themselves in as many ways as possible. This process has given rise to a neologism that describes an idea which spreads through the media like a virus in an organism:

83   Matheson, *Rhetoric of the Reformation*, 20–1, 239.

84   Anon., *Histoire memorable de la persecution & saccagement du peuple de Merindol & Cabrieres & autres circonvoisins, appelez Vaudois* (Geneva, 1555), sig. *4v; translated by Maxwell-Stuart (ed.), *The Occult in Early Modern Europe*, 168.

Media viruses spread through the datasphere the same way biological ones spread through the body or a community. [...] Once attached, the virus injects its more hidden agendas into the datastream in the form of ideological code-not genes, but a conceptual equivalent we now call 'memes'.[85]

To carry the analogy further, 'memes' affect the collective organism, society at large, or for want of a better word 'public opinion'. The themes, topoi or ideas that can be found in religious propaganda could be more usefully described as 'memes'. Their recurrence in many different sources suggests they enjoyed a wide distribution not only in print, but also in the predominant medium of orality.

Indeed Catholic authors added credence to their accusations by resorting to the ubiquitous 'rumour' that has been described as the oldest media in the world.[86] For example, Simon Vigor wrote: '[Margaret of Spain] was horrified at hearing what was said [...]'.[87] Protestant authors, such as des Gallars and Chandieu, were particularly quick to accuse Catholic writers of spreading false rumours: '[...] monks flock to hear the news [...] spies report to our betters [...] and spread false rumours and feed the population with nonsense and lies'.[88] The best example of the relationship between written propaganda and the spread of rumours by word of mouth is provided by the affair of the rue St Jacques: '[It] was at the origin of the commonly held belief that assemblies were excuses for orgies and that there were witnesses to that effect'.[89] The speed with which

---

85   Douglas Rushkoff, *Media Virus! Hidden Agendas in Popular Culture* (New York, 1991), 9–10.
86   Jean-Noël Kapferer, *Rumeurs: Le Plus Vieux Média du Monde* (Paris, 1987); Gabriel-André Pérouse, 'De la rumeur à la nouvelle au XVIe siècle Français', in M. T. Jones-Davies (ed.), *Rumeurs et Nouvelles au temps de la Renaissance* (Paris, 1997), 93–106.
87   Ceneau, *Response Catholique*, sig. E1r; Vigor, *Oraison Funebre*, sig. F2v.
88   Des Gallars, *Seconde Apologie ou Defense des Vrais Chrestiens, contre les calomnies impudentes des ennemis de l'Eglise catholique. Ou il est respondu aux diffames redoublez par un nommé Demochares docteur de la Sorbonne* (Geneva, 1559), sig. D7r.
89   Antoine de la Roche Chandieu, *Histoire des Persecutions, et martyrs de l'Eglise de Paris, depuis l'an 1557. Jusques au temps du Roy Charles neufviesme* (Lyon, 1563), sig. x7v.

information travelled is demonstrated by the rapid spread of the homicidal fury that seized regional capitals in the aftermath of the St Bartholomew's day massacre. Probably the most pervasive rumour, after the politicisation of the conflict, was that Huguenots were engaged in a vast conspiracy that encompassed the whole of Christendom. This is what Jean de la Vacquerie wrote in 1560, two years before the taking of Orleans and Lyon by the Protestants:

> Married women plot the death of their husbands, and all the assembly is in league to arm against the salvation and the honesty of the republic: They take counsel and machinate among themselves to determine how they can bring about the end of, or deprive them of their offices, those magistrates who are contrary to them: in order to replace them some of their faction; and by these means hold the reins of the government of the republic, after having removed the good rectors and the governors of the cities.
>   Who knows if they don't raise funds to buy offices and introduce their friends and correligionaries in the presidial courts? So that they can spread their venomous doctrine in all impunity, and when they are arrested, so that they can find patrons and defenders instead of judges punishing them: this is the way they have gained Geneva, Lausanne, and many other cities of Switzerland and Germany. This is what they will achieve in our country of Gaul, if we are not careful and repress their audacious effrontery.[90]

This rumour was circulated at the time of the purge of the *Parlement* of Paris orchestrated by the Cardinal de Lorraine and Antoine de Mouchy that culminated in the execution of Anne du Bourg in March 1560. This is also the time when the University and the *Parlement* of Paris began to criticise the Crown, shortly after Catherine de Medici appointed Michel de L'Hospital as chancellor. While the Crown pursued a policy of conciliation with the Protestants, at least until the surprise of Meaux in 1567, the Catholic establishment used propaganda to promote persecution in the face of a pluralism it abhorred. Catholic propaganda offers us an inestimable insight into the mentality of the first decades of the French Wars of Religion, a

---

90   Jean de la Vacquerie, *Catholique Remonstrance aux Roys et Princes Chrestiens, a tous magistrats & gouverneurs de Repub. touchant l'abolition des heresies, troubles & scismes qui regnent aujourd'huy en la Chrestienté* (Paris, 1560), sigs. F1r–v.

sensitive period which can be characterised as 'make or break' for the Reformation. The overall impression, expressed perhaps for the very first time, is that the Catholic riposte to the Reformation in France was far richer than it was given credit for. This sometimes crude response was probably more popular than the arguments of the Reformers, however more sensible and better articulated they might seem to the modern reader.[91] By the time Calvinism started making inroads into France, the use of the vernacular and printing as a way of reaching the wider audience of those not literate in Latin was well established among Catholic circles. The situation is completely different from the Lutheran Reformation where it was the Reformers themselves who orchestrated vicious attacks against the Papacy. In France, it was the Catholic theologians, notably from the University of Paris, who spearheaded the use of propaganda to debase Protestantism.

The versatility of Catholic propaganda is shown by its use of the 'battle of the sexes' and the popular topos of the 'world upside down'. In a striking reversal of the German situation, it was the Catholics who appealed to consensus values found in popular culture. Although French Protestants also used these images, they were hampered by the Genevan distaste for crude and inflammatory propaganda. Catholics used the full array of medieval stereotypes to good effect, using female attributes to describe heresy. Accusations of sexual impropri-eties, of which Catholic propaganda is replete, can be explained through the traditional association between heresy and adultery. Catholic propaganda consistently attempted to sway opinion in favour of further persecution, and posited a major obstacle to the establish-ment of religious pluralism in France. The Edict of Nantes could only be promulgated once Catholic propaganda had been silenced. With the benefit of hindsight it could be argued that by converting to Catholicism, Henri IV had understood the lesson that the League had taught Henri III. By 1600, the French Crown had recognised public opinion as a political force to be reckoned with and propaganda would be harnessed by Richelieu and his successors to promulgate the King's will.

---

91   Mark U. Edwards, *Printing, Propaganda, and Martin Luther* (London, 1994), 76–81.

RICHARD BONNEY

'God, Fatherland and Freedom': Rethinking Pluralism in Hungary in the Era of Partition and Rebellion, 1526–1711[1]

I cannot better explain... the whole dispute between the Emperor and the Hungarians than by acquainting you, that the latter pretend their kingdom is founded upon the same constitutions in reference to the House of Austria as Scotland is in regard to the crown of England; viz, that they have an independent government whereas the Court of Vienna would willingly reduce them to the form of Ireland, and treat them as a people reduced by conquest,

---

1 The author is grateful for the comments of Dr János Barta (University of Debrecen), but any mistakes remain his own. A useful introduction to the subject is provided by J. Bérenger, *Tolérance ou paix de religion en Europe centrale, 1415–1792* (Paris, 2000). A remarkable evidential base has been assembled by Béla Köpeczi: Köpeczi, *La France et la Hongrie au début du xviiie siècle. Étude d'histoire des relations diplomatiques et d'histoire des idées* (Budapest, 1971). Though not mentioned in the frontispiece, this was a translation of a work which appeared earlier in Hungarian in 1966. Another remarkable publication is the annotated French and Hungarian edition of Rákóczi's memoirs, which also has a detailed chronology of the revolt: I. Kovács and B. Köpeczi (eds), *Mémoires du Prince François II Rákóczi sur la guerre de Hongrie depuis 1703 jusqu'à sa fin* (Budapest, 1978). For the years 1661–1700, there is a great deal of useful information to be gleaned from *State Papers Foreign. Germany (Empire) and Hungary, 1661–1700 (SP 80/11–17)* (List and Index Society, 223, 1987) (hereafter *State Papers, 1661–1700*). Though disappointing as a posthumous work, there is nevertheless useful information to be gleaned from W. B. Slottman, *Ferenc II Rákóczi and the Great Powers* (New York, 1997). The most succinct but well documented recent account is C. W. Ingrao, *In Quest and Crisis: Emperor Joseph I and the Habsburg Monarchy* (West Lafayette, Ind., 1979), ch. 5: 123–60. A condensed version of this paper appeared as Bonney, '"For God, Fatherland and Freedom": Rethinking Pluralism in Hungary in the Era of Partition and Rebellion, 1526–1711', in K. Papp, J. Barta et al (eds.) *The First Millennium of Hungary in Europe* (Debrecen, 2002), 377–96.

which has not been their case hitherto, though it is likely to be their inevitable misfortune, if they do not get out of this war with some success.

The English envoy, reflecting upon the difficulties faced by the Rákóczi revolt prior to its suppression and the conclusion of the Peace of Szatmár in 1711, made this telling comparison between the relationship between Hungary and Austria on the one hand and Scotland, Ireland and England on the other.[2] In both cases, the relationship was contentious because it was simultaneously a religious and a political issue. The chief aim of this chapter, which needs to be read in conjunction with a more detailed analysis of the limits of pluralism in early modern France,[3] is to suggest that the complexity of pluralism from the point of view of the historian arises precisely from the interaction of religious and political issues. Both as a theoretical construct and in actual historical experience, a state could be pluralist in terms of its political structures but exclusivist in terms of its religious position (viz, the kingdoms of Aragon, Valencia and Catalonia in the sixteenth century); conversely, a state which was pluralist in its religious position could be exclusivist in its political stance (viz, the Ottoman state except in relation to its vassal states).

The Hungarian experience between the national disaster at Mohács in 1526 and the Peace of Szatmár in 1711[4] is therefore of

2   The remark, made in Nov. 1704, was quoted by M. A. Thomson, 'Self-determination and collective security as factors in English and French foreign policy, 1689-1718', repr. in *William III and Louis XIV. Essays, 1680–1720 by and for Mark A. Thomson*, ed. R. M. Hatton and J. S. Bromley (Liverpool, 1968), 280.

3   R. J. Bonney, 'The Limits of Pluralism in Early Modern France', in K. C. Cameron, M. Greengrass and P. Roberts (eds.) *The Adventure of Pluralism in Early Modern France* (Berne, 2000), 205–26. An important article by Philip Benedict has identified some of the issues: P. Benedict, '*Un roi, une loi, deux fois*: parameters for the history of Catholic–Reformed co-existence in France, 1555–1685', in O. P. Grell and R. W. Scribner (eds.) *Tolerance and Intolerance in the European Reformation* (Cambridge, 1996), 65–93.

4   This chronology is also proposed by L. Benczédi, 'The warrior estate in the seventeenth century with special reference to the Thököly uprising, 1678–1685', in J. M. Bak and B. K. Király (eds.), *War and Society in East Central Europe. III. From Hunyadi to Rákóczi. War and Society in Late Medieval and Early Modern Hungary* (Brooklyn, NY, 1982), 351.

much greater international importance than is sometimes imagined and its significance is heightened by the fact that the medieval kingdom had been a multi-nation state. For here we have a testing ground for the various issues of religious and political pluralism over almost two centuries, with a tripartite division of the kingdom into potentially competing blocs torn between two great powers, the Habsburg dynasty and the Ottoman state. How should this experience of potentially dual loyalty or double rule be viewed? Should it be seen simply as a national catastrophe? The Catholic kingdom (whose millennium was celebrated in the year 2000) was no longer unified and no longer exclusively Catholic in 1526. In spite of his own personal sympathies, as a result of the pressure of the diet, the last Jagiello king had allowed the enactment of three laws against Lutheranism in 1523 and 1525.[5] What was the political price to be paid for liberation from the Ottoman yoke?[6] In any balancing of a 'political price' for freedom, the loss of unity has to be set against the fact that the divisions within Hungary before the conquest were far-reaching; in Norman Housley's view, it was a case of 'kingdom against kingdom' not just in the events of 1514, but in 'the first quarter of the [sixteenth] century in its entirety'.[7] Moreover, were there not religious disadvantages to the expulsion of the Ottomans? If Rákóczi himself and most of his advisers were Catholics, 'the long history of Habsburg persecution there made it easy for the Maritime Powers to believe that all the rebels were victims of religious

5   K. Peter, 'Hungary', in R. W. Scribner, R. Porter and M. Teich (eds.), *The Reformation in National Context* (Cambridge 1994), 158. D. P. Daniel, 'Hungary', in A. Pettegree (ed.), *The Early Reformation in Europe* (Cambridge, 1992), 58.

6   Cf. two quotations from *The Corvina History of Hungary from Earliest Times until the Present Day*, ed. P. Hanák (Budapest, 1991), 67: 'in 1699 the Treaty of Karlowitz was signed. After 150 years of subjugation, Hungary, with the exception of the *Temesköz* area, was finally free from Ottoman dominion.' Ibid., 69: 'After 150 years of Ottoman domination, Hungary's territorial unity was restored. However, the country had to pay a high price for the expulsion of the enemy. The Turkish yoke had been removed, only to be replaced by Habsburg oppression.'

7   N. J. Housley, 'Crusading as Social Revolt: the Hungarian Peasant Uprising of 1514', *JEH*, 49 (1998), 11–28 at 26.

intolerance'.[8] Rákóczi, it has recently been argued, 'won over much of the country's non-Catholic majority by promising to restore religious freedom, together with those places of worship that had been seized under Leopold'.[9] In the end, it was the Calvinist gentry who elected him prince of Transylvania and sought to crown him king.[10] *Kuruc* ideology in Transylvania, at least from Bocskai in 1605 onwards, had linked resistance to Habsburg claims to the struggle for political and religious liberties. In Robert Evans's judgement, this alternative set of values 'meant the survival, not only of Protestantism, but of confessional pluralism'.[11]

I

The greater understanding of the historical significance of pluralism in recent times, and its considerable contemporary relevance, suggests that a more balanced assessment of gains and losses needs to be drawn during the nearly two centuries between Mohács and Szatmár. Two observations are pertinent at the outset. The first is the need to avoid teleology. This has been persuasively argued by David Nirenberg in his study of the persecution of minorities in the Middle Ages. He argues that 'discourse and agency gain meaning only in relation to each other':

> thus when medieval people made statements about the consequences of religious difference, they were making claims, not expressing accomplished reality, and these claims were subject to barter and negotiation before they could achieve real force in any given situation... The more we restore to those outbreaks of violence their own particularities, the less easy it is to assimilate

8   J. P. Spielman, *Leopold I of Austria* (London, 1977), 197; Thomson, 'Self-determination and collective security', loc. cit.

9   C. Ingrao, *The Habsburg Monarchy, 1618–1815* (Cambridge, 1994), 116.

10   R. J. W. Evans, *The Making of the Habsburg Monarchy, 1550–1700. An Interpretation* (Oxford, 1979), 266.

11   Ibid., 267.

them to our own concerns, as homogeneity and teleology are replaced by difference and contingency.

He adds as another 'perhaps more provocative, criticism of the teleological model' that it has 'overlooked the fundamental interdependence of violence and tolerance in the Middle Ages'.[12] These remarks may be equally valid for the period when the Reformation begins to make its impact in the various European countries. We should neither view the events of the years between 1526 and 1711 from the perspective of the late medieval monarchy under the Jagiellons nor should we view it with hindsight, after the phenomenal growth of Austrian Habsburg power, the baroque *trompe-l'oeil* after 1700.[13] Thus older statements relating to the national character of the Hungarian state over very long periods of history have to be viewed with considerable caution. Few would now subscribe to the view propounded in 1910 by Henry Marczali that

> the alliance with the Turks at a time of constitutional and religious struggle involved a denial of the nation's past and future. It is this fact that accounts for the tragic fate of men like Bocsay and Gabriel Bethlen (*sic*), who were the leaders not only of their party but of their nation: they could achieve victories, excite enthusiasm and command devotion, but they were never able to revive the whole energy of the national spirit.[14]

Even Marczali had commented that 'it was natural and almost necessary that the interests of the weaker Protestantism should be identified with those of Islam, the foe of Christianity'.

The second observation concerns the experience of Islamic rule in other areas of Europe and the reputation of the Ottoman state as a relatively advanced champion of religious pluralism in the sixteenth century. By the mid-sixteenth century, those advocates of toleration who noted that the Ottoman State harboured 'several religions and

12   D. Nirenberg, *Communities of Violence: Persecution of Minorities in the Middle Ages* (Princeton, N. J, 1996), 6–7.
13   C. Capra, 'The Eighteenth Century. I. The Finances of the Austrian Monarchy and the Italian States', in R. J. Bonney (ed.), *Economic Systems and State Finance* (Oxford, 1995), 295.
14   H. Marczali, *Hungary in the Eighteenth Century* (Cambridge, 1910), 248.

various sects in its borders' were said by Christian advocates of persecution to injure the reputation of Christian princes: 'they want to measure their empires according to the tyranny of the Turks and dispose Christian customs in accordance with the monstrousness of the laws of the Turks'.[15] In the view of many sixteenth- and seventeenth-century Christians, Islamic pluralism ought to set no precedent for Christians. Nevertheless, the force of two contemporary arguments in favour of 'Calvino–Turcism'[16] needs to be recognised. The first is that it was only after the Ottomans were chased out of Hungary that 400 temples or so were expropriated and the Protestants were persecuted; in contrast, under Ottoman rule, Protestant rights had been secure.[17] As Béla Köpeczi puts it,

> Hungarian public opinion in the first half of the seventeenth century was highly impressed by the economic and cultural development and relative religious tolerance that had come into being in a Transylvania subordinated to the Turks, circumstances that demonstrated that the latter did not interfere in home affairs anywhere as much as the Habsburgs.[18]

In May 1661, Henry Oldenburg in England confirmed that German and Hungarian Christians were willing 'to live under ye Turk, because of liberty of conscience', while after 1662 some English Nonconformists believed that they would be better treated under the Ottomans than under the established Anglican church.[19]

A second contemporary argument concerns the reputation of the Ottomans with the French Protestants: the Huguenots made the telling

15   D. G. Mullan ed., *Religious Pluralism in the West* (Oxford, 1998), 124.

16   R. J. W. Evans, 'Calvinism in East Central Europe: Hungary and her Neighbours', in M. Prestwich (ed.), *International Calvinism, 1541–1715* (Oxford, 1985), 179.

17   Köpeczi, *La France et la Hongrie*, 470.

18   B. Köpeczi, 'The Hungarian Wars of Independence of the Seventeenth and Eighteenth Centuries in their European Context', in Bak and Király, (eds.), *From Hunyadi to Rákóczi. War and Society in Late Medieval and Early Modern Hungary*, 445–53, at 447. However, two similar vassal states, the Romanian principalities of Wallachia and Moldavia were Greek Orthodox states without any sign of religious tolerance.

19   N. Matar, *Islam in Britain, 1558–1685* (Cambridge, 1998), 106–7.

comparison between the treatment of the Protestants in France and Hungary and their attitude was overwhelmingly favourable to the Ottomans. Louis XIV clearly sought to champion the rights of Hungarian Protestants (among others), while persecuting his own Protestant subjects.[20] In so doing, the French king was said by his propagandists to be following the message of the gospel in helping unjustly oppressed Christians: 'the king and the Turks are acting in the spirit of Jesus Christ. The ruler of Hungary, on the other hand [that is, Leopold I], is acting like a perfect Muslim.'[21] More generally, the positive reputation of the Ottomans with regard to other religions was attested even by some Catholics. The comment of the great sixteenth-century jurist Jean Bodin in the *Six Books of the Republic* (1576) is symptomatic of this attitude:

> The great emperor of the Turks doth with as great devotion as any prince in the world honour and observe the religion by him received from his ancestors; and yet determineth he not the strange religions of others; but to the contrary permitteth every man to live according to his conscience; yea and that more is, near unto his palace at Pera suffereth four divers religions, *viz.* that of the Jews, that of the Christians, that of the Grecians, and that of the Mahometans...[22]

20   Köpeczi, *La France et la Hongrie*, 499 ('les Turcs [...] leur sont pourtant beaucoup plus favorables, pouisque au lieu de les persécuter, comme les papistes font, ils observent religieusement les traités faits avec eux au sujet de la religion'). French Protestants would have rejected as specious the argument that Louis XIV's persecution of the Huguenots was political in motivation: ibid., 471.

21   Köpeczi, 'The Hungarian Wars of Independence', 451. This late use in 1692 of the term 'Muslim' as a pejorative epithet should be noted.

22   Jean Bodin [trans. R. Knolles, 1606], *The Six Bookes of a Commonweale [...]*, ed. K. D. McRae (Cambridge, Mass., 1962), 537 (spelling modernised). Quoted from a modern translation by D. J. Vitkus, 'Early Modern Orientalism', in D. R. Blanks and M. Frassetto (eds), *Western Views of Islam in Medieval and Early Modern Europe. Perception of Other* (Basingstoke, 1999), 226. The four religions thus defined were Judaism, Christianity according to the Roman rite, Christianity according to the Greek rite and Islam. The use of the term 'Islam' became more common in the seventeenth century, as against the terminology e.g. of French writers in the sixteenth century which (with the exception of Bodin) was usually pejorative.

II

If we consider the Hungarian case in the light of the suggested model for the levels of pluralism in a society (see Appendix, p. 120) then clearly in 1514 and as late as 1525 Hungary conformed to the first level, where there is no pluralism at all. This situation, where there is no acceptance or coexistence with religious minorities, may be termed 'confessional exclusivism'. The outsider is stigmatised as the enemy; when the conflict is religious, the enemy is demonised and the conflict is therefore sanctified. Insurrection to secure religious freedom or 'rights' may become a form of religious war in such circumstances and the forcible elimination of heretics becomes a process of sanctified violence or holy war. The Dósza revolt in 1514 was resolutely orthodox in its Catholicism; indeed the very orthodoxy of the Hungarian *cruciferi* is problematic, because the crusade–revolt aimed at the overthrow of the *status quo* but the ideas and goals of the movement were inspired and rendered coherent by the cross which worn by its participants.[23]

Repressive legislation came to an end in 1525 and was in any case unenforceable after the military collapse the following year. Not until 1548 were there further attempts to pass laws in Royal Hungary against Protestants. In that year, Lutherans and Catholics joined in an effort to expel Anabaptists and Swiss Sacramentarians from the kingdom.[24] As in Germany, the dispute was over which Confession of Augsburg was acceptable (was it the 1530 version, the *invariata*, as the Lutherans wanted, or the *variata* of 1540?) As confessional divisions hardened, both groups disassociated themselves from Anabaptists and anti-trinitarians.[25] However, in Habsburg-controlled Royal Hungary, the adherence to the ruler's religion was not

---

23   Housley, 'Crusading as Social Revolt', 28.
24   L. Makkai, 'The Crown and the Diets of Hungary and Transylvania in the Sixteenth Century', *Crown, Church and Estates. Central European Politics in the Sixteenth and Seventeenth Centuries*, ed. R. J. W. Evans and T. V. Thomas (New York, 1991), 86–7.
25   Daniel, 'Hungary', 67.

obligatory because of the statute law of patronage (*jus patronatus*) dating from the Middle Ages: according to this, the landed gentry and privileged districts and cities had the right to appoint ministers, priests and teachers. These entrenched patronage rights ensured the success of the Reformation by the later sixteenth century, so that at least 90 per cent of the population in Royal Hungary adopted Protestantism according to either the Lutheran or the Reformed confession.[26]

Thus the divided Hungarian kingdom in the 1530s and 1540s seems to conform largely to level two, where the majority culture merely coexists with minorities *de facto* (this might be termed 'confessional coexistence'): hostility to the minority religions and cultures remains and the legitimacy of their existence is challenged. This state of affairs may contain the feature of 'culture wars' between cultures within the same state which remain totally separate. The early Reformation in Hungary was taken up first by the towns with German populations: Transylvania's Saxons were probably 'the first to read the pamphlets of the Reformation, and the first modern printing press in Hungary was established in 1529 in the Saxon town of Szeben'.[27] The councils of the towns in Hungary which had turned to the Reformation provided financial assistance for students to study at Wittenberg and elsewhere in Protestant universities in Germany.[28] In contrast, Calvin was almost unknown in Hungary in the 1540s and there was little contact with Geneva even at the end of the century. When the first Swiss-inspired advances were made, it was in an initiative from Bullinger at Zurich in 1549, who sent the Swiss Reformed Confession (the *Consensus Tigurinus*) to eastern Europe for approval.[29]

By the 1560s, Royal Hungary had also attained level two in our model: the majority culture, in this case that of the Habsburg Emperor and his court, merely coexisted with the religious minorities *de facto* in a form of 'confessional coexistence', the difference being that the

---

26   Makkai, 'The Crown and the Diets of Hungary and Transylvania', 86.

27   Peter, 'Hungary', 164.

28   Daniel, 'Hungary', 62–3.

29   Evans, 'Calvinism in East Central Europe', 171, 176 (denial of service to 'János Kalviny').

so-called religious minorities actually constituted the majority of the population. In Royal Hungary, a law was enacted by the diet against the Arians (anti-Trinitarians) in 1572.[30] A law against Calvinism was proposed to the Hungarian diet but was not enacted. The decisive factor was political, in the negative sense of fear of the Counter-Reformation and of the Ottomans, and also in the positive sense, of an embattled population seeking self-help in constitutional and religious terms.

The advance of the Reformation in its diversity was most marked in Transylvania, which enjoyed the greatest autonomy under Ottoman suzerainty and for a time seems to have attained level four (a mixture of religions and cultures existing side by side, with none predominating). The problem of religious diversity was confounded with that of ethnic diversity (the *unio trium nationum*, the confederation of the three 'nations' of Magyar nobility, Saxons and Szeklers or Székelyek, which had been formed in 1437 for the suppression of the peasants in revolt against their landlords, continued to reflect ethnic divisions).[31] Edicts of toleration, which recognized confessional differences, were passed in 1557 and 1563.[32] The apogee of the movement for civic toleration came on 28 January 1568, with the legislation of Sigismund II János Zápolyai in Transylvania ensuring toleration for the four existing confessions (Catholic, Lutheran and Reformed; the Unitarian confession was added in 1571) so long as they did not introduce further doctrinal innovation: 'we demand that in our dominions there shall be freedom of conscience.'[33] Moreover, the diet at Torda proclaimed that villages were allowed to 'keep any preacher whose preaching pleases it... because faith is a gift of God'. Freedom of worship was also allowed for the Orthodox Church and for the Jews, so that in Transylvania 'there prevailed a pluralism

30   Makkai, 'The Crown and the Diets of Hungary and Transylvania', 87.
31   Ibid., 88.
32   G. H. Williams, *The Radical Reformation* (London, 1962), 712–13, 715–16.
33   E. Cameron, *The European Reformation* (Oxford, 1991), 332; J. Lecler, *Toleration and the Reformation*, trans. T. L. Westow (2 vols., New York and London), 1:402; E. M. Wilbur, *A History of Unitarianism in Transylvania, England and America* (Boston, 1945), 40, 48.

unprecedented in Europe'.[34] Zápolyai was the first (and to date the only) important European ruler to convert to Unitarianism;[35] he did so under the influence of Giorgio Biandrata, the Piedmontese physician who became leader first of the Polish and the Hungarian Unitarians. It was as Zápolyai's physician that Biandrata spread his ideas and succeeded in converting the most influential Calvinist preacher, Ferenc Dávid.

The regime of civic toleration was inherited by the first powerful prince of independent Transylvania, the Catholic István Báthory, and his 'confessionally mixed advisers with their Italianate and Renaissance culture'[36] and subsequently, once he became king of Poland in 1574, his elder brother Christoph. At a time when the Emperor Maximilian II described himself as 'neither a Catholic nor a Protestant, but a Christian',[37] István Báthory said that he was ruler of the people, not of their consciences.[38] Promotion to public office was open to Calvinists and Lutherans. He became increasingly suspicious of Unitarianism however, although this was, if anything, the predominant Protestant confessional identity in Transylvania in the early 1570s.[39] The spiritual focus of Unitarianism was Kolozsvár, where a prolific press was managed by Dávid's associate Kaspar Heltai. István Báthory forbade them to print books without his prior permission. The movement was fatally weakened for religious and political reasons. Biandrata and Socinus (Fausto Paolo Sozzini) attacked Dávid's suspension of the sacraments and the worship of Christ; they succeeded in having him arrested on the prince's authority and in November 1579 he died in prison. The political threat came from a failed rebellion of the Székely population under Kaspar Békés in 1575 with

---

34 Makkai, 'The Crown and the Diets of Hungary and Transylvania', 90.
35 Wilbur, *A History of Unitarianism*, 49.
36 Evans, 'Calvinism in East Central Europe', 173.
37 L. W. Spitz, 'Imperialism, Particularism and Toleration in the Holy Roman Empire', in A. Soman (ed.), *The Massacre of St Bartholomew: Reappraisals and Documents* (The Hague, 1975), 73.
38 Williams, *The Radical Reformation*, 726.
39 Wilbur, *A History of Unitarianism*, 62–3, 67–8, 90.

which Unitarianism was strongly linked.[40] The doctrinal innovation of Dávid could be said to have infringed the legislation of 28 January 1568, and the subsequent interpretation placed on it with regard to Unitarianism at the Diet of Torda in 1572, while a failed rebellion inevitably carried its own price. But clearly there were limits as to Biandrata's view of tolerance, since he had instigated the arrest of Dávid, his own former colleague.[41] Socinus, who is best known as the organizer of Polish Unitarianism after 1579, formulated views in his treatise *De Ecclesia*, which distinguished between *adiaphora* and fundamental articles or essentials. He rejected the interference of the state in the interior discipline of the church; denied the prince any power over religious matters; and contested the right of the civil authority to banish, imprison or execute heretics. Socinus' tolerance was arrived at by way of a mystical spiritualizing individualism. Membership of a church was not necessarily a test of Christian values:

> Nothing prevented [it] then [in the time of St Paul], and nothing prevents now the possibility of accepting and keeping the true doctrine of Christ without binding oneself to any outward church if, rightly or wrongly, one came to suspect all of some error concerning salvation.[42]

Transylvania became an autonomous principality in 1571[43] and developments there cannot be taken as representative of Hungary as a whole. Since Socinus removed himself to Poland, his views cannot be taken as representative even of Unitarian opinions in Transylvania, let alone Hungary. It seems reasonably clear that as the warring between Unitarian factions developed, so the Reformed confession under Péter Méliusz's leadership strengthened.[44] Christoph Báthory was more

---

40   Wilbur, *A History of Unitarianism* 54–6; Cameron, *The European Reformation*, 332; Williams, *The Radical Reformation*, 726–7.
41   Lecler, *Toleration and the Reformation*, i. 412–13.
42   Ibid., 1: 413–15. Williams, *The Radical Reformation*, 749–56.
43   L. Makkai, 'István Bocskai's Insurrectionary Army', in Bak and Király (eds.), *From Hunyadi to Rákóczi. War and Society in Late Medieval and Early Modern Hungary*, 276; B. K. Király, *Hungary in the Late Eighteenth Century. The Decline of Enlightened Despotism* (New York and London, 1969), 115 n. 1.
44   Evans, 'Calvinism in East Central Europe', 172–3; Cameron, *The European Reformation*, 280.

inclined than his younger brother to promote Catholic interests and fell increasingly under Jesuit pressure, ordering the arrest of Dávid in 1579.[45] Developments affecting the Székely population, including their enserfment or enfranchisement, remained key factors in the ability of the Transylvanian rulers to mobilize a field army between the reigns of Sigismund II János Zápolyai (who ordered enserfment in 1562) and Sigismund Báthory (who restored their liberty in 1595). It was the enfranchised Székely serfs who provided the army of 20,000 men mobilised by Báthory's general, István Bocskai, in his campaign against the Turks in Wallachia in 1595.[46] There can be little doubt that Sigismund Báthory sought, in his new status as Prince of the Holy Roman Empire, to reduce Transylvania to a Catholic confessional state; to this end, he had five Unitarian magnates who opposed his policies executed in 1595. Political instability unsettled this policy (the government changed twelve times in six years) and it was left to the depredations of the army under Giorgio Básta to continue the oppression of the Protestant confessions by military means. If Unitarianism was particularly hard hit, all forms of worship other than according to the Catholic rite were prohibited in the last stages of Básta's military autocracy.[47]

Bocskai's volte-face, from a commander in the Habsburg interest against the Turks in 1595 to a commander in the Ottoman interest against the Habsburgs in 1604, can only be explained by personal ambition and the possibilities of realising his objectives given the accumulated grievances of Hungary and Transylvania resulting from the fifteen-year war against the Turks. In Royal Hungary, Rudolf II's prosecution of influential magnates, the expropriation of Protestant churches at Kassa and the arbitrary addition of a clause favouring the Counter-Reformation to the resolutions of the Pozsony Diet of 1604 provided the stimulus to rebellion.[48] Five *hadjú* captains promised

45   Williams, *The Radical Reformation*, 727, 730.
46   Makkai, 'István Bocskai's Insurrectionary Army', 275–96.
47   Wilbur, *A History of Unitarianism*, 94–103.
48   G. Schramm, 'Armed Conflict in East-Central Europe: Protestant Noble Opposition and Catholic Royalist Factions', in Evans and Thomas (eds.), *Crown, Church and Estates*, 180, 186.

Bocskai on 14 October to 'defend Christianity, our country and dear fatherland, and especially the one true faith' and to support his military leadership 'to rescue this dear fatherland'. Ideas of a Transylvanian alliance with the Hungarian estates against the Habsburg ambition of *dominium absolutum*,[49] exploiting anti-German and anticlerical sentiments (the reformed pastors wanted to 'send the tonsured, chanting priests back to Rome') and perhaps enfranchising the largely serf *hadjúk* population seem to have merged rapidly in the Bocskai revolt. On 20 November 1604, Bocskai received Ahmed I's warrant (*berat*) as prince of Transylvania; on 20 April 1605 the diet of Royal Hungary at Szerencs recognised him as protector of Hungary, but the nobility made it clear that it wanted the *hadjúk* controlled.[50] 'As the first Reformed prince of Transylvania, Bocskai was able to dictate terms in the rest of Hungary',[51] with his *Apology* of 1605 published abroad in several languages[52] much as William of Orange's had been. In the Peace of Vienna of 23 June 1606, Bocskai ensured that the *hadjúk* were transformed into a free peasantry that was tax exempt but obliged to perform free military service. Their position in Royal Hungary was seen as comparable to that of the Székelyek in Transylvania, while Bocskai's attitude has been considered 'unique among Hungarian magnates'.[53]

The religious concessions were equally important. Freedom of religion was granted to the noble and burgher estates 'without prejudice to the Catholic religion'. Bocskai died suddenly in December 1606. When Rudolf II refused to implement the peace, the diet of Royal Hungary came out openly against him and persuaded his brother, the ambitious Archduke Matthias, to lead their movement. Rudolf abdicated and Hungary (as well as Austria and Moravia) fell to Matthias. As king, Matthias gave way to the estates at the Diet of Pozsony in November 1608 on the principle of religious self-determination for village communities. Protestant peasants on the

---

49   Ibid., 187 (Bocskai's propaganda against Sigismund III of Poland).
50   Makkai, 'István Bocskai's Insurrectionary Army', 280, 282, 285–6, 289, 281.
51   Evans, 'Calvinism in East Central Europe', 177.
52   Evans, *The Making of the Habsburg Monarchy*, 267.
53   Makkai, 'István Bocskai's Insurrectionary Army', 292–3.

lands of a Catholic lord could no longer be forced to follow the religion of their master. In Royal Hungary a measure limiting the *jus patronatus* was enacted (this had been the policy in Transylvania since 1588). Transylvania had, in the end, set the pace of pluralism for Royal Hungary: a new interpretation was placed on article 31 of the Hungarian Golden Bull of 1222, which was taken to mean that the Hungarian nobility possessed a clear right of rebellion (*jus resistendi*) in the case of autocratic rule or a threat to its privileges.[54]

After 1613, Transylvanian policy under Bethlen Gábor was to establish a Protestant alternative for Hungary by military force and alliances with foreign powers, including the Ottomans. Ferdinand of Styria was deposed as king of Hungary and Bethlen was elected king by the diet in the summer of 1620 in the presence of an Ottoman delegation; Osman II authorised the diet to elect a king 'well disposed' towards him.[55] Despite his military victories, Bethlen's support in Hungary collapsed and a series of treaties – Nickolsburg (1621), Vienna (1624) and Pozsony (1626) – extricated him from the wars while preserving the status quo in constitutional and religious terms. Between 1630 and 1648 György I Rákóczi was more cautious in his policies, though he, too, knew how to exploit grievances in 1644–5, when he went to war in alliance with France (an alliance that was recalled by Ferenc II Rákóczi in his revolt after 1701).[56] Under pressure from the Ottomans, Rákóczi abandoned his foreign alliances

---

54 Evans, 'Calvinism in East Central Europe', 177 n 26. K. Benda, 'Habsburg Absolutism and the Resistance of the Hungarian Estates in the Sixteenth and Seventeenth Century', in Evans and Thomas (eds.), *Crown, Church and Estates*, 126-8; Makkai, 'The Crown and the Diets of Hungary and Transylvania', 90. It was not, therefore, an innovation of the Treaty of Linz of 1645 as maintained by Király, *Hungary in the Late Eighteenth Century*, 117;
J. Bérenger, 'Le royaume de France et les "Malcontents" de Hongrie. Contribution à l'étude des relations entre Louis XIV et Imre Thököly, 1678–1689', *Revue d'histoire diplomatique*, 87 (1973), 277–319, at 281–2. Article 31 was revoked by the Hungarian diet in 1687, which at the same diet acknowledged the Habsburg right of succession to the Hungarian throne.

55 K. Péter, 'Two Aspects of War and Society in the Age of Prince Gábor Bethlen of Transylvania' in Bak and Király (eds.), *From Hunyadi to Rákóczi. War and Society in Late Medieval and Early Modern Hungary*, 307.

56 Köpeczi, *La France et la Hongrie*, 166–7.

at the Peace of Linz in 1645.[57] The religious and constitutional terms of the peace were subsequently ratified by Ferdinand III the following year in his desire to keep Hungary pacified while pursuing his other military objectives in the Thirty Years' War.[58]

Relative military and political ascendancy for the autonomous Transylvanian principality was gained at a cost: Calvinism became the state church; Sabbatarians and heterodox Calvinists (Independents or Puritans) were persecuted; a new confession of faith (the Dées agreement or *Complanatio Deesiana*) was imposed on Unitarians, who were subject to civil punishment if they pursued doctrinal innovation beyond the agreement (this was imposed by the Diet, the Unitarians excepted, and thus given the force of law in 1638).[59] From level four in our model, the mixture of religions and cultures existing side by side, with none predominating, Transylvania sank rapidly to level two, that of mere confessional coexistence, with all four confessions defined and limited in theological development. György II Rákóczi's ambitions in Poland, which came to shattering defeat in 1657, left a politically divided Transylvania which encouraged the Turks to crush its independence and install the pliant Mihály I Apafi as ruler.[60] Apafi was a devoted Calvinist who was prepared to see the Unitarians excluded from membership of the diet in 1670. This might give grounds for considering that Transylvania seemed on the way to becoming a Calvinist confessional state, except that 'the free practice of their religion' for the 'four received confessions' was emphasised in treaties and negotiations between Leopold I and Apafi in 1686–8.[61]

With Transylvania reduced by the Turks to impotence, and a twenty-year armistice agreed with the Ottomans after 1664, the

---

57   B. Croxton, *Peacemaking in Early Modern Europe. Cardinal Mazarin and the Congress of Westphalia, 1643–1648* (Selinsgrove, 1999), 189.

58   K. Péter, 'The Struggle for Protestant Religious Liberty at the 1646–47 Diet in Hungary', in Evans and Thomas (eds.), *Crown, Church and Estates*, 261–8; Evans, *The Making of the Habsburg Monarchy*, 121.

59   Evans, *The Making of the Habsburg Monarchy*, 270–1. Idem, 'Calvinism in East Central Europe', 181–7; Wilbur, *A History of Unitarianism*, 117–19.

60   Evans, *The Making of the Habsburg Monarchy*, 269; Idem, 'Calvinism in East Central Europe', 186–7.

61   Wilbur, *A History of Unitarianism*, 125–6, 128.

Emperor Leopold I was in a position to launch a concerted assault on the *acatholici* of Royal Hungary, as Vienna contemptuously referred to its perceived 'heretics'. This amounted to an attempt to reduce it to category one in our model, a confessionally exclusivist state. The maxim of 'burning the Hungarians' laws on their heads' was possibly quoted to Leopold I around 1680,[62] but clearly applies to the repression of the earlier period. The key figures in this repression were the king's confessor, the Jesuit Father Müller,[63] Cardinal Kollonich (so cordially hated in Hungary that he would 'infallibly have [had] his throat cut' if the rebels had been able to seize him)[64] and the primate archbishop and Chancellor Szelepcsényi (who pursued a policy of repression yet detested Kollonich).[65] Szelepcsényi presided over the tribunal at Pozsony in 1673–4, which passed sentence upon 336 Protestant ministers because of their religion.[66] There is evidence that Lutherans and Calvinists responded differently to the assault: whereas Lutheran pastors were prepared to sign statements of complicity in the rebellion (complicity being assumed because of religious allegiance), the Calvinists preachers refused outright.[67] The Papacy was active in support of the assault on Protestant rights, seeking the recall of Habsburg troops from Germany for use in 'God's service against the infidels', since Ottoman intervention was feared on the side of the

62 Benczédi, 'The Warrior Estate in the Seventeenth Century with Special Reference to the Thököly Uprising, 1678–1685', 358, 365.
63 J. Bérenger, 'La Hongrie des Habsbourgs au xviie siecle. République nobiliaire ou monarchie limitée?', *Revue Historique*, 238 (1967), 31–50 at 48; J. Bérenger, *Finances et absolutisme autrichien dans la seconde moitié du xviie siècle* (Paris, 1975), 62, 219. The influence of the Jesuits on Leopold was a theme of Rákóczi's memoirs: Kovács and Köpeczi (ed.), *Mémoires du Prince François II Rákóczi*, 59.
64 *State Papers, 1661–1700*, 168, 171–2, 296; Evans, *The Making of the Habsburg Monarchy*, 251–2.
65 *State Papers, 1661–1700*, 171; Evans, *The Making of the Habsburg Monarchy*, 260–1.
66 I. Bitskey, 'The Collegium Germanicum Hungaricum in Rome and the Beginning of the Counter-Reformation in Hungary' in Evans and Thomas (eds.), *Crown, Church and Estates*, 118.
67 Bérenger, 'Le Royaume de France et les "Malcontents" de Hongrie', 279.

rebellion.[68] In the 1680s, during the last years of the pontificate of Innocent XI, papal finance to the Habsburg military effort in Hungary was crucial to its success.[69] The predominant theology of the repression was Marian in inspiration: the idea of a *Regnum Marianum* went hand in hand with the cult of St Stephen who had made Hungary a haven of Latin Christianity under siege from the Orthodox and the pagans.[70] Though temporarily suspended on 8 October 1681 because of the Ottoman threat, the policy was resumed in the legislation of 1687, according to which religious affairs were construed as part of the royal prerogative and removed from the jurisdiction of the Hungarian diet. This was followed up with the *Explanatio Leopoldina* (4 December 1691), which remained in force until 1731: this arbitrarily changed all the previous legislation on religious matters, restricted Protestant rights of worship and required Protestants to celebrate Catholic holidays as well as, in the case of guild members, to participate in Catholic processions.[71] This legislation was the culmination of twenty years of royal policy seeking to implement confessional exclusivism, level one in our model. The main hope for the Protestants lay in the success of armed resistance.

The original pretext for the Catholic offensive was provided by the Wesselényi conspiracy, although its leading participants were in fact Catholic malcontents.[72] A Protestant rebellion in Upper Hungary in 1672 served as a further justification. Before 1678 the Turks were reluctant to intervene directly, although they seem to have offered military supplies to Apafi of Transylvania and the Hungarian Protestants. The leadership of the 'exile' (*bujdosó*) movement from 1672 to 1678 rested in the hands of a group of between twelve and fifteen 'deputies' who were all members of the wealthiest landed

---

68   *State Papers, 1661–1700*, 76, 203; Evans, *The Making of the Habsburg Monarchy*, 261.

69   Bérenger, *Finances et absolutisme autrichien*, 413–14.

70   Marczali, *Hungary in the Eighteenth Century*, 250–2; Evans, *The Making of the Habsburg Monarchy*, 256.

71   Király, *Hungary in the Late Eighteenth Century*, 118.

72   Evans, *The Making of the Habsburg Monarchy*, 261–3; Idem, 'Calvinism in East Central Europe', 190; Király, *Hungary in the Late Eighteenth Century*, 117–18.

nobility in Royal Hungary and sought to establish a noble republic there.[73] Since appeals to the Emperor had failed, the 'exile' movement clearly sought support from abroad, stressing the need for the United Provinces and England to defend Protestant rights abroad.[74] The key military support was that offered by the Ottomans, with the prospect of diplomatic assistance (and from 17 November 1676, a subsidy) from France.[75] The Emperor's offers of peace were not trusted, since the Protestants had been deceived in the previous expectations of liberty of conscience (and Leopold broke off discussions once he had secured peace with France). Transylvania, for example, was insistent on the free exercise of religion. The revolt took on a whole new momentum once Imre Thököly, the twenty-two-year-old son of a Calvinist nobleman whose estates had been confiscated after the Wesselényi conspiracy, assumed military leadership in April 1678.[76] Against the Catholic theological vision of a *Regnum Marianum*, the rebels asserted an alternative vision on the coins they struck in the autumn of 1678. On one side of the coin was the image of St George, with the inscription SANCTE GEORGI PATRONE AEQUITUM. The reverse side of the coin showed a ship in violent storms with the motto POST TEMPESTATEM SERENITAS.[77]

During the Dutch war (1672–8), French policy was to finance a diversion by the rebels in Hungary to limit the capacity for action of the Habsburg forces in the western theatre of war; a draft treaty was drawn up in November 1676 and ratified the following year. The French negotiators secured Malcontent agreement to free rights of

---

73   Benczédi, 'The Warrior Estate in the Seventeenth Century with Special Reference to the Thököly Uprising, 1678-1685', 357; *State Papers, 1661–1700*, 110; Bérenger, *Finances et absolutisme autrichien*, 99.

74   *State Papers, 1661-1700*, 100, 143, 171.

75   P. Roy, *Louis XIV et le second siège de Vienne, 1683* (Paris, 1999), 34–5.

76   *State Papers, 1661–1700*, 174, 193–4, 202; J. P. Spielman, *Leopold I of Austria* (London, 1977), 86.

77   *State Papers, 1661–1700*, 200 (24 Oct./3 Nov. 1678). The significance of St George is two-fold. Firstly, he had been the patron of warriors and especially crusaders in the Middle Ages; secondly, as one of the Fourteen 'Holy Helpers' he had been venerated in Hungary, Germany and Sweden in the later Middle Ages. D. H. Farmer, *The Oxford Dictionary of Saints* (Oxford, 1978), 156, 166.

worship for Catholics of the Latin rite, who thus demonstrated their commitment to confessional pluralism.[78] Whereas in 1668 Louis XIV had been prepared to abandon the Hungarian rebels because of a peace treaty with the Emperor, in 1679 this was no longer the case.[79] Thököly was encouraged by the French negotiators to adopt an intransigent position, precisely so that the Emperor would not be able to renew hostilities in Germany.[80] The pliant Mihály I Apafi made his peace with the Emperor, thus removing Transylvania from potential hostilities at least at first. Thököly and the Malcontents were encouraged by him to settle with Leopold, who made the appropriate concessions to religious liberty on 8 October 1681. On 11 December, Thököly was promised 100,000 *écus* by the French government if he took to arms in the spring of 1682.[81] The French expectation was that the Turks would follow suit and thus that France would gain its powerful war by diversion on the eastern front the following year.[82] Then, on 6 August 1682, the Turks went much further than before and recognized Thököly as ruler of Upper Hungary under Ottoman protection. Though a Calvinist, Thököly was able to gain the support of the Catholic nobility in 1682–3, a development which, while crucial for the chances of success of his movement, nevertheless carried the risk that they would later revert to Habsburg allegiance. The collapse of the movement was inevitable once the Ottomans arrested Thököly in October 1685 (albeit he was held at Buda only for three months).[83]

78   Bérenger, 'Le royaume de France et les "Malcontents" de Hongrie', 291–5.

79   Louis XIV was obliged to cease all assistance under the terms of the Peace of Nimwegen; but he accepted on 16 December 1679 the proposal to establish in Hungary and Transylvania 'un parti… dont on pourrait à tout événement tirer de l'utilité pour les affaires de Pologne et même pour l'Empereur de ce côté là': Roy, *Louis XIV et le second siège de Vienne*, 36–7.

80   Bérenger, 'Le royaume de France et les "Malcontents" de Hongrie', 298–300.

81   Roy, *Louis XIV et le second siège de Vienne*, 59 (the instructions were received by Vitry in January 1682).

82   Bérenger, 'Le royaume de France et les "Malcontents" de Hongrie', 310–12.

83   J. Stoye, *The Siege of Vienna* (London: Collins, 1964), 15–16 (the title of king of Hungary), 47 (prince of middle Hungary); Benczédi, 'The warrior estate in the seventeenth century with special reference to the Thököly uprising, 1678–1685', 359, 361–2; Evans, *The Making of the Habsburg Monarchy*, 264; Spielman, *Leopold I of Austria*, 120.

By November 1690, he had to retreat into Moldavia and Wallachia; but these setbacks did not stop Thököly and the Turks continuing joint military incursions in August 1693, including the siege of Belgrade. Support had faded for his rebellion by May 1695, when he was said to have hardly more than 500 rebels in his forces.[84] However, as late as 1704, in spite of a long exile in the Ottoman state, Thököly retained support among the Lutherans of Transylvania; Rákóczi claimed that he feared that his return would have destabilized relations between the religious parties there and would not have been in the interests of Catholicism.[85] The following year, the French envoy confirmed the potential for religious factionalism in Transylvania: Catholics supported Rákóczi; Calvinists, the younger Apafi; Lutherans, Thököly; and the Unitarians whichever 'is the strongest party'.[86]

III

The restriction of Hungarian privileges and the defeat of Thököly's rebellion resulted from the determination of Leopold I and his chief adviser between 1693 and 1699, Count Franz Ulrich Kinský, to resist any long-term compromise either on religious or political independence. Influenced by his Bohemian origins and his position as Chancellor of Bohemia, Kinský was inclined towards removing all Hungarian rights, on the model of the revision of the Bohemian constitution in 1627. The more moderate counsels of the Chancellor Strattman, who was of German origins, prevailed until his death in 1693 and influenced the arrangements for Hungary in 1687 and for Transylvania in 1690.[87] Kinský was thought by the English envoy to be of 'a Jesuiticall persecuting principle' so that no concessions could

84   *State Papers, 1661–1700*, 250, 287, and 298.
85   Kovács and Köpeczi (eds.), *Mémoires du Prince François II Rákóczi*, 86.
86   Köpeczi, *La France et la Hongrie*, 83, 106.
87   Spielman, *Leopold I of Austria*, 134, 164–5; Bérenger, *Finances et absolutisme Autrichien*, 56–62; Evans, *The Making of the Habsburg Monarchy*, 272.

be made to 'that brave unhappy man' Thököly.[88] By 1696 Kinský's policy had won: direct political control was being exercised by the Habsburg monarchy in both Hungary and Transylvania. The renewed Ottoman offensive, which aimed to restore Transylvanian independence, could have undermined this victory for Catholic confessional absolutism. Eugène of Savoy's crushing victory at Zenta on 11 September 1697 ended the Ottoman hopes of restoring their own power and Transylvanian autonomy. Though there were later periods of Ottoman resurgence, and Eugène only received the biretta and sword from the Papacy in 1716 (in recognition of his outstanding military services to Christendom and the Catholic Church), once he had recovered the Bánát, there is little doubt that 'the Turks were in decline in Europe' after Zenta.[89] As Béla Köpeczi remarks, 'in the end Thököly fell victim to the Turkish alliance and the disastrous decline of the Ottoman Empire'.[90]

The Peace of Karlowitz (26 January 1699) was Kinský's work, although the Allies had a hand in it. At these negotiations, the States General of the United Provinces instructed their envoys to intercede with Leopold I to secure freedom of conscience for the Hungarian and Transylvanian Protestants; they asked William III to instruct his envoys to do likewise.[91] But they asked in vain. With the expulsion of the Turks, in spite of all Leopold's formal undertakings (the *Explanatio Leopoldina* of 1691 had warned that religious freedom in the reconquered lands was purely voluntary and only temporary), the Hungarian lands were on the way to being returned by force to Catholic confessional exclusivism, level one in our model. The commission for the reconquered lands (*Neo-Acquistica commissio*) was presided over by the hated Cardinal Kollonich from 1688.[92] Significant clerical landholdings were re-established, since the Ottoman restrictions on the activities of the Catholic clergy were

---

88   *State Papers, 1661–1700*, 290; Slottman, *Ferenc II Rákóczi and the Great Powers*, 107.
89   N. Henderson, *Prince Eugen of Savoy. A Biography* (London, 1964), 43, 225.
90   Köpeczi, 'The Hungarian Wars of Independence', 448.
91   *State Papers, 1661–1700*, 310.
92   Evans, *The Making of the Habsburg Monarchy*, 252 n. 38.

removed at a stroke.[93] The removal of Protestant civil rights, especially rights to office, the work of the *Carolina resolutio* of 1731,[94] was the logical outcome of the victories of the 1690s. The pace of Catholic exclusivism was curtailed by Rákóczi's rebellion for 'God, Fatherland and Freedom' (*cum Deo pro patria et libertate*) between 1703 and 1711, which temporarily deposed Habsburg power in Hungary and Transylvania.[95] Could Catholic exclusivism have been prevented altogether?[96] The great achievement of the rebellion, settled by the negotiators at the Peace of Szatmár in May 1711 (in the absence of Rákóczi and in spite of his letter of

93   Bérenger, *Finances et absolutisme autrichien*, 120; Evans, *The Making of the Habsburg Monarchy*, 238, 271–2. The English envoy at Vienna noted the intransigent attitude of the Jesuits to Protestant churches in Transylvania as early as April 1692: *State Papers, 1661–1700*, 275. Leopold's vow to rebuild all the (Catholic) churches of Hungary destroyed during the war: ibid., 284 (August 1693). After the fall of Buda, write A. N. Kurat and J. S. Bromley, 'the whole Hungarian resistance broke down in consequence and Thököly had to abandon his remaining towns to the judicial terror supervised by General [Antonio] Caraffa at Eperjes': Kurat and Bromley, 'The retreat of the Turks, 1683–1730', in J. S. Bromley ed., *New Cambridge Modern History. VI. The Rise of Great Britain and Russia, 1688–1715/25* (Cambridge, repr. 1971), 619.

94   Király, *Hungary in the Late Eighteenth Century*, 119; Marczali, *Hungary in the Eighteenth Century*, 255.

95   A. Várkonyi, 'Rákóczi's War of Independence and the Peasantry', *From Hunyadi to Rákóczi. War and Society in Late Medieval and Early Modern Hungary*, 369–91 at 369; 'For God and Liberty': Köpeczi, *La France et la Hongrie*, 395.

96   Kovács and Köpeczi (ed.), *Mémoires du Prince François II Rákóczi*, 60: '...si j'exhortois les esprits à la charité et à la tolérance réciproque, ne pouvant approuver qu'on employât la violence dans la conduite des consciences, on m'accusoit de favoriser le parti des Anticatholiques de n'avoir qu'une Religion feinte et dissimulée.' This had been the criticism of Michel de L'Hospital in France in 1562–8. In fact, Rákóczi made it clear that his compromises between the religious factions were made without prejudice to the Catholic faith: ibid., 117. As with de L'Hospital, he made it clear that his ultimate aim was the reunion of Protestants within the Catholic church, but by pacific means: ibid., 14 ('...aiant établi l'union des esprits, je pourrois par des voies douces et pacifiques ramener les Religions séparées à la véritable Unité catholique'). Since the obstacles to unity were overwhelming it is a matter of speculation whether or not it would have taken the form of a Uniat church.

protest), was a limitation on the activities of the commission for the reconquered lands (*Neo-Acquistica commissio*).[97] Ferenc II Rákóczi, the grandson of György II and stepson of Thököly, had been educated by the Jesuits and in later life became a Jansenist.[98] Contemporary observers of the rebellion noted that he was a 'très bon catholique'; he was called a fervent Catholic though most of his officers were Protestant; he was someone who was 'très exact dans la pratique de la religion'.[99] With regard to Hungarian affairs, he was said to know how to maintain co-operation between the different religious interests.[100] Rákóczi was projected by the diet (and projected himself) as *père de la patrie*,[101] almost as a king of France would have done, and certainly as distinct from Muscovite autocracy. The early propaganda of the revolt, such as in the call to mobilization of 6 May 1703 stressed that the movement was for all Hungarians without class or religious distinction against the German nation which was oppressing the kingdom. Later, more considered, statements such as Paul Ráday's *Animadversiones apologicae* (1706), stressed that Transylvania had never accepted direct imperial control or the terms of the Peace of Karlowitz. Noble rights of rebellion under the terms of article 31 of the Hungarian Golden Bull of 1222 were reasserted and it was required that freedom of worship should be guaranteed under the terms of the decisions of the Diet of Szécsény in 1705. The Jesuits were said to have violated the laws of the land and were to be expelled from Hungary. The rebels made the disavowal of the decisions of the Diet of Pozsony of 1687 the cornerstone of their programme. They made it clear that they regarded its decisions as illegal promulgations

---

97   Köpeczi, *La France et la Hongrie*, 298.

98   Evans, *The Making of the Habsburg Monarchy*, 238, 265; Köpeczi, *La France et la Hongrie*, 602; J. Bérenger in F. Bluche (ed.), *Dictionnaire du grand siècle*, (Paris, 1990), 1298 (*s.v.* Rakoczi).

99   Köpeczi, *La France et la Hongrie*, 88, 112, 114.

100 Ibid. 117: 'il sait accorder, par rapport aux affaires d'Hongrie, les différentes religions que l'on y exerce'; ibid., 145: Louis XIV recognized that at the diet of Szécsény in 1705 his 'prudence... ait suspendu les différends que la religion pouvait exciter en cette occasion' (5 Nov. 1705).

101 Ibid. 197 (20 Aug. 1707); Kovács and Köpeczi (ed.), *Mémoires du Prince François II Rákóczi*, 151.

which had been wrung from the body under duress from the Austrian Habsburg government.[102] It seems clear that the rebellion did succeed in winning some permanent gains for the Hungarian Protestants.[103]

Yet when it came to the search for foreign assistance to the rebellion, the apparent religious consensus underpinning the revolt began to show signs of strain. This was already evident in September 1704, when the Protestants in Hungary made it clear that they sought English and Dutch mediation and distrusted Rákóczi's dealings with France. They feared 'some stricter engagements' secretly taken with the Franco-Bavarian alliance, and would have been even more apprehensive had they known that before the outbreak of the revolt, in November 1701, Rákóczi had already appealed to Louis XIV for support.[104] Religious difficulties might well have surfaced at the Diet of Szécsény in 1705, precisely because the question of an alliance with France was openly discussed.[105] In the event, the projected French alliances of 1708 envisaged the re-establishment of the liberty of the estates of the kingdom of Hungary and the principality and estates of Transylvania (in two separate documents), but Louis XIV recognized by this date that the projected alliances were of no value either for his service or for the good of the rebellion,[106] such had been the decline of French power during the War of the Spanish Succession. The military disasters at Blenheim, Ramillies and Turin had taken their toll.

102　Köpeczi, *La France et la Hongrie*, 48, 385; Slottman, *Ferenc II Rákóczi and the Great Powers*, 299; Kovács and Köpeczi (eds.), *Mémoires du Prince François II Rákóczi*, 58.

103　The Protestants had about a thousand churches c.1700. They regained some 600 churches; although some 443 of these were lost between 1711 and 1781, this still resulted in a net gain of some 150 churches between 1699 and 1781. K. Domonkos, *Müvelödés a XVIII. Svázadi Magyarországon* (Budapest, 1980), 83. The author is grateful to Dr. Janos Barta for this reference.

104　Kovács and Köpeczi (eds.), *Mémoires du Prince François II Rákóczi*, 82 (for the dashed hopes of a junction with Bavarian forces after Blenheim). Köpeczi, *La France et la Hongrie*, 36, 102 n. 29.

105　Ibid. 128, 137–8.

106　Ibid. 260–2. Count Wratislaw had warned Rákóczi not to trust in French promises: Kovács and Köpeczi (ed.), *Mémoires du Prince François II Rákóczi*, 135.

Rákóczi had sought to act without the help of the Ottoman state which, as has been seen, was weakened by military defeat and was also doubtful about the chances of success for the revolt. The primary motive in rejecting the traditional Ottoman alliance, in the view of Louis XIV, was because Rákóczi and his supporters wished to appear as liberators of their oppressed homeland.[107] On the other hand, the French king tried to incite the Ottoman state to attempt to reverse its military defeats by using the Rákóczi revolt for its own purposes.[108] Rákóczi's relations with the Ottomans eventually broke down in June 1707, once it was clear that there was no prospect of military support.[109] It seems probable that Catholic support for the rebellion would in any case have been alienated by such an alliance, as also by the Protestants' championing of an alliance with the defeated Charles XII of Sweden after Poltava.[110]

IV

This survey began with the comparison between the relationship between Hungary and Austria on the one hand and Scotland and England on the other. The parallel between Hungary and Scotland can be overdrawn. Though this had not been the case under James I[111] and Charles I, the mid-seventeenth century crisis in the British monarchies had led to a partial settlement of the religious and constitutional disputes, confining the Scots Kirk to the kingdom of Scotland which also, until the Act of Union of 1707, possessed its own Parliament.

---

107   Köpeczi, *La France et la Hongrie*, 97.
108   Ibid., 80 (6 Aug. 1703).
109   Ibid., 205.
110   Ibid., 276. Kovács and Köpeczi (ed.), *Mémoires du Prince François II Rákóczi*, 193: the Catholic nobility broke ranks with the rebellion once Clement XI clearly supported Joseph's title as King of Hungary and instructed the clergy to do likewise.
111   A. R. MacDonald, *The Jacobean Kirk, 1567–1625: Sovereignty, Polity and Liturgy* (Aldershot, 1998).

England, for example, definitively rejected Scots Presbyterianism in 1648–9. For a few years, in the 1640s, there had been a dangerous intrusion of the various religious and constitutional issues from each of the separate kingdoms (England, Scotland and Ireland) into the other. The norm, however, was for a separate political and religious arrangement in each of the kingdoms forming the composite British monarchy.

The history of Royal Hungary under Leopold I, in contrast to the Scots and Irish parallel, shows the constant interaction of religious and constitutional issues within a single state structure. For Jean Bérenger, the status of Royal Hungary in the second half of the seventeenth century was halfway between that of the remodelled constitution of Bohemia after 1627 and the freedom enjoyed by the *Sejm* and the nobility of Poland.[112] Rákóczi's memoirs allude to his fears that without a clear victory or an acceptable negotiated settlement, Hungary would be reduced to the status of Bohemia after the defeat at the White Mountain.[113] The Polish parallel is interesting because of Rákóczi's ambition to become king of Poland, an ambition which the French envoy thought was fatal to his cause.[114] A relatively simple comparison, however, shows that aristocratic 'freedom' had gone much further in Poland by the later seventeenth century than in Royal Hungary. The *Sejm* met biennially and controlled the taxation required for military campaigns.[115] The Diet in Royal Hungary, in contrast, met only five times in the second half of the seventeenth century (in 1655, 1659, 1662, 1681 and 1687). After 1687, Leopold summoned only two assemblies of magnates (in 1696 and 1698).[116] This is in contrast

112   J. Bérenger, 'La Hongrie des Habsbourgs au xviie siecle', at 31. The English diplomat George Stepney raised comparisons with Bohemia, Silesia, Moravia and also with Scotland and Ireland in the same paragraph: Slottman, *Ferenc II Rákóczi and the Great Powers*, 282.

113   Kovács and Köpeczi ed., *Mémoires du Prince François II Rákóczi*, 146, 194.

114   Köpeczi, *La France et la Hongrie*, 275, 288.

115   J. Jedruch, *Constitutions, Elections and Legislatures of Poland, 1493–1977: A Guide to their History* (Washington, DC, 1982); A. Filipczak-Kocur, 'Poland-Lithuania before Partition', *The Rise of the Fiscal State in Europe, c.1200–1815*, R. J. Bonney ed., (Oxford, 1999), 443–79, especially figs. 14.9 and 14.10.

116   Bérenger, 'La Hongrie des Habsbourgs', 35.

to Bohemia, where the remodelled constitution allowed for annual meetings of the Diet in the second half of the seventeenth century.[117]

The irregularity of the meetings of the Diet of Royal Hungary meant that either no taxation was granted (and therefore none levied) or else the government had to act unconstitutionally and take what it needed by force using the army. This was part of the significance of what Bérenger calls the *régime d'exception* from 1670 to 1681, an experiment which he considers came to an end at the Diet of Sopron in 1681.[118] Yet can the *régime d'exception* really be considered to have ended in 1681? The religious disagreements at the diets of 1662 and 1681 had not gone away; the crown was determined to destroy elective monarchy at the diet of 1681, a task which it completed in 1687. Above all, the war went on and the army needed resources: nearly half the Habsburg army was tied down in Hungary by early 1711.[119] Aristocratic critics could claim, with some justification, that supporters of absolutism on the French model had demolished the old system without determining first whether its replacement was 'possible, indeed practicable' in Hungary.[120] While there may be something to be said for Cardinal Kollonich's view, expressed in a memorandum of 1681, that the threat to the liberties of Hungary came from noble rebellions rather than the crown,[121] attempts could have been made to summon diets in those parts of Royal Hungary under the control of the Habsburg monarchy. The argument looks like the classic absolutist assertion of overriding 'necessity' (the term used in Kollonich's memorandum) rather than a respectful commitment to

---

117   Bérenger, *Finances et absolutisme autrichien*, 138.
118   Ibid., 332–3. Bérenger, 'La Hongrie des Habsbourgs', 49–50.
119   Ingrao, *In Quest and Crisis*, 159.
120   Slottman, *Ferenc II Rákóczi and the Great Powers*, 252. Count Mansfield on 12 Nov. 1699.
121   Bérenger, 'La Hongrie des Habsbourgs', 38. Rákóczi admitted that there was a measure of continuity in what he termed as seven revolts (including his own): Slottman, *Ferenc II Rákóczi and the Great Powers*, 310 n 5; Kovács and Köpeczi (ed.), *Mémoires du Prince François II Rákóczi*, 57: 'je rapporte ceci entant que les violations des Libertés et leur réparations ont été la cause des guerres, et non entant que celles-ci concernoient la propagation des Religions heterodoxes…'

Hungarian liberties. Kinský was also clear about the necessity of bypassing the Hungarian diet in 1698; yet of course one year's financial emergency could have ended up as a semi-permanent system of military requisition of taxation, a *contributa continuata* without aristocratic control or even influence (though whether force alone without consent could extract the money was open to doubt).[122] When Joseph I summoned the diet of Royal Hungary to Pozsony in April 1708, it was the first time that it had met in over twenty years, and it was immediately paralyzed by religious dissension. Joseph claimed that his reign marked a break with his father's tyranny and that he would restore religious freedom: yet he passed over the Protestant grievances.[123]

The parallel between Transylvania and Scotland is closer. For if Scotland saved the English crown from the dangers of Arminianism in 1640, Transylvania – still the land of three nations and four faiths at the time of the Rákóczi rebellion[124] - had traditionally acted as the bastion of Protestant rights in Hungary.[125] It was the refusal of Joseph I to recognize the independence of Transylvania in July 1706 that reinforced the conviction of the Hungarian rebels that the Emperor sought to oppress Hungary.[126] Conserving Transylvania in its status of 1691 and preventing its union with Hungary were the central principles of Joseph's policy. Count Wratislaw followed Kinský's policy, which was that by separating the two states, Protestants would be denied the possibility of playing a significant political role in

---

122　Slottman, *Ferenc II Rákóczi and the Great Powers*, 228, 231, 234–6, 240.
123　Ingrao, *In Quest and Crisis*, 127, 146-7, 151.
124　Kovács and Köpeczi (eds.), *Mémoires du Prince François II Rákóczi*, 85.
125　Ibid. 55–6: 'on observera un admirable tissu des oeuvres de la Providence, principalement en ce qu'elle a donné au Roi Jean, Hongrois, la Transsilvanie et les Parties du Royaume de Hongrie qui y sont annexées, comme un Etat séparé, dans lequel on conserva le modèle de la Liberté donnée par Les Loix à la Nation. Cette forme fut toujours conservée sous les Princes de Transsilvanie...'
126　Count Wratislaw stated that Joseph would never allow Rákóczi to keep Transylvania: Kovács and Köpeczi (eds.), *Mémoires du Prince François II Rákóczi*, 134; Köpeczi, *La France et la Hongrie*, 177–8; Ingrao, *In Quest and Crisis*, 129–30; Slottman, *Ferenc II Rákóczi and the Great Powers*, 407–9.

Hungary's future.[127] Anything else, in the Habsburg view, would let the Turks back into influence over Hungarian affairs: Transylvanian semi-autonomy or a joint protectorate were Ottoman ploys to be rejected outright.[128] Whereas in the Act of Union of 1707 the Scots Parliament was abolished (and has only been reestablished since 1999) the Transylvanian diet survived after the rebellion until 1761.[129] What had changed was the reality and practice of confessional pluralism: Transylvania was still called a principality of three nations and four religions during the Rákóczi rebellion;[130] under Maria Theresa, Transylvania became the place which received Protestants who had been forcibly evicted from Hungary.[131]

As for Hungarian Protestantism in general, religious equality was destroyed by Act 30 of the Hungarian Diet of 1715 and the *Carolina resolutio* of 1731. It has even been claimed (incorrectly) that Joseph II's Patent of Toleration of 1781 was 'insufficient to wipe out the repercussion of nearly a century of persecution'.[132] The *juramentaum*

---

127   Ingrao, *In Quest and Crisis*, 137–8; Slottman, *Ferenc II Rákóczi and the Great Powers*, 238, 403.
128   Slottman, *Ferenc II Rákóczi and the Great Powers*, 62–3, 116.
129   Ingrao, *The Habsburg Monarchy*, 163: 'in Transylvania her military governor completed the process of emasculating that principality's diet at least a decade before it held its last meeting in 1761.' *The Corvina History of Hungary from Earliest Times until the Present Day*, Hanák ed., 76: 'The now defunct Principality of Transylvania remained separated from Hungary. Instead, it was governed as a grand duchy and subordinated to Vienna.' John Stoye perhaps exaggerates the extent of the incorporation of Transylvania into the Habsburg lands: 'When Apafi formally surrendered his claim, in April 1697, a distinct phase of Austrian expansion in this period was complete. Transylvania, the great auxiliary of Ottoman domination in the plains, or of successful rebellion in Upper Hungary against the Habsburgs, had at length disappeared.' J. W. Stoye, 'The Austrian Habsburgs', in J. S. Bromley ed., *New Cambridge Modern History. VI. The Rise of Great Britain and Russia, 1688–1715/25* (Cambridge, repr. 1971), 582. Rákóczi recalled Apafi's treaty with Leopold and insisted on the diet electing his successor: Kovács and Köpeczi (ed.), *Mémoires du Prince François II Rákóczi*, 135.
130   Köpeczi, *La France et la Hongrie*, 115.
131   Ingrao, *The Habsburg Monarchy*, 170.
132   Király, *Hungary in the Late Eighteenth Century*, 118–22; Marczali, *Hungary in the Eighteenth Century*, 254–5.

decretale, the oath invoking the names of the Virgin Mary and the saints, could be taken only by a Catholic. It had seemed perfectly normal to István Verböczi to prescribe such an oath in the *Tripartitum opus...* of 1514. For at that time, in the aftermath of the great peasant rebellion of that year, his was the authoritative statement of the constitution, affirming the nobles' independence from the elective monarchy and their supremacy over the peasantry. But what had seemed relevant in the era of the Dósza revolt, before Luther's break with Rome, could hardly seem relevant two hundred years later, when the Austrian Habsburg monarchy had abolished elective monarchy and established a form of absolute rule. It is the late success of confessional absolutism in Hungary which perhaps is the most telling divergence between developments there and elsewhere in Europe.

The parallel with Louis XIV's France after the revocation of the Edict of Nantes was made by Marczali[133] and remains persuasive, if not quite for the reasons he advanced. What Protestant contemporaries of Louis XIV could not at first quite comprehend was that the Bourbon monarchy seemed to have renounced its positive achievement in European state-building in the era of Louis XIII and Richelieu: this had been the creation of an alliance system with Protestant states in the interests of the European balance of power and reasonable treatment for Protestants at home. At a time when, in the United Provinces and England after 1689, some notable gains had been made in the cause of religious pluralism (though not for

---

133   Marczali, *Hungary in the Eighteenth Century*, 255. At 256, Marczali made the interesting comment that Prince Eugène's advice may have delayed the full implementation of confessional absolutism. His biographer comments: 'He hated fanaticism whether in politics or religion. He was a believer and read the scriptures regularly' but 'in all his long years of war against the Turks he never saw himself as a crusader engaged in some mission for Christianity. He was opposed to Papal intervention in temporal affairs. Moreover as Governor-General of the Netherlands he did everything he could to uphold the rights of Jansenists against Papal oppression.' Henderson, *Prince Eugen of Savoy*, 246. For Leopold's unwillingness to listen to Eugène's political views: Slottman, *Ferenc II Rákóczi and the Great Powers*, 213. Under Joseph, his absence at the war front limited his political influence: Ingrao, *In Quest and Crisis*, 226. For Eugène as a (relative) radical: J. I. Israel, *Radical Enlightenment. Philosophy and the making of modernity, 1650–1750* (Oxford, 2001), 65–6.

Catholics), in France the clock seemed to have been turned back. How much more so in Hungary a generation later – for, if the interpretation of this survey is correct, from being in the *avant-garde* of political and religious pluralism in the era of partition and rebellion between 1526 and 1711, Hungary in the era of the strict application of the *decretalis* oath had fallen very much into the European rearguard. It was not until Joseph II's reign that nearly a century of persecution was halted with the Patent of Toleration of 1781; not until after 1811 were full legal and civil rights given to religious minorities.[134]

Appendix: Suggested Model for the Levels of Pluralism in a Society

In this scheme, pluralism does not deal with the truth claims of religions and other systems of belief and practice: instead, it asks how such systems can co-exist harmoniously in civil society. Cf. Chancellor Michel de l'Hospital's distinction between a religious and a civil constitution in France (1562): 'It was not a matter of establishing the faith, but of regulating the State. One could be a citizen without being a Christian, and one did not cease to be the king's subject by separating from the Church.'

> (1)   The first level is where there is no pluralism at all, a situation where there is no acceptance or coexistence with religious minorities. This might be termed 'confessional exclusivism'. The outsider is stigmatized as the enemy; when the conflict is religious, the enemy is demonized and

---

134   J. Whaley, 'A tolerant society? Religious toleration in the Holy Roman Empire, 1648–1806', *Toleration in Enlightenment Europe*, ed. O. P. Grell and R. Porter (Cambridge, 2000), 188. For the 'broad measure of support' for full religious toleration and removing disabilities on non-Catholics: R. J. W. Evans, 'The Habsburgs and the Hungarian problem, 1790–1848', *TRHS*, 5th ser., 39 (1989), 53.

the conflict is therefore sanctified. Insurrection to secure religious freedom or 'rights' may become a form of religious war in such circumstances and the forcible elimination of heretics becomes a process of sanctified violence or holy war.

(2) A second level is where the majority culture merely coexists with minorities *de facto* (this might be termed 'confessional coexistence'): hostility to the minority religions and cultures remains and the legitimacy of their existence is challenged. This state of affairs may contain the feature of 'culture wars' between cultures within the same state which remain totally separate.

(3) A third level is where there may be a majority confession, but minorities enjoy rights *de jure*, so that a culture of citizenship for all faiths and cultures begins to emerge (this might be termed 'civic toleration').

(4) Finally, a fourth level is where there is a mixture of religions and cultures existing side by side, with none predominating (the completeness of such pluralism depends on prevailing attitudes as to whether this is a desirable, harmonious and permanent state of affairs).

In this scheme, a vital factor in hindering any development from level one to a higher level of pluralism is the prevalence of fear and distrust within the majority community and the belief that the new religion does not seek coexistence but confessional exclusivism. Rules of good behaviour on the part of proselytisers, those subject to proselytism, and behaviour applicable to all, are useful but are essentially unenforceable.

Nature of church–state relations (e.g. hostile separation; separation; establishment (including *de facto* disestablishment); and intermediate separation) are relevant, but are not necessarily the decisive consideration.

JUDITH POLLMANN

From Freedom of Conscience to Confessional Segregation? Religious Choice and Toleration in the Dutch Republic[1]

On the early morning of 3 September 1605 an anxious young school-master made his way to the *Grote Kerk* in the Holland city of Hoorn. As he was still able to recall ten months later, the sermon that morning was on Matthew 20:28. Yet it was not the sermon that was to make this into such a memorable occasion. No, that was because, on this day, Israel Jacobszoon van der Meersch, the son of Mennonite parents, the husband of a Mennonite wife, who himself had received adult baptism seven years earlier, at last openly acknowledged what he himself had known for some time, that he was attracted to the Reformed faith.[2]

The anxiety with which he had made his way to Church proved entirely justified. When his coreligionists found out where he had been, and that was soon enough, they responded, as Isaac recalled, as if 'I had deserved death on that morning'.[3] So vehement was the

---

1   This article could not have been written without the generous help of Jan de Bruin, who helped me find my way in the Streekarchief West-Friesland, its archivist Piet Boon, who gave me access to his notes on the Van Der Meersch family, Adriaan Plak of the Studiezaal Mennonitica in Amsterdam University library, who not only found the answers to some of my questions, but who also pointed me to further primary sources, and Professor Paul Hoftijzer, who shared his data on Pieter van der Meersch with me. The members of the religious history seminar of the University of Birmingham helpfully commented on an early draft of this paper. Joanna Innes alerted me to useful information on religious surveys in England. I am very grateful to them all.

2   Add MS 24, 339, Songbook of Israel Jacobszoon van der Meersch. The account of this eventful day and its aftermath in *Het 36. Liet*, 56r–8r. It was to be sung to psalm 81, and is dated on 8 July 1606.

3   Ibid. 57r 'al had ic die doot verdient die voor-noene'.

barrage of 'shameful reproach' that Israel could initially barely bring himself to speak, the words stifled in a stream of tears. But these were not tears of remorse – Israel believed that he had been right, and eventually expressed this to his coreligionists. Seeing how serious the matter was, they adjusted their tactics – they now began to speak kindly, plead with him, and were prepared to give him time to change his mind. But Israel could not find peace:

> so that I abstained myself from them, their teaching was like smoke, and my eye could not suffer it, since truth told me to build on her. And so that I would find more certainty, I set myself a time of penance before the Lord, and cast myself down to pray and to read. And oh, I found an inner joy, so that I with gladness have joined GOD's community as a proper member.[4]

On 9 February 1606 the consistory of the Reformed Church accepted him as a member, and three days later he took Reformed communion for the first time. A year later his wife, Marrichjen Jans, joined him at the Reformed communion table.[5] Israel was by no means the only Mennonite to convert to the Reformed faith. When the Dutch Revolt broke out there had probably been more Mennonites than Calvinists in the Netherlands, yet in the new Republic the Mennonites were slowly but steadily to lose ground to the Reformed.[6] What makes Israel unique, however, is that he decided to set his experiences down

---

4   Ibid. 57v: 'Soo dat ic mij ooc/van haer heb onthouwen/haer leer was mij rooc/mijn oogh' leed het niet/Want die waerheijt riet/mij op haer te bouwen.//Opdat ik te bet/versekert mocht wesen/heb een tijt gezet/van boet voor den HEER/ic sloegh mij ter neer/met bidden en lesen.//Och ic heb de vreucht/inwendich vercreghen/dat ic met geneucht/in GODES gemeent/mij ooc heb vereent/als een Lidt ter deghen'.

5   He noted the dates of his entry into the Reformed church and first communion in the margins of Ibid. 57v–58r. Notes by his grandson Pieter van der Meersch, Ibid. 44v and 106v mention the date of Marrichje's entry into the Reformed Church. Pieter may have gleaned this information from another text, perhaps a family bible. He also copied a detailed account of Israel's adult baptism in 1598, Ibid. 106v, which was printed in G. Kalff, *Verslag van een onderzoek in Engelsche bibliotheken in 1910* (The Hague, 1911), 47–55.

6   A. Th. Van Deursen, *Mensen van klein vermogen. Het 'kopergeld' van de Gouden Eeuw* (Amsterdam, 1992), first published as *Het kopergeld van de Gouden Eeuw* (Assen, 1978–81), 340.

on paper. Hundreds of thousands of Netherlanders changed confession in this period, but very few of them explained why they did so and barely anyone left as full an account as Israel van der Meersch.[7]

The two poems in which Israel accounted for his decision belong to a collection of sixty-five songs that he began in 1598, when he was courting his future wife with the first of the many pious verses he was to write for her.[8] The last of the *liedjes* dates from 1637, four years before his death. Although Israel had no conscious autobiographical agenda, the collection tells us quite a bit about his life. Thus, we know of his early friendship for his wife's uncle, the Mennonite elder and preacher Dirck Pietersz Koot, who had baptised him in Nieuwe Niedorp.[9] Of the fact that in 1612 he survived the plague.[10] Of his opinion of the 'evil teachings' of the Remonstrants, and his admiration for Stadholder Maurits.[11] Of his daughters' weddings, and their efforts at school – in 1627 his daughter Barbertje was poetically admonished to do her best.[12] His collection of occasional, pious poetry was cherished by his children; his grandson, the Leiden bookseller Pieter van der Meersch, who was to annotate the manuscript with much useful information and who added a few religious entries of his own, remembered how his mother had encouraged him to learn some of the texts by heart, and recite them for her.[13] Such evidence on the way domestic and occasional poetry was used and cherished is rare indeed

---

7   Judith Pollmann, 'A different Road to God. The Protestant experience of conversion in the sixteenth century' in P. van der Veer (ed.), *Conversion to modernities. The globalization of Christianity*, (New York and London, 1996), 47–64 and Judith Pollmann, *Religious choice in the Dutch Republic. The reformation of Arnoldus Buchelius, 1565–1641* (Manchester, 1999).

8   Songbook, 2v–3r *Dat 1 Lietgen*, of June 1598. Other songs dedicated to his wife ibid. 5v–6r, 18v–19r, 37r–38v, 42r.

9   He dedicated several songs to him. See ibid. 43v–44r, where also notes by Pieter van der Meersch on this man, 52v–53v.

10   Ibid. 61r–62v.

11   Ibid. 63v–68r. Both date from 1618. *Het 39 Lietgen* was dedicated to his children 'tot waerschouwinge van alle quade leeringen des tijts'. He signed his laudation on Maurits with the motto 'Goet prins-gesint'.

12   Poems for his children e.g. ibid. 74r, 78v–79v, 90v–91r, 93v–94v. His song for Barbertje on 80r.

13   Ibid. 90v–91r, 93v–93r, 102v–102r.

and would deserve some study in its own right; for the purposes of the present chapter, it is the two poems in which Israel explained his decision to become Reformed, which are of most significance.

These two poems shed a fascinating light on a process on which we know all too little, that of religious choice in the Dutch Republic. First of all, they remind us that such choice existed. Despite the initial commitment of William of Orange and other Dutch rebels to a policy of religious coexistence, the Dutch Republic that came into being in 1579 had soon banned Catholic worship, and had given the Reformed Church the status of 'public' church. Reformed congregations were granted the use of the existing church buildings, Reformed ministers were to be paid out of public funds (or rather the sequestered possessions of the old Church), and the Reformed church was to provide essential religious 'public' services: baptism, marriage and burial (although the latter without a religious ceremony). It led public prayers for victory and mercy and it advised the secular authorities. Its consistories administered charity and attempted to control education.[14]

Yet the Reformed Church was denied, and indeed denied itself, a position as a State Church that could have gained it control over all citizens of the United Provinces. It limited access to communion to its membership, and such membership did not come by virtue of being a citizen of the United Provinces. For membership one had to qualify, by subscribing to the Dutch confession of faith, by showing a minimum knowledge of Reformed doctrine and by living 'honestly'. Membership brought the privilege of access to the Lord's Supper, but it also implied submitting to church discipline, the control over life, morals and doctrine by the consistories. In that sense the Reformed Church was thus a voluntary church, a pure gathering of the faithful, that insisted that discipline was a matter for the Church alone, and that

14   On the growth of the Reformed Church, see A. Th. van Deursen, *Bavianen en slijkgeuzen. Kerk en kerkvolk ten tijde van Maurits en Oldenbarnevelt* (Assen, 1974).

was governed by consistories in which lay elders retained considerable control.[15]

Where did this leave the non-Reformed Dutch population? On the one hand, they were denied the right to public worship. Yet in article 13 of the 1579 Union of Utrecht, the rebellious provinces had also agreed that 'no one shall be persecuted or examined for religious reasons'. Even if the Dutch were denied freedom of worship, they were thus given freedom of conscience, the freedom to think and believe what they wanted, and the promise that they were not to be coerced in matters of faith.[16] As a consequence, it was impossible to force the residents of the United Provinces to attend the public church, let alone to impose Reformed discipline on all. Only Zeeland seems to have made an early attempt to make churchgoing compulsory, but the edict was apparently mainly intended (and applied) to stop Sunday trading.[17] Within their own homes, Dutch believers could effectively do as they pleased – retain images, say their prayers, read any religious book, and to gather friends and family for religious purposes. It was the latter freedom that enabled non-Reformed worship to survive the ban. Catholics, Lutherans and Mennonites, and eventually also Jews and the adherents of a myriad of dissenting Protestant groups, met at private homes, and worshipped there.

This did not go unchallenged. Reformed consistories might insist on their right to be selective about their membership, but they still aspired to reform society at large, and continuously demanded that the secular authorities suppress non-Reformed forms of worship.[18] Yet

---

15   Alastair Duke, 'The Ambivalent Face of Calvinism in the Netherlands, 1561–1618' in A. Duke, *Reformation and Revolt in the Low Countries* (London, 1990), 269–93.

16   M. E. H. N. Mout, 'Limits and Debates. A comparative View of Dutch Toleration in the sixteenth and early seventeenth Centuries' in C. Berkvens-Stevelinck *et al.* (eds) *The Emergence of Tolerance in the Dutch Republic* (Leiden, 1997), 37–47.

17   H. A. Enno van Gelder, *Getemperde vrijheid. Een verhandeling over de verhouding van kerk en staat in de Republiek der Verenigde Nederlanden en de vrijheid van mening in zake godsdienst, drukpers en onderwijs gedurende de 17e eeuw* (Groningen, 1972), 48.

18   Jonathan Israel, 'The Intellectual Debate about Toleration in the Dutch Republic' in Berkvens-Stevelinck, *The Emergence of Tolerance*, 3–47.

although this resulted in occasional (and sometimes intensive) harassment by zealous officials, the States-General did not have the right to police the country, and the patchwork of jurisdictions within the provinces made effective enforcement of the many bans against non-Reformed worship extremely difficult. Moreover, the authorities justified the ban on Catholic worship as a security issue, and although they fostered the Reformed Church, many of the Dutch regents were neither willing nor able to enforce a godly reformation from above. For some, it was simply a practical issue. As long as there was a war to be won, it was impossible for the authorities to divert their energies to enforcing the new religion. Moreover, trade demanded that they would not be too rigid about confessional issues. But in the early Republic by no means all of the political elite was committed to Calvinist orthodoxy. Even if Catholic town councillors were to become something of a rarity, for quite some time many of the regents were not themselves members of the Reformed Church. Although he attended the Reformed Church, the Amsterdam patrician Cornelis Pieterszoon Hooft, for instance, remained fiercely committed to the idea that the Revolt had not been fought for the Reformed religion but for 'liberty' and freedom of conscience. His wife, Anna Blaeu, was a Mennonite, who continued to practise her own faith, and he respected her freedom to choose.[19]

It was because of such attitudes that what had begun in private homes could often turn into semi-public worship. In some towns Lutherans were granted the freedom to build churches early on. Anabaptist gatherings, who showed little inclination to take the public stage, were usually left in peace. And Catholic missionary priests showed such tenacity, and often had such powerful protection, that it proved impossible to stop Catholic worship. In practice there developed a system in which non-Reformed communities could often buy immunity from official harassment by paying a fixed sum of so-called 'recognition' money to local sheriffs.

Some parts of the Republic, it is true, were much less tolerant of dissent than others. Peter van Rooden has argued that the 'tolerant'

---

19   H. A. Enno van Gelder, *De levensbeschouwing van Cornelis Pieterszoon Hooft, burgemeester van Amsterdam, 1547–1626* (Amsterdam, 1918), 6.

Dutch society of the textbooks actually extended no further than Holland, Zeeland, and a part of Friesland. In the Eastern provinces, the arrangements for toleration were effectively no different from the settlements that had emerged in the Empire.[20] Maarten Prak has shown that a range of towns in the Eastern Netherlands – Kampen, Arnhem, Nijmegen, Zwolle and Utrecht – made Catholic immigrants ineligible for citizenship in the 1620s, and not only reiterated these laws in the 1660s but also enforced them.[21] And whereas most towns in Holland, Zeeland and Friesland created a form of civic marriage that enabled dissenters to contract a legal marriage without church intervention, and did not demand that all children were baptised in the public Church, this was often different in the Eastern and Northern Provinces.[22]

The lands of the 'Generality', the overwhelmingly Catholic territories in the South that had been reconquered in the 1620s, formed a third and even less tolerant zone. Denied the right to constitute a province, they were ruled directly by the States-General, and from 1648 onwards these areas were, as Van Rooden put it, ruled much as the English ruled the Irish. A Reformed elite was superimposed on a society that had been profoundly influenced by the Counter-Reformation. Marriages conducted by Catholic priests were no longer recognised (although Catholics eventually were given the possibility of marriage before the magistrates), Catholic schools were closed, officeholders all had to be Protestant.[23]

Yet however intensive the harassment of non-Reformed communities might be in some places, it remained true that even there no one was forced to join the Reformed Church. Decisions to join could be made freely, and individually. And Israel's case demonstrates that they were not made lightly. What had prompted his decision? The

---

20 Peter van Rooden, *Religieuze regimes. Over godsdienst en maatschappij in Nederland, 1570–1990* (Amsterdam, 1996), 21–2.
21 Maarten Prak, 'The Politics of Intolerance. Citizenship and Religion in the Dutch Republic' in R. Po-Chia Hsia and H. van Nierop (eds), *Calvinism and Toleration in the Dutch Republic* (Cambridge, 2002).
22 Van Gelder, *Getemperde vrijheid*, 107.
23 Van Rooden, *Religieuze Regimes*, 21; Willem Frijhoff en Marijke Spies, *1650. Bevochten eendracht* (Den Haag, 1999), 383–5.

poem in which he recounted his first visit to the Reformed Church and the response of his coreligionists, did not say very much about the reasoning that had preceded his decision. Yet in a poem that he wrote in October 1605 and that he dedicated to a friend, Jan Meindertszoon, he was somewhat more explicit.[24] First, Israel told his friend that he had discovered 'a Light in front of me' that 'came to bring me the Truth'. Although the light had shown him 'the way of the Gospel' he had initially not dared to accept it, 'not as yet having discovered the value of the smooth pearl'.[25]

Of course, it was not as if Israel was unfamiliar with the Gospel. His earlier poems show that he had always been a very pious young man, and we may assume that he had been brought up in a climate of intense Mennonite godliness. His father, Jacob van der Meersch, had been a 'French schoolmaster' in Hoorn, and both his profession and his Flemish surname suggest that he had probably originally come as a refugee from the South.[26] That he gave his son, who was born around 1573, the name Israel may also point to the fact that the family was in

24   Songbook, 107r–108v. It was added by Pieter van den Meersch, who copied it from an unknown manuscript, at the end of the collection, and dated on 14 October 1605, i.e. in the period between Israel's first visit to the Reformed Church and the moment he actually joined. It was to be sung to the melody of Psalm 6.

25   Ibid. 107r 'Ik sag een Licht voor d'oogen/een Licht quam mij vertoogen/ de Waerheit heel gelijk [...]//Al scheen het licht seet klare/mij lichtende te gare/op t'Evangelis pat/ik durfd'noch niet aenvaerden/ik kend noch niet de waerden/al van die Peerl glat.'

26   Some information on Jacob van der Meersch and his family can be gleaned from his will, Archiefdienst Westfriese Gemeenten, Notary archives, 2037, 291r–92v, 29 July 1593. On Jacob's activities as a schoolmaster, see J. Steendijk Kuypers, 'De Franse School in Hoorn (1578–1793)', *Oud-Hoorn* 7 (1985), 63–5. On the name Van der Meersch, Piet Boon, 'De kaarten van de Westfriese zeekerende dijken uit 1638', *Caert-Thresoor* 7 (1988) 61–7, there 66. In 1593, Jacob published a book of didactic riddles, many of which were of a religious nature. It was reprinted in 1614, with some verses by Israel, as J. van der Mersch, *Tgroot Raedtsel-boeck inhoudende dry hondert nieuwer Raedtsels met duytlegginge van dien tot oeffeninge van de eerbare ende leersame Jeucht* (Amsterdam, 1614). The flyleaf contains some notes in a later hand, which mention that he died in 1595, and that his grave and coat of arms are to be found in the 'Hooftkerk' in Hoorn.

religious exile.[27] It is not surprising, then, that Israel's upbringing steeped him in the language of Scripture. He set several of his early songs to psalms, and in a song on the Trinity that he dedicated in 1604 to Dirck Pieterszoon Koot, the Mennonite *vermaner* who had baptised him, he referred to no fewer than 36 Scripture passages.[28]

It was thus not his discovery of Scripture, but of the Reformed interpretation of it, that had changed Israel. Yet what exactly it was that attracted him to it, or what he had come to dislike about Mennonite teachings, is not quite clear. His comments on the Reformed doctrine were not particularly specific. He had seen light, found truth, received knowledge. His problem with the Mennonites was mainly that they were so divided over doctrine.[29] The internal divisions among the Mennonites had already become proverbial and the *Waterlander* community to which he himself belonged was locked in bitter conflicts with the so-called Flemish and Frisian Mennonites in Hoorn.[30] In the circumstances it was perhaps not so surprising that

27   Pieter van der Meersch noted in Songbook 4v that his father was twenty-seven years old when he married Marritje Jans in 1600. She was twenty-two.

28   Ibid. 52v–53r.

29   As early as 1600, he expressed anxiety about the existence of so many different versions of religious truth. Scripture warned believers to heed 'false prophets', but how, he asked his God, was he to decide 'which volck (community) was moved by Your Spirit?', ibid. 7v., Song for Julius Jacobszoon, 1 April 1600 'Voor veel valsche propheten/hebt ghij ons gewaerschout/Och dat ick nu cond weeten/Op welcke dat het hout//[…]//Daer heb ick seer mijn leven/becommert in geweest/Wat volck wordt gedreven/O Heer door Uwen geest//'. Although it is possible that he was already considering a move to the Reformed Church, his use of the word volck – a term that was often used by Mennonite groups to describe themselves – suggests that he was referring to the competing Mennonite communities.

30   Ibid. 108r 'Ook kan ik wel betoogen/ dat 's in de Leer geboogert/heel sijn gedeelt van een/of sij al een van Namen/sijn Mennisten te samen/elk gaet sijn weg vast heen'. There are no registers of the Waterlander community for this period, but a mid-seventeenth century document describing the conflicts within the Mennonite community around 1600 mentions a prominent Waterlander elder called Dirk Pietersz van Niedorp, who is likely to be the same person as the Dirk Pietersz Koot who had baptised Israel in Nieuwe Niedorp in 1598. See J. G. de Hoop Scheffer, 'Eene geschiedenis van de doopsgezinden, van hunne geschillen en hereenigingen, door een doopsgezinde in 1647', *Doopsgezinde*

Mennonite believers like Israel could be longing for some doctrinal certainty and cohesion.

But whatever drove Israel to prefer Reformed doctrine, his poem also tells us that his discovery of its truths had not immediately led to the conclusion that he should leave the Mennonite community. As he explained to his friend, the memory of his father and mother had held him back. How could he 'despise the faith of my beloved parents'? It was a dilemma that all converts faced, a dilemma that had probably vexed his grandparents, before him, and they may well have arrived at a similar solution. For Israel concluded that to remain a Mennonite, despite his doubts, was not really to follow his parents' example. They had simply not been aware of the light, yet had they found it, 'they would immediately have followed it'. Why then should he forego the truth 'now that the Lord was teaching me properly'? His parents would have done exactly the same.[31]

Even so, he had for some time also wondered whether doctrine was really so important:

> I imagined that it did not really make such a difference if I stayed where I was. Because I could live anew there too, by turning to the Lord [...] and I so fancied that it might be the best way after all not to consider their doctrine, but their way of life [i.e. of his fellow Mennonites].[32]

---

    bijdragen (1876), 13–41, at 37. On these conflicts, see Samme Zijlstra, *Om de ware gemeente en de oude gronden. Geschiedenis van de dopersen in de Nederlanden, 1531–1675* (Hilversum, 2000), 382–9.

31   Ibid. 'Ik woud ook soo diep niet trachten/noch het Geloof verachten/ van mijn Ouders bemint [...] //Nochtans hoe ik mij paide/de waerheit vast ontleide/hoe meer ik wert ontrust/ te doen (dagt ik) ter stede/niet als mijn Ouders dede/die sulcx niet was bewust//En hadden sij 't gevonden/sij souden tot dier stonden/dat hebben na gegaen/nu mij de Heer der Heeren/de waerheit regt gaet leeren/waerom soude ik 't versmaen'.

32   Songbook, 107v 'Mij selfs ging ik inbeelden/dat het soo veel niet scheelden/of ik bleef daer ik was/Want nieu hier ook gaet leeven/hem tot de Heer te keeren/dagt ik toen op dit pas//En liet mij soo aen kallen/dat het noch wel van allen/mocht sijn de rechte hoop/ik en sache niet soo seere/op hunne gront der leere/als op hun levensloop.'

Doctrine was, then, not the only thing that mattered; Israel had considered that religion was not just about teaching, it was also about a way of life. He could start a new life for himself by turning to God and perhaps it did not matter so much where he did that. Moreover, he had apparently found little fault with the piety of his coreligionists. Had religion *just* been about pious living, he could have stayed where he was.

There were thus three central considerations that played a role in Israel's decision making: doctrine, family tradition, and good living. In his case, doctrine had weighed most heavily. For others in his society that was not always the case. Catholics often defended their continued allegiance to the old church with reference to tradition. Thus, the Utrecht nobleman Johannes de Wit said that he wanted to stay 'in Peter's ship, outside which I have learned that there is no salvation. There my dearest parents placed me [...] therein I shall live and die happily'.[33] A pious way of life was decisive for others. Neeltje Jans of Monnickendam defended her defection from the Reformed Church to the Mennonites by saying that 'those with whom she now went seemed much better and more godly than those in the [Reformed] Church'.[34] And there were and remained many Christians who thought as Israel had done when he was hesitating about the importance of doctrine, that one could be pious in any Church, or even outside one. The Reformed theologian Jacobus Trigland lamented the existence of the many 'libertine spirits' who:

> adhere neither to the Reformed Church nor to any sects outside it, thinking that they can achieve salvation [...] by living virtuously and civilly under their government and thus quietly serving God by themselves according to their own understanding.[35]

---

33   Letter from Johannes de Wit to Lambert van der Burch, 13 August 1614 in 'Brieven van Joahnnes de Wit aan Arend van Buchel en anderen', A. Hulshof and P. S. Breuning (eds), *Bijdragen en Mededelingen van het Historisch Genootschap* 60 (1939), 87–208, 169.

34   Cited in Van Deursen, *Bavianen en slijkgeuzen*, 152.

35   Cited in Benjamin Kaplan, *Calvinists and Libertines. Confession and community in Utrecht, 1578–1620* (Oxford, 1995), 80.

Even many of those who frequented the Reformed Church which Israel now called his own had not actually become members of that Church. In a groundbreaking study of Dutch Calvinism between 1580–1620, A. Th. van Deursen demonstrated in the 1970s that the membership of the Reformed Churches long remained very small indeed. Traditionally, Dutch scholars had measured the growth of Reformed Churches by counting the number of baptisms. Yet as van Deursen pointed out, Reformed Churches actually baptised all children, irrespective of the faith of their parents. To measure actual commitment to the new religion, he said, one should look at the number of *lidmaten*, members of the Church, those had made a confession of faith, and were admitted to the Lord's Supper. In a score of Holland towns and villages he found that members and their children only formed a small minority of the population. Yet that did not mean the Churches were empty, or that everyone else was Catholic. Van Deursen pointed to the existence of a large category of believers who were known as the *liefhebbers* (or sympathisers) of the Reformed religion. People, that is, who came to Church, but who were shying away from full membership.[36]

Subsequent research has confirmed that there was a very large group of people in the early Republic who never took communion, and who did not fall under any form of Church discipline. In Haarlem, for instance, it appears that by 1620 about half of the population was not a member of any Church. The Reformed *lidmaten* and their children made up about 20% of the population, an equal proportion was Catholic, and another 10% or so belonged to Lutheran and Mennonite Churches. In Utrecht, a Catholic bulwark, Calvinists and their children at that time made up only about 13% of the population. About a third of Utrechters was not religiously affiliated. Although we do not have exact figures for Hoorn, the situation there is unlikely to have been very different.[37]

---

36   van Deursen, *Bavianen en slijkgeuzen*, 128–60.
37   Joke Spaans, *Haarlem na de reformatie. Stedelijke cultuur en kerkelijk leven* (The Hague, 1989), 104. Similar conclusions can be drawn for Delft from A. P. F. Wouters, *Nieuw en ongezien. Kerk en samenleving in de classis Delft*

When Israel moved to the Reformed Church, he thus *remained* a member of a religious minority. It was of course a privileged minority, the only one that could worship in public, a minority that enjoyed the protection of the authorities, that increasingly claimed a monopoly on all political offices, and tried to control education. To join such a privileged minority had its practical benefits – had he remained a Mennonite schoolmaster, Israel might eventually well have found his livelihood under threat. But he was clearly not just a conformist. When, in 1615, Contra-Remonstrant believers seceded from Hoorn's Reformed Church in protest against the Arminian preachers who were protected by the authorities, Israel and his wife were again among the dissidents.[38]

Both the highly principled line which Israel took in matters of faith, and the angry response of his coreligionists when he became Reformed, point to the fact that, however multi-confessional a society this was, it was not ecumenically inclined. Preachers and priests in all churches spent much of their time vilifying other faiths and believers took confessional difference extremely seriously. Yet, whilst there were occasional religious riots, they were surprisingly few and far between. Scholars have long wondered how it was possible that this society managed to handle confessional divisions with as little bloodshed as it did. One solution is to assume that believers of different confessions tried to stay out of each other's way as much as possible, under the guidance of a state that contained potential conflict. In the late 1970s, van Deursen stressed that Golden Age believers of all denominations 'from within the fortification of their church-walls, saw only heretics outside and never fellow Christians of another confession'.[39] If that were true, it could only have been through a form of social and cultural apartheid, more or less in the style of Dutch society between 1850 and 1950, that such divisions did not lead to open violence.

en Delfland, 1572–1621 (Delft, 1994), 234, 242–3, and for Utrecht from Kaplan, *Calvinists and Libertines*, 117, 255, 277–8.

38   Archiefdienst Westfriese gemeenten, Archief Hervormde Gemeente Hoorn, no. 581, list of members taking communion in the Ramen, 1615.
39   Van Deursen, *Mensen van klein vermogen*, 338.

Recently, however, this model has been challenged. Scholars now argue that it was not confessional segregation, but the fluidity of the confessional situation, the fact that religion was a matter of choice, that made grassroots toleration imperative. The existence of *liefhebbers* and other uncommitted believers created a grey area, which made it extremely difficult to draw strict confessional boundaries. Moreover, the highly individual nature of religious decision-making also meant that many families were confessionally divided. Couples were not necessarily of the same confession. Parents, siblings, cousins, made different choices. However committed believers were to the doctrines of their Church, few early modern Dutch people could afford to sever links with the kinsfolk on whose support they depended for survival. And even those whose families were all confessionally united would meet people of other faiths in the *gebuurten* – the neighbourhood organizations – in guilds, chambers of rhetoric and civic militia companies (although the pacifist Mennonites of course refused to serve in the latter). This meant that, regardless of confessional commitment, there was continued need to communicate with those whose faith one did not share.[40] It was for this reason that the town governments in the early Republic often continued to promote the old ideals of Christian and civic concord, and continued to deploy a meta-confessional language of religious peace and unity.[41]

At first sight it may not seem so easy to fit people like Israel into this picture. How could a man of his convictions have overlooked confessional difference when it came to his everyday contacts? The response of his Mennonite coreligionists suggests that, initially at least, he and his wife were facing the destruction of their existing

40   Kaplan, *Calvinists and Libertines*, 291–4. L. C. J. J. Bogaers, 'Geleund over de onderdeur. Doorkijkjes in het Utrechtse buurtleven van de vroege Middeleeuwen tot in de zeventiende eeuw', *Bijdragen en Mededelingen betreffende de Geschiedenis der Nederlanden*, 112 (1997), 336–63; Willem Frijhoff, 'Dimensions de la coexistence confessionelle', in Berkvens-Steverlinck *et al.* (eds), *The Emergence of Tolerance in the Dutch Republic*, 213–37; Wiebe Bergsma, *Tussen Gideonsbende en publieke kerk. Een studie over het gereformeerd protestantisme in Friesland, 1580–1650* (Hilversum, 1999), 295–342; Pollmann, *Religious Choice*, 164–203.
41   Spaans, *Haarlem na de reformatie*, 195–9, 121, 238.

social network within the Mennonite community. When he joined the Reformed Church he was probably 'banned' by the community, whose members would be expected to avoid contact with him. In fact, Israel and Marrichjen were lucky that the fairly moderate Waterlanders did not insist that people who had been excommunicated be shunned by their spouses, as happened in other Mennonite communities. Even so, that Marrichjen chose to become Reformed, too, may have had to do with the fact that she could not face life in a community that despised her husband.[42]

Like the Mennonite communities, the Dutch Reformed Churches attached much importance to the 'purity' of their gatherings, and insisted on a clear division between those within, and those outside, the membership. Considering the divisions between the godly and the ungodly in England, and the intense concern with election among English Puritans, one might assume that predestinarian theology dictated social separation to the Reformed.[43] Yet as Philip Benedict has pointed out, in this respect continental Calvinists differed much more from their English counterparts than is usually acknowledged.[44] Election actually played a very minor role in their piety which, unlike in England, did not centre around the problem of how to reach assurance about one's state before God. Of course continental Calvinists thought that predestination mattered. After all, the Gomarist–Arminian controversy over predestinarian theology brought the Republic to the brink of civil war. Yet unlike their English co-religionists they had an adequate institutional way of expressing the difference between the godly and the ungodly – their Churches were voluntary gatherings, and had church discipline to safeguard their purity. Consequently, they were much less concerned about visibly, socially separating themselves from the reprobate than their English counterparts. Even the movement for Further Reformation that began

---

42   Zijlstra, *Om de ware gemeente*, 272–3.
43   Patrick Collinson, 'The Cohabitation of the Faithful with the Unfaithful' in Ole Grell *et al.* (eds), *From Persecution to Toleration. The Glorious Revolution and Religion in England*, (Oxford, 1991), 51–76.
44   Philip Benedict, 'The Historiography of continental Calvinism' in Hartmut Lehmann *et al* (eds), *Weber's Protestant Ethic. Origin, Evidence, Context*, (Cambridge, 1993), 309–25.

to emerge in the Republic in the 1630s, and that was heavily influenced by William Perkins and other Puritan thinkers, did not initially change this. When and where that happened, in the later seventeenth century, it was only in small groups and conventicles on the margins of the Reformed church that Dutch Calvinist piety began to resemble that of the Puritans, and that visible segregation from the world became a key concern.[45]

Despite the exclusive character of Mennonite communities, as a schoolmaster it is unlikely that Israel's existing contacts could ever have been limited to the Mennonites alone. His friendship with Jan Meindertszoon, who presumably was Reformed himself, is likely to have predated his conversion to the Reformed church. And although we do not yet know enough about the confessional affiliations of Israel's friends and acquaintances to establish with any certainty to what extent his social circle became exclusively Reformed, we know that at least some of his Mennonite contacts survived his conversion. Thus, he did not hesitate to contribute a poem to a 1609 book that commemorated the Mennonite artist, poet and art critic, Karel van Mander.[46] From what we know of others in his society, moreover, it seems highly unlikely that his contacts became limited to the Reformed community alone. For believers like Israel, whatever his own doctrinal preferences, it was clearly extremely uncomfortable to conclude that only the Reformed would be saved. The memory of their parents alone made that impossible. And since Reformed doctrine made a theoretical allowance for the salvation of people outside the Church, they did not have to force themselves to think so. The

---

45 F. A. van Lieburg, 'From Pure Church to Pious Culture. The Further Reformation in the Seventeenth-Century Dutch Republic' in W. Fred Graham (ed.), *Later Calvinism, International Perspectives*, Sixteenth Century Essays and Studies, XXII (Kirksville, Mo. 1994), 409–29; F. A. van Lieburg, *Levens van vromen. Gereformeerd piëtisme in de achttiende eeuw* (Kampen, 1991).

46 *Epitaphien ofte grafschriften ghemaect op het afsterven van Carel van Mander, in sijn leven cloeck schilder ende poet* [...] (Franeker and Haarlem, 1609), 53. One could also think of the poem he wrote for the 1617 edition of Theodorus Velius, *Chroniick van Hoorn* (Hoorn, 1617), although it should be noted that we are not altogether sure how committed Velius himself remained to the Mennonites.

Catholic Church was less flexible in this respect, but we know that even zealous Catholics felt they needed to make exceptions. In a similar predicament to Israel, the Catholic convert Joost van den Vondel did on the one hand assert that non-Catholics were heretics who would go to hell, whilst simultaneously 'hoping for the best' for his Mennonite grandfather, 'because of his simple piety'.[47]

The presence of relatives, neighbours and colleagues of other faiths made it extremely difficult just to judge by confessional norms. As I have argued elsewhere, Dutch believers therefore operated two norms of piety at once – one that was based on confessional conviction, the other that focused on a non-confessionally determined concept of experienced piety.[48] We have seen that Israel was familiar with such a distinction. That is why he had wondered whether 'good living' was not a more important benchmark for religiousness than doctrinal purity. He had, of course, eventually concluded that doctrine was so crucial that he had to leave his community, but that probably did not stop him from continuing to recognise that there was a second measure for religiousness: a pious, Christian lifestyle. We certainly know that other Reformed hardliners were capable of this. The ortho-dox Calvinist elder Arnoldus Buchelius, for instance, maintained friendships with Catholics and Mennonites, and managed to both consider Remonstrants as a moral danger and 'pests of the Republic', and to form a warm personal friendship with the Remonstrant scholar and poet Caspar Barlaeus, whom he praised for his piety. Willem Frederik, the deeply Reformed stadholder of Friesland, too, acknow-ledged that there were different ways of measuring Christianity, when he wrote in 1647: 'The zeal of a papist, the well-living of a Men-nonite, the doctrine of a Calvinist, together make a true Christian.'[49]

---

47   Geeraardt Brandt, 'Het leven van Joost van den Vondel', in Joost van den Vondel, *Poëzy, of Verscheide Gedichten*, 2 vols. (Franeker, 1682), II, 76.

48   Pollmann, *Religious Choice*; Judith Pollmann, 'The bond of Christian piety. The individual practice of tolerance and intolerance in the Dutch Republic' in Hsia and Van Nierop, *Calvinism and Toleration*.

49   Pollmann, 'The Bond of Christian Piety'; G. J. Visser and G. van der Plaat (eds), *Gloria parendi. Dagboeken van Willem Frederik, stadhouder van Friesland, Groningen en Drenthe, 1643–1649, 1651–1654* (The Hague, 1995), xxiv.

Yet if the individual nature of religious choice in the early Republic ensured that confessional apartheid was not an option, it is often argued that it did not stay that way. Simon Groenveld, for instance, recognises that the growth of confessionalism was very slow, but argues that between 1650 and 1750 Dutch society had indeed become *verzuild*, confessionally segregated. Stable denominational subcultures had been formed, dissenters and eventually Catholics provided charity and education within their own communities, and social interaction between believers of different confession diminished.[50] Jonathan Israel, too, has stressed the slow but steady growth of confessionalism, and actually thinks that it contributed to the rise of a more tolerant attitude among the authorities. Thus, the fact that 'confessional lines had stabilised', was, according Israel,

> doubtless the most important reason why confessional tensions began to ease from around 1630 [...] Consequently, Dutch civic and provincial identities set aside their previous anxieties, and became more relaxed in their attitude to dissenting churches.[51]

From around 1650 the authorities indeed seem to have accepted that the Republic was to remain a multiconfessional society. In the *Grote Vergadering* of 1651 the provinces formally recognised that the Reformed Church was the privileged church, and committed themselves to maintaining the orthodoxy that had been redefined in the Synod of Dordt in 1618–19. All officeholders were to be 'reformed'. The placards against Catholics would remain in force. Yet the meeting also acknowledged, and formalised, the position of dissenting Protestants. These would be tolerated, but were instructed not to claim the public stage or to try and expand. Whereas it should be stressed that the initial effect of the *Grote Vergadering* was a renewed campaign to Calvinise public life and eradicate Catholic worship, particularly in the Generality Lands, it simultaneously demonstrated that the elite had

---

50 Simon Groenveld, *Huisgenoten des geloofs. Was de samenleving in de Republiek der Verenigde Nederlanden verzuild?* (Hilversum, 1995).
51 Jonathan Israel, *The Dutch Republic. Its Rise, Greatness and Fall, 1477–1806* (Oxford, 1995), 388–9.

had to abandon the fiction that the Republic was confessionally united.[52]

Yet were policy changes really the result of a stabilization of confessional lines? Had all believers now found a confessional home? And did the new generations that were born in confessionally committed families, unlike Israel van der Meersch, stick to the choices of their parents, and segregate into clearly demarcated confessional subcultures? The research on which both Israel and Groenveld relied for this assumption indeed suggests that the group of unaffiliated disappeared from the Dutch confessional landscape. Quite when this happened is not so clear, but the first national religious survey that we possess, dating from 1809, suggests that almost everybody at that date considered themselves to belong to a Church, and that the Reformed churches had been the main beneficiaries of this process. Most dissenting Protestants had lost ground, Catholics had recovered somewhat in the eighteenth century, but their gains were by no means spectacular.[53]

However, as Juliaan Woltjer has pointed out, the population survey of 1809 categorised believers according to the Church in which they had been baptised, not according to membership, as Van Deursen's work has taught us to do.[54] If we apply that measure, we find that the unaffiliated group shrunk much more slowly than has usually been assumed and never disappeared. In 1645, it was estimated that in the Holland villages of West- and Oost-Graftdijk only 150 of the 400 people who attended the Reformed church were actually members of the Church.[55] Wiebe Bergsma has shown that

---

52   F. G. M. Broeyer, 'IJkpunt 1650. Andere gezindtheden met tollerantie getolereert' in C. Augustijn and E. Honée, *Vervreemding en verzoening. De relatie tussen katholieken en protestanten in Nederland, 1550–2000* (Nijmegen, 1998), 34–67.

53   Hans Knippenberg, *De religieuze kaart van Nederland. Omvang en geografische spreiding vanaf de Reformatie tot heden* (Assen, 1992); J. A. de Kok, *Nederland op de breuklijn Rome-Reformatie* (Assen, 1964).

54   J. J. Woltjer, 'De plaats van de calvinisten in de Nederlandse samenleving', *De Zeventiende Eeuw*, 10 (1994), 19.

55   A. Th. van Deursen, *Een dorp in de polder. Graft in de zeventiende eeuw* (Amsterdam, 1994), 83.

around 1660 at least a quarter of the Frisian population was still unaffiliated, and has presented strong evidence that this did not change in the eighteenth century.[56] A similar picture emerges from an excellent study of the Zuidholland village of Maasland by the demographer Dirk Jan Noordam, that yields most of the information necessary to establish the confessional spread among the population at large. In 1730 there were 497 people over 25 years of age in Maasland. In this group, 279 persons were members of the Reformed Church. If we assume that the proportion of people over 25 in the Catholic community was the same as among the Reformed, there must have been 98 Catholic adults. This left 120 people over 25 without formal affiliation, that is almost a quarter of the adult population. Forty years later, in 1770, there were 703 adults over 25. Of these, 359 were members of the Reformed Church, about 108 were Roman Catholic, and 236 people, about a third of the adult population, were unaffiliated.[57]

Even so, the reason why eighteenth-century historians have tended to ignore the continuing discrepancy between the numbers of members and *doopleden*, is that some contemporary sources did so, too. The 1809 survey was the first national religious headcount, but individual localities had produced such surveys earlier on, and these, too, tended to assign a confessional colour to virtually all households. How can we explain this? One option is to assume that experience now taught that virtually all people who were baptised in the Reformed Churches would eventually also become members. The large number of unaffiliated adults in Maasland can then be explained by the fact that many people only joined the Church when they were well advanced into adulthood, or even when they were quite old.[58] This would match findings in the early seventeenth century, when many women, for instance, did not join until after they had become

---

56   Bergsma, *Tussen Gideonsbende*, 96–150, 186.
57   Dirk-Jan Noordam, *Leven in Maasland. Een hoogontwikkelde plattelands-samenleving in de achttiende en het begin van de negentiende eeuw* (Hilversum, 1986), 64, 78.
58   Noordam, *Leven in Maasland*, 116–17, 128 shows that many people were not yet *lidmaten* at the time they married, when they were on average 27–28 years old.

widows, and not many new members were qualified as 'young'. Whereas scholars have usually seen this a sign that it took these first generations time to adjust to the Reformation, the fact that this pattern persisted may suggest that Reformed church membership was a choice that was made at particular and late points of the lifecycle.[59] Van Deursen noted, for instance, that for some men in the village of Graft the decision to join the Church coincided with the moment that they took over as head of the family.[60] When he visited the village of Bozum in 1754, minister Elco Alta was particularly surprised that many older 'Reformed' people in the village had not yet joined the Church.[61]

Yet recent research by Joke Spaans also suggests a second, different possibility. In her view, the growing recognition of non-Reformed communities, and the emergence of Catholic, Mennonite and Lutheran charities was not the result of growing toleration but, rather, related to administrative concerns. The growing willingness to recognise dissenting churches in Friesland was a response to difficulties the authorities experienced in caring for the growing number of urban poor who relied on support from city funds. In Friesland non-Reformed Churches were therefore often effectively *forced* to start developing their own institutions.[62] In Haarlem, too, it took a move to exclude all Catholics from civic charity, before they could be induced to set up their own charitable institutions.[63] Communities gained recognition in return for compliance with these moves, whilst for the authorities there was the added benefit of gaining greater control over what went on in the non-Reformed Churches.

---

59 Wouters, *Nieuw en ongezien*, 259–68; Pollmann, 'Women and Religion in the Dutch Golden Age', *Dutch Crossing*, 24 (2000), 162–82.
60 Van Deursen, *Een dorp in de polder*, 86–7.
61 Bersgma, *Tussen Gideonsbende*, 147.
62 Joke Spaans, 'De katholieken in de Republiek na de Vrede van Münster', *De Zeventiende Eeuw*, 13 (1997), 253–60; Joke Spaans, *Armenzorg in Friesland. Publieke zorg en particuliere liefdadigheid in zes Friese steden. Leeuwarden, Bolsward, Franeker, Sneek, Dokkum en Harlingen* (Hilversum, 1997), 228–82.
63 J. A. F. de Jongste, *Onrust aan het Spaarne. Haarlem in de jaren 1747–1751* (Dieren, 1984), 51.

One of the consequences of such policies was, however, that it became necessary to assign a religion to all households. In Haarlem, a religious survey directly preceded the move to exclude Catholics.[64] In Leeuwarden the label of Reformed was given to anyone who did not claim to belong to a church: the category of the 'Reformed poor' there was one that was separate from 'deacons' poor', the actual members of the Reformed Church and their families. That it seemed desirable to call these unaffiliated people 'Reformed', and eventually even to let them wear a badge with the letter R may have had to do with the fact that these people were simply more Reformed than anything else. Yet legal handbooks too, as Spaans points out, suggest that 'Reformed' had simply become a label for anyone who was not explicitly committed to one of the tolerated churches.[65] It is not difficult to see why this would have become attractive. It was administratively convenient, it took account of the fact that some people who were not members of the Reformed church would eventually become so, and it also usefully created a cosmetic appearance of Reformed strength. But it said perhaps rather little about the religious convictions of those who were labelled Reformed.

A second indication for the ongoing fluidity of confessional lines, is the number of mixed marriages. Research has found that Reformed consistories in Holland were particularly active in disciplining members for engaging in mixed marriages in the period 1630–60, and it is possible that the subsequent drop in the number of cases meant that the problem simply disappeared.[66] Youngsters could, however, avoid discipline altogether by postponing their decision to join the Church until after they had found a marriage partner. Both in Graft and Maasland, it was very common to do so.[67] Consistories were thus only ever likely to report on a fraction of the actual number of mixed marriages,

---

64   Ibid.
65   Spaans, *Armenzorg*, 257, 315.
66   Manon van der Heijden, *Huwelijk in Holland. Stedelijke rechtspraak en kerkelijke tucht, 1550–1700* (Amsterdam, 1998), 235–7.
67   Van Deursen, *Dorp in de polder*, 86; Noordam, *Leven in Maasland*, 116. He draws the conclusion that members married later than non-members, but it rather seems to be an indication that few people joined the Church at an early age.

those involving members, just as they would only discipline *lidmaten* who changed religion, but were helpless when *liefhebbers* did so. We thus need to look at other evidence. Research in Leiden, Amsterdam and Maasland indicated that mixed marriages became quite rare, but this may be due to the problematic assumption that both partners in marriages conducted in the Reformed Church would usually be Reformed. The Reformed churches in fact married anyone who was baptised and, as Rommes has pointed out, by no means all non-Reformed believers objected to a Reformed wedding ceremony. The fact that a civic marriage was considerably more expensive, may also have played a role in this.[68] Some recent studies, in fact, suggest that mixed marriages occurred frequently. In Harlingen around 1665, more than a quarter of Mennonite newlyweds married a non-Mennonite spouse.[69] Recent recearch on Bergen op Zoom, a city in Brabant where the Reformed steadily lost ground to the Catholic majority, shows that 11% of all marriages in the eighteenth century there was between people of different confessions, with the Reformed being most likely to contract a marriage with someone from another faith.[70] And Rommes has demonstrated that about 40% of Utrecht's Lutherans in the eighteenth century married people of another faith.[71]

In practice, then, the confessional boundaries between 1650 and 1750 were probably by no means as clearly drawn as has often been suggested. The Reformed Churches could not call the majority of the Dutch population their own in the sense that they could command their doctrinal loyalty or exercise church discipline over them. Believers had a choice to join a Church, and they still exerted it. For most Protestants, their choice may have been limited to the decision whether or not, and when, to place themselves under church discipline. Nor perhaps, as often as they once had done, did believers use their freedom to leave the faith of their fathers. Even so, the shrinking

68   Noordam, *Leven in Maasland*, 116, 130; Ronald Rommes, *Oost, West, Utrecht best. Driehonderd jaar migratie en migranten in de stad Utrecht* (Amsterdam, 1998), 53.
69   Bergsma, *Tussen Gideonbende*, 337.
70   Charles De Mooij, *Geloof kan Bergen verzetten. Reformatie en katholieke herleving te Bergen op Zoom, 1577–1795* (Hilversum, 1998), 582.
71   Rommes, *Oost, West, Utrecht best*, 190–1.

numbers of Mennonites and Remonstrants suggest that some people must have continued to break away from what might have become family traditions, whilst Ronald Rommes noted that many Utrecht families that had been Lutheran in the seventeenth century, by the eighteenth century had become Catholic or Reformed.[72] Confessional divisions thus were much less stable than has been suggested. It was only within the officeholding elite that confessional conformity became a *sine qua non* for survival.

It seems unlikely, then, that we can explain the greater political willingness to recognise non-Reformed churches with reference to the stabilising of confessional boundaries. Yet at the same time it seems a far too optimistic assessment of the powers of the Dutch authorities to maintain, as some scholars have done, that the later seventeenth and eighteenth centuries at last witnessed an effective campaign for confessionalisation on the part of the authorities.[73] Administratively, it was possible to turn unaffiliated people into Protestants. Administratively, it became much easier to isolate Catholics from the rest of the population. In addition, Churches increased their control over the recipients of church charity in the course of the eighteenth century. Yet because of people's ability to make their own religious choices, there remained many shades of grey within the Dutch religious landscape. Churches had a limited grip on believers, and the impetus to ignore confessional difference in day-to-day contacts remained very much alive. As Rommes points out, a large number of Utrechters, even in the eighteenth century, must have had relatives whose religion differed from their own.[74] Confessional allegiance was strong, but it could simply not be the only norm by which people operated.

In the spring of 1734, parts of the Republic were shaken by a rumour about an impending Catholic takeover, to take place on 24 June. It was a special date, one of the rare occasions on which Corpus Christi and the Feast of the Nativity of St. John the Baptist would coincide. Prophecies that, on this day, Catholic subjugation was come to

---

72   Ibid. 190–1, 197–8.
73   Joke Spaans, 'Religie in Amsterdam in de Gouden Eeuw', *Jaarboek Amstelodamum*, 91 (1999), 104–7.
74   Rommes, *Oost, West, Utrecht best*, 198.

an end, triggered a wave of Catholic enthusiasm and Protestant panic, which resulted in some anti-Catholic violence, and in the arrest and trial of several Catholics who had spread the prophecy and who had in some cases even presaged a massacre of all Protestants. It is hard to imagine a clearer example of the inter-confessional tensions that continued to live under the surface of this multi-confessional society.[75] Yet it was not just the state that defused such tension, it was the reality of everyday coexistence. Frisian records of the trials that followed the panic, reveal that Catholic and Protestant neighbours had discussed the rumours during the visits they routinely paid each other; one of the Catholic accused could bring seventeen Reformed *lidmaten* to testify in her favour, and the Catholic milkmaid Griete Ates promised one of her Protestant customers that she would see to it that he was spared in the impending bloodbath.[76] Dutch believers were not either tolerant or intolerant, they tended to be both; fiercely committed to confessional difference and often deeply opposed to tolerant policies, much of this aggression was suspended in day to day contacts with people of other faiths.

Of course, confessionalism grew over time. Yet Israel van der Meersch's conversion reminds us that it is far too simple to assume that believers, once raised in solid post-Reformation confessionalism, would never question the truths in which they had been raised. And particularly when they were surrounded and in constant contact with believers of other confessions, when pious literature of all confessions freely circulated and other corporate loyalties remained of significance, voluntary religion did not automatically result in segregation. Pieter van der Meersch, having learned his grandfather's pious poems by heart as a child, was and remained a deeply religious man. Unlike his grandfather, he probably did not break away from the Church in which he had been brought up; he married and was buried in the Reformed Church, although we do not know whether he was ever a

---

75   Willem Frijhoff, 'De paniek van juni 1734', *Archief voor de geschiedenis van de katholieke kerk in Nederland* 19 (1992), 170–233.

76   Ibid. 223–4.

member.[77] Trading in Catholic martyrologies, Remonstrant theology, Socinian scholarship and Mennonite ethical manuals, as well as in Reformed authors, doctrinal purity to him was perhaps of less importance than it had been to his grandfather.[78] Like him, he had the choice to mould his own confessional life, to be committed to his faith in a way over which neither the state nor the Church had any automatic control.[79] And however Reformed his upbringing, it did not limit his contacts to the Reformed community alone. That he catered for readers of all confessions may just have been the result of sheer commercial good sense, but that he left all his books not to a co-religionist, but to a Catholic, the Jansenist Hugo van Heussen, suggests that for Pieter van der Meersch religious and social divisions had never come to coincide.[80] It is no surprise, then, that, looking back on his grandfather's agonising conversion, he pointedly wrote that he himself one day hoped to be reunited in heaven, not just with his parents, ancestors and friends, but also with all others 'who have died in Christ'.[81]

77   Gemeentearchief Leiden, Kerkelijke ondertrouwregisters, 21 June 1668. He married Wyvetje van Groeneveld and was buried in the Pieterskerk. I thank Piet Boon and Paul Hoftijzer for making this information available to me.
78   The Short Title Catalogue for the Netherlands lists twenty-three of the books he traded, included works by the Remonstrant Stephanus Curcellaeus and the Socinian Stanislaw Lubieniecki, as well as a Catholic martyrology by Opmeer.
79   Pieter apparently cherished this freedom. When, in 1705, he edited one of his grandfather's poems, a eulogy of the city of Hoorn, he inserted a stanza of his own that read 'To force Conscience is unheard of here, Religion here is free – all can be confident and sure – of any tyranny.' Songbook, 110v–111r 'Men maekt hier ook geen mentij/te dwingen de Conscientie/De Godsdienst is hier vrij:/elk kan en mach bij desen/gerust en seker wesen/van alle Tyranny'.
80   Gemeente Archief Leiden, Notary Archives 1723, No. 19, Will of 16 March 1713. I thank Paul Hoftijzer for this information.
81   Songbook, 108v.

John Coffey

Scepticism, Dogmatism and Toleration in Seventeenth-Century England

'At the back of many people's minds', writes the historian of ideas Richard Tuck, 'is a rough history of the modern world in which the dissolution of strongly-held beliefs [...] was a precondition for extending toleration to men who would once have been attacked as heretics'.[1] When we moderns speak about the demise of persecution and religious uniformity and the rise of toleration and pluralism, we tend to cast dogma as the culprit and scepticism as the liberator. In this sense, we are all heirs of the Enlightenment. In the late 1980s, for example, during the controversy over the *fatwa* against Salman Rushdie, the former Labour party leader, Michael Foot, put it this way:

> How the world in general, and Western Europe in particular, escaped from this predicament, this seemingly endless confrontation [between religions], is one of the real miracles of western civilisation, and it was certainly not the work of the fundamentalists on either side. It was done by those who dared to deny the absolute authority of their respective gods; the sceptics, the doubters, the mockers even, the men like Montaigne who saw where the endless bloodletting would lead, and how each side must be ready to abjure absolute victory.[2]

Foot's essential point – that religious dogmatism kills while religious scepticism heals – may seem like straightforward common sense. Jonathan Israel has pointed out that William of Orange, who contributed as much as any early modern statesman to the cause of toleration, was a man of 'decidedly tepid' faith. Israel writes,

1   R. Tuck, 'Scepticism and toleration in the seventeenth century', in S. Mendus (ed.), *Justifying Toleration* (Cambridge, 1988), 21.
2   L. Appignanesi and S. Maitland (eds), *The Rushdie File* (London, 1991), 244.

One might agree or disagree with the proposition that the advancement of the cause of religious toleration in early modern Europe in general was a function of the steady waning of religious fervour in the post-Reformation context. But in William's own case his emphatic espousal of the cause of toleration does appear to have gone hand-in-hand with a marked lack of religious commitment.[3]

However, although religious scepticism and 'waning fervour' clearly played a role in the demise of persecution, the picture is by no means as simple as Michael Foot suggested. Richard Popkin, the leading historian of early modern scepticism, has argued provocatively that dogmatic millenarians 'did at least as much to create modern tolerant societies as the deist and nonreligious groups in Europe and America in the seventeenth and eighteenth centuries'. He suggests that a 'benign egalitarian millenarianism' played an important role in promoting tolerance, particularly of Jews and American Indians.[4]

This chapter reflects further on the respective roles of scepticism and dogmatism in the development of toleration, with particular reference to seventeenth-century England. The English experience usually occupies a significant place in histories of toleration, and rightly so.[5] The development of English tolerationism was to have important long-term consequences beyond the British Isles. For Enlightenment intellectuals like Voltaire, pluralistic England offered a radical alternative to the religious uniformity which had been pursued in France since the Revocation of the Edict of Nantes by the Edict of Fontainebleau (1685).[6] Moreover, England's radical tolerationists had

3   J. Israel, 'William III and Toleration', in O. Grell, J. Israel and N. Tyacke (eds), *From Persecution to Toleration* (Oxford, 1991) 131.

4   R. Popkin, 'Skepticism about Religion and Millenarian Dogmatism: Two Sources of Toleration in the Seventeenth Century', in J. Laursen and C. Nederman (eds), *Beyond the Persecuting Society: Religious Toleration before the Enlightenment* (Philadelphia, 1998), 232–50, at 245, 242.

5   See for example, H. Kamen, *The Rise of Toleration*, (London, 1967), ch. 7: 'The English contribution'; P. Zagorin, *How the Idea of Toleration Came to the West* (Princeton, 2003), ch. 6: 'The great English toleration controversy, 1640–1660'.

6   Discussed by Brian Strayer, 'The Edict of Fontainebleau (1685) and the Huguenots: Who's to Blame?', see below.

created colonies in America that allowed greater religious freedom than England itself: namely, Pennsylvania, Rhode Island, and the Carolinas. Finally, seventeenth-century English tolerationists like Locke and Milton were widely read in the eighteenth century, and their arguments shaped the thinking of the Founders of the United States – one could argue that the English tolerationist tradition reached its fulfilment with the First Amendment to the American Constitution.

I wish to focus particularly on the half century between 1640 and 1690. This period witnessed two very significant developments. Firstly, this was the age of the great English toleration debate, inaugurated in 1644 by Henry Robinson's *Liberty of Conscience,* Roger Williams' *Bloudy Tenent of Persecution,* William Walwyn's *Compassionate Samaritan,* and John Milton's *Areopagitica* and culminating in Locke's famous *Letter concerning Toleration* published in English in 1689. Secondly, the fifty years from 1640 to 1690 saw the splintering of English Protestantism. In 1640, only a few thousand Protestants dared to worship outside the established church in illegal, clandestine conventicles. By 1690, Dissenters probably numbered more than a quarter of a million, constituted about 5% of the population, and were worshipping openly and erecting new meeting houses at a rate which appalled conservative Anglicans. The Act of Toleration in 1689, despite all its limitations outlined by David Wykes,[7] marked a decisive turning point. The age of uniformity and persecution was over, the age of pluralism and toleration had begun. Seventeenth-century England has a significant place in the history of religious toleration, and it provides an ideal testing ground for theories about the relationship between scepticism, dogmatism and tolerance.[8]

I will make four points. Firstly, radical scepticism about religion was a relatively rare phenomenon in seventeenth-century England, and in any case, it did not necessarily favour toleration. Secondly, the kind

---

7   Below, D. L. Wykes, '"So Bitterly Censur'd and Revil'd": Religious Dissent and Relations with the Church of England After the Toleration Act'.

8   For complementary overviews, see J. Coffey, *Persecution and Toleration in Protestant England, 1558–1689* (Harlow, 2000); A. R. Murphy, *Conscience and Community: Revisiting Toleration and Religious Dissent in Early Modern England and America* (University Park, 2001).

of scepticism which did contribute to toleration was usually a mitigated and devout scepticism, built on the theological conviction that as fallen human beings we are all profoundly fallible. Thirdly, the very idea of toleration flourished in the seventeenth century because it was touted as a basic item of Christian dogma, the solemn duty of every true Christian. Finally, it is hard to see how religious pluralism could ever have developed without fresh kinds of religious dogmatism. The fragmentation of Western Christendom in the early modern period occurred because of a series of passionate heretical and schismatic movements. Lutherans, Anabaptists, Calvinists, Socinians, Separatists, Baptists, Independents and Quakers were not normally noted for their easy-going outlook or their ability to see the other person's point of view.

I   Radical Religious Scepticism and Toleration

Our first problem in dealing with scepticism is a problem of definition. Alan Levine has identified three basic types of scepticism. First, *Academic scepticism*, which originated in Plato's Academy and received its classic expression in the writings of Carneades and Cicero. Academic sceptics denied the existence of epistemological certainty, but they did not believe that scepticism should degenerate into total doubt. Instead, by examining both sides of every controversy, the philosopher could arrive at judgements based on probability. Second, *Pyrrhonian scepticism*, which also has its roots in Greek philosophy, in the thought of Pyrrho of Elis. The Pyrrhonist went further than the Academic sceptic, and argued that we cannot even know whether or not knowledge is possible; the only sensible policy is to suspend judgement. Finally, *Fideism*, a form of scepticism originating within Christianity in the late medieval and early modern periods. Fideists argued that although knowledge cannot be acquired through reason or the senses, it is available through faith and divine revelation.[9]

Levine's distinction between these three forms of scepticism is admirably clear, but it does not really help us to unlock seventeenth-century English discourse on toleration. Pyrrhonian scepticism was rare indeed in seventeenth-century England, and even Fideism was uncommon in an age when most Christians believed that belief in God was rationally demonstrable. Academic scepticism was a more significant force, and we shall see that it played a significant role in tolerationist argument. However, I suspect that when Michael Foot and others speak about 'sceptics', they have in mind not Academic sceptics, or Pyrrhonists, or fideists, but those seventeenth- and eighteenth-century figures who questioned the truth of Christianity. These thinkers may not have entertained doubts about the human capacity for knowledge *per se*, but they were decidedly sceptical about the doctrines of traditional Christianity. So in this section, I will focus on what I shall call radical religious scepticism, especially scepticism about the Christian religion.

It should be said at the outset that radical religious sceptics did make a significant contribution to the development of toleration in Europe, both in terms of the idea and the policy of toleration. The Dutch Jew, Benedict Spinoza, who was deeply sceptical about both Judaism and Christianity, was also one of the most radical tolerationists of the seventeenth century. As Jonathan Israel has pointed out, Spinoza's doctrine of toleration went further than that of John Locke.[10] Indeed, Israel has provided a powerful restatement of the claim that it was the sceptical rationalists of the Radical Enlightenment (inspired by Spinoza) who created the modern idea of a free society, one in which there is freedom of thought, freedom of religion, freedom of expression, free speech, a free press, and even

9   A. Levine, *Early Modern Skepticism and the Problem of Toleration* (Lanham, 1999), 10–11.

10   J. Israel, 'Spinoza, Locke and the Enlightenment Battle for Toleration', in O. P. Grell and R. Porter (eds), *Toleration in Enlightenment Europe* (Cambridge, 2000), 102–13.

sexual freedom.[11] Certainly, from the late seventeenth century onwards, radical religious sceptics (mainly Deists) were among the most thoroughgoing proponents of toleration in Europe and America. Writers like the English Deist John Toland and the French *Philosophe* Voltaire campaigned tirelessly for toleration, whilst political leaders like Frederick the Great and Thomas Jefferson (both of whom were sceptical Deists) used their position to ensure that freedom of religion was extended in their nations.

However, without in any way denying the significance of the eighteenth-century Enlightenment, we should point out that the great toleration debates of early modern Europe were already well under-way before the rise of radical religious scepticism. Seventeenth-century England witnessed the development of far-reaching theories of toleration, but denial of the Christian religion was a rarity. Social historians have found evidence of sceptical irreligion among ordinary people, but the trend in recent years has been to argue that most early moderns were genuine Christian believers, even if they did not always lead lives of exemplary piety.[12] And although Deism did emerge as a significant force in the 1690s, the great majority of English intellectuals in the seventeenth century were committed (if sometimes heterodox) Christian believers.[13] For example, although writers like Hobbes, Spinoza and Richard Simon pioneered the development of biblical criticism after 1650, the age of biblical literalism took a long time to draw to a close.[14] In the early eighteenth century, Isaac Newton was still engaging in the kind of literal historicist reading of

11   J. Israel, *Radical Enlightenment: Philosophy and the Making of Modernity, 1650–1750* (Oxford, 2001), esp. chs. 4, 5, and 15.

12   See for example, M. Ingram, *Church Courts, Sex and Marriage in England, 1570–1640* (Cambridge, 1987) ch. 3; M. Spufford, (ed.), *The World of Rural Dissenters* (Cambridge, 1995); J. Maltby, *Prayer Book and People in Elizabethan and Early Stuart England* (Cambridge, 1998).

13   On the challenge of identifying 'unbelievers' in the period, see the thoughtful discussion of G. Aylmer, 'Unbelief in Seventeenth-Century England', in D. Pennington and K. Thomas (eds), *Puritans and Revolutionaries: Essays in Seventeenth-Century History Presented to Christopher Hill* (Oxford, 1978), 22–46.

14   See P. Harrison, *The Bible, Protestantism and the Rise of Natural Science* (Cambridge, 1998), passim.

Daniel and Revelation promoted by his Cambridge predecessor, Joseph Mede, more than half a century earlier. Both Newton and his successor as Lucasian professor, William Whiston, also attempted to mesh the new science with literalist readings of Genesis – Whiston argued, for instance, that Noah's universal flood had been started by a comet crashing to earth.[15] By the time that radical religious scepticism had become a major intellectual force, ideas of toleration had been in circulation for decades.

Moreover, the assumption that radical religious scepticism naturally led to toleration should be treated with some caution. As Richard Tuck has demonstrated, the relationship between scepticism and toleration was somewhat ambivalent. Although Tuck thinks that there is 'a certain emotional kinship' between scepticism and tolerance, he suggests that early modern scepticism could be allied to a programme of 'ideological repression'. He illustrates this with reference to Thomas Hobbes, who combined a sceptical approach to religion with a defence of the magistrate's sovereign authority over public doctrine and practice.[16]

In recent years, Hobbes's attitude toward toleration has attracted a great deal of attention, and several scholars (including Tuck himself) have presented us with 'a more tolerant Hobbes'.[17] They point out that Hobbes was a bitter foe of the intolerant clerical elites who tried to police early modern religious beliefs. In Parts III and IV of *Leviathan*, he launched a powerful attack on the 'divine right' claims of popes, prelates and presbyters, and defended the authority of the magistrate

---

15   J. Brooke, 'The God of Newton', in J. Fauvel *et al* (eds), *Let Newton Be! A New Perspective on His Life and Works* (Oxford, 1988), 175–6.

16   Tuck, 'Scepticism and Toleration', 21–35.

17   A. Ryan, 'Hobbes, Toleration and the Inner Life', in D. Miller and L. Siedentrop (eds), *The Nature of Political Theory* (Oxford, 1983), 197–218; A. Ryan, 'A more Tolerant Hobbes', in S. Mendus (ed.), *Justifying Toleration*, ch. 2; R. Tuck, 'Hobbes and Locke on Toleration', in M. Deitz (ed.), *Thomas Hobbes and Political Theory* (Lawrence, 1990) ch. 8; J. Sommerville, *Thomas Hobbes: Political Ideas in Historical Context*, (London, 1992), ch. 6; G. Burgess, 'Thomas Hobbes: religious toleration or religious indifference?', in C. Nederman and J. Laursen (eds), *Difference and Dissent: Theories of Toleration in Medieval and Early Modern Europe* (Lanham, 1996), ch. 8.

and the liberty of the individual against the might of established churches. As Glenn Burgess has noted, Hobbes argued that the sovereign has a duty to avoid making unnecessary laws that might jeopardise public peace, especially laws that impose on conscience. In chapter 46 he insisted that inquisitions into the private religious beliefs of his subjects were 'against the law of nature'. The sovereign should be satisfied with 'the Conformity of their Speech and Actions', and should not pry into 'the very Thoughts, and Consciences of men, by Examination, and Inquisition of what they Hold'.[18] In chapter 47, Hobbes even seemed to celebrate the voluntaristic individualism which now prevailed in England, where uniformity was no longer enforced and each person was allowed to attend the congregation of his choice: 'And so we are reduced to the Independency of the Primitive Christians to follow Paul, or Cephas, or Apollos, every man as he liketh best'.[19] Hobbes may have given his sovereign the power to determine the doctrine and worship of his people, but he clearly did not envisage a sovereign who was a zealous hunter of heretics.

Since Hobbes himself was decidedly heterodox in his own opinions, this is hardly surprising. *Leviathan* cast doubt on the Mosaic authorship of the Pentateuch and advanced a potent philosophical critique of traditional ideas of angels, miracles, prophecy and hell, laying some of the groundwork for the biblical criticism and theological scepticism of the Enlightenment. It landed Hobbes in hot water with his erstwhile Anglican friends, and after the Restoration the philosopher lived in fear of persecution. According to John Aubrey, Hobbes heard 'a report that the Bishops would have him burn't for a Heretique. So he then feared the search of his papers, and burned the greatest part of these verses'. Preoccupied by this threat, Hobbes wrote several short works arguing that there was no valid basis for punishing heresy under English law.[20]

---

18   Burgess, 'Thomas Hobbes', 145–9. The key passage is in R. Tuck (ed.), *Leviathan* (Cambridge, 1991), 229, ch. 30.
19   Hobbes, *Leviathan*, 479.
20   See P. Milton, 'Hobbes, Heresy and Lord Arlington', *History of Political Thought*, 14 (1993), 534–79.

It is quite clear, therefore, that Hobbes the religious sceptic was an inveterate critic of the traditional theological argument for the persecution of heresy. He expressly discouraged the magistrate from conducting inquisitions into the thoughts and private opinions of his subjects. However, it is worth remembering that the bulk of persecution in Stuart England was directed not against hidden heresy, but against outward schism and nonconformity. Both before and after the Puritan Revolution, Dissenters were persecuted in large numbers primarily for their failure to conform to the established church. There were, of course, theological justifications for this persecution of schism derived from St Augustine, but defenders of religious coercion also employed political arguments resting on the Erastian emphasis on the magistrate's authority over public worship. Many Anglicans argued that the magistrate must be able to impose a single form of public worship on his people, for reasons of political order. The magistrate, they maintained, had the authority to determine rites and ceremonies not prescribed by Scripture (*adiaphora*, or things indifferent), and to order public worship as he chose, for the sake of peace. His subjects were obliged to conform.[21]

As Johann Sommerville has pointed out, Hobbes agreed with his Anglican contemporaries on the magistrates' authority to order the public worship of the Christian Commonwealth, and to punish dissenters.[22] Although Hobbes denied the sovereign any authority to pry into private opinions, and permitted freedom of 'private' (i.e. 'secret') worship,[23] he was insistent that the sovereign could regulate public worship and prosecute nonconformists. In *Leviathan*, the sovereign was 'Gods Supreme Lieutenant', Judge and Interpreter of religious doctrine; the 'chief Pastor' of the Commonwealth; and 'the

---

21   On the Augustinian and Erastian arguments for religious persecution see M. Goldie, 'The theory of religious intolerance in Restoration England', in O. Grell, J. Israel, and N. Tyacke (eds), *From Persecution to Toleration* (Oxford, 1989), ch. 13; Coffey, *Persecution and Toleration*, ch. 2. Dissenting views of *Adiaphora* are discussed by Paul Lim, '*Adiaphora*, Ecclesiology and Reformation: John Owen's Theology of Religious Toleration in Context', below.

22   Sommerville, *Thomas Hobbes*, 155–6.

23   *Leviathan*, 249, ch. 31.

Supreme Ecclesiastical Power'.[24] As such, he was to establish the 'Uniforme' 'Publique Worship' of the Commonwealth, prescribing what 'Actions, and Gestures, of an indifferent nature' were 'to be Publiquely and Universally in use'.[25] He also had authority to determine the public religious doctrine and teaching of the Commonwealth, so that 'any private men, that stubbornly defend some Doctrine, prohibited by their lawfull Soveraigns' were to be considered 'Haeretiques'.[26]

One of the most revealing examples used in *Leviathan* is that of the biblical figure, Naaman. Naaman was the heathen general who believed in the God of Israel but was given permission by the prophet Elisha to continue bowing before his idols. Hobbes's point was that Naaman's body bowed to the idol Rimmon, but his mind remained free to worship his God.[27] The Hobbesian subject was required to render outward conformity, but continued to possess inward freedom of thought. The Hobbesian sovereign had authority over 'the externall acts and profession of Religion', but he did not have the authority over 'the *inward* thought, and *beleef* of man'.[28]

In recent years, some scholars have been unduly impressed by Hobbes's stress on the immunity of '*inward* thought, and *beleef*'. We need to remember that even the most hardline defenders of persecution protested that they were not advocating thought control. The Scottish Presbyterian, Samuel Rutherford, insisted that the godly magistrate would not interfere with the 'internal liberty [...] to think, understand, judge, conclude'.[29] Persecutors were primarily interested in outward conformity. Even if they wanted to, they could not control inward thoughts and, in any case, individuals who kept their heterodox opinions to themselves were no threat to religious uniformity. Those who did suffer for heresy in Protestant England were those who insisted on teaching and propagating their beliefs, and who stubbornly

24   Ibid. 306, 322, 378.
25   Ibid. 252–3, ch. 31.
26   Ibid. 399, ch. 42.
27   Ibid. 343–4, ch. 42.
28   Ibid. 323, ch. 40.
29   Samuel Rutherford, *A Free Disputation against Pretended Liberty of Conscience* (1649), 46.

refused to recant or conform even after many warnings.[30] Hobbes had no time for zealots like this; he displayed little imaginative sympathy for persecuted religious dogmatists who refused outward conformity. As far as he was concerned, those who failed to follow Naaman's example, and refused to conform outwardly would have to pay the price. Self-appointed 'Martyrs' were a menace to the peace of the Commonwealth, because they insisted on disobeying their prince whenever he commanded worship that was contrary to their conscience.[31] *Leviathan* argued for freedom of internal thought, not for freedom of nonconformist worship or expression. Its argument would have been cold comfort to most religious dissenters. Nonconformists were not satisfied with being allowed to think what they liked within the safety of their own minds or to enjoy 'private worship' in the safety of their own homes, but insisted on meeting together in substantial conventicles. As Glenn Burgess rightly concludes, 'Hobbes's tolerance is extraordinarily narrow, extending only to private beliefs and not at all to religious practices'.[32]

Moreover, despite the claims of Tuck,[33] it is doubtful that Hobbes was particularly sympathetic to Protestant Dissenters after the Restoration. In his history of the Civil War, *Behemoth* (written in 1668 but not published until after his death), Hobbes does lament the folly of the English government in imposing the Prayer Book on the Scots,[34] but he also castigates the Puritans for their pigheaded refusal to submit to their lawful sovereign. In stark contrast to chapter 47 of *Leviathan*, the Independents are now identified as 'seducers' of the people. Along with the Baptists and other sects, the Independent tolerationists are condemned for advocating 'liberty in religion' and 'private interpretation of the Scripture'.[35] The main character in the dialogue complains that

---

30   See Coffey, *Persecution and Toleration*, 99–102, 114–15.
31   Hobbes, *Leviathan*, 343–5.
32   See Burgess, 'Thomas Hobbes', 155.
33   R. Tuck, *Thomas Hobbes* (Oxford, 1989), 32–7, portrays Hobbes as aligned with tolerationists after the Restoration.
34   F. Tonnies (ed.), *Behemoth, or the Long Parliament*, (Chicago, 1990), 28.
35   Ibid. 3.

> after the Bible was translated into English, every man, nay, every boy and wench, that could read English, thought they spoke with God Almighty, and understood what he said, when by a certain number of chapters a day they had read the Scriptures once or twice over.

His interlocutor, a young man, wonders why the Bible was ever translated into the vernacular, since this was bound to produce 'diversity of opinion, and consequently (as man's nature is) disputations, breach of charity, disobedience, and at last rebellion'. The main character agrees that this was foolish, and argues that the solution to the problem is to make the king 'chief judge of the rectitude of all interpretations of the Scripture'.[36] As in *Leviathan*, Hobbes explains that his ideal magistrate would not make unnecessary laws about religion, but that if the magistrate did authorise 'unnecessary doctrines', 'it is the duty of every subject not to speak against them', and 'the wisdom of all such powers to punish such as shall publish or teach their private interpretations, when they are contrary to law'.[37]

Written in the wake of the Clarendon Code, the re-imposition of religious uniformity, and the renewal of the persecution of Dissent, this hardly suggests much sympathy for intransigent Dissenters who appealed to private conscience to justify their failure to conform. Hobbes may have disapproved of the heavy-handedness of the Clarendon Code, but he also condemned nonconformity. During the Restoration, he was very concerned to protect heterodox philosophers (like himself) who were willing to keep their heads down and conform outwardly. By contrast, he showed little interest in defending the Dissenters who were being imprisoned and fined in their thousands for refusing to conform to the publicly prescribed worship of the established church.[38]

---

36   Ibid. 21–2, 53.
37   Ibid. 55.
38   However, there is now an intriguing debate between historians who see Hobbes as a source for Restoration anti-tolerationists (like Samuel Parker) and those who see him being used by tolerationists (like Andrew Marvell). Compare G. Schochet, 'Between Lambeth and Leviathan: Samuel Parker on the Church of England and Political Order', in N. Phillipson and Q. Skinner (eds), *Political*

In the end, the contrasts between Hobbes and tolerationists are more striking than the similarities. Tolerationists insisted that *peace* could be secured by granting toleration and permitting religious pluralism; Hobbes believed that peace could only be achieved when the sovereign imposed a uniform public worship and the subjects yielded outward conformity. Tolerationists questioned the *magistrate's authority* over religion; Hobbes defended it. Tolerationists sympathised with the *martyrs* who had died for their faith; Hobbes regarded martyrs as dangerous subversives. Tolerationists often claimed that the individual had a *right* to freedom of religion; Hobbes emphatically denied this.[39] The conclusion of James Farr seems persuasive: 'Hobbes was not writing *about* toleration, and such strains of it that we find in his work exist alongside more virulent strains of intoleration'.[40]

Hobbes illustrates the problems with making a tight connection between scepticism and tolerance. The sceptics, doubters and mockers whom Michael Foot celebrates may have had no *theological* motive for persecution, but they could easily find a *political* one. Anticlerical unbelievers tended to find strong religious belief disturbing, and some were prone to jump to the conclusion that it was socially or politically pernicious and ought to be regulated or even suppressed. Historically, the militant anticlericalism of religious sceptics has often proved fertile ground for persecution. As Richard Popkin has reminded us, the tolerant Deism of the American Founding Fathers needs to be set alongside the intolerant Deism of the French Revolution.[41] In the

Discourse in Early Modern England (Cambridge, 1993), ch. 9; with J. Parkin, 'Liberty Transpros'd: Andrew Marvell and Samuel Parker', in W. Chernaik and M. Dzelzainis (eds), *Marvell and Liberty*, (London, 1999), ch. 12.

39   See *Leviathan*, 223, ch. 29.

40   J. Farr, 'Atomes of Scripture: Hobbes and the Politics of Biblical Interpretation', in Dietz (ed.), *Thomas Hobbes and Political Theory*, 190. For further challenges to the tolerationist reading of Hobbes see Murphy, *Conscience and Community*, 233–9; and M. P. Thompson, 'Hobbes on Heresy', in J. C. Laursen (ed.), *Histories of Heresy in Early Modern Europe: For, Against and Beyond Persecution and Toleration* (New York, 2002), 77–99.

41   R. Popkin, 'The Deist challenge', in Grell, Israel and Tyacke (eds), *From Persecution to Toleration*, 213–4; Popkin, 'An Aspect of the Problem of

twentieth century, the avowedly atheistic regimes of the Communist world have not been renowned for their tolerance.[42] Instead of taking the trouble to cultivate an imaginative appreciation of religious belief and otherness, radical sceptics often settled for denouncing it as a dangerous pathology, thus fostering new kinds of hostility and prejudice. Abandoning traditional religion did not make sceptics immune from the impulse to persecute.

Thus in trying to explain the rise of toleration and religious pluralism in the seventeenth century, we should not exaggerate the role played by radical scepticism. The 'doubters' were not necessarily more tolerant than the believers, and they were thin on the ground in Stuart England. In the eighteenth century, of course, religious scepticism became far more widespread, as the impact of radical Enlightenment ideas began to be felt, and eighteenth-century Deists were able to contemplate a broader toleration than most seventeenth-century Protestants.[43] Yet by this stage, a significant degree of toleration and pluralism had already become well entrenched in England, the Netherlands and a number of the American colonies. Although eighteenth-century rationalists like Voltaire and Jefferson were to make great contributions to the cause of religious toleration, they were building on the achievements of other, more conservative figures. If we are to understand seventeenth-century tolerationism, we need to look beyond the tiny numbers of radical sceptics.

Religious Freedom in the French and American Revolutions', *Proceedings of the American Catholic Philosophical Association* (1976), 146–61.

42   See T. Beeson, *Discretion and Valour: Religious Conditions in Russia and Eastern Europe* (London, 1982); M. Bourdeaux *et al*, *Religious Minorities in the Soviet Union* (London, 1984); P. Marshall, *Their Blood Cries Out: The Worldwide Tragedy of Christians who are Dying for their Faith* (Dallas, 1997), ch. 4.

43   See J. Champion, *The Pillars of Priestcraft Shaken: The Church of England and its Enemies* (Cambridge, 1992); Champion, *Republican Learning: John Toland and the Crisis of Christian Culture, 1696–1722* (Manchester, 2003). For a revisionist attempt to cut the Deist movement down to size see S. J. Barnett, *The Enlightenment and Religion: The Myths of Modernity* (Manchester, 2003), ch. 3.

II   Mitigated Scepticism and Toleration

However, the importance of scepticism to the development of toleration cannot be disregarded. If radical scepticism towards religion was rare in the seventeenth century, the mitigated scepticism associated with Academic sceptics was much more common. As Gary Remer has demonstrated, Erasmus and his followers drew heavily on the Academic sceptics' stress on probability. Erasmus, for example, suggested that although the fundamentals of Christianity could be known with certainty, non-essentials could only be grasped as probabilities. On such non-essentials, Erasmus recommended that Christians should tolerate diversity of opinion. Those inspired by Erasmus – including Jacob Acontius and William Chillingworth – were among the leading advocates of religious toleration in the sixteenth and seventeenth centuries, and they appealed to uncertainty and fallibility to undermine the case for persecution. These devout sceptics did not doubt the truth of Christianity, but they acknowledged the real possibility that they themselves might misunderstand or misrepresent that truth. Conscious of their own fallibility, they were tentative in their own assertions and willing to acknowledge that they still had much to learn when it came matters of Christian truth.[44]

In many cases, this theological openness reflected the Protestant conviction that truth had been lost during the medieval apostasy of the church and would be gradually recovered in the latter days. John Milton's great defence of the freedom of the press, *Areopagitica* (1644), rested firmly on this assumption. Milton compared Truth to a beautiful woman, 'a perfect shape most glorious to look on', whom the enemies of God had 'hewed into a thousand pieces, and scattered them to the four winds'. Ever since, said Milton, believers had been wandering the earth 'gathering up limb by limb'. This work would carry on until the Second Coming of Christ, and in order that it might proceed, it was vital that Parliament allowed freedom of the press.

---

44   G. Remer, *Humanism and the Rhetoric of Toleration* (University Park, 1996). The tolerationist implications of 'Christian skepticism' are also explored in Murphy, *Conscience and Community*, 103–10.

Milton was no radical sceptic, but he was suspicious of theological dogmatism, and hostile to the idea that God's truth had been signed, sealed and delivered in the neat package of Calvin's *Institutes*. 'We have looked so long upon the blaze that Zwinglius and Calvin hath beaconed to us, that we are stark blind', he wrote.[45] His attitude recalled that of the Pilgrim Fathers' pastor, John Robinson, who declared, 'The Lord has more truth and light yet to break forth out of his holy word'.[46]

This notion of progressive revelation, of the Spirit leading the church into new light, counted against the hasty censure of innovative religious ideas. John Goodwin, the radical Independent tolerationist, praised the wisdom of Gamaliel, the Jewish leader who had argued against killing the early Christians on the grounds that if they were wrong their cause would collapse, whilst if they were right their persecutors would be fighting against God (Acts 5.33–40). There was a kind of 'uncertainty principle' underlying Goodwin's case. His sermon on Gamaliel was entitled *Theomachia: Or the Grand Imprudence of Men Running the Hazard of Fighting against God* (1644). Persecutors were taking a risk, for how could they be sure that the earnest heretics they punished were not godly martyrs? The history of the Reformation itself demonstrated that truth was often called heresy, and that persecutors pulled up good wheat along with the tares they sought to destroy. In *Hagiomastix* (1647), Goodwin developed this sceptical argument at length. He noted that the Presbyterians themselves were 'confessedly fallible'. Yet in their Blasphemy Ordinance of 1646 they had identified certain teachings as 'manifest' or 'certain' heresy. To Goodwin this was sheer presumption on the part of fallible men, and to underline the point he repeatedly printed the word 'CERTAINTIE' in capital letters.[47] Goodwin was clearly influenced by Academic scepticism, and he wrote the foreword to the English translation of the famous tolerationist work by Acontius, *Satan's Stratagems* (1648). He maintained that once it was recognised

---

45   M. W. Wallace (ed.), *Milton's Prose* (Oxford, 1925), 311–12.
46   Quoted in G. Nuttall, *The Holy Spirit in Puritan Faith and Experience* (Chicago, 1992), 22.
47   *Hagiomastix* (1647), esp. 22–35.

that many of the doctrinal beliefs of Christians were based on probability, not on certainty, the epistemological foundation of persecution would be undermined. When persecutors admitted even a slight possibility of doubt, they became hesitant to execute other men for heresy.[48]

Other tolerationists echoed Goodwin. The Baptist, Samuel Richardson, made much of the argument from human fallibility. No one thinks he is in error, Richardson pointed out, though it is certain that all human beings err. There was no infallible human judge in matters of religion, and the Presbyterian clergy should not be set up as such. Moreover, 'all truth is not among one sort of men', and even error served a purpose, for 'if there were no error, it could not be known what is truth, or [it would] not be so glorious'.[49] Similar arguments came from the father of the latitudinarians, William Chillingworth. Chillingworth saw no reason why Protestants should be bound by every word of Luther or Calvin, any more than Roman Catholics should be bound by all the assertions of their theologians. On matters necessary to salvation made plain in Scripture, certainty was desirable and possible, but on secondary matters things were different:

> though we wish heartily that all controversies were ended, as we do that all sin were abolished, yet we have little hope of the one or the other until the world be ended: and in the meanwhile think it best to content ourselves with, and to persuade others unto, an unity of charity, and mutual toleration; seeing God hath authorised no man to force all men in unity of opinion.[50]

The sceptical argument simply confirmed the suspicion of conservative Protestants that tolerationists were sinking in a swamp of indifference and doubt. Yet this was not exactly true. Tolerationists were certain about many things, and often preserved Erasmus's distinction between the sure and certain fundamentals of the faith, and

---

48   For an in-depth exploration of Goodwin's thought see J. Coffey, *John Goodwin and the Puritan Revolution* (Woodbridge, forthcoming).

49   Richardson, *An Answer to the London Ministers Letter* (1648), 31.

50   William Chillingworth, *The Religion of Protestants*, in his *Works*, 3 vols, Oxford (1838), 1: 214–6.

the uncertain non-essentials. Indeed, the problem with sceptical arguments for toleration is that they only extend as far as the tolerationist's own scepticism. When the tolerationist feels certain that some belief or practice is wrong, he has no sceptical case for toleration, and is forced either to abandon toleration or to find another basis for it. In the seventeenth century, when the existence of God was widely regarded as certain and demonstrable, mitigated scepticism did not point to toleration for atheists. Nevertheless, mitigated Academic scepticism of the sort popularised by Erasmus did provide a basis for mutual tolerance among Christians. In England, those Protestants who were willing to acknowledge grey areas of theology accepted that the interminable debates between Protestants were unlikely to be resolved on this side of heaven. The Bible itself was not lucid enough on secondary matters to solve all disputes, and even the godliest Christian still saw as through a glass darkly (1 Corinthians 13.12). The participants in these controversies ought to resign themselves to living with their differences, and refuse to employ coercion to bring their debates to a quick resolution. To do otherwise would be to employ popish means, to set oneself up as an infallible authority when the only infallible authorities were God and his Word.

This tradition of Christian fallibilism was ably summed up by John Locke. Locke clearly saw himself as an earnest Christian; he believed in the existence of God, in Christ as Redeemer, and in the Bible as God's revelation to mankind. Yet he also believed that dogmatism was inappropriate in many areas of controversy between Christians. The debates which had swirled around the doctrine of the Trinity, for example, were difficult and obscure, and human beings were fallible and fallen. Thus it was wise to be tentative and charitable in one's judgements, instead of imposing them dogmatically on others. In a letter to the Dutch Arminian, Philip van Limborch, Locke wrote, 'May others forgive my mistakes! I declare war on no one on account of difference of opinions, myself an ignorant and fallible manikin. I am an Evangelical Christian, not a Papist'. He went on to explain that there were only two kinds of Christians. Papists were those (in whatever denomination) who regarded themselves as infallible, and 'arrogate to themselves dominion over the consciences of others'. Evangelicals, on the other hand, were those who, seeking truth alone, desire themselves and others to be convinced of it only by proofs and reasons; they are gentle to the errors of others, being not unmindful of their own weakness; forgiving human frailty and ignorance, and seeking forgiveness in turn.[51]

For devout sceptics like Locke, then, tolerance was a question of Christian character. Persecutors were arrogant and self-confident, sure that they knew God's mind as well as he did himself. Tolerationists, by contrast, were deeply conscious of their own finitude, fallenness and fallibility. Their lives were characterised by humility.

III   Dogmatism and Toleration

Yet in a fundamental sense, tolerationists were dogmatists too. Anyone who has read seventeenth-century tolerationist tracts will have been struck by the intensely biblical character of the arguments. There were, of course, prudential or 'interest' arguments for toleration, and many writers claimed that a policy of toleration was in the national interest because it would encourage economic growth or political stability.[52] But the core of the tolerationist case was theological. As Perez Zagorin concludes in his recent study, 'the idea of toleration was itself very largely inspired by religious values and was fundamentally religious in character'.[53] Tolerationists had to persuade other Christians that they had a solemn duty to tolerate schism and heresy. They argued that persecution was diametrically opposed to the witness of Christ and his Apostles.[54]

I will illustrate this with reference to Roger Williams, William Penn and John Locke. My choice of these figures is not random, for

---

51   E. S. Beer (ed.), *The Correspondence of John Locke*, 8 vols. (Oxford, 1978), 6: 495.

52   See Murphy, *Conscience and Community*, 115–16, 146–50.

53   P. Zagorin, *How the Idea of Toleration Came to the West*, 289.

54   The theological character of English tolerationist argument is also emphasised in Murphy, *Conscience and Community*, esp. 12–14, 96–103, 226–33.

these were the English tolerationists involved in the establishment of the tolerant and pluralistic colonies of Rhode Island, Pennsylvania and the Carolinas. Williams, Penn and Locke were not simply interested in toleration for their own sect, and they were not mere theorists whose lofty ideas had no impact on empirical reality.

Roger Williams was perhaps the most influential tolerationist of the 1640s.[55] Although he had emigrated to New England in the previous decade, he had been expelled from Massachusetts Bay for his radical ideas, and had established the settlement of Rhode Island. In 1643, he returned to England to acquire a charter for the colony, and in the following year he published *The Bloudy Tenent of Persecution*. The book opened with a startling proposition:

> It is the will and command of God, that since the coming of his Son the Lord Jesus, a permission of the most Paganish, Jewish, Turkish, or anti-christian consciences and worships be granted to all men in all nations and countries: and that they are only to be fought against with that sword which is only, in soul matters, able to conquer: to wit, the sword of God's Spirit, the word of God.[56]

The phrase 'since the coming of his Son the Lord Jesus' was central to Williams's case for toleration, which rested on a radical distinction between the age of the Old Testament and the age of the New. Under the Old Covenant, he argued, God's people had been a single ethnic group united in a unique covenant with the Lord. Israel was a theocracy, and in order to preserve its special character, the magistrate had to punish idolatry, blasphemy, heresy and schism. But with the coming of Christ, everything changed. God's people were now a multi-ethnic group called out from among many nations. The political nation itself, therefore, was desacralised. There was no such thing as a Christian nation, and the magistrate was merely responsible for preserving the bodies and goods of men. Although he could

---

55   Among the many books on Williams, see especially E. Morgan, *Roger Williams: The Church and the State* (New York, 1967); W. C. Gilpin, *The Millenarian Piety of Roger Williams* (Chicago, 1979); T. D. Hall, *Separating Church and State: Roger Williams and Religious Liberty* (Chicago, 1998).

56   Roger Williams, *The Bloudy Tenent of Persecution*, E. B. Underhill (ed.) (London, 1848), 2.

enforce the principles of natural law (embodied in the second table of the Ten Commandments), he had no warrant to meddle in matters of religion. The church was no longer to be tied to the state. Instead, it was to be an association of 'volunteers', 'like unto a Corporation, Society or Company of East Indie or Turkie merchants'.[57] The tragedy of Christendom, according to *The Bloudy Tenent*, was that it had turned its back on the New Testament vision of the church. With the conversion of the Roman Empire in the fourth century, Christians had returned to the Israel model and the radical difference between the age of Israel and the age of the Church had been forgotten. In a delightful phrase, Williams declared that 'Christianity fell asleep in Constantine's bosom'.[58] His mission was to issue a wake-up call.

Williams's argument was a radical one, for it pointed towards a separation between church and state. Yet its primitivist logic was profoundly appealing to the godly; the notion of toleration may have been disturbingly novel, but the idea of returning to the New Testament pattern was reassuringly familiar. In the years following the publication of *The Bloudy Tenent*, a significant minority of radical Puritans embraced its point of view. In the Whitehall debates of 1648, for example, the arguments of Williams were reiterated by Independents, Baptists and Levellers.[59] This radical Puritan case for toleration was not based primarily on devout scepticism, but on the dogmatic conviction that Christians must recover the purity of the primitive church. Protestant persecutors were treading along a popish path, for they were perpetuating the mistakes of medieval Christendom. They must be warned of the error of their ways and called back to the truth.

The radical Puritan argument was later adopted by the Quakers.[60] In his writings on toleration, William Penn insisted that persecution was 'anti-protestant' and 'anti-Christian'. Protestant Christianity was

---

57   Ibid. 46.
58   Ibid. 154.
59   See J. Coffey, 'Puritanism and Liberty Revisited: the Case for Toleration in the English Revolution', *Historical Journal*, 41 (1998), 961–85.
60   See J. Coffey, 'Restoration Quakers and the Theology of Tolerance', *Q/W/E/R/T/Y: Arts, Litteratures & Civilisations du Monde Anglophone*, 8 (1998), 231–9.

all about returning to the model of the primitive church, and the primitive church had not persecuted its enemies. The 'plainest testimonies of divine writ', claimed Penn, 'condemn all force upon conscience'. To persecute was to overturn Christianity itself, for Christ had

> defined to us the nature of his religion in this one great saying of His, my kingdom is not of this world. It was spiritual, not carnal, accompanied with weapons, as heavenly as its own nature, and designed for the good and salvation of the soul, and not the injury and destruction of the body: no gaols, fines, exiles, etc. but sound reason, clear truth and a strict life. In short, the Christian religion entreats all, but compels none.[61]

The same arguments can be found in Locke's *Letter concerning Toleration* (1689). Going beyond the traditional Protestant claim that persecution was the mark of the false church, Locke opens his *Letter* by declaring that Toleration is 'the chief Characteristical Mark of the True Church'. He writes

> the Gospel frequently declares that the true Disciples of Christ must suffer Persecution; but that the Church of Christ should persecute others, and force others by Fire and Sword, to embrace her Faith and Doctrine, I could never yet find in any of the Books of the New Testament.

The Old Testament, of course, was a different matter, but like Williams, Locke takes care to consign the Mosaic Law to a past dispensation. Christians are to be identified by their 'Charity, Meekness, and Good-will in general towards all Mankind'. Cruelty is not only 'inhumane', it is also 'unChristian'.[62]

Locke reminds us that tolerationists were above all trying to establish toleration as a Christian dogma and a Christian practice. In the words of Andrew Murphy, they 'attempted nothing less than a

---

61   W. Penn, 'The Great Case of Liberty of Conscience', in E. B. Bronner (ed.), *The Peace of Europe, The Fruits of Solitude and Other Writings* (London, 1993), 157, 161–3.
62   John Locke, *A Letter Concerning Toleration*, J. Tully (ed.) (Indianapolis, 1983), 23, 30, 44–5, 32, 25.

massive reconstruction of what it meant to be a Christian'.[63] By and large, early modern tolerationists did not suggest that truth was unattainable, and that men must therefore stop persecuting others. On the contrary, they claimed that they were rediscovering New Testament Christianity, a faith that had been tragically corrupted during the centuries of the church's apostasy. Persecution had arisen because Christians had abandoned the primitive pattern, and as long as it continued it would inhibit the recovery of truth in all its primitive glory. But by repudiating persecution, believers could contribute to a restoration of the Christian faith. Tolerationists were not so much disillusioned sceptics, as zealous prophets calling fellow believers back to their roots.

The primitivist dimension of tolerationist argument has been highlighted by the philosopher Jacques Derrida. Derrida notes with interest that even the sceptical Voltaire appealed to the example of the early church when arguing for toleration. 'When Voltaire accuses the Christian religion and the Church', writes Derrida,

> he invokes the lesson of originary [sic] Christianity, 'the times of the first Christians', Jesus and the Apostles, betrayed by 'the Catholic, Apostolic and Roman religion'. The latter is 'in all its ceremonies and in all its dogmas, the opposite of the religion of Jesus.

Voltaire was far from exceptional – other eighteenth-century Deists like Frederick II, Tom Paine, Jefferson and Diderot all made the same appeal to the teaching of Jesus and the example of the Apostles. Derrida concludes that

> the concept of tolerance, *stricto sensu*, belongs first of all to a sort of Christian domesticity. It is literally, I mean behind this name, a secret of the Christian community. It was printed, emitted, transmitted and circulated in the name of the Christian faith.[64]

John Plamenatz once observed that liberty of conscience was:

---

63   Murphy, *Conscience and Community*, 12–3.
64   J. Derrida, 'Faith and knowledge', in Derrida and G. Vattimo (eds), *Religion* (Cambridge, 1998), 22.

first asserted and cherished in an age of strong beliefs. It was first asserted among peoples who adhered, as the Greeks and Romans did not, to dogmatic religions, among peoples who had been taught for centuries that nothing was more important than to have the right beliefs.

Plamenatz suggested that though this stress on the importance of right beliefs was the source of fanaticism and persecution, it was also the source a new conception of freedom. Because of the division of Christendom in the early modern period, one proposition ('Faith is supremely important, and therefore all men must have the one true faith') gradually gave way to another ('Faith is supremely important, and therefore every man must be allowed to live by the faith which seems true to him').[65]

Plamenatz was reflecting on another strand in the tolerationist argument, the emphasis on individual faith and conscience, but his argument reinforces the claim that dogmatic convictions were not always at loggerheads with toleration. The *primitivist* case for toleration rested on the unequivocal belief that religious coercion was antithetical to the teaching and example of Jesus. The *rights of conscience* argument was built on a deep respect for earnest religious belief, a respect that arose not from scepticism but from the conviction that every individual had a solemn duty to seek God with all his heart, soul, mind and strength, and that God alone was Lord over conscience. Plamenatz's conclusion seems very appropriate: 'Liberty of conscience was born, not of indifference, not of scepticism, not of mere open-mindedness, but of faith'.[66]

65   J. Plamenatz, *Man and Society* (London, 1963), 1: 50.
66   Plamenatz, 50.

IV Dogmatism and Religious Pluralism

If dogmatism underwrote tolerationism, it also assisted the growth of religious pluralism in seventeenth-century England. Protestants who broke with the national church to form their own movements were rarely as modest and tentative in their faith as John Locke. Separatists, Baptists and Quakers were passionate in their denunciation of the Church of England and unwavering in their sense of their own rectitude. They had to be. To separate oneself from the established church was to take a momentous step. Schism was a grave sin, and leaving one church to join another was not the casual affair that it was later to become. Since the parish was at the centre of communal life, separation from the church involved cutting oneself off from neighbours and friends. As if this was not enough, separatists knew that they could face fines, imprisonment, corporal punishment, or exile. Half-a-dozen Separatists had been executed under Elizabeth I, and many more had emigrated to the Netherlands and America before 1640. During the Restoration, thousands were imprisoned, and approximately 450 Quakers died in English gaols.

Thus to separate from the Church of England, people had to be very sure that they were doing the right thing. Those who could see both sides of an argument and were impressed by the complexity of the issues were unlikely to make the break. In modern times, ecumenically-minded Nonconformists have often been embarrassed by the attitudes and actions of their abrasive ancestors.[67] Secular historians like Christopher Hill have taken a mischievous delight in pointing out the gulf between the polite and respectable Quakers of today and the fierce and confrontational Quakers of the 1650s. Although the Quaker tradition of prophetic protest has continued, modern Quakers do not condemn the Church of England as Antichrist

---

67   See William Lamont in Bonney and Trim (eds), *Development of Pluralism in Britain and France.*

or interrupt parish services to hurl abuse, as did the women discussed by Mary Trim.[68]

Quakers, of course, were uniquely vitriolic in their attacks on the established church, though even they learned to moderate their rhetoric during the Restoration. Presbyterians, on the other hand, were deeply attached to the ideal of a national, established church, and only left it in the early 1660s after agonies of conscience. Yet once again, it was the conscientious convictions of Presbyterians which forced them to separate from the national church. Had they been less precise and more broadminded, they could have put aside their scruples and conformed.[69] England became a profoundly pluralistic nation largely because English Puritans were so unwilling to compromise their strongly held beliefs.

The dogmatism of the Dissenters carried them through the storms of persecution. Whereas radical sceptics tended to be conformists (in the mould of Hobbes's Naaman), Dissenters were prepared to be martyrs.[70] They resisted all attempts to coerce them back into the national church, and stubbornly maintained their separate identity. Sustained by disciplines of prayer, fellowship, biblical meditation and communal worship they displayed strength of character which proved impossible to break down. Although recent research has emphasised the sporadic character of persecution, and stressed the active measures the victims took to evade and counteract repression,[71] the traditional stress on the courage of Dissenters is still valid. Many spent years in Restoration gaols with hardly a sign of faltering or weakness. In them, Anglican persecution met its match. Their attitude is epitomised by the Quaker leader, George Fox. Voltaire called him 'a holy mad-man' and

68   Below, M. Trim, '"In This Day of Perplexity": Seventeenth-century Quaker Women'.
69   See Paul Lim's discussion of Presbyterians, below.
70   For a searching study of the mentality of early modern Christian martyrs see B. Gregory, *Salvation at Stake: Christian Martyrdom in Early Modern Europe* (Cambridge, 1999), ch. 4: 'The willingness to die'.
71   See C. Horle, *The Quakers and the English Legal System, 1660–1688* (Philadelphia, 1988).

one can see why.[72] Fox was dogmatic and irrepressible, despite his sufferings. In Lancaster gaol, the smoke from the chimney was so thick that he could barely see a burning candle, and the rain continually soaked his clothes and bedding. Yet Fox was unbroken: 'I was grown very weak in body', he admitted, 'but the Lord's power was over all [...] For while I was in Lancaster prison I answered several books'.[73]

To modern secular liberals, religious Dissenters like Fox seem a strange lot – dogmatic, disputatious, passionate, God-ridden 'funda-mentalists', far removed from the light irony favoured by 'us liberal gentlefolk' (to borrow a nice phrase from Richard Rorty). Yet the courage and sheer intransigence of Dissenters played a vital role in the emergence of modern pluralism. By separating from the national church and creating religious movements independent of the state, Dissenters placed enormous pressure on religious uniformity. Campaigns of persecution aimed to restore national religious unity, but they proved a dismal failure. Not only did persecution fail to drive large numbers of Dissenters back into the arms of the state church, it also caused considerable unease among Anglicans themselves. The ideal of uniformity no longer matched the reality of pluralism. Although many still held on to the ideal, and hoped that either coercion or comprehension would come to its rescue, others abandoned it. If the so-called Act of Toleration in 1689 was the result of political contingencies, it also reflected the fact that the stubborn reality of Dissent was impossible to eradicate or ignore. If we find religious dogmatism uncongenial, we should reflect on the fact that whereas sceptics tended to lie low and conform, dogmatists were willing to stand out and be martyred. If it were not for religious dogmatists, there would not have been much pluralism to tolerate.

---

72   Voltaire, *Selected Writings*, C. Thacker (ed.) (London, 1995), 17. The quotation
     is from the third of Voltaire's *Letters concerning the English Nation*.
73   George Fox, *Journal*, N. Penny (ed.) (London, 1924), 233–5.

V   Conclusions

The role of dogmatism and devout scepticism in the emergence of toleration casts doubt on Michael Foot's simple dichotomy between reactionary 'fundamentalists' and progressive 'sceptics'. In reality, the picture is a great deal more complicated. Sceptics certainly did play a part, particularly in the eighteenth century, but in the sixteenth and seventeenth centuries the leading tolerationists were mostly devout believers. And there is an irony in our modern tendency to celebrate diversity whilst cherishing irenical attitudes, for the emergence of religious pluralism in early modern England owed more to militants than it did to moderates.

MARY TRIM

'In this Day of Perplexity': Seventeenth-Century Quaker Women

This chapter considers the religious awakening of women from many levels of English society in the mid-seventeenth century and their response to the preaching of the charismatic George Fox and his early 'Publishers of Truth.' Believing that the movement was apocalyptic, a revival of the power and faith principles of the early Christian church, and an answer to the unrest of the times, women embraced its eschatological message in total commitment. Their resultant behaviour tends to have been misunderstood to some extent in historical studies, but the twentieth-century publication of Quaker women's writings and new explorations into their visionary views, theology, ministry and modes of witness, place their lives in more positive perspective, as does application of twentieth-century research into male and female differences in brain function.

Two time periods under discussion indicate a change in the role of Quaker women, firstly, from their rise and response, 1650–64, a time marked by unorthodox witness of Christian faith, by religious views that conflicted with those of other nonconformists and persecution of women and children. The lives of four remarkable Quaker women who lived during this early period are considered and their shared attributes are placed in synthesis. The second period, 1664–1700, concerns the changing role of Quaker women and the gradual shift from movement to sect, to survival in a pluralist society.

I

During the tumultuous days of seventeenth-century England, especially in the years that preceded 1688, it is evident from women's writing of the period that a mental state of perplexity was a common undertow in the lives of females, be they wives, sisters and mothers, spinsters or even children. Not at the front-line of political, economic and religious crisis, but expected to fulfil their designated roles in the social order as homemakers and dutiful daughters, they nevertheless experienced the effects of their changing society with its contrasting extremes of wealth and poverty, the demands of church tithes – difficult for impoverished tenants – the effects of seemingly unjust government and the multiplicity and diversity of religious and political proposals. About their lives, wave after wave of deep conviction and individualism rose and fell, or mingled in the tide of what is loosely termed Puritanism, begun but not fully resolved in the English Reformation of Elizabeth I's reign.

Unrest came in cumulative effect through the despotism of Charles I, distress of civil war where sometimes neighbour fought against neighbour and brother versus brother, causing distress to the females of a household, plus the promises of the Protectorate of Oliver Cromwell, the uncertainties of the interregnum and the momentum of various political-religious, or religious, dissenting and declamatory separatist voices. Additionally there rose questions that concerned the respective roles of women and men. In reference to Cambridgeshire alone, Spufford recognises that 'spiritual seeking and unrest was extremely widespread [...] and that the Quaker position was reached or nearly reached, before the arrival of the Quakers'.[1] The Puritan leader, Richard Baxter, recognised the unrest that was abroad: 'No person more fit for a Quaker, a Papist, or any sectary to work upon, than a troubled mind'.[2]

1   Margaret Spufford, *Contrasting Communities* (Cambridge, 1974), 283.
2   Richard Baxter, *The practical works of the Rev. Richard Baxter*, W. Orme (ed.), 23 vols (London, 1830), 12:500, quoted in Richard T. Vann, *The Social Development of English Quakerism 1655–1755* (Cambridge, 1969), 30.

Women of the 1640s and early 1650s felt impelled to assert their voices in response to the tangled state of society. About three hundred women visionaries emerged from a widespread range of social class and communities: Baptist, Brownist, Familist, Fifth Monarchist, Independent, Leveller, Presbyterian, Puritan Royalist, Ranter, Royalist, Shaker and followers of mysticism.[3]

The greatest number of women visionaries came from among the Friends, or Quakers as they were called in jibes. During 1660–5 there were about two hundred and forty recognised as prophets[4] representing the whole spectrum of society, although Barbour considers that many had been domestic servants, 'and the prominence of such women [...] shows their indifference to social standing and convention'.[5] Most of these came from the northern and Midlands counties of England though others came from the south and west.

Early Quaker women preached, prophesied, protested and proselytised, concerned to proclaim their apocalyptic vision. Central to their messages was the equality of sexes as they responded to the inner light of Christ in their hearts, believing that Acts 2:17–18 applied to themselves as 'daughters' and 'maidservants' on whom the Holy Spirit would be poured in the last days. A reading of their tracts shows their concern for a purified society, ready for the end of time and judgement. Barbour identifies these aspects as being linked to Puritanism and the intensity of their experience to that of Luther and Wesley.[6] Public response accelerated, possibly reaching 60,000 within a decade; it might have seemed as if all England would embrace Quakerism within one generation if the pace was maintained.[7]

However, Quaker men and women became caught up in harassment due to a backlash from the Blasphemy Act of 1650, aimed at Ranters with whom Quakers were frequently confused, although twentieth-century research reveals that Quaker tracts in the 1650s have

---

3   Phyllis Mack, *Visionary Women: Ecstatic Prophecy in Seventeenth-Century England* (Berkeley, 1992), 413–14. I am indebted to Mack for her comprehensive research that has considerably opened up the area of study.
4   Ibid. 415–20.
5   Hugh Barbour, *The Quakers in Puritan England* (New Haven, 1964), 92.
6   Ibid. 1–2.
7   Barry Reay, *The Quakers and the English Revolution* (London, 1985), 11.

a style that is distinct from Ranters, or from Calvinists.[8] From 1661, with the implementation of the Clarendon Code, persecution of all dissenters became the rule, while local prejudices and oppression increased. Hester / Esther Biddle, a Quaker prisoner in Newgate Prison in 1662, wrote from her heart, saying:

> O Lord, thy seed to Heaven doth cry for delivery
> *In this day of perplexity.*[9]

But women did more than 'cry for delivery.' They also acted.

II   The Rise and Response of Quaker Women, 1650–64

The role of women in Quaker society can be seen in two distinct phases. The first commenced at the beginning of 1649, as a result of the confident and charismatic George Fox's belief in his commission 'to change the real world'.[10] An examination of his testimony contributes to an understanding of the impact of his appeal to a distressed, confused society that might be comforted with new, transcendent solutions:

> But with and by this divine power and spirit of God, and the light of Jesus, I was to bring people off from all their own ways to Christ, the new and living way, and from their churches, which men had made and gathered, to the Church in God, the general assembly written in Heaven, which Christ is the head of, and from off all the world's worships, to know the spirit of truth in the inward parts [...] And I was to bring people off from all the world's religions, which are vain [...] And I was to bring people off from Jewish ceremonies [...] and

---

8   Barbour, *The Quakers*, 95.
9   Hester Biddle, 'O Zion's King, thy beauty bright', poem following *The trumpet of the Lord Sounded Forth*, in Paul Salzman (ed.), *Early Modern Women's Writing: an Anthology 1560–1700* (Oxford, 2000), 165–6. Italics mine.
10   John Punshon, *Portrait in Grey: a Short History of the Quakers* (London, 1991), 51.

from men's inventions and windy doctrines [...] and all their vain traditions, which they had gotten up since the apostles' days.[11]

Here Fox expressed the bulwark teachings of Quakerism: leaving the formalised religion of the Christian churches and listening to the Holy Spirit as He impressed within hearts and minds. This power-enabling emphasis on the individual gave the movement direction and impetus which continued into the second phase of seventeenth-century Quaker women, 1664–1700, when earlier perceptions and behaviours became irrelevant and when heterodoxy gave way to pluralism.

One important recognition prevailed through both periods: Quaker women centred their faith in Jesus Christ, not so much as their visible or ascended Lord, but as light-giver of truth within. This is reflected in their frequent usage of the image of light and in the descriptive title of this group of Protestant separatists who linked together in fellowship known as 'Children of Light'.[12] Quaker women used this or similar expressions often, saying 'O! hearken unto the Light of Christ in your consciences', as did Esther Biddle; 'The Light which I with many thousands have believed in, and found, saves from sin [...]' is the expression of Rebecca Travers, who frequently links Light and the Spirit.[13] Margaret Fell writes persuasively of 'the light which comes from Jesus Christ, which is the messenger of the Living God, sent from God'[14] Barbara Blaugdone refers to the time when her mind was directed toward 'the Light of Christ'.[15]

---

11   Ibid. 46.

12   Reay, *The Quakers and the English Revolution*, 9.

13   Rebecca Travers, 'A Testimony for God's Everlasting Truth, as it hath been learned of and in Jesus' (London, 1669), repr. in Mary Garman *et al* (eds), *Hidden in Plain Sight* (Pendle Hill, 1996) (hereafter cited as Garman, *Hidden*), 317–38.

14   Margaret Fell, quoted in Catherine M. Wilcox, *Theology and Women's Ministry in Seventeenth-Century English Quakerism: Handmaids of the Lord* (Lampeter, 1995), 31.

15   Esther Biddle, *The Trumpet of the Lord Soundeth Forth as a Warning unto these Three Nations,* in Garman, *Hidden*, 129–34. She is the same person whom Salzman names as Hesther. Barbara Blaugdone, *An Account of the Travels, Sufferings and Persecutions of Barbara Blaugdone* (London, 1691), 5, 9.

The first prominent Quaker woman is Elizabeth Hooten, wife of a prosperous yeoman in Skegby, Nottinghamshire, and mother of five children. She had been active in Baptist worship and witness before becoming convinced to join the Friends by Fox in 1647. She then made her home available for meetings and became the first Woman Quaker minister, travelling widely, not only through England but also in America. She is one of the twelve women numbered in the 'Valiant Sixty' who first spread through England, taking the 'message of glad tydeings'.[16] Indeed, 55% of the early Friends, but no more, according to Vann's research, may have been women.[17]

Why did early Quakerism speak so clearly to women? Certainly it was founded on the vision and dynamism of Fox, but very quickly women embraced his ideals, interpreted and applied them. Was its appeal purely because of the perplexing time in place and history, or did it concern sociological impact, or its psychological effect? Probably all these reasons hold partial keys to the answer, yet there is another dimension which Punshon identifies:

> It [Quakerism] can be seen as an ideal, a technique, a refuge, an expression of deeper things in another guise. But to those who first came to it, it provided an experience of the Christian faith like no other they had known. All the first Quakers came into the society from elsewhere. The sects and churches from which they came had failed to meet their needs. Nowhere did they find rest for their souls until they heard and responded to the first Quaker preachers, or 'publishers of truth' as they came to be known.[18]

The female response can also be viewed from the traditional view of feminine qualities, those of 'humility, receptivity and emotionalism', while it is also important to recognise that in the Quaker conception of the self, emotional behaviour was not regarded in a negative light.[19] Sarah Cheevers said,

---

16   Elfrida Vipont, *George Fox and the Valiant Sixty* (London, 1975), 129.
17   Richard T. Vann, *The Social Development of English Quakerism, 1655–1755* (Cambridge, 1969), 83.
18   Punshon, *Portrait*, 34.
19   Mack, *Visionary*, 18, 135.

we cannot hold our peace; the God [...] of glory doth open our mouth, and we speak to his praise, and utter his voice, and sound forth his word of life, and causeth the earth to tremble [...] my heart, soul and spirit that is wholly joined to the Lord, stream forth to you..[20]

Today we can read such behaviours in the light of Freudian theory as self-nullification, the ultimate goal of the person who absorbs self in religion.

Even further insights can be found when the findings of twentieth-century research into the brain differences between sexes are applied to seventeenth-century Quaker women, particularly those studies that concern the left and right hemispheres of the brain. These stress different perceptions, priorities and behaviour, with women 'concerned with people, morality and relationships'.[21] Women are seen to be especially intuitive and less able to separate emotion from reason because of the way the female brain is organised. The female brain has emotional capacities on both sides of the brain, plus there is more information exchanged between the two sides of the brain. The emotional side is more integrated with the verbal side of the brain. A woman can express her emotions in words because what she feels has been transmitted to the verbal side of her brain.[22]

In light of these studies in brain differences and what Witleson refers to as women's 'preferred cognitive strategy',[23] plus the concept of self nullification from a Freudian and Christian, self-sacrificial point of view, it becomes more obvious why uninhibited emotion and talk became characteristics of early Quaker women. Not only does it explain their responses but it also answers, in essence, an important biological root of Quakerism's early appeal to women. Yet it should

20   'Sarah Cheevers Epistle to Friends to read at Bull and Mouth', LSF, Portfolio MSS 31/60. See Mack, *Visionary*, 136, for a discussion of this issue and the catatonic ecstasy of a traditional visionary compared with the suspended ego of the Quaker prophet.
21   Anne Moir and David Jessel, *Brain Sex* (London, 1989), 98.
22   Ibid, 48. For substantiative bibliography concerning studies in brain differences, see 200–1.
23   Sandra Witleson, 'Sex Differences in the Neurolgy of Cognition: Social, Educational and Clinical Implications', in E. Sullerot and O. Thibault (eds), *Le Fait Fèminin* (France, 1978), 287–303.

also be noted that some, in their renunciation of self, exhibited contemporary feminine behaviour turned upside down, as will be shown, when they resembled aggressive Old Testament, male prophets.

An example of Quaker women collectively being prepared to defy the Law, applying what they deemed biblical principles, came when 7,000 of them opposed the system of tithes and sent their protest to parliament in 1659. The organisational effort, time, and the risk-taking involved must have been immense. Calling themselves Handmaids and Daughters of the Lord, they declared:

> We whose hands are hereunder written do testifie and declare against the oppression of Tithes, and against the injustice of them, which hath come up since the dayes of the Apostles in the Apostacy, and set up by the commands of men, the author of which was the Pope.[24]

Some aspects of the rationale of this unique document may be disputable, but its sincerity and brave cry for justice is indisputable.

Many early Quaker women felt impelled to talk publicly about their new liberation, to which their faith experience in the Inner Light amounted. In the street, in the marketplace, in graveyards and churches, court rooms and in any public place where they could find an audience, they made proclamations that were often charged with charismatic emotion. With the same fervour they wrote in various modes: tracts of warning, journals, autobiographies, spiritual journeys, travel narratives, theological works, letters and epistles. These were the woman whom Richard Farnsworth described as weaker vessels, yet filled by the Lord with wisdom and the rule of the Holy Spirit.[25] They were afire and would not be stopped in spite of threats, imprisonment and demeaning punishments.

24   'These several papers was sent to the Parliament the twentieth day of the fifth
     month, 1659. Being above seven thousand names of the Handmaids and
     Daughters of the Lord' (London, 1659), 1, repr. in Garman, *Hidden*, 58–128.
25   Richard Farnsworth, *Woman Forbidden to Speak* (London, 1654), 4.

III   Early Unorthodox Witness

Some traditional historians have regarded early Quaker women in a negative light, and this perception is understandable when placed against acceptable standards of behaviour for women of their day. One, Jane Holmes, preached eloquently in the streets of Malton in 1652, urging shopkeepers to burn their wares of extravagant ribbons and laces which were in stark contrast to the simple attire worn and advocated by Quaker women. Causing a street fire was, however, unusual and disruptive behaviour. Another, Elizabeth Adams, broke a jar at the door of parliament in 1656, assuming a Jeremiahic, symbolic protest. Again, in 1657, she rode silently through Canterbury on horseback, holding high two lighted torches that symbolised the Light that bystanders should seek. In another instance, Sarah Goldsmith made herself a full-length coat of sackcloth, let her hair hang loose and smeared herself with ashes. She then walked through Bristol until she reached the high cross in the marketplace, all as a sign to testify against the pride of the city.

Going excessively beyond symbolic enactment, however, was the part played by women followers of leading Quaker, James Nayler, who encouraged rather than rebuked Ranterish behaviour among hysterical women,[26] and for a time defected from the Quaker movement. He assumed what appeared to be a Messianic stance in entering on a donkey to Bristol in 1656, escorted mainly by women who sang, 'Holy, holy, holy, Lord God of Israel' and kissed his feet, then laid garments before him on the muddy road. In punishment, he was close to receiving the death penalty, but was instead awarded the lesser punishment of being branded on his forehead, bored through the tongue, whipped and pilloried. At the pillory site near the Royal Exchange in London, three women, acting the parts of Mary, mother of Jesus, Mary Magdalen and Mary, mother of Cleophas at the cross, displayed a placard that declared, 'This is the king of the Jews'.[27] The

---

26   See Isabel Ross, *Margaret Fell: Mother of Quakerism*, 3rd edn (York, 1996), 102.

27   Reay, *The Quakers*, 55.

enactment possibly began as a dramatic idea but it was one that could be, and clearly was, misinterpreted by the audience, who saw it as blasphemy.[28] However, as Reay and Hill observe, 'above all [...] it was the Quaker movement and the government's religious policy that were in the dock'.[29]

Unwelcome and uninvited dramatisation by Quaker women extended into the sanctity of churches also, reminiscent of the style of Old Testament prophets or medieval players. For example, in 1661, Elizabeth Simcock held a lantern, a candle and sheet of white paper in a Cheshire church. She then proceeded to burn the paper, break the lantern and declare, 'Even as you see this paper consumed with the fire so shall the wicked be consumed before the Lord for he is consuming fire'.[30] In other instances they interrupted services, pronouncing woe to the clergy.

Even more extreme and misunderstood were the behaviours of shaking, staring, weeping and quaking, demonstrated by Quaker women, supposedly as a manifestation of the Holy Spirit; or the insults, provocative statements, shouted or screamed by such as Esther Biddle, Katherine Evans, Margaret Killam and Elizabeth Hooton in public protest.[31] The latter even harangued Oliver Cromwell and King Charles II,[32] apparently having no fear of, or respect for, authority. Moreover, they stood out as different in appearance from contemporary English women. Quakers appeared without lavish makeup, in plain dress without buttons, lace or trimming, simply heeled, prepared to chastise a community, be they neighbours or community leaders or clergy, even prepared to leave their children or give birth in prison when imprisoned for militant conduct. On the other hand, it is

28   Ibid. 54.
29   Ibid. He describes the event as 'This symbolic entry'.
30   Mack, *Visionary*, 168.
31   Ibid. 139.
32   Elizabeth Hooton to Oliver Cromwell, 1653, LSF, Portfolio MSS 3/3,10 quoted in Emily Manners, *Elizabeth Hooton, First Quaker Woman Preacher, 1600–1672* (London, 1914), 10; Hooton to Charles II, Portfolio MSS 3/43, quoted in Manners, *Elizabeth Hooton*, 49. Quoted in Mack, *Visionary*, 127–8.

fair to point out that they were approaching a pacifist position even before 1660,[33] believing that the ultimate battle was a spiritual one.

IV   Quakerism and Other Religious Movements

At the heart of Quakerism were aspects that gave grounds for division and misunderstandings, be they by the established Church of England, Nonconformist ministry and believers, other heterodox groups or the bureaucracy of the legal system. There was the dichotomy of, on one hand, the unorthodox conduct of some early Quaker women, whereby they aroused hostility and, on the other hand, observation of others who behaved with 'personal integrity and an extraordinary capacity for physical and emotional restraint'.[34] Again, there was the momentum of the movement that threatened to disturb a fractured peace, attracting citizens who felt called and chosen, who would no longer defer anyone, whether Church of England priest, Presbyterian merchant or magistrate. The following synopsis highlights only a few of the differences between themselves and others:

Quakers, John Bunyan and Ranters

Bunyan disagreed with Quakers' views in several areas. He associated their beliefs with those of Ranters stating, 'only the Ranters made them threadbare in the alehouse, and the Quakers have set a new gloss upon them again, by an outward legal righteousness'.[35] In 1657, he

---

33   Reay, *The Quakers*, 41.
34   Mack, *Visionary*, 132.
35   John Bunyan, quoted in Christopher Hill, *A Tinker and a Poor Man: John Bunyan and his Church, 1628–1688* (New York, 1989), 81.

opposed the teaching of the Inner Light,[36] and when Women's Meetings became topical, because he regarded woman in the Genesis account of creation as subordinate to man, he disagreed with the freedom of women to preach. Thus he wrote another tract in 1683, in opposition to separate women's meetings for worship.[37] Conversely, Fox was at pains to distinguish Friends from anarchic or incendiary groups like Fifth Monarchists or Ranters, while Margaret Fell, in 1665, wrote an exposure of Ranters' teachings, and the London Friends condemned a number of Quaker women for 'Ranterish' behaviour in 1657.[38]

Quakers and Baptists

The Quaker belief in baptism by the Holy Ghost rather than by immersion, and their rejection of the celebration of the Lord's Supper, placed them in immediate disagreement with the various groups of Baptist believers, many of whom had joined the early Quakers – another cause of irritation. The seventh-day Sabbath, observed by the Seventh-day Baptists and others, was also unequivocally rejected by Quakers. For the Quaker women, 'He (Christ) was their Sabbath rest, their Passover meal, their Priest, Prophet, teacher, leader, husband and light.'[39]

36   John Bunyan, *A Vindication of Gospel Truths Opened According to the Scriptures* (1657), in T. L. Underwood (ed.), *The Miscellaneous Works of John Bunyan*, Vol 1 (Oxford, 1980).
37   Bunyan, *A Case of Conscience Resolved* […] (1683) in T. L. Underwood (ed.), *The Miscellaneous Works of John Bunyan*, Vol 4 (Oxford, 1989).
38   Mack, *Visionary*, 202, 339.
39   Wilcox, *Theology and Women Ministry*, 40; see Bryan Ball, *The Seventh-Day Men: Sabbatarians and Sabbatarianism in England and Wales, 1600–1800.* (Oxford, 1994).

Quakers and Muggletonians

When Ludowijk Muggleton and John Reeve identified themselves as the two witnesses of the Spirit in the book of Revelation, with Muggleton assuming a Messianic role, they were rejected by most Quakers and much bitterness ensued. Muggleton subsequently wrote to Elizabeth Hooton, 'I do pronounce Elizabeth Hooton, Quaker [...] cursed and damned, both in soul and body, from the presence of God, elect men and angels, to eternity'.[40]

Other Differences

Social order concerned both Diggers and Quakers though their view-points arose from different epistemologies. For Diggers, reason, 'the life of the spirit' which resulted from practical living rather than from education, was all important, whereas to Fox, the intuitive, 'spirit of discerning' was the energising force in society.[41] Certainly, the militarist background of Fifth Monarchists, Levellers, and Diggers among Quaker converts is identified by Reay.[42] Shakers shared the same tremblings as Quakers, but the latter did not accept their identification of John Reeve as Messiah.[43] Agreement with female autonomy was also important in the Philadelphian Society for the Advancement of Piety and Philosophy but they were a community of mystics and intellectuals. As far as Catholicism was concerned, it is evident from Quaker writings that they condemned them as the beast of Revelation, as had Protestants from earlier centuries, and as did Milton, Bunyan and others. In preaching style, the Quakers' evangelical mode contrasted with the sober, intellectual style of

---

40   See Manners, *First Woman Preacher*, referred to in Mack, *Visionary*, 248.

41   Gerrard Winstanley, *Fire in the Bush: The Spirit Burning Not Consuming, but Purging Mankinde* (1650), reprinted in George H. Sabine (ed.), *The Works of Gerrard Winstanley*, (Ithaca, 1941), 478; George Fox, *The Journal of George Fox*, John L. Nickalls (ed.) (london, 1975), 9.

42   Reay, *The Quakers*, 19.

43   Mack, *Visionary*, 105; see Terrie Dopp Aamodt's chapter in the companion volume.

Puritans and Anglicans, each party misunderstanding the Quaker attitude toward Scripture; and there were also acrimonious disputes between Quakers and those whose faith was based on the Bible alone.[44] The ultimate aggravation must have been that these followers of Fox, often uneducated, presumed themselves to be called to proclaim the end-time and did so in unconventional, unacceptable ways, contradicting the established church, insisting that they resumed the life blood of the true church as it emerged from the wilderness of apostasy.[45]

V   Persecution of Women and Children

Early hostility rose from a public which was disturbed by, and disliked or misunderstood, the behaviour of those who were different, especially from women who publicly rebuked their fellow citizens and pronounced doom. There may also have been arousal of xenophobia in country communities which lived in their own confined areas. Thus, Quaker women visionaries suffered punchings, stonings and general harassment, sometimes being linked with witches. Records of assizes[46] indicate tension in a society where conventicles were banned (from 1664), and the unconventional Quakers, who dressed and spoke differently, who refused to bow their heads or to remove their caps and hats in deference to authority, were held responsible for anarchy. An extreme instance was the martyrdom of Margaret Newby, a widow with several children, in 1657, but the time of greatest hardship came

---

44   Wilcox, *Theology*, 57–61.
45   Punshon, *Portrait*, 60. See also George Fox, *The Journal of George Fox*, Nickalls (ed.), and other early Quaker manuscripts.
46   See, for example, David L. Wykes, 'They "assemble in greater numbers and (with) more daring than formerly"': The Bishop of Gloucester and Nonconformity in the late 1660s', *Southern History*, 17 (1995), 24–39; 'At the Generall Quarter Sessions of the Peace holden at Hertford [...] 1668', Bod. Lib. MS Rawlinson C.719.

with the methodical persecution of all dissenters during the 1660s. In a fair analysis, Quaker scholar, Punshon, notes that:

> The persecution Friends suffered was neither as systemic nor as horrendous as the treatment meted out to the continental Anabaptists or the Protestant martyrs in England. It was arbitrary and callous, cruel even, but the Quaker sufferings were caused far more by local prejudices than a deliberate policy of vindictiveness on the part of the state. In the period 1652–1660 there are plenty of examples of appeals to central government putting right illegal or badly judged actions by provincial magistrates. In some places like their strongholds in the northern counties, Bristol and London, the Quakers suffered few disturbances. Elsewhere, and at certain times, the authorities set out to harass them with some severity.[47]

Persecution extended to children who suffered physically and psychologically for their insistence on living and worshipping as Quakers, either with their families or when their parents were imprisoned. From Quaker records, particularly from 'The Minutes of the Meeting for Sufferings' and from Joseph Besse's two folio volume *Collection of the Sufferings of the People Called Quakers* (1753) comes the most comprehensive picture of the persecution of the young. Chasing, pinching, beating and threats of whipping were the common forms of terrorising juveniles. They were also fined relatively large sums of money, one shilling each in the case of Lydia Herfant, Mary Kent and Sarah Kent who were sent to gaol in August 1666, 'where they lay for a long time'.[48]

On occasion, however, juvenile persecution went beyond threats and fines. In 1662, Mary Gibbons, aged fourteen, and Joanna Taylor, aged thirteen, were imprisoned in the gallery of Newgate Prison, while at Bridewell, eight girls aged from eight to twelve years were held

---

47   Punshon, *Portrait*, 64.

48   Joseph Besse, *A Collection of the Sufferings of the People called Quakers for the Testimony of a Good Conscience from the Time of their being distinguished by that name in the year 1650 to the Time of the Act commonly called the Act of Toleration, granted to Protestant Dissenters in the first year of the reign of King William the third and Queen Mary in the year 1689*. Taken from *Original Records and other authentik Accounts, I and II* (London, 1753), I:10.

captive.[49] None of these children should have been incarcerated, for all were aged under sixteen years and so their treatment was illegal. However it is fair to recognise that militia who were sent to break up clandestine meetings may have had difficulties in recognising what ages children were and, in the heat of an encounter and keen for prisoners, took them all. On the other hand, there were those in authority who appear to have made an issue of harrying children for long periods.

During the 1680s that abuse and imprisonment of children noticeably increased. On 5 June 1680, six boys were put in stocks at Bristol, although only for one hour, it must have been an hour of torture and fear. At the same time, a number of girls were threatened with identical punishment and all had their hats forcibly removed. In total about thirty children were involved.[50]

A number of significant features stand out in relationship to the faith development and religious stamina of Quaker children. Firstly, expressions of love and tenderness by Quaker mothers toward their children, despite strict training that included plainness of dress and language.[51] Secondly, there was home instruction and modelling of their distinctive faith, so much so that in 1655 eight-year-old Mary Fell wrote out the 'light' she believed God had given her. Addressed to 'Priest Lampitt', the local rector, she declared:

> Lampitt,
> The plaiges of god shall fall upon thee and the seven viols shall bee powered upon thee and the milstone shall fall upon thee and crush thee as dust under the Lords feete how can thou escape the damnation of hell.
> This did the Lord give mee as I lay in bed.[52]

Her sister, Rachel, when six years old in 1659, signed the petition against tithes and when aged eleven years stood beside her mother in the dock when on trial at Assizes.

---

49   Ibid. I: 67–8.
50   Ibid. II, 129.
51   Mack, *Visionary,* 348, 359, 372. This tenderness is expressed in their private
      letters.
52   Ross, *Margaret Fell,* 27.

Literacy was a third factor, important to Puritans, Quakers and Baptists, all of whom wrote books for children during the seventeenth century. The Quakers went so far as to have their own list of recommended reading for children. Associated with literacy were at least seventeen Quaker boarding schools, operating by 1671, distributed through eleven counties of England, some for boys, some for girls, others being for mixed groups. Such aspects of child training may have been a key to Quaker success in maintaining their sect, even after persecution. In contrast, some other religious groups, including the Seventh-day Baptists,[53] did little to encourage child faith and suffered the consequence of diminishing adherents and eventual annihilation.

VI   Women of the Light

Esther Biddle, Rebecca Travers, Margaret Fell and Barbara Blaugdone are four remarkable women whose experience demonstrates the range of early Quaker women's ministry.

Esther Biddle

For Esther Biddle (1629–96), the light of the 'Spirit of Truth' led her along the route of prophecy. Born in 1629, a convinced Friend in 1654 and wife of a London shoemaker, she was mother to four sons, one of whom may have born while she was in prison for her faith.[54] Fox mentions her once in his journal where he tells of a woman who prophesied to him that Charles II would be restored to the English throne. Knowing that Biddle might be charged with treason if she said

---

53   Ball, *Seventh-Day Men*, 325.
54   Lydia Rickman, 'Esther Biddle and Her Mission to Louis XIV', *Quaker History* 47 (1955), 41.

this publicly, he advised her to 'wait upon the Lord and keep it to herself'.[55]

Biddle published eight broadsides and tracts between the years 1659 and 1662. Of these her major work was *The Trumpet of the Lord Soundeth forth into these Three Nations*, written in 1662 while a prisoner in Newgate Prison. It is an impressive piece of writing, well constructed, cohesive in argument and powerful in rhetoric. She begins by addressing the city of London, then addresses the king, urging him to 'hearken unto the Light of Christ'. As she proceeds, she addresses rulers, judges and justices, before making exhortations to England, Scotland and Ireland. Finally she turns her attention to those in royal or high estate:

> Oh! let your King and Queen, Dukes and Earls, Lords and Ladies, Judges and Rulers and all Bishops, Deacons, Priests and People in these three Nations and all the World, consider their wayes, worships and religions, and fear and tremble before the mighty God who hath the hearts of Kings and Rulers in his hand [...] what is the Pope or the Kings of the Earth, will he not bring them to judgement, and turn them to dust again from whence they came.[56]

She rounds off her treatise with autobiographical information addressed to other Friends, confirming that

> I was once of this Religion which is now in Power [...] but now Glory be to the Lord, I am set at Liberty from this vain religion [...] whilst I have breath [...] shall bear my testimony against it, for I know the powerful God is risen to throw it down, and wo[e] be to all that uphold it.[57]

This commitment led her to travel to at least six countries beyond England as a missionary and to suffer imprisonment fourteen times.

---

55   Journal of George Fox, 342.
56   Paul Salzman (ed.), *Early Modern Women's Writing: an Anthology, 1560–1700* (Oxford, 2000) 148–66; also in Garman, *Hidden*, 132.
57   Garman, *Hidden* 134–5.

Rebecca Travers

For Rebecca Travers (1609–88) the 'Light and the Spirit' guided her into theology and debate, rather than to the usual witness of experience. Well read in the Scriptures, raised a Baptist and perhaps used to polemic in that environment, as a Quaker she wrote approximately nine tracts. The most memorable is:

> A TESTIMONY for God's EVERLASTING TRUTH, as it hath been learned of and in JESUS; testifying against Such as through unbelief have departed from, or been disobedient to the Spirit that convinces the World of Sin: Among whom R.C. hath appeared with his many things to oppose and withstand the one thing, the Spirit of life, that sets free from Sin and Death, which is the Truth which the people called Quakers have and do testifie to and of.[58]

This tract was an answer to an anti-Quaker publication by Robert Cobbit. In her rebuttal, Travers raises some major issues: the nature of Christ, his ascension, the work of the Spirit and the supernatural nature of Quaker faith. She also appeals to Cobbit and to other readers to seek and know God and find his transforming grace. Five times imprisoned herself, when free she spent time visiting women prisoners and became a great encourager of Women's Meetings.

Margaret Fell

The name of Margaret Fell (1614–1702) is the one most celebrated of all the names of early Quaker women. She is regarded as a pioneer of Feminism, often spoken of as the 'Mother of Quakerism', or the 'Nursing Mother Of Quakerism',[59] although Bonnelyn Kunze suggests that 'Mother Superior' would be a more appropriate title.[60] The 'Light which comes from Jesus Christ' led her into a quieter role than that of Biddle and Travers, nevertheless her presence was strongly felt in

---

58   Printed in Garman *et al* (eds), *Hidden*, 152–64.
59   Punshon, *Portrait*, 13. He quotes Caton, who lived with the Fell family, 19.
60   Bonnelyn Young Kunze, 'The Family, Social and Religious Life of Margaret Fell', (Ph.D. diss. University of Rochester, 1986), 389.

Quakerism and the wider community throughout her ministry as writer, preacher and polemicist for women's rights.

Fell came from a privileged background, being the daughter of a well-to-do gentleman, John Askew of Marsh Grange, Lancashire. Her great grandmother is believed to have been Anne Askew, who, for reading the Bible in Lincoln Cathedral and other places, was burnt at the stake in 1546.[61] Of her mother, Margaret Pyper, little is known, but it is recorded that Fell received a house and estate as marriage dowry and £3000 at her father's death which indicates that she came from a prosperous family.[62] When she was about eighteen years old, she married Judge Fell of Swarthmore Hall, near Ulverston in Lancashire, one of the gentry of the north-west, member for Lancaster of the Long Parliament, 1645–7. For at least twenty years after her marriage she actively sought to know and serve God, took much interest in the Puritan parish and 'went often to hear the best ministers that came into our parts […] whom we frequently entertained at our house […] and had often Prayers and Religious Exercises in our Family'.[63]

To appreciate Margaret Fell's actions as a Quaker, one needs to understand her background and also her husband's position and character, as these may well have contributed to the generosity she exhibited in hospitality and her confidence in approaching royal, legal and governmental circles. Trained in law, and a barrister, her husband, Thomas Fell was appointed Vice-Chancellor of the Duchy of Lancaster in 1649, and Attorney for the County Palatine of Chester. He also held the office of Chancellor of the Duchy Court at Westminster and was Attorney-General of the North Wales Counties. He later became a circuit Judge of Assize for Chester and North Wales. In Whitelock's Memorials, he is referred to as a 'good lawyer and a good man'.[64] Although he never became a Quaker himself, he

61   Isabel Ross, *Margaret Fell: Mother of Quakerism,* 3rd edn (York, 1996), 5.
62   Ibid. 5. There are a number of sources for the life of this remarkable woman who deserves more than the cursory glance this chapter offers Also helpful is Garman, *Hidden,* 155–8, 444–5. Margaret Fell's *Works* (London, 1710) also relates about her birth, education, life, conversion and travels.
63   Margaret Fell, *A Brief Collection of Remarkable Passages and Occurrences Relating to Margaret Fell,* Fox (London, 1710), 2. See Garman, *Hidden,* 245.
64   W. R. Williams, *The Welsh Judges* (London, 1899), 58.

was generous with his home and means, allowing Friends to gather there in Meetings or to stay as guests. Furthermore, he treated Quakers who were on trial fairly and sympathetically.

Margaret Fell's introduction to Quakerism came in 1652. Out for the day, but leaving at home her son and six daughters, aged from nineteen down to two years of age, the Mistress of Swarthmore Hall, discovered on her return that the already renowned Quaker preacher, George Fox, had visited during her absence. She learnt, as well, that Fox had debated there with the local rector, an Independent, who had also called. That very evening, Fox returned and preached in her home, and 'opened us a book that we had never read in, nor indeed had never heard that it was our duty to read in it (to wit) the Light of Christ in our consciences, our minds never being turned towards it before'.[65] It was the turning point in her life. From 1653 until 1698, Margaret Fell wrote at least twenty-seven *Epistles*, most of them being printed in her *Works* (1710). Additionally, she wrote to, and spoke 'often'[66] with King Charles II, and later James II, about the state of the nation and Quakerism. She also addressed petitions to them, and to other people in positions of power, on behalf of George Fox and other imprisoned Quakers. Fines and her generous hospitality accounted for the loss of much of her wealthy estate but in 1663 she received the savage sentence of *praemunire* which meant that she could no longer have the king's protection and must forfeit all her estate and be imprisoned for life.

Subsequently a prisoner in Lancaster prison for four years, 1664–8, although in very dismal, damp surroundings, she wrote many letters to her family and epistles to encourage Friends, as well as five books that represent the range of her vision. The first of these was addressed to both Jews and Gentiles, *A Call to the Universal Seed of God* (1664) in which she appealed for an inward, spiritual religion, centred in Jesus Christ. The second, published in 1666, focused on the role of women, and could be regarded as a pioneering feminist work:

---

65   Quoted in Ross, *Margaret Fell*, 11.
66   Margaret Fell, *A Relation of Margaret Fell, her Birth, Life, Testimony, and Sufferings for the Lord's Everlasting Truth in her Generation* in Garman, *Hidden*, 244–54; and in *A Brief Collection*, 1–13.

Women's Speaking Justified, Proved, and Allowed of by the Scriptures, All Such as Speak by the Spirit and Power of the Lord Jesus. The third, *The Standard of the Lord Revealed*, was based on biblical scholarship, designed to show how God worked through the Jews until the coming of Christ and thereafter through the Holy Spirit. It was sent to London for publication in 1666 but the Great Fire delayed its appearance until 1667. The fourth indicates its audience in the title: *A Touch-Stone; or, a Tryal by the Scriptures of the Priests, Bishops and Minister* (1666). Here, in 115 pages in her collected *Works*, she argues, among other emphases, that the inspiration of the Spirit is more reliable than university education; that ecclesiastical courts were grossly intolerant; and that Roman Catholic priests kept their followers in ignorance of the Bible. The fifth was again a work addressed to Jews, *A Call unto the Seed of Israel* (1688), for whom she clearly felt concern.

It is interesting to observe the selflessness of Margaret Fell as she pleaded for compassion and mercy to all, yet did not allow room for the diverse views or individualism of others. Nevertheless, while a daughter of her century, she possessed profound perception and prophetic insight, recognising that 'The Truth is one and the same always, and though ages and generations pass away, and one generation goes and another comes, yet the word and power and spirit of the Living God endures for ever, and is the same and never changes'.[67]

She married George Fox in 1669, a year after she was released from Lancaster Castle on order of the King and Council. She had been a widow for eleven years but many of the years of marriage to George Fox were spent apart, due to their separate missionary travel and Fox's imprisonments. Furthermore, while Margaret's home, Swarthmore, in northern England was now his home, he preferred to live in London where he was most needed by Friends and their work. 'We were very willing', she wrote, 'to live apart for some years upon God's account, and his truth's service [...].'[68]

67   Fell, *Works*, 47. See also Ross, *Margaret Fell*, 29.
68   Margaret Fox, in *Leeds Journal*, 76. See Ross, *Margaret Fell*, 311.

As one reads Margaret Fell's work, one cannot help but be impressed by her resolution to follow 'the Light of Christ' in her conscience. A cultured, gracious, godly woman, always an intelligent encourager of women and their meetings, her work, *Women's Speaking Justified*, is regarded as an early example of feminist writing. Its merit and place in history is acknowledged in a collection beside other *English Women of Letters 1660–1800*.[69]

Barbara Blaugdone

The ministry of Barbara Blaugdone (1606–1701) embraces all the fields of Quaker women's endeavour. Hers was an unusual life in which, as a late-comer to Quakerism, she felt compelled to preach, to prophesy, to write and to embark on missionary journeys. Her experience is both typical and atypical of that of her Quaker sisters, yet exemplifies many aspects of their witness.

Blaugdone's published writing was restricted to one short testimony, *An Account of the Travels, Sufferings and Persecutions of Barbara Blaugdone: Given forth as a Testimony to the Lord's Power, and for the Encouragement of Friends*, printed and sold by T. S. at Shoreditch in 1691. In it she gives reasons for writing her spiritual biography:

> And I have written these Things that Friends may be encouraged, and go on in the Faith, in the Work of the Lord: For many have been the Tryals, Tribulations and Afflictions the which I have passed through, but the Lord hath delivered me out of them all; Glory be given to him and blessed be his Name for ever, and evermore.[70]

Blaugdone begins her story with reference to her childhood concern to know and to please God. Omitting details of several decades of her life, she then quickly moves on to refer to the ministry of two Yorkshire Friends, John Audland and John Camme, at Bristol

---

69   Uphaus and Foster, *The 'Other' Eighteenth Century: English Women of Letters, 1660–1800* (East Lansing, 1991), 17–22.

70   Blaugdone, *Account*, 38.

in 1654 where, preaching in an orchard to three to four thousand people at a time, they aroused the wrath of some local clergy and also proselytised one quarter of the Broadmead Baptist Church membership.[71]

Blaugdone, then about forty-eight years old, was impressed by these men, as much by their deportment and behaviour, 'before ever they opened their Mouths', as by what they preached. She tells of that day:

> [...] they directed my Mind unto the Light of Christ, therein to wait, which I was diligent to do, and found the Vertue of it; and as the Evil was made manifest, I departed from it, and willingly took up the Cross, and yielded obedience unto it, in plainness of Speech and in my Habit.[72]

It is reasonable to assume that the period of Blaugdone's waiting was probably for clear recognition of the Inner light in her own life, as verification of call. A private process, it agrees with the accounts of many Friends that '[...] no man had made them a Quaker'.[73] The immediate outcome of Blaugdone's conversion was ostracism, especially by her former friends among eminent gentry and aristo-cracy; by loss of employment as a governess and imprisonment for up to three months. This was to be the pattern of her life and missionary journeys thereafter, for forty-seven years until her death at the age of ninety-five.

What is known of the life of Barbara Blaugdone is largely limited to her own *Account*, although, according to Brailsford, Besse's chronicler reports that Barbara was 'a woman of good parts and education'; that she set herself in her young widowhood to supplement her income by teaching.[74] Brailsford adds in comment, that 'Without stretch of fancy one can trace the pedagogue in her later acts and speeches; like the apostolic bishop, she was apt to teach, and never lost the self-confidence which is born of authority.'

---

71   Mabel Richmond Brailsford, *Quaker Women, 1650–1690* (London, 1915), 163.
72   Barbara Blaugdone, *Account,* 5. Her spiritual biography is also in: Garman, *Hidden.* 274–84; Mabel Richmond Brailsford, *Quaker Women,* 164–76.
73   Vann, *Social Development,* 9.
74   Brailsford, *Quaker Women,* 165.

An example of Blaugdone's ease with language and her confident usage, is evident from the start of her work, especially in the rhetoric of:

> And so, dear Friends, the cross is the Way to the Crown of Life, and to the Crown of Glory; and they that continue Faithful and Obedient, they obtain the Eternal Crown, which they that are disobedient, lose.

Here can be seen the effective use of alliteration and the easily flowing pattern that provides a balance of two types of crowns and two types of responses, a technique which leads to the climax of the ultimate reward. Then follows, in stark, dramatic contrast, six plainly expressed words of doom.

Blaugdone's writing style seems reminiscent of the rhetoric of an evangelical preacher; or, again, of the rhythm and melodic devices of poetry. Indeed, the passage quoted above could be easily set out in poetic form. Certainly it reflects an educated, literate, informed writer, especially as one notes the cohesive structure of Blaugdone's entire work, as well as her use of an established literary form of the Renaissance and seventeenth century, an epistle or spiritual narrative.[75] At the same time, Blaugdone's narrative can seem 'humble, even apologetic'[76] when she mentions her care as she listened to, and spoke as impressed by, the Holy Spirit, ('quietly'; 'never hasty nor forward')[77] and went about public ministry in churches and other places. Judith Applegate, a Quaker scholar, suggests, appropriately, that Blaugdone's model was the missionary journeys of Paul in 2 Corinthians: 11:23–33,[78] and the likeness is evident in its level of confidence and faith, the detailed account of places visited and the record of acceptance or persecution.

As far as the autobiographical writing of Quaker women generally is concerned, there was no stereotypical style, and they expressed themselves with a range of voices. Women of humble,

---

75   Judith Applegate in Garman, *Hidden*, 151, 164; Margaret J. M. Ezell, *Writing Women's Literary History* (Baltimore, 1993), 34.

76   Applegate in Garman, *Hidden*, 161.

77   Blaugdone, *Account*, 9.

78   Applegate in Garman, *Hidden*, 161.

working-class backgrounds wrote with the confidence of new status, while among the upper class Mack points out the easy confidentiality of the upper-class Mary Penington, the mystical ardour of Elizabeth Bathurst; and the contemplative poetry of Mary Mollineux.[79] To these should be added Margaret Fell's intimate, personal tone and Barbara Blaugdone's forthright descriptive manner which incorporates the cumulative technique of folk-lore that adds event to event and thereby builds intensity, though in general, Nigel Smith is correct when he speaks of the Quakers' 'flat style' compared with the radical content of Digger and Ranter publications.[80]

VII Early Quaker Women's Attributes

What are some aspects that Quaker women visionaries had in common? My own reading suggests, firstly, confidence born of conviction, balanced by humility. Blaugdone's confidence in her call grew from her year of waiting in which she fasted, 'and in that time the Lord caused me to grow and to prosper in the Truth: And then I was made to go and to call the People'.[81] Margaret Fell and her daughters also practised fasting.

Secondly, women visionaries assumed a prophetic role. In Blaugdone's case, she tells of a letter she wrote to a judge who had caused her to be incarcerated in Dublin, warning him that he would soon die. Following her release, procured by gentry friends,

---

79   Mack, *Visionary*, 377.
80   Nigel Smith, 'Hidden Things Brought to Light: Enthusiasm and Quaker Discourse', in Thomas N. Corns and David Loewenstein (eds), *The Emergence of Quaker Writing: Dissenting Literature in Seventeenth-Century England* (London, 1995), 57.
81   Blaugdone, *Account*, 10.

[…] I was moved to go to the Steeple-house, where this judge was, and the Lord was with me, and I Cleared myself of him; and he went to Bed and Died that Night: And […] they all said, That I was a true prophetess unto him.[82]

On another occasion, when foul weather for six days and nights threatened to overthrow the ship on which Blaugdone was sailing to Corke, sailors conspired to throw her overboard, holding her responsible, Jonah-like, because she was a Quaker. In response, Blaugdone felt moved to go up on deck to reassure and pray with them, and the ship eventually put into harbour at Dublin without loss or damage. Blaugdone claimed that the sailors acknowledged her prophetic role, saying that she was better than a priest in their eyes because she had prayed for them. On a second occasion it was said that her prayers caused a storm to cease and the preservation of all aboard.[83]

Blaugdone's prophetic role, like that of many of her contemporary women prophets and the Old Testament, biblical model, Deborah (Judges, chs. 4–5), not only encompassed proclamation and forecasts of future events but also included a pastoral role. In Blaugdone's situation she was able to seek out former friends among the gentry as well as supporting the community of Friends.

Thirdly, like nearly one hundred other early Quaker women who displayed similar zeal, and courage, Blaugdone became a missionary. For example, the sixteen-year-old Elizabeth Fletcher, having previously preached in Oxford, travelled to Ireland in 1655; Elizabeth Harris, Mary Fisher and Ann Austin went to America at about the same time, and Mary Fisher, walked 500 miles alone in Turkey to address the Sultan. Others went to Holland, Malta and other lands where, again, they were often misunderstood and punished. Blaugdone records in detail her own intensive journeys through England and Ireland. Wherever she went, she paid all her own expenses; unlike some others, she had no children to leave, nor a husband, as she had apparently become a widow of means when young.

---

82   Ibid. 35.
83   Ibid. 21–2, 36–7.

Fourthly, like her sisterhood of Quaker visionaries, Blaugdone's burden was for the 'Truth' which, meant, listening for the 'Power of God'.[84] She describes the beginning of her public work:

> And when I had laboured pretty much at home, he called me forth to labour abroad, and I stood so in dread, awe and fear of the Lord, that his Spirit strove much with me, before I could open my mouth; and the Lord came unto me in a Meeting, That the Lord would have War with Amelek from Generation to Generation: And the Power and Spirit of the Lord was so strong in me, that it set me upon my Feet, and constrained me to speak the words; for I was never hasty nor forward.[85]

Such waiting and listening for individual spiritual guidance meant opposition to the established church and its practices, and especially rejection of the instruction of 'bad priests', to whom Blaugdone refers in several instances. Witnessing, in some places, prompted positive results: interest and conversions. Of her experience in Dublin, Blaugdone reported, 'This my service for God was great, and he made it to prosper'.[86]

A fifth aspect, demonstrated in Blaugdone's experience, was the profound sense of community that Quakers shared, where the collective identity mattered to one another, especially as the years passed and they moulded more and more together due to their shared sufferings and societal isolationism. Despite the emphasis on individual call and response, the collective identity and unity of the group mattered most.[87] In one example of mutual support, Blaugdone tells of going to Basingstoke especially to support two Friends, Thomas Robinson and Ambrose Riggs, who had been put into prison. She delivered a letter for them from John Camme by poking it into the chink of a door, then went to the Mayor to plead on their behalf, and 'in a few days the Friends had their Liberty'.[88] When a vessel on which she was travelling to Ireland broke up in a storm off Dungarvan

---

84   Ibid. 8.
85   Ibid. 9.
86   Ibid. 26.
87   Mack, *Visionary*, 208, 210.
88   Blaugdone, *Account*, 21.

and others drowned, Blaugdone, 'ordered of the Lord to stay in the Ship',[89] was ultimately rescued by the sacrificial effort of another Friend passenger, assisted by the ship's Master.

An egalitarian community did not mean that relationships were always easy. Mack's study shows that several women experienced difficulty concerning the authority of Quaker male leadership to direct their activities.[90] Other men and women failed to receive the sympathy and support which they sought. According to Margaret Fell's biographer, she was 'often deeply hurt by the opposition she encountered from some Friends'.[91] In one instance of difference there were conflicting views as Margaret (by this time Margaret Fox) urged Friends to maintain the old standards, while other (men) sought to shun persecution following the Second Conventicle Act. Blaugdone wrote to George Fox in 1656, two years after her conversion, deferentially seeking his advice regarding her prophetic call.[92] However, after thirty-two years in her Quaker affiliation, she wrote to George Fox in 1686 with a tone of dissension mixed with compliance:

> I have not received one line from thee this great while though I writ to thee twice, now this thing was with me to lay before the King [...] I leave it with thee as thou shalt order it, I have not showed it to anyone here because they see not themselves joining it [...] I have been and still am a great sufferer [...] I believe thou art not insensible of it.[93]

A sixth shared characteristic was that of the inevitable punishment and persecution of dissenters, of which Blaugdone suffered much, being imprisoned in numerous places. She was stabbed in Bristol, whipped and imprisoned in Exeter where she fasted for fourteen days and imprisoned for six weeks in Marlborough where she fasted for six days, abstaining from both bread and water. In Exeter she was whipped until blood ran down her back, yet she sang through-

---

89   Ibid. 29.
90   Mack, *Visionary*, 210.
91   Ross, *Margaret Fell*, 287.
92   Swarthmore Mss 3/194, quoted in Barbour and Roberts (eds), *Early Quaker Writings, 1650–1700* (Grand Rapids, 1973), 479–80.
93   LSF, Portfolio MSS, 1/41

out.[94] In 1664, two hundred and nineteen Quakers of the Bristol Meeting were imprisoned, including fifty-five women. Blaugdone, now fifty-eight years of age was one of them, crowded into one room of Bridewell Prison where there were only four or five beds. The report printed in Besse comments that 'this was very hard to a woman of substance and credit, accustomed to live neatly', and it was not long before three young women had died in prison of the close confinement and the unsanitary conditions'.[95] On another occasion a huge dog was set upon Blaugdone, which creature can perhaps be seen as a symbol of the many forms of persecution undergone by Quaker women and children.

In a paraphrase of the words of Paul[96] and Blaugdone combined, Blaugdone might have said:

> Are they Quakers? So am I. Are they ministers of Christ (I speak with care), I am more. In labours more abundant, in punishments above measure, in prisons more frequent, in deaths oft [...] beaten, stoned, stabbed, shipwrecked; in perils of water, in perils of robbers, in perils by gypsies, in peril of a butcher's cleaver at my head, in perils on long Downs; rejected by relations and former friends; my bed a pig-sty trough [...] I speak my experience of the Dealings of the Lord with me [...] and I can speak it to the glory of God, he never moved me to any thing, but that he gave me Power to perform it [...][97]

VIII Quaker Women's Changing Role, 1664–1700

From the mid-1660s on, Quakerism began a new phase when it moved beyond the independence of a young movement to gradually assume the structure of a sect. The need for organisation came about through many causes. There was the consequence of an influx of adherents and the decades of persecution with their subsequent limitations of

94   Blaugdone, *Account*, 11–15.
95   Besse, 1:52. See Brailsford, *Quaker Women*, 291.
96   2 Corinthians 11:22–30.
97   Blaugdone, *Account*, 8.

movement and action. There was also the recognition of the dangers of an exaggerated spirit of individualism, demonstrated in the James Nayler experience and by other misled Quakers, as well as the decline of the Ranter movement. Times were changing; neither had the Lord come, nor had the prophesied Millennium of Revelation, Chapter 20. Where and how would Quaker women find their place in the changed arena? Would they maintain their faith?

The equality of women with men had been an important early tenet and this remained (and remains) unchanged, even when Women's Meetings became an official part of the movement's organisational structure from the 1670s on. Now, however, the emphasis was on what Fox called 'Helps Meet', in reference to Genesis 2:18, with 'Mothers in Israel' supporting each other's faith, nurturing the Christian family and home, helping the poor, counselling the dying and doing other good works. It was a far less up-front role and non-confrontational. Indeed, as Wilcox says, by the close of the seventeenth century, Quakers (including Quaker women) viewed themselves 'not as the army of the Lamb marching upon the world, but rather as a small remnant', with its echoes of Revelation 12:17. Further change came as educated men became apologetic theologians for Quakerism, rather than women writers who did not have the same educational opportunities nor late-century encouragement in the now pluralist society.[98]

Meetings exclusively for women became part of the formalised structure, venues where matters of home, family, female gender and concern, were central. At the same time, 'a woman's right to speak publicly was safeguarded by the Quakers' view of inspiration. All alike could be moved to speak the word of God, regardless of age, sex or social standing'.[99] There is a hint of irony in Wilcox's comment that 'the meetings provided women with a context in which they could speak without being condemned for taking up valuable time that should have been given over to more important speakers (i.e. men)'. In later years the separation of the men's and women's meetings

---

98 Wilcox, *Theology*, 120. A similar process occurred among early nineteenth-century women: see Penny Mahon's chapter in the companion volume.
99 Wilcox, *Theology*, 254.

appeared increasingly to be an exclusion from the place where power was centred in Quakerism, the men's Yearly Meeting.[100] It must be noted, however, that a precedent had already been established by women themselves, for they had actually initiated meeting together from about 1659 in order to plan ways of helping their fellow Friends, collecting money for prisoners and their families and writing encouraging letters.[101]

These Women's Meetings were crucial for Quaker women. They supported each other's faith, gave witness to their own visions, helped the poor or sick, counselled the dying. Now the sometimes noisy public stance of the past gave place to the quieter, nurturing role – self-perpetuating of the sect – which they could do very effectively. Rebecca Travers describes the state of the London Women's Meeting of 1676:

> The ancient love among the brethren waxes cold: too much love of this world stains our pristine glory, when it was said, even by our enemies, they so love one another that we shall never be able to break them. But the Women's Meetings are accompanied with the power and presence of the Lord as ever – our service is great, and our supply faileth not.[102]

Much of the success of the seventeenth-century Women's Meetings can be attributed to the contribution of Margaret Fell/Fox and her daughters who perpetuated their mother's vigour and dedication.[103] Days of perplexity appear to bring forth charismatic leaders, of whom Margaret Fell/Fox was one.

Criticism of separate women's meetings by such as John Bunyan in his tract *A Case of Conscience Resolved* (1683) did not deter Quaker women as the end of the century drew nearer. The clerk of the Lancashire Women's Meeting, Sarah Fell, wrote in 1689:

---

100   Ibid.
101   The founding of the Women's Meetings and their activities during the early decades has been described by Irene L. Edwards in 'The Women Friends of London: The Two-Weeks and Box Meetings', *Journal of the Friends' Historical Society*, 47 (1955): 2–221. See also Garman, *Hidden*, 10.
102   LSF, Barclay MSS. See Brailsford, *Quaker Women*, 329.
103   Ross, *Margaret Fell*, 286.

IN THE UPPER ROOM: THE WORK OF THE WOMEN'S MEETING. They were all gathered together in an upper room [...] with the women and Mary the mother of Jesus [...] and the holy ghost was poured upon them, so plentifully, that the multitude were all amazed [...] Therefore let all mouths be stopped, which would limit the spirit of the Lord God in male or female, which he hath not limited; but the Lord hath regard unto and takes notice of the women, and despises them not.[104]

IX Conclusions

Women of all religious persuasions were involved in, and concerned by, the perplexities of the seventeenth century. During the mid-seventeenth century, Quaker women, from servant girl to aristocratic lady, responded to an apocalyptic vision, believing that the Spirit of God led them by an inner light of wisdom and discernment in an intensely personal experience of knowing Christ. As they responded, they set aside notions of conformity to gender roles or circumspect behaviour in an attitude of abnegation.[105] This led them into the role of visionary women whose chief desire was to proclaim that the end time was at hand and to prepare England for judgement: 'Christ was come and coming again after the apostasy, and was being revealed in his light as judge, prophet and king'.[106] Their theology and view of eschatology were unwelcome to many, misunderstood and/or regarded with suspicion. Added to this was the confusion and perplexity brought into society by their gender – the fact that it was women who preached, prophesied, protested and proselytised, frequently in an unfeminine, disruptive mode with quaking, shouts and tears did not help their acceptance in society.

Change came, even within twenty years, both within and without the fellowship of Quakerism. Perhaps Mack is correct when she suggests that the seeds of change may have been inherent as the

---

104   Mack, *Visionary*, 326.
105   This commitment echoes Paul's self-renunciation, expressed in Philippians 3:8.
106   Wilcox, *Theology*, 41.

movement began; that even by the end of the 1640s the age of independent female prophecy had come to an end.[107] Their own success could be interpreted as making them victims of change, so that their roles gradually mellowed and, subsequently extinguished their charismatic zeal. It was the pragmatic need for organisation and structure, in order to form a cohesive, now greatly swollen community, that accelerated flux within. A further reason was the heightened persecution from without. In a seeming lament for the loss of innocence, the Quaker historian, William Braithwaite, notes that:

> Quakerism [...] began as fellowship, thrilling with intense life, with the great purposes of God ringing in its ears and driving it forth to adventurous, if sometimes mistaken service, and later, by [...] the accretions of habit, the stereotyping force of tradition, and the pressure of the outside world, it established a strong organisation and lost something of its soul.[108]

Braithwaite's reference to 'mistaken service'[109] prompts examination and in doing so, raises questions. Were the Quaker women who gave up so much for their faith misled all along? Was the meaning of their witness completely clear, or overdressed with eloquence, conspiracy or alarmist theory? Was the imminent kingdom they announced to be literal, spiritual only, or both? What of their claim of being witnesses to the final redemption of the whole world? When Margaret Fell wrote of 'the Lord's Everlasting Truth in her generation',[110] was she implying consciously, or unwittingly, that the 'Lord's Truth' held generational relevancy in the unforeseen future; that the seventeenth-century women's cry to the world to receive the bridegroom had been a misplaced sense of earth's 'midnight'?[111] Punshon's analysis is that

---

107 Mack cites as evidence Patricia Crawford's work, 'Women's Published Writings 1600–1700', in Mary Prior (ed.), *Women in English Society, 1500–1800* (London, 1985), 211–82. This area may need further research to give the full picture.

108 William Braithwaite, *The Second Period of Quakerism* (York, 1979), 324.

109 Ibid.

110 Fell, *Remarkable Passages*, 1.

111 See Matthew 25:6. The role of Christ as bridegroom, husband and spouse is referred to by many Quaker women. See Dorothy White, *A Trumpet of the Lord*

Fox and his fellows were quite clear that they were proclaimers and witnesses of the final redemption of the whole world, and no account of Quaker origins is adequate that fails to give fullest weight to this aspect of their thought.[112]

Another question concerns the reliability of the women's knowledge of Scripture. In response, it must be recognised that seventeenth-century society was so permeated with biblical knowledge that both those who could read, and those who were illiterate, knew, and could quote from, the Bible; and it was the source upon which their consciences drew. Wilcox's study into women's ministry and their theology in the seventeenth century[113] indicates the centrality of the work of Christ in early Quaker thought; that they emphasised 'the *inner* revelation of Scripture'[114] and showed deep respect for Scriptural authority. Richard Hubberthorne, a Quaker who in 1660 explained his faith to Charles II, said, '(the work of the light) leads up in the fulfilling of Scripture, not in the opposition to it'.[115]

Of Past and Present

A study of seventeenth-century Quaker women and the ensuing questions prompt insights into the pluralist state of the Christian Church in the twentieth and twenty-first centuries. Modern Christians of many groups will recognise similar patterns in their own backgrounds or personal experience. Similar historical stages are discernible: the initial evangelistic fervour with its vision of truth and the return of primitive faith, perfection and the immediacy of the kingdom of God; then a gentle subsidence into a state of acquiescence; then the need to find new roles to justify call and place in society, followed by awareness of need for societal acceptance and respectability. Thus ensues the change from movement to sect to denom-

---

of Hosts (1662); Mary Penington, *Some Account of Circumstances in the Life of Mary Penington from her Manuscript left for her family* (London, 1821).

112   Punshon, *Portrait*, 60.
113   Wilcox, *Theology*.
114   Ibid. 68 (italics mine).
115   Ibid. 61 (*sic*).

ination, despite the founders not seeking to form a new ecclesiastical group.[116]

Others features will be recognisable, for many have preached and believed in a restoration of apostolic truth, yet experienced a period of great disappointment as eschatological expectation was unfulfilled, or, at least, fulfilled in a very different way from that expected. Certainly religious toleration was not envisaged either by the Royalist Church of England members, or by Presbyterians of the seventeenth century. Was Biddle's prophecy that the hierarchy of the Church of England or Catholicism would be thrown down a false message or a conditional one?[117]

Other similarities between the seventeenth-century past and the twenty-first century indicate that many have sensed new manifestations of Pentecost; many have seen 'apostasy' from membership and then return, even as happened in the early days of Quaker women;[118] some still view themselves as the 'remnant'.

Moreover, women prophets and so-called 'Messiahs' have come and gone,[119] while confusion and misunderstandings between the different parts of the body of Christ about their specific teaching, emphases and goals still exists, despite a spirit of ecumenism. Not only does a study of Quaker women echo the past but it also radiates nuances for present and future Christian faith, a minority belief system in the Western world. The work of Christian women historians has brought about fresh and discerning insights during the twentieth century as they look critically and analytically at their denominational stories. Moreover, the rise of Feminist critiques in the 1960s and 1970s has offered new approaches and methodologies, while Christian women apologists are writing and/or preaching again as women's ordination grows more and more accepted, though often not among

---

116   B. R. Wilson (ed.), 'Introduction', to *Patterns of Sectarianism: Organisation and Ideology in Social and Religious Movements* (London, 1967).

117   Biddle, *Trumpet*, 9–15. Also expressed in *One Warning more to the Bishops, Priests, Deacons, Friers and Jesuites*, 16. See Garman, *Hidden*, 129–36.

118   Mack, *Visionary*, 210.

119   E.g. in the eighteenth century, Mary Lee, founder of the Shakers; and in the nineteenth and early twentieth centuries, Ellen G. White, co-founder of the Seventh-day Adventists, and Mary McKillop. the first Australian saint.

the evangelical minorities who are, in some respects, the Quakers' heirs.

Theories of Morality and Faith

The tolerance of other points of view in a pluralist society is a characteristic of Kohlberg's twentieth-century theory of moral development, set as the ultimate Moral level, Stage Six: the Universal-Ethical-Principle Orientation.[120] At this highest level, abstract and ethical principles are embraced through personal decision; they are not concrete moral rules as are the Ten Commandments. They concern justice, reciprocity and equality of human rights, with respect for every individual's dignity of personhood. This theory may be regarded by some as more Humanist than Christian and of limited application.

The theory of faith development from a Christian perspective, addressed by James W. Fowler, appears more relevant as a descriptive measure. Like Kohlberg, he identifies six stages. Moving beyond the influence of home, family and authority voices, Stage Four often 'develops under the tutelage of ideologically powerful religions, charismatic leadership or ideologies of other kinds. It often finds it necessary to collapse these polar tensions in one direction or the other'.[121] It is probable that this is the level of early charismatic movements. At Stage Five, the person recognises the integrity and position of others, which is a move into a pluralist point of view. Stage Six, that of Universalising Faith, considered rare, is

> what Christians and Jews call the Kingdom of God [...] a live, felt reality for the person of faith. Here one dwells *in* the world as a transforming presence, but

---

120   L. A. Kohlberg, 'Moral Stages and Moralization. The Cognitive-developmental Approach.' in Thomas Lickona (ed.), *Moral Development and Behaviour* (New York, 1976), 34–5. See also Thomas C. Hennessy (ed.), *Values and Moral Development* (New York, 1976), 2–3.

121   James W. Fowler, 'Stages in Faith: The Structural-Developmental Approach', in Hennessy (ed.), *Values and Moral Development*, 184.

is not *of* the world [...] Such persons are ready for fellowship with persons at any of the other stages and from any other faith tradition.[122]

The 'set of spiritual rules of extraordinary potency, handed on from father to son and mother to daughter in the families of Friends' is well recognised in a long view of the history and development of Quakers by G. M. Trevelyan. He concludes that 'The finer essence of George Fox's queer teaching [...] was surely this – that Christian qualities matter much more than Christian dogmas. No Church had made that its living rule before'.[123]

Another word should come from Newgate Prison in 1662, from Hester Biddle whose poem drew attention to the day of perplexity. Her poetic vision exudes confidence that perplexity will ultimately give way to Omnipotence; and the unchanging, basic faith that made the Quakers, like other dogmatic minorities examined by John Coffey, ultimately unconquerable:

> O Zion's king, thy beauty bright
> Hath filled our hearts with great delight;
> Thy city pure our eye doth see,
> In which alone dwells purity [...]
> O Lord we will serve thee whilst we have breath.[124]

But the final word belongs to Margaret Fell, Quaker visionary of discernment:

> The Truth is one and the same always, and though ages and generations pass away, and one generation goes and another comes, yet the word and the power and spirit of the Living God endures for ever, and is the same and never changes.[125]

---

122   Ibid. 185.
123   G. M. Trevelyan, *English Social History* (London, 1942), 267.
124   Hester Biddle, in Paul Salzman (ed.), *Early Modern Women's Writing: an Anthology, 1560–1700* (Oxford, 2000), 166.
125   Fell, *Works*, 47.

CHRISTOPHER DURSTON

'Settling the Hearts and Quieting the Minds of All Good People': The Major-Generals and the Puritan Minorities of Interregnum England[1]

In the late summer of 1655 Oliver Cromwell decided to appoint a number of his closest military colleagues as major-generals and to dispatch them to the English provinces to act as representatives of his government at a local level. They were entrusted with a wide range of responsibilities, in particular with the overseeing of local security arrangements and the regulation of the moral behaviour of the people. Although these were daunting undertakings, over the course of the next few months the major-generals displayed great energy and commitment, and by the second half of 1656 they believed they were making real progress. Large numbers of former royalists had been disarmed, forced to provide security for their future good behaviour, and obliged to pay an extraordinary or decimation tax. In some parts of the country, too, suspect clergymen had been ejected, alehouses had been shut down, unruly rural sports and pastimes had been outlawed, and moral transgressors had been hauled before the courts and prosecuted for their crimes. In the autumn of 1656, however, this reform programme began to lose impetus. When the second Protectorate parliament met in mid-September, it was decided that the major-generals were needed at Westminster, and their absence from their districts during the autumn months inevitably led to the scaling down of their work. At the end of 1656 one of their number, John Desborough, attempted to obtain parliamentary sanction for the

1   I should like to thank Barry Coward, Sue Doran and Jackie Eales for their helpful comments during the writing of the piece. An earlier version of the article was published in the journal *History* in April 2000. I should like to thank the editor of that journal for permission to publish it here.

indefinite continuation of the decimation tax which underpinned their rule; his move, however, misfired disastrously, for in late January 1657 the House of Commons voted to end the tax and as a result effectively brought the major-generals' experiment to a close.[2]

Historians have traditionally laid great stress on the unpopularity of the major-generals, particularly in their role of moral policemen. In the later seventeenth century Edward Hyde, Earl of Clarendon, reflected that they had 'carried themselves like so many bassas [bashaws], with their bands of janizaries towards the people, and were extremely odious to them of all parties'.[3] Clarendon, of course, was a far from unbiased commentator, but the rather more impartial Samuel Rawson Gardiner also claimed two centuries later that as 'discouragers of vice and encouragers of virtue' they had 'roused the most virulent opposition', and David Watson Rannie commented at about the same time that their 'efforts on behalf of religion and morals' had met 'the inevitable fate of unpopularity'.[4] In the 1940s, Wilbur Abbott declared that they had raised 'deep and bitter discontent everywhere' and that 'men of all parties [...] longed for their downfall'.[5] More recently Ivan Roots has suggested they were viewed as a 'monstrous apparition', David Underdown has argued that they 'incensed the country gentry, moderate and Royalist alike', Clive Holmes has commented that they were 'the epitome of central interference in local government and their operations aroused very considerable antipathy', and Mark Kishlansky has claimed they were 'detested in the localities'.[6]

2   For more details of these events see Christopher Durston, 'The Fall of Cromwell's Major-Generals', *English Historical Review*, 113 (1998), 18–37; and Christopher Durston, *Cromwell's Major-Generals: Godly Government during the English Revolution* (Manchester, 2001).

3   Edward Hyde, Earl of Clarendon, *The History of the Rebellion and Civil Wars in England*, W. Dunn Macray (ed.) (6 vols, Oxford, 1888), 6: 16–17.

4   S. R. Gardiner, *The History of the Commonwealth and Protectorate, 1649–1656* (4 vols, 1965 edn), 4: 29; D. W. Rannie, 'Cromwell's Major-Generals', *English Historical Review*, 10 (1895), 500.

5   W. C. Abbott, *The Writings and Speeches of Oliver Cromwell* (4 vols, Oxford, 1937–47), 4: 59, 62.

6   Ivan Roots, 'Swordsmen and Decimators: Cromwell's Major-Generals', in R. H. Parry (ed.) *The English Civil War and After 1642–1658*, (London, 1970),

While these assessments are not without some foundation, their frequent restatement has tended to obscure another important aspect of the rule of the major-generals: the fact that within each of the English and Welsh counties there existed a small but dedicated cadre of 'well-affected' local Puritans who welcomed the soldiers with open arms, seeing them as the harbingers of the godly reformation for which they had been waiting in vain since the parliamentary victory in the civil war ten years earlier. This chapter investigates the composition and attitudes of these Puritan minorities and the nature of their relationship with the major-generals in 1655 and 1656, looking in particular at how they responded to the news of the generals' deployment in the provinces, how they co-operated with them in their work, and how ultimately they came to terms with the failure of the initiative.

I

The major-generals had been conceived as a means of increasing the security of the Protectorate state in the aftermath of the abortive but alarming royalist insurrections of the spring of 1655. To this end, they were instructed to proceed quickly against all those involved in the recent uprisings, and to disarm, monitor the movements of, and charge a punitive decimation tax upon any landowners who could be shown to have supported Charles I or his son during the previous fourteen years. From the outset, however, they were also given the not inconsiderable additional task of improving the moral calibre of the English people. Their orders required them to 'encourage and promote godliness and virtue and discourage and discountenance all profaneness and ungodliness'. More specifically, they were instructed to close down brothels, gaming houses and unlicensed alehouses; set to work,

79; David Underdown, 'Settlement in the Counties', in G. E. Aylmer (ed.), *The Interregnum: The Quest for Settlement*, (London, 1972), 172; Clive Holmes, *Seventeenth-Century Lincolnshire* (Lincoln, 1980), 214; Mark Kishlansky, *A Monarchy Transformed: Britain, 1603–1714* (London, 1996), 210.

imprison or transport the idle and dissolute; suppress a range of rural sports, including horse-racing, bear-baiting, and cock-fighting; punish all those who profaned the Sabbath, swore, indulged in illicit sexual activity, or were married in a religious rather than civil ceremony; and eject from their livings all ministers and schoolmasters whose opinions or lifestyles the government considered unacceptable. Cromwell and his colleagues, who were doubtless aware that this represented a formidable workload, were convinced that their royalist enemies posed an equally serious threat to the regime's survival and the nation's moral good. They thus saw security and reformation as indivisible twin goals and believed that neither would be achieved if pursued independently, for just as the godly reformation could not be brought about until the regime was secure, so real security would only be established when godly reforms had begun to take firm root. Cromwell specifically acknowledged this at the opening of the second Protectorate parliament when he declared that these objectives were 'scarcely distinct' and added: 'I think reformation, if it be honest and thorough and just, it will be your best security'.[7]

In view of the scope and challenging nature of their responsibilities, the major-generals clearly needed all the local support they could muster. They had at their disposal the experienced and ideologically committed troops of the new county militias raised during the early summer, and they also relied very heavily upon the regime's 'well affected' civilian supporters within the individual shires of their districts. The central government had begun to select those who would assist the major-generals in August 1655, and in late October they formally appointed 'commissions for securing the peace of the commonwealth' for every English and Welsh county and instructed the new commissioners to work closely with their local major-general.[8] A number of individuals were later added on the recommendation of the generals after they had taken local soundings. While no definitive lists of the commissioners appear to have survived among the Interregnum State papers, the names of many of those who were active can be found attached to the letters they wrote to

7   Abbott, *Writings and Speeches of Cromwell*, 4: 270.
8   Gardiner, *Commonwealth and Protectorate*, 3: 321–2.

Cromwell and his secretary of state, John Thurloe, over the next few months.

The number of commissioners varied from shire to shire but within most counties somewhere between ten and thirty individuals appear to have become involved in the work. A few, such as Cornelius Holland, who was named in both Berkshire and Buckinghamshire, and James Chadwick, who was named in Nottinghamshire and Derbyshire, served for more than one county. Many of them were civilians, but the officers of the county militias were also named, and, despite the fact that it was not at all clear whether they had any legal authority within corporations, they came from both urban and rural areas. While a few commissioners, such as Jonathan Bruen of Cheshire, John Bingham of Dorset, Sir William Brownlow of Lincolnshire, Sir Thomas Barnardiston of Suffolk and Samuel Dunch of Berkshire, were substantial figures from the pre-civil war, magisterial county elites, the majority of them were more minor landholders. This fact was acknowledged early on by William Goffe, the major-general for Sussex, Hampshire and Berkshire, who reported to Thurloe in November 1655 that 'the stresse of this businesse must lie upon the middle sort of men'.[9] Goffe's perception is confirmed by a recent study of the Staffordshire commissioners which has shown that the commissioners for that county came predominantly from the ranks of the lesser gentry and prosperous middling people.[10] Undoubtedly, however, some of the commissioners were of meaner extraction. In the seventeenth century the Suffolk royalist, Roger Coke, dismissed them as 'mean and profligate rascals', and in the early eighteenth century the hostile Tory historian, Laurence Echard, also claimed that they were 'the dregs of the people, tho' others of better note were

---

9   Bod. Lib., Rawlinson MSS, John Thurloe's State Papers, A 32, fos 171–4; most of these letters are transcribed as Thomas Birch (ed.), *A Collection of the State Papers of John Thurloe Esq.* (7 vols, 1742).

10   John Sutton, 'Cromwell's Commissioners for Preserving the Peace of the Commonwealth: A Staffordshire Case Study', in I. Gentles, J. Morrill and B. Worden (eds), *Soldiers, Writers and Statesmen in the English Revolution*, (Cambridge, 1998), 151–82.

sometimes mingled with them'.[11] More recently, John Morrill has remarked of Charles Worsley's period of rule in Cheshire that 'the rise to greater prominence of low born men was a marked feature of his administration'.[12]

Many of the new commissioners had been active as members or officers of parliamentary county committees and as justices of the peace in the 1640s and 1650s. The great majority had also been named both to the county committees charged in 1654 with the ejection of scandalous and insufficient ministers and schoolmasters, and to the militia commissions established in the wake of the royalist uprisings of the spring of 1655.[13] Significant numbers, too, had either been in arms for parliament during the civil war or were still serving as army officers. The great majority was conspicuous as staunch supporters of the godly cause.

In a number of counties some of those nominated as commissioners centrally subsequently declined to act. In Derbyshire Colonel Thomas Sanders refused and in Hampshire Colonel Richard Norton expressed reservations, although William Goffe thought they were 'easy to be answered'.[14] At the end of December James Berry informed Thurloe that, while most of the commissioners named for North Wales were 'very forward to give assistance', a couple of them were 'disatisfyyed or rather not satisfyed to act', adding: 'there is some little scruple in some, and they scarce know what it is'.[15] Early in the new year, John Desborough reported from Bristol that 'sundry'

11   Roger Coke, *A Detection of the Court and State of England during the Last Four Reigns and Interregnum* (2 vols, 1694), 2: 53; Laurence Echard, *The History of England from the Beginning of the Reign of Charles I to the Restoration of King Charles the Second* (London, 1718), 777.

12   J. S. Morrill, *Cheshire, 1630–1660: County Government and Society during the English Revolution* (Oxford, 1974), 285.

13   The names of many of the active commissioners can be found attached to the letters they wrote to Thurloe and Cromwell, which are preserved among the Thurloe State Papers in the Bod. Lib. Rawlinson MSS; for the commissions of ejectors see C. H. Firth and R. S. Rait (eds), *Acts and Ordinances of the Interregnum*, (3 vols, London, 1911), 2: 968–90; the militia commissions are given at PRO SP, 76A, 26–33.

14   Bod. Lib., Rawlinson MSS, A 32, fos 805–8, 809–12.

15   Ibid. A 33, fos 726–9.

of the commissioners named for that county borough had 'craved time to consider [...] and at last made their excuses', and that as a result he had been forced to replace them with others 'that will effectually carry it on'.[16] In neighbouring Gloucestershire two of the commissioners sent excuses, pleading toothache and gout respectively; Desborough, who was clearly not entirely convinced of the genuineness of these ailments, commented wryly to Cromwell: 'but the best is they are diseases not catching, for the work goes pleasantly on'.[17]

The best documented case of refusal to act concerned Thomas Grove of Wiltshire. Grove was a Presbyterian gentleman who had been expelled from the Long Parliament by Pride but had sat again in the 1654 parliament. In early December 1655 Desborough informed Thurloe and Cromwell that all the Wiltshire commissioners were willing to act with the one exception of Grove, whom he described as 'honest and able, though tender'. He enclosed a letter which Grove had sent him, in which the writer had explained that ill-health had prevented him from attending the commissioners' first meeting, but that even if he had been well he would have requested more time to consider whether or not to act, because: 'I cannot undertake any business of consequence till I have had some serious thoughts about it and have debated it with mine own weak judgement, that so my conscience may be clearly satisfide in what I doe'. Grove went on to make clear that, while he had no objection to 'the grounds of the design' and was also sure that 'the old enimies have their old hearts and their old hatred still', he was none the less concerned that 'there may be some scruple in the manner of doing this'. He assured Desborough that if he could convince himself that 'the way and manner be as righteous and warrantable as the thing is good and desirable' he would act 'as cordially in it as any man in England'.[18] Elected to the second Protectorate parliament in the summer of 1656, Grove subsequently withdrew from the house in protest against the exclusion of members, but he later returned and in 1657 he was closely associated with the kingship group.

16   Ibid. A 34, fos 173–6.
17   Ibid. A 34, fos 173–6.
18   Ibid. A 33, fos 225–32.

Some other commissioners who did act may have done so with reluctance. William Boteler initially encountered some hestitancy amongst the Northamptonshire commissioners; in early November he informed Thurloe that only a few of them had turned up to their first meeting in Northampton, and that some of those that had attended 'were not very harty in our worke' but rather 'a little timorous and seeming averse' to the business of assessing their neighbours for the decimation tax. Whether through threats or encouragement, within a day or so he had persuaded them to act and could report back that 'they have all of them putt their hands to the plough; and shame will not let them now looke back'.[19] A week later he confirmed that 'they came on (some of them especially) a little slowly at first, yet now go on without any rubb'.[20]

A few commissioners, too, may have served not out of zeal for the major-generals' cause but rather from a desire to gain power, to influence the course of events or to protect their royalist friends and neighbours. According to Lucy Hutchinson, James Chadwick, one of the Nottinghamshire commissioners, was a time-serving opportunist, whose apparent godliness was merely a sham and who was addicted to a 'thousand cheates and other base wayes'.[21] Similarly, one of the Gloucestershire commissioners, Christopher Guise, had a royalist father and a distinctly ungodly reputation as a womaniser. His largely fruitless attempts to help his royalist neighbours to evade the decimation tax enraged his fellow commissioners, who prevailed upon Desborough to intervene to prevent his election to parliament in August 1656. Guise was so shocked by the 'hate' that Desborough displayed against him at the poll that he seriously feared for his safety.[22]

In many counties those commissioners who were less than fully committed to the work of the major-generals played at best only a

19   Ibid. A 32, fos 293–6.
20   Ibid. A 32, fos 385–8.
21   Lucy Hutchinson, *Memoirs of the Life of Colonel Hutchinson*, John Sutherland (ed.) (Oxford, 1973), 71–2.
22   Godfrey Davies (ed.), *Memoirs of the Family of Guise*, Camden Society, 3rd ser. 28 (London, 1917), 129–30.

minor role on the commissions and left the brunt of the work to be conducted by their more committed colleagues. These active commissioners were often local military figures and zealous Puritans who were unswervingly committed to the work of the major-generals and utterly uncompromising in their approach to those of their neighbours whom they considered to be its enemies. In Kent, for example, in addition to the three commissioners who refused to serve at all, another thirteen attended fewer than seven of the commission's twenty-three meetings. Most of the work was thus left to a sub-group of thirteen commissioners, which included no fewer than nine soldiers as well as the unpopular regicide, Sir Michael Livesey.[23] In Warwickshire the equivalent sub-group of active commissioners included the two godly merchants from Coventry, Thomas Basnet and Robert Beake, the governor of Warwick Castle, Colonel Joseph Hawkesworth, the former sequestration commissioner, William Thornton, and the former county committeeman and major of foot, Waldive Willington.[24]

It was the members of these sub-groups who were to work most closely with the major-generals and to devote themselves unstintingly to the work of improving the regime's security and bringing about the long-awaited reformation of manners. United by their strong support for Cromwell's government and their staunch Puritanism and believing that they were doing God's express bidding by disabling and punishing His enemies, they set to work with a vengeance about their tasks of levying the new tax, purging the ministry, and clamping down on the immorality which they believed to be endemic in local society – a collective approach to public affairs nicely signalled by the name of one of the Lincolnshire commissioners: Robert Vigerous.

---

23   Peter Bloomfield 'The Cromwellian Commission in Kent, 1655–57', in Alec Detsicas and Nigel Yates (eds), *Studies in Modern Kentish History* (Maidstone, 1983), 22. Bloomfield based this article on their minute book, then held at the Centre for Kentish Studies in Maidstone (reference U2341). Unfortunately, it could not be consulted for this study because it has subsequently been lost.

24   Staffordshire Records Office, D793, 95, Commissioners for Warwickshire to Sir Hervey Bagot, 29 Nov 1655; for more details on these men see Ann Hughes, *Politics, Society and Civil War in Warwickshire, 1620–1660* (Cambridge, 1987).

II

The eagerness of the most active commissioners to assist with the work is a frequent theme of the correspondence received by Cromwell's secretary, John Thurloe, during the weeks which followed the major-generals' arrival in their associations. James Berry, for example, wrote from Herefordshire that the commissioners there had begun to act 'with much readines and (indeed I thinke) joy', adding that:

> some that have seemed disatisfyed and have declined action formerly have now declared their hopes of good by this dispensation and are resolved to assist in this worke and are persuaded it will bring forth some desirable reformation.[25]

Thomas Kelsey similarly commented that the commissioners for Kent 'unanimously seeme to be very hartie and cordiall to the work', and William Boteler remarked of the Bedfordshire commissioners that 'God hath wrought a good promptitude in the harts of our honest friends in other places to this great worke; yet I am apt to thinke more than ordinary in these gentlemen'.[26] An account of Charles Worsley's first meeting with the Lancashire commissioners, meanwhile, which appeared in the government newspaper, *Mercurius Politicus*, suggested that:

> there appears daily more and more Ground of encouragement for Acting, for the good people doe not a little rejoyce and seem to be abundantly affected therewith and promise to set heart and hand to this good work.[27]

It is possible, of course, that some of the heady optimism which pervades these reports was the product of wishful thinking or Panglossian self-delusion on the part of the major-generals and their masters in London. On the other hand, several of the generals who had clearly not set out for their districts with very great expectations were

---

25   Bod. Lib, Rawlinson MSS, A 32, fos 793–6.
26   Ibid. A 32, fos 517–20, 683–6.
27   BL, Thomason Tracts, E.489.14, *Mercurius Politicus*, 8–15 Nov 1655.

genuinely taken aback by the degree of enthusiasm they encountered. Hezekiah Haynes, Charles Fleetwood's deputy in East Anglia, wrote from Norwich in early November to inform Thurloe: 'I did not expect it would have had so good an acceptance with them; and I desire to bless the Lord for his goodness therein and to take encouragement from this good beginning to trust him in what remains'.[28] Several weeks later he again commented: 'Truly I could not have expected that readyness to this worke as I find in the gentlemen now mett', and a few days afterwards he declared, this time from Cambridge: 'still it pleaseth the lord to unite the hearts of our friends beyond expectation in this worke'.[29] Thomas Kelsey was another who was surprised by the zeal of the active commissioners; in late November he informed Thurloe from Maidstone: 'I must confess the Lord hath given my unbelieving hart the ly, by vouchsafing unto mee more of his presence and comfort in thes uncouth imployment then I could expect'.[30]

The positive tone of the generals' own reports was replicated in the correspondence which some of the commissions themselves sent to Thurloe and Cromwell during this period. Their letters, which were received from all parts of the country, thanked the government profusely for sending down the generals, expressed great keenness to assist with the work, and promised to carry it out as speedily and diligently as possible.[31] In a typical example sent to Thurloe on 16 November, the commissioners for Bedfordshire declared themselves highly satisfied that the government had decided 'to purpose such a way for settling the hearts and quieting the minds of all good people by this course now proceeded in'.[32] A few days later, the Suffolk commissioners declared to Cromwell: 'We are very clear in our opinions that this undertaking is not only honourable in itself but also the most probable and likely means to secure the peace and happiness of this commonwealth'.[33]

---

28   Bod. Lib., Rawlinson MSS, A32, fos 215–18.
29   Ibid. A 32, fos 711–14, 931–4.
30   Ibid. A 32, 683–6.
31   For examples see Ibid. A 32, fos 529–32, 691–4, 719–22; A 33, fos 157–60, 355–8, 359–62, 702–5; A 34, fos 767–70; A 36, fos 117–20.
32   Ibid. A 32, fos 529–32.
33   Ibid. A 32, fos 691–4.

A number of these letters reveal quite clearly that what the newly appointed commissioners found especially appealing about the arrival of the major-generals in their counties was the fact that it presented them with a heaven-sent opportunity to settle some old scores with their royalist and ungodly neighbours. The Suffolk commissioners declared their gratitude that God had made Oliver Cromwell 'the instrument of our deliverance from that implacable generation of men', and expressed great satisfaction that the raising of the decimation tax would reduce the financial burden on 'the good and peaceable people of this nation who have a long time born the heat of the day'.[34] According to William Boteler, the Bedfordshire commissioners had declared that they would 'make it their business to finde out and give me notice of all their prophane and idle gentry and others whose lives are a shame to a Xn [Christian] Commonwealth'.[35] Thomas Kelsey meanwhile informed Thurloe that the Kentish commissioners 'rejoyce to see such a checke and discouragement is put upon their old enemy'.[36] In late November the Cheshire commissioners told Cromwell they had 'long been desirous that the first and continued causers of the disturbance of our peace might not equally have shared our so dearly purchased freedom', and in mid-December the Essex commissioners assured him that it was right that 'those who will not be convinced, reclaimed and won by lenity should have the streighter reins of government imposed for a curb and terror unto them'.[37] In January 1656 the Nottinghamshire commissioners similarly informed him that in their view the work was 'composed of great justice and mercie, wisdom and equitie of justice in chargeinge the guiltie and easing the guiltlesse'.[38] In March the Buckinghamshire commissioners expressed the view that the decimation should not be considered 'an extraction of vitals, but the correction of distempered humours that the whole body may be brought into a right frame again', adding

34   Ibid. A 32, fos 691–4.
35   Ibid. A 32, fos 655–8.
36   Ibid. A 32, fos 683–6.
37   Ibid. A 32, fos 887–90; A33, fos 385–8.
38   Ibid. A 34, fos 767–70.

the whole tenour of the worke speakes good, the uniting of the fellow sharers in the grace of Christ, the exciting of magistrates and ministers to the faithful discharge of their dutyes, the bridleing of idle and licentious persons, who threaten an innundacon of sinn and consequently of wrath and ruine.[39]

Such expressions of support were a welcome source of reassurance for those at the centre; in mid-December Thurloe wrote back by return of post to tell Haynes how pleased Cromwell had been to receive the supportive comments in the letter from the Essex commissioners.[40]

III

The commissioners' first priority was the assessment and collection of the decimation tax. This required them to summon before them all former royalists who they believed might possess land worth at least £100 per annum or personal property worth £1,500 or more, and to establish accurate valuations of their real and personal estates so that they could determine the amount they were liable to pay. In theory, all this needed to be done before 21 December 1655, the date prescribed by the government for the payment of the first six months' instalment of the tax. In the larger counties this involved conducting detailed interviews with scores of aggrieved royalists in a little over a month.

In most counties the commissioners set about this task with real urgency. Boteler reported that the Northamptonshire commissioners had assessed around thirty individuals in one week in early November, and Haynes testified that during the same period the Norfolk commissioners had completed most of their work by sitting for ten days without a break.[41] In mid-December Berry informed Thurloe that those named in North Wales were 'hard at it' at Wrexham, and had

39   Ibid. A 36, fos 229–32.
40   Ibid. A 33, fos 461–4.
41   Ibid. A 32, fos 385–8, 647–50; for most of the extant decimation lists see 'The Cromwellian Decimation Tax of 1655. The Assessment Lists', in J. T. Cliffe (ed.) *Camden Miscellany*, Camden Society, 5th ser. 7 (London, 1996), 403–92.

met daily for over a week.[42] Some of the commissioners were exceptionally eager to play their part; in January 1656 William Goffe reported to Thurloe that Walter Everenden, was so keen on the decimation work that he travelled more than sixty miles from Rye to Chichester for meetings of the Sussex commissioners.[43]

Some historians have argued that in their dealings with their local royalist communities the commissioners showed restraint and tact, and tried to soften the impact of the major-generals' instructions. In his study of civil war and Interregnum Somerset, David Underdown suggested that the commissioners in that shire were 'relatively moderate' in their assessment of royalists for the tax. He claimed that they accepted without question some absurdly low estimates of personal wealth and that they displayed none of the 'vindictive zeal' which had characterised the earlier administration of the notorious local parliamentarian, Colonel John Pyne.[44] His conclusion seems to have been based largely on comments made by one of the bailiffs of the Seymour family in a letter of January 1656, in which the writer states that the commissioners 'act very mildly and will do my lord all the services they may'.[45] Ivan Roots has similarly pointed out that in mid-December 1655 Thomas Crompton, one of the Staffordshire commissioners expressed considerable embarrassment about having to ask his royalist friend, Sir Richard Leveson, to enter a bond for his future good behaviour. After offering to bring the bond to his house so that Leveson could avoid the trouble of travelling in 'difficult and tedious' weather, he assured him 'you may be confident I will use you with what civility my commission and instructions give me leave'.[46]

It would, however, be a mistake to conclude on the basis of the above evidence that throughout the country the commissioners' proceedings with regard to the decimation tax were marked by

---

42   Bod. Lib., Rawlinson MSS, A 33, fos 373–6.
43   Ibid. A 34, fos 225–8.
44   David Underdown, *Somerset in the Civil War and Interregnum* (Newton Abbot, 1973), 180–2.
45   HMC, *Bath MSS*, 4: 281–2.
46   Ivan Roots, 'Swordsmen and Decimators', 84; the letter in question is from Staffordshire Record Office, Leveson Correspondence, D 593, P/8/1/46, Crompton to Leveson 18 Dec 1655.

moderation and leniency. For, while a few of the commissioners may have been discomforted and embarrassed at having to deal with their often more socially elevated neighbours, many others were clearly not; evidence from a number of other counties makes it clear that the generals and the commissioners went to considerable lengths to maximise the yield from the tax, and frequently protested vigorously at what they saw as the central government's over-readiness to exempt some prominent individuals from payment.

In a number of counties the commissioners were clearly not prepared to trust their royalist neighbours' own valuations of their estates. In Sussex they compared the figures presented by the royalists with their own estimates based on the information in the county sequestration books; delivering their first set of returns to Thurloe in late November, Goffe assured him that if they had under-assessed anyone it was only because of a lack of information, and added: 'wee may go higher when we have cleare grounds so to doe'.[47] The Lancashire commissioners also declared themselves unwilling to accept uncorroborated valuations, and those in Lincolnshire sent out messengers to check out the accuracy of the royalists' own assessments.[48] In Cheshire they attempted to achieve accurate valuations by comparing the royalists' own estimates with existing estate surveys, and told the government they intended to conduct fresh ones in disputed cases, and according to Haynes in Norfolk they assessed estates more carefully than the sequestrators had in the 1640s.[49] In November 1655 William Boteler told Thurloe that it was 'the great desire' of the Bedfordshire commissioners to go 'to the utmost bounds of their power' against one royalist who owned valuable woodland in the county.[50] The Essex commissioners even decimated the estate of their major-general's elder brother, Robert Haynes.[51] Instances of open defiance of the commissioners or refusal to pay appear to have been uncommon, but when they did occur the commissioners were

47   Bod. Lib, Rawlinson MSS, A 32, fos 525–8, 809–12.
48   Ibid. A 32, fos 289–92; A 34, fos 561–4.
49   Ibid. A 32, fos 647–50, 871–4.
50   Ibid. A 32, fos 655–8.
51   Cliffe, 'Assessment Lists', 434, 461.

quite prepared to take severe action. When James Compton, Earl of Northampton, publicly refused to give security for his good behaviour, William Boteler and the Northants commissioners threw him in prison, and when Sir John Monson similarly refused to co-operate with the Lincolnshire commissioners, they quartered fifty cavalry on his home and later sequestered his estate.[52]

Again, many of the commissioners clearly believed that the threshold for the tax had been set too high and that as a result many guilty men of modest means were escaping payment altogether. Worsley informed Thurloe in November that the only complaint of the Staffordshire commissioners about the decimation work was that 'the tax was too litle'.[53] Writing to Thurloe from York in mid-December, Robert Lilburne, John Lambert's deputy in Yorkshire, commented that most of the Yorkshire commissioners

> were very desirous the rule might have been £40 and £500, for most of your desperate people, which are a more considerable number than those that are taxt, escape, I may say, unpunished.[54]

The commissioners for North Wales also asked for a reduction in the lower limit as many of their most culpable delinquents fell below it, and those in Northamptonshire called for very low minimum levels of £20 worth of land and £300 of personal estate, 'many of that degree being as dangerous and disaffected to the present government as those of higher quality'.[55]

Soon after the assessment process had begun, it became clear that a sizeable group of royalists was managing to evade payment of the tax by successfully petitioning Cromwell and the council for exemptions or suspensions. By the early spring of 1656 it was a commonplace within the royalist community that the local commissioners were much more hard-line than their masters and that claims for

---

52   Bod. Lib, Rawlinson MSS, A 32, fos 385–8; M. M. Verney, *Memoirs of the Verney Family* (4 vols, 1894), 3: 258; *Calendar of State Papers Domestic 1655–1656*, 50.

53   Bod. Lib., Rawlinson MSS, A 32, fos 679–82.

54   Ibid. A 33, fos 417–20.

55   Ibid. A 32, fos 617–20, 773–6.

leniency would receive a more favourable response in London than in the counties. Writing to a friend in March 1656 from the capital where he was pursuing his own claim for exemption, John Frechevile commented that 'London is thought to be the fittest place for one whom the state makes a rogue to worke in'. He went on to cite the case of the wealthy royalist peer, William Cavendish, Earl of Devonshire, who he claimed had been treated 'most civilly' by Cromwell and his council and had obtained a temporary suspension of payment, but had nonetheless been decimated by 'the implaceable officers in the countrye'.[56]

On a number of occasions the local commissioners went so far as to flout direct orders from London to release individuals from the tax. Frechevile was right about William Cavendish, and his own case also proved his point because, while he was pursuing his case in London, Whalley and the Lincolnshire commissioners sequestered his estate for non-payment.[57] Similarly, despite the fact that Cromwell had excused Thomas Knyvett of Ashwellthorpe in Norfolk from payment in January 1656, the Norfolk commissioners continued to proceed against him and in April they wrote to the Protector to explain why they believed he should pay.[58] The commissioners for Middlesex and Westminster similarly ignored instructions to suspend proceedings against William Russell, Earl of Bedford, and continued to demand £300 from him.[59]

In the light of the above evidence, it is difficult to accept David Underdown's view that the commissions for securing the peace were 'generally less severe than their counter-parts on the old county committees had been'.[60] In many instances the commissioners acted with harshness and obduracy rather than lenience, and much of the royalist community certainly seems to have viewed them as anything but mild. Sir William Sancroft commented to a relative in mid-November that it was 'the opinion of all knowing men I meet with that

---

56   HMC, *Portland MSS*, 2: 141.
57   Ibid. A 35, fos 77–8.
58   Ibid. A 37, fos 361–4; Abbott, *Writings and Speeches of Cromwell*, 4: 82.
59   Bod. Lib., Rawlinson MSS, A 34, fos 357–60, 643–6.
60   Underdown, 'Settlement in the Counties', 175.

there is the greatest and sharpest persecution now falling upon the whole Royall party that they ever yet felt'.[61] A month later one of Sir Edward Nicholas's informants told him that: 'the lieutenants are very severe in exacting the tenths and every gentleman must give in the number of servants, and security for their deportment, so that all show of liberty is lost'. He clearly hoped that the rigour of the major-generals' proceedings might provoke a royalist backlash, for he added: 'I pray the sense and memory of it be not lost too, if they be long used to the burden'.[62] A few days later he again commented that the royalists were 'under the lash' and again predicted that the recent developments might encourage active resistance.[63] In March Nicholas himself reported that as a result of the actions of the generals and their commissioners 'people who never thought of going beyond seas are now meditating how to get out of England speedily'.[64]

IV

In addition to their involvement in the decimation work, local Puritans also supported their major-generals by acting with them to combat what they saw as the disorderliness, immorality and ungodliness of their neighbours and by helping them to remove from the parochial ministry those clergy whom they regarded as politically and religiously incorrect. In August 1654 the government had passed an ordinance 'for ejecting scandalous, ignorant and insufficient ministers and schoolmasters'.[65] This measure had established county commit-tees of 'ejectors' to hear evidence against suspect individuals, but during the following twelve months only a few of these groups appear to have been very active. Hopeful that the major-generals would be

---

61   Bod. Lib., Tanner MSS, vol. 52, fo. 97.
62   PRO, SP 18/102/60A, Ross to Nicholas, 24 Dec 1655.
63   PRO, SP 18/102/76, Ross to Nicholas, 29 Dec 1655.
64   PRO, SP 18/125/54, Nicholas to Jane, 21 Mar 1656.
65   Firth and Rait, *Acts and Ordinances*, 2: 968–90.

able to remedy this situation, the government instructed them to re-activate the local committees of ejectors and oversee their efforts to purge the local ministries. It also ordered them to imprison any ejected ministers who continued to preach, administer the sacraments or marry couples, and to ensure that none of them was employed as a private chaplain or tutor in any royalist household in their districts.[66]

Although some of the major-generals were in the event too preoccupied with their other responsibilities to take this aspect of their brief as fully on board as they would have liked, a number of them, in particular John Desborough, Hezekiah Haynes, Charles Howard, Robert Lilburne, Edward Whalley and Charles Worsley, did manage to devote a significant amount of time to this work. In a number of their counties additional ejectors were nominated by the generals and these new men – many of whom also sat as commissioners for securing the peace of the commonwealth – were galvanised into taking action, frequently proving just as vindictive towards their clerical as their lay enemies. Thomas Holbech, the rector of Chastleton in Oxfordshire, was ejected in late 1655 on the grounds that he had been sequestered and ejected from the vicarage of Epping at the beginning of the civil war. Writing to his friend William Sancroft in March 1656, he commented that he had hoped to keep his royalist past a secret but that 'the malice of some made that knowne soon enough to cut the throate of any such purpose'. He added that the local major-general, Charles Fleetwood, might perhaps have shown him some favour, 'but he acts not at all in person and his commissioners I have noe great fancy unto'.[67] Walter Bushnell, the incumbent of Box in Wiltshire, was another minister who was ejected in 1656. He was so incensed by the way he was hounded and eventually driven from his living by the Wiltshire ejectors that at the Restoration he published a detailed account of the proceedings against him, in which he accused them amongst other things of repeatedly interfering with witnesses and evidence, and relying on the testimony of professional informers.[68]

---

66   Gardiner, *Commonwealth and Protectorate*, 3: 322–4.
67   Bod. Lib. Tanner MSS, vol. 52, fo. 113; see also fos 100, 104, 109, and 141.
68   BL. E.1837.1, *A Narrative of the Proceedings of the Commissioners appointed by Oliver Cromwell for the Ejecting of Scandalous and Ignorant Ministers in*

Thomas Grantham, who was ejected from the living of Waddington in Lincolnshire by five ejectors, three of whom were also commissioners for securing the peace of the commonwealth, similarly complained in print about 'oppressing, hungry, barking, sharking, hollow bellyed committeemen'.[69] The diary of the Essex clergyman, Ralph Josselin, provides another interesting illustration of the uncompromising approach adopted by some of the ejectors. At the end of February 1656 Josselin, the minister of Earls Colne, was summoned along with all the other clergy and schoolmasters in his county to a meeting of the Essex ejectors at Chelmsford. Despite the fact that he was a close personal friend of Haynes and generally well disposed towards Cromwell's government, he was deeply troubled by the 'rigour' of the proceedings and by the extreme hostility the ejectors displayed towards himself and his clerical colleagues. He afterwards commented in his diary:

> for my part I saw no beauty in the day, neither doe I joy to see ministers put under the lay power, and thus on their head. Such is the affection of some that would be counted the first friends of god and religion [that they] hoped wee should have been sent from thence to the Barbados, lord remember us for we are become a reproach.[70]

In the event only the relatively small number of around 150 ministers seems to have been ejected throughout the whole of England as a result of charges of scandal or insufficiency brought against them during the period of the major-generals' ascendancy. The failure to achieve a more substantial purge of the parochial ministry was not, however, the result of any lack of motivation on the part of the local Puritan cliques who assisted the major-generals. It proceeded instead from the length and complication of the procedures that had to be followed before a minister could be removed, the short amount of time

the *Case of Walter Bushnell, clerk* (1660). The answer of one of the commissioners can be found at E.187.5, *An Answer of Humphrey Chambers, Rector of Pewsey [...] to the Charge of Walter Bushnell* (1660).

69   BL, E.1710.2, *A Complaint to the Lord Protector* (1656), 15.

70   Alan Macfarlane (ed.) *The Diary of Ralph Josselin, 1616–1683* (London, 1976), 362–3.

available to the generals before their withdrawal from the provinces in the autumn of 1656, and the absence of any widespread support for the ejectors on the part of the laity.

V

Among the commissioners who proved most active in the sphere of moral reformation were those who worked with Edward Whalley in the east Midlands and Charles Worsley in the north-west of the country. Whalley informed Thurloe in January 1656 that his Lincolnshire commissioners had 'had many plowes agoing', and, despite the continuing demands of the decimation work, were ejecting clergy, suppressing beggars and closing down alehouses 'which were growne to incredible numbers'.[71] Several months later he wrote from Nottingham to report that he and the commissioners of that county

> make it our whole busynes to promote the publique [good], and the lord hath not left us without our encouragement in our undertaking [...] you may ride over all Nottinghamshire and not see a beggar or a wandering rogue.

He added: 'I hope suddenly to have it so in all the counties under my charge'.[72] Whalley also launched the Puritan equivalent of a one-man charm offensive, in what he claimed was a largely successful attempt to win the backing of the godly clergy of his counties. At the beginning of December 1655, he told Thurloe that in Lincolnshire, Leicestershire and Coventry:

> there is a great change in godly ministers; they exceeding well resent [approve of] the busynes. I make it a great part of mine busynes to discuss with as many as I thinke feare God and labour to satisfye them and to gayne their affections by giving them more than an ordinary respect which I thinke they well deserve; they have and I hope shall have as much encouragement as I can give them in

71   Bod. Lib., Rawlinson MSS, A 34, fos 427–30, 561–4.
72   Ibid. A 37, fos 570–3.

the wayes of godlines; they express great affections to his Highness and pray for him in theyr pulpits.[73]

Charles Worsley, meanwhile, and the most active commissioners in Cheshire, Staffordshire and Lancashire were engaged in their own Herculean efforts to effect a moral reformation within their local communities. In early November Worsley told Thurloe that he had been encouraging the 'best of people' within the towns of his area 'to be puttinge in execution the laws against drunkennesse, sweringe, profaining the Lord's Day, and other wickednesses', and had found that 'God hath already put into his people prayinge sperit for this great and goode worke'.[74] He had in fact written to a number of Independent congregations of his association inviting them to send him a list of their reform aspirations and their grievances against their ungodly neighbours. One response from 'the Church of Christ meeting at Altham' in Lancashire exhorted him to establish a magistracy of 'just men fearing God and hating covetousness' and to purge the local ministry of 'profane and heretical ministers who fill most pulpits in the country'; it also encouraged him to punish drunkards and sabbath-breakers, suppress alehouses and take action against non-attendance at church.[75]

Worsley needed little encouragement to pursue these objectives. Within a few weeks he was reporting good success against drunkards and profaners, 'for some towns have made proclamation and take a very strick course and make diligent search every night for such'. Clearly very pleased with his progress, he remarked: 'I cannot but admire at the freenesse of good people of severall judgements to promote this work'.[76] In December he reported that so many trans-gressors had been arrested that the gaols of his association were almost full.[77] During the early months of 1656 his commissioners in Lancashire and Cheshire ordered the closure of as many as 200

73   Ibid. A 33, fos 39–40.
74   Ibid. A 32, fos 373–6.
75   Henry Fishwick (ed.), *The Notebook of the Reverend Thomas Jolley*, Chetham Society, new ser., 33 (1895), 127–8.
76   Bod. Lib., Rawlinson MSS, A 32, fos 871–4.
77   Ibid. A 33, fos 515–18.

unlicensed alehouses in the Blackburn area and a similar number in and around Chester. The Cheshire commissioners also continued to secure large numbers of 'suspicious idle and lewd persons', and imprisoned along with them 'several persons' who had flouted the 1653 civil marriage act by marrying in religious ceremonies. Worsley commented of all this work: 'Those things give matter of rejoicing to the good, and is a terror to the bad'.[78] This relentless pressure for moral reformation in the north-west was sustained into the early summer, but the effort proved too much for Worsley himself and in early June he died after a brief illness. The Cheshire commissioners were clearly very upset by his death, which they described to Thurloe as

> a loss we cannot but be deeply affected with, having had so large and manifest experience of his sincere, zealous and upright endeavours both to [the] discharge of his trust and [the] comfort and satisfaction of good men's spirits.[79]

VI

What then were the impact and repercussions of all this activity? As is made clear in a number of the comments quoted above, in the autumn of 1655 the government and its supporters had had very high hopes of the major-generals. This sense of optimism and purpose had persisted throughout the winter months and by the spring of 1656 some of those who had been active in the shires believed they could see signs that their reform work was beginning to bear fruit. Edward Whalley indeed had perceived some change for the better from as early as the new year when he had reported optimistically to Thurloe:

> our presence I fynde is desired in all places and gives lyfe to all proceedings; besides they look upon it as a favour to them to have us in theyre county [...] You cannot imagine what an awe it hath strucke into the spirits of wicked men,

---

78 Ibid. A 34, fos 693–4; A 35, fos 104–5.
79 Ibid. A 39, fos 366–7.

> what incouragement it is to the godly, yea and I may say through God's mercy how it reconciles them amongst themselves through our weake endeavours.[80]

Charles Worsley was another who believed his tireless efforts were bringing the desirable results. He wrote to Thurloe from Cheshire in March 1656 to assure him:

> Wee are in a very good condition in this county [...] this worke stirs up the good people to informe us of the conversation of all men, their carridge and behaviour, so that, truly, I thinke the good sober people never were in better hart than now, and so much owned.[81]

The following month Rowland Dawkins, James Berry's deputy in South Wales, wrote to Cromwell outlining a similarly positive assessment of the progress in Glamorgan and declaring:

> The effects of our work are very observeable; our enemies being much terrifyed, our freinds encouraged, our peace as much as may be by ev'ry humane ordinance and more (for wee hope this is of God) secured, and sin and wickednesse suppressed. And though it be a dealinge that hath severity in it, compared with what hath bene formerly shewed that party, and therefore greivous to them and best pleasing to us, yet the good people of this countrey judge it very necessary and just; such indulgence hath but hardened them in their mallignity.[82]

But, despite the fact that these men firmly believed that their godly reformation was well underway by the spring of 1656, by the end of the summer it had become all too clear that they had overstated their degree of success and that the reality in the localities was far less acceptable to the government and its allies than these wildly over-optimistic reports suggested. Following the government's decision in July 1656 to summon a second Protectorate parliament, the August election campaign revealed that, while the generals and their commissioners might have succeeded in cowing the enemies of the godly

---

80   Ibid. A 34, fos 561–4.
81   Ibid. A 36, fo. 341.
82   PRO, SP/18/126/50.

into temporary submission, they had made little real progress in their attempts to change their hearts and minds.

Throughout the country the elections were seen as a referendum on the rule of the generals and their godly allies and as such were intensely contested. Desborough reported from the south-west that there were 'great contendings and strugglings in all parts' and that 'the honest people' were 'like to meet with great opposition';[83] Haynes meanwhile remarked that in East Anglia 'every man layd about him, as if his all lay at stake'.[84] In a sermon preached at Stowmarket on the day of the Suffolk poll, the Puritan minster of Lavenham, William Gurnall, made a passionate, last-minute appeal to the voters to return godly MPs, declaiming:

> This day the temper of this nation will be discovered; [there is] no way that I know like this to feel how its pulse beats; and for my own part [...] I cannot look upon it otherwise then as our owning or disowning God to be our God to rule over us; and if the nation do but vouch God to be their God, by a godly choice, I shall not bury my hopes for their future happiness [...] drive him away and Oh how unhappy are thou O England, if thou mayst still have thy God and will not.[85]

He went on to declare that any elector who voted for an unworthy candidate was 'a forsworne wretch' and that 'if thou gettest this brand upon thy forehead once, go where thou wilt, thou dragest a chaine after thee that will bind thee over to the fearful expectation of God's wrath'. This last comment was probably an implicit reference to the Book of Revelation, where a brand on the forehead was identified as one of the defining marks of the Beast, condemning those who carried it to be 'tormented with fire and brimstone'.[86]

In the event, Gurnall's threats and encouragements were widely ignored and, as he had clearly feared, the outcome of the poll proved an extreme disappointment to the godly. All over the country the voters turned their backs on anyone associated with the 'swordmen

---

83   Bod. Lib., Rawlinson MSS, A 41, fos 432–5, 436–9.
84   Ibid. A 41, fos 492–4.
85   BL, E.889.6, William Gurnall, *The Magistrates Pourtraiture* (1656), 26.
86   See Revelation 14: 9.

and decimators' and elected instead many of their most prominent
adversaries. Hezekiah Haynes was one of the more eloquent godly
commentators on these depressing events. On 15 August he told
Cromwell that he and his allies were 'not in these parts without our
dissatisfaction', adding ruefully:

> such is the prevalency of that spirit which opposeth itself to the work of God
> upon the wheele, that the spirits of those that are otherwise minded have been
> much perplexed and discouraged from almost appearing at the election, seeing
> no visible way of ballancing that interest.[87]

A few days later he wrote to tell Thurloe that there was 'a clear
combination' in Norfolk to elect opponents of the regime 'by which
choyce the prophaine malignant and disaffected party and scandelous
ministry are only gratified'. He also informed him that 'if something
[...] be not done for the encouragement of your friends, their spirrits
will in all likelyhood dispond verie much'.[88] A week later one of the
Norfolk commissioners, John Balleston, confirmed his bleak assessment, commenting in a letter he sent him on 1 September: 'We may
perceive by the appearance at the elections the affections of the
people, and I much greve to see what a poor number appered hartilie
for our friends [...] Maney of our seeming friends proved very faynt'.[89]

Thomas Kelsey and the commissioners for Kent were similarly
shocked by the outcome of the county poll at Maidstone. In a letter of
26 August, Kelsey informed the Protector that in Kent the cavaliers
had joined forces with the Presbyterians against 'Swordmen,
Decimators, Courtiers' and 'all those persons that owned Your
Highnes and [the] present government'. He further told him that the
success of this combination of opponents had left the commissioners
very apprehensive about the coming parliament and anxious to see
some sort of purge of members before it met. They were particularly
alarmed that some of the newly elected MPs had declared 'that they
would downe with the Maior Generalls and Decimators and the new
militia', and were convinced that there was

---

87   Bod. Lib., Rawlinson MSS, A 41, fos 492–4.
88   Ibid. A 41, fos 572–5.
89   Ibid. A 42, fos 7–10.

such a perversenesse in the spirits of those that are chosen, that without resolution of spirit in your Highnes and the Councell to maintayne the interests of God's people (which is to be preserved before a thousand Parliaments) against all opposition whatsoever we shalle returne againe to our Egiptian taskmasters.[90]

As these Kentish commissioners had predicted, the election results and the subsequent departure of the generals for Westminster a few weeks later did indeed begin to turn the tables decisively against the local Puritan minorities. All their hopes that with the help of the major-generals they could at long last create godly commonwealths in their provincial worlds were dashed and they were left prey to the powerful local interests they had done so much to antagonise earlier in the year. The deep disappointment of the godly at the withdrawal of the major-generals pervades the whole of a remonstrance that the pastors of a number of the independent churches in Gloucestershire sent the Protector in late 1656 or early 1657. Expressing great unease at the recent turn of events and the rumours that Cromwell might soon be offered the crown, they declared:

We cannot but lay before you to what a height the malignant and persecuting spirrit is of late risen in this nation, how they openly boast of laying levell the Lord's blessed work among his poore people and what affronts and violence they meet withall from that party, especially upon the rumour of the Major-Generalls being voted downe, under whom the Lord's people had comfortable protection.[91]

Despite the failure of the generals and commissioners to achieve their reform aspirations, however, their period of power was of considerable and lasting importance for the political and religious history of the Interregnum. For, through their enthusiastic collection of the decimation tax and their strenuous efforts to eject ungodly clergymen and to purge local society of its irreligious and immoral elements, they had poured a large quantity of salt into the still unhealed wounds inflicted on local society in the 1640s and had

90   PRO, SP/18/129/156, Kelsey to Cromwell, 26 Aug 1656.
91   J. Nicholls (ed.), *Original Letters and Papers of State Addressed to Oliver Cromwell*, (1743), 140.

violently re-activated the old conflicts and animosities that most men and women had been trying hard to forget.

In a letter to Thurloe from Leicester at the end of November 1655, Edward Whalley wrote that he believed the major-generals were obeyed by some men out of 'fear' and by others out of 'respect'. He then struck through 'respect' and substituted for it the word 'love'.[92] Just over a year later in January 1657, the peace of the Bull Inn in Lewes was rudely shattered by a drunken brawl which erupted after one drinker had stated that the decimation tax was 'a mercy in the protector and council in that the cavaliers had forfeited both life and goods', and another had declared 'the plague of God take the decimators and all those that devised decimation'.[93] It is the contention of this essay that the principal objection of the English provinces to the rule of the major-generals was not that it represented rule by the army, nor that it was an unwelcome intrusion by central government into local affairs, but rather that it had empowered deeply unpopular local cliques of Puritans and allowed them to tear away from within at the still fragile fabric of post-war English local society. The fabric survived, but the episode drove another large nail into the coffin of godly rule and paved the way for the emphatic national repudiation of Puritanism which followed the return of Charles II in 1660.

92   Bod. Lib., Rawlinson MSS, A 32, fos 805–8.
93   Ibid. A 46, fos 131–4.

PAUL C.-H. LIM

Adiaphora, Ecclesiology and Reformation: John Owen's Theology of Religious Toleration in Context[1]

> That they had neither care of the truth,
> nor love of peace, nor conscience of scandal,
> nor would by any means be prevailed on
> to lay down their malice and animosities.
> Emperor Constantine[2]

I

In the historiography of early modern Britain, the question of toleration and liberty – political, ideological and religious – has been of paramount importance, whether in reception, repudiation or in re-appraisal of this admittedly modern concept. Among other groups, the Independents have commanded much attention for their putative role in championing religious liberty during the Civil War. Whiggish historians such as W. K. Jordan have found in the Independents and radical Puritans a fertile seedbed for the rise of religious toleration in the modern western world. However, the historiographical paradigm of a steady progression toward greater ideological and religious tolerance and diversity has been questioned by revisionist historians,

---

1   I would like to thank John Coffey, Eamon Duffy and Brent Whitefield for comments on an earlier draft of this paper.
2   Socrates, *Historia Ecclesiastica,* i. 34, cited in John Owen, *Of Toleration,* in W. H. Goold (ed.), *The Works of John Owen,* (16 vols, London, 1850–3), 8: 185. [Hereafter cited as *Works*].

finding instead in early modern England a transitional existence
which, rather than influencing the rise of modernity, owed its
existence to and was influenced by the habits of thought of the late
middle ages, thus giving a more nuanced reading of a society where
ideas of tolerance and intolerance were often locked in intense battles.[3]
    Blair Worden has questioned the by-then historiographical truism
– of W. K. Jordan, William Haller, S. R. Gardiner, to name a few –
that the Independents were instrumental in the rise of religious liberty
and toleration in early modern England.[4] In a seminal article,
'Toleration and the Cromwellian Protectorate', Professor Worden has
convincingly argued that 'puritan theological conservatism' was a
keystone in 'the formation of the government's doctrinal policies in
the Protectorate'.[5] Avihu Zakai and Carolyn Polizzotto have echoed
Worden's position and reconstructed the Independents' stance on
religious toleration during the English Civil War and during the early
1650s, showing that the Independents were more concerned with
preservation of doctrinal orthodoxy rather than liberty for its sake.[6]
More recently, however, John Coffey and Norah Carlin have each
questioned the revisionist perspective, and argued that even within the

3   See Ole Peter Grell and Bob Scribner (eds), *Tolerance and Intolerance in the
     European Reformation* (Cambridge, 1996).
4   W. K. Jordan, *The Development of Religious Toleration in England* (4 vols,
     London, 1932-40); William Haller, *Liberty and Reformation in the Puritan
     Revolution* (New York, 1955); S. R. Gardiner, *The First Two Stuarts and the
     Puritan Revolution* (London, 1878), 136. See also Joseph Lecler, *Toleration and
     Reformation* (2 vols, London, 1960), 2: 453–61; George Yule, *The Independents
     in the English Civil War* (Cambridge, 1958), 13, 45; A. S. P. Woodhouse (ed.),
     *Puritanism and Liberty: Being the Army Debates (1647–49) from the Clarke
     Manuscripts* (London, 1938); Henry Kamen, *The Rise of Toleration* (New York,
     1967), 170.
5   Blair Worden, 'Toleration and the Cromwellian Protectorate', in W. J. Sheils
     (ed.), *Persecution and Toleration* (Studies in Church History 21, Oxford, 1984),
     207.
6   Avihu Zakai, 'Religious Toleration and Its Enemies: The Independent Divines
     and the Issue of Toleration During the English Civil War', *Albion* 21 (1989), 1–
     33; idem, 'Orthodoxy in England and New England: Puritans and the Issue of
     Religious Toleration, 1640–1650', *Proceedings of the American Philosophical
     Society* 135 (1991), 401–41; Carolyn Polizzotto, 'The Campaign against *The
     Humble Proposals* of 1652', *JEH*, 38 (1987), 569–81.

context of mid-seventeenth-century politics and religion, some Puritans were clearly proponents of tolerance.[7]

In the case of John Owen we have an interesting picture – a potential dilemma. Historically it has been assumed that Arminianism and other theologically liberalising tendencies were largely responsible for theories of toleration in the seventeenth century and paved the way for modern liberal political and religious discourses.[8] Despite the number of historians who have been so inclined, looking across the 'historiographical divide' between the Interregnum and the Restoration,[9] there were a number of dissenting theorists of liberty of conscience who were committed Calvinists, not just Arminians. How can we account for this? A simple explanation would be to blame it on the *volte-face* of the erstwhile Calvinist ecclesiastical architects of the Cromwellian church – Owen, Thomas Goodwin and Philip Nye, among others. Another answer might lie in their theological convictions applied in different contexts. Admittedly their attitudes, and particularly Owen's, toward theological and religious dissent was different before and after the Restoration; however, it is important to recognise, as I hope to show, that it was a principled stance which has its ideological foundation in Owen's pre-Restoration theory of liberty of conscience.

Referring to the views of religious conscience and toleration of John Owen, Sir Charles Wolseley, John Humfrey, Slingsby Bethel and William Penn, respectively, Gary De Krey noted that 'each of these

7   John Coffey, 'Puritanism and Liberty Revisited: The Case for Toleration in the English Revolution', *Historical Journal* 41 (1998), 961–85; idem, *Persecution and Toleration in Protestant England, 1558–1689* (London, 2001); Norah Carlin, 'Toleration for Catholics in the Puritan Revolution', in Grell and Scribner (eds), *Tolerance and Intolerance*, 216–30.

8   Though this has usually been associated with Whiggish historiography, even revisionists such as Blair Worden, at least by implication, assume that Arminianism, and especially its 'sinister' sibling Socinianism, tended to foster a *zeitgeist* of tolerance and ideological mutuality. See Worden, 'Toleration and the Cromwellian Protectorate', 202–3.

9   Recent historiography has emphasised the continuity of the issues and personnel that shaped the trajectory of the Restoration ecclesiastical and political settlement. See for example, Tim Harris, Paul Seaward, and Mark Goldie (eds), *The Politics of Religion in Restoration England* (Oxford, 1990).

spokesmen for conscience deserves treatment in his own right'.[10] His call for a more fruitful engagement with the political and theological thought of the above five thinkers, especially of Owen, has yet to be responded to.[11] This essay, then, is part of the effort to fill the historiographical lacuna to provide a contextual reading of John Owen's theology of religious toleration during the Interregnum and the Restoration. Three important criteria in Owen's tolerationist thought will suggest themselves: the rhetoric against imposition of the *adiaphora*, the developed position of Congregationalism and the vision of primitive ecclesiology,[12] and the drive to complete the work

10   Gary S. De Krey, 'Rethinking the Restoration: Dissenting Cases for Conscience, 1667–1672', *H.J.* 38 (1995), 54. Juxtaposing this with Geoffrey Nuttall's comment that 'the more positive, and to some extent new, religious motives which lay behind the Congregational men's opposition to persecution and compulsion in matters of faith have perhaps been insufficiently appreciated', a study of Owen's theology of liberty of conscience perhaps finds further justification. See G. F. Nuttall, *Visible Saints: The Congregational Way, 1640–1660* (Oxford, 1957), 104.

11   To be sure, Christopher Hill, Richard Ashcraft and J. Wayne Baker have treated Owen's theory of religious toleration. However, their treatment has given us either a picture of an erstwhile radical tamed by the adverse turn of events during the Restoration, or that of the radical influence on John Locke, both of which historians such as Gordon Schochet, Richard Greaves and Gary De Krey have challenged. See Christopher Hill, *The Experience of Defeat: Milton and Some Contemporaries* (London, 1984), 170–8; Richard Ashcraft, *Revolutionary Politics and Locke's Two Treatises of Government* (Princeton, 1986), xii–xiii, 42–7, 62–6, 70–4; J. Wayne Baker, 'Church, State, and Toleration: John Locke and Calvin's Heirs in England, 1644–1689', in Fred Graham (ed.), *Later Calvinism: International Perspectives* (Kirksville, 1994), 525–43. For countervailing views, see Gordon Schochet, 'Radical Politics and Ashcraft's Treatise on Locke', *Journal of the History of Ideas*, 50 (1989), 491–510; Richard Greaves, *Deliver Us From Evil: The Radical Underground in Britain, 1660–1663* (Oxford, 1986); idem, *Enemies Under His Feet: Radicals and Nonconformists in Britain, 1664–1677* (Stanford, 1991); De Krey, 'Rethinking the Restoration', 55–6, 67–9, 74, 79.

12   By espousing a congregational autonomy in deciding these controverted points, the Independents diffused the ecclesiastical policy-making power-base, from Lambeth to localities. As R. S. Paul points out, it was this different conception of ecclesiology that drove a wedge between the Presbyterians and the Independents. See his *Assembly of the Lord: Politics and Religion in the*

of reformation.[13] *Adiaphora* became a contentious issue during the Reformation debates, more in England than other European countries. It was usually defined as that which was 'neither good nor bad, neither commanded nor proscribed' in the Word of God, thus (apparently) leaving it to human decisions, without causing harm to the consciences of those who dissented.[14] We will briefly look at the Interregnum context of Owen's position on liberty of conscience, then focus on his Restoration debates on conscience and toleration, especially with Samuel Parker and Edward Stillingfleet.

II

The exact date of Owen's embrace of Congregationalism is difficult to ascertain. From his rare autobiographical reference in his *Review of the true Nature of Schism*, we learn that it was through reading John Cotton's *Keys of the Kingdom of Heaven* (1644) that Owen 'was prevailed on to receive [...] those principles which I had thought to have set myself in opposition unto', thus providing 1644 to be the *terminus a quo*.[15] In June 1645, John Owen was a signatory to a letter written by Thomas Goodwin and other concerned English divines to the Massachusetts General Court, pleading for clemency toward 'some Anabaptists in that Jurisdiction' who were dissenting from the

Westminster Assembly and the 'Grand Debate' (Edinburgh, 1985), 31, 191–4, 199–206, 487–91.

13   John Wilson, *Pulpit in Parliament: Puritanism during the English Civil Wars, 1640–48* (Princeton, 1969).

14   See Bernard Verkamp's *The Indifferent Mean: Adiaphorism in the English Reformation to 1554* (Athens, 1977) and J. H. Primus, *The Vestments Controversy* (Kampen, 1960).

15   *Works*, 13: 223. cf. Nuttall, *Visible Saints*, 16. The best introduction to Owen's life and thought is Peter Toon, *God's Statesman: The Life and Work of John Owen, Pastor, Educator, Theologian* (Exeter, 1971).

ecclesiastical imposition of the Colonial authorities.[16] As the debate in the Westminster Assembly on the issue of toleration and church polity was raging, Owen published 'A Country Essay', an appendix to *A Vision of Unchangeable Free Mercy,* his sermon delivered at the House of Commons on 29 April 1646. Owen warned Parliament and the divines whose zeal for establishing reformed orthodoxy – in doctrine, polity and worship – often found expression in demonizing their ideological 'others':

> Now, I am mistaken if this principle, that the civil magistrate ought to condemn, suppress, and persecute every one that he is convinced to err, though in smaller things, do not at length, in things of greater importance, make Christendom a very theatre of bloody murders, killing, slaying, imprisoning men round in a compass; until the strongest becomes dictator to the rest, and he alone be supposed to have infallible guidance, – all the rest to be heretics, because overcome and subdued.[17]

In this 'Essay', Owen even mentioned the difficulty attendant to 'judge of heresies and heretics', citing Luther, Beza, and Gregory of Nazianzen as those who divulged the abuses – political and ecclesiastical – of the early ecumenical councils.[18] Elsewhere he argued that the persecutorial syllogism, 'He is to suppress evil deeds; heresy is an evil deed: therefore that [heresy] also' was a 'paralogism [...] so foul and notorious' in its logic and utterly devoid of force in argumentation.[19] To demonstrate the evil of magisterial imposition of doctrinal issues and resorting to violence to stamp out heresies, Owen recounted that the early church maintained its pristine doctrinal coherence and clarity, all without recourse to either magisterial intervention or violence:

---

16 The text of this letter is found in *Winthrop Papers*, V, *1645–1649* (Boston, 1947), 23–5.

17 *Works*, 8: 63.

18 Ibid. 8:61. Luther's critique of the Council of Nicea is found in 'Of Councils and the Church', in Jaroslav Pelikan and Helmut Lehmann (eds), *Luther's Works* (55 vols, Philadelphia, 1958–75), 41: 3–178.

19 *Works,* 8: 168.

For three hundred years the church had no assistance from any magistrate against heretics; and yet in all that space there was not one long-lived or far-spreading heresy, in comparison of those that followed. As the disease is spiritual, so was the remedy which in those days was applied; and the Lord Jesus Christ made it effectual [...] but for corporeal punishment to be inflicted on them, in their writings not a syllable.[20]

Ironically, if not tragically, the official sanctioning of Christianity in the Roman empire, Owen argued, brought about the very opposite result of seeing heresies abound: 'Witness Arianism, which had almost invaded the whole world'.[21] Here we notice that, for Owen, primitive ecclesiological purity was compromised by the involvement of the magistrate in spiritual things. The desire to re-discover the pristine purity of the church and the communion of saints was a powerful impetus behind the Congregationalist vision of the church.[22]

By March of 1646, however, judging from Ralph Josselin's diary, Owen seems to have 'proposed a new project for gathering of churches', indicating Owen's move closer toward Independency. And in two years, when Essex ministers were discussing a feasible Presbyterian ecclesiastical settlement, Owen objected to it and 'conceived this too broad, and would have first a separacion to bee

20   Ibid. 183.
21   Ibid. 184. This is not to say that Owen was entirely critical of Constantine. Despite the coalescing of the start of the decline of Christian purity and Constantine's adoption of Christianity as state religion, Owen reported that it was Constantine who proclaimed that 'liberty of worship is not to be denied; and therefore the Christians, as others, should have liberty to keep the faith of their religion and heresy'. Eusebius, *Ecclesiastical History*, x. 5., cited in *Works*, 8: 185.
22   See William Bartlet's significant treatise which amply reflects the ecclesiological concern of the Independents, *Iconographia, Or a Model of the Primitive Congregational Way* (London, 1647). See also Nuttall, *Visible Saints*, 1–2, 43–70, 131–55; T. D. Bozeman, *To Live Ancient Lives: The Primitivist Dimension in Puritanism* (Chapel Hill, 1988). The best treatment of the fascination with the renaissance ethos among English Puritans is J. S. Coolidge, *The Pauline Renaissance in England: Puritanism and the Bible* (Oxford, 1970).

made in our parishes; and that by the minister, and those godly that joyne unto him, and then proceed to choosing'.[23]

Owen's role in presenting *The Humble Proposals* of 1652 and his attack on Socinianism, however, help to contextualise the limits of liberty of conscience.[24] For Owen, only the consciences of those who were 'Reformed, Protestant' and Trinitarian could be tolerated.[25] During the early years of the Cromwellian government, one of the most subversive religious threats came from the Socinianism of John Biddle whose *A Twofold Catechism* caused the Independents to think soberly about the terms and limits of orthodoxy and toleration. It was in this context that the Council of State called upon John Owen to confute Biddle's 'soul-destroying' heresies.[26] Owen's point-by-point refutation of Biddle was published as *Vindiciae Evangelicae*. For our purposes, what is noteworthy is Chapter XXXIV where Owen calls into question Biddle's insistence on the set form of prayer, especially the Lord's Prayer as part of public worship. For Owen, there was no exegetical proof that Jesus meant to impose this – word and spirit – for future generations as part of public worship. And even if he had 'prescribed us a form', that would not weaken Owen's argument since that would simply mean that no human can 'dare to prescribe another'. This refusal to allow for human imposition in public worship was a hallmark of Owen's theology of liberty of conscience which came to the fore in the Restoration debates. As we will see, for Owen, the forms and fixed ceremonies were part of worship in the Old Testament era, but with the advent of Christ, especially after Pentecost, God had given New Testament believers a genuine freedom and liberty in the Spirit. Thus to go back to set forms of prayers as part of public

---

23   Alan MacFarlane (ed.), *The Diary of Ralph Josselin 1616–1683* (Oxford, 1976), 57, 121 [31 March 1646 and 31 March 1648].

24   See Polizzotto, 'The Campaign against *The Humble Proposals* of 1652', 569–81.

25   This was the phrase used to describe the type of Christians whose liberty of conscience would be protected in the Commonwealth. See *Commons Journal*, 7: 397 (7 December 1654).

26   *Calendar of State Papers Domestic 1654*, 3. For John Biddle, see *DNB* and H. J. McLachlan, *Socinianism in Seventeenth-Century England* (London, 1951).

worship was retrogressive.[27] Owen's attack on Biddle over set forms of prayer for public worship was also the very bone of contention between the Puritans and the Laudians; thus, attacking set forms of prayer as part of the warped theological framework of a heretic would serve Owen's polemical purposes well.

Therefore it is not surprising that Thomas Long, who emerged in the Restoration as a leading Anglican polemicist, took up the cudgel to defend the legitimacy of the Lord's Prayer in public worship, and that the Church and the magistrate could sanction its use. Citing Calvin,[28] Beza,[29] the Lutheran theologian Martin Chemnitz[30] and David Paraeus[31] as authorities, Long insisted that there was a general consensus as to the usefulness of the Lord's Prayer, even in public worship. To hit a bit closer to home, Long argued that 'our Assembly' (the Westminster Assembly), and John Ball also endorsed an edifying usage of the Lord's Prayer.[32]

Despite the litany of Protestant and Puritan authorities arrayed to confute Owen, Long did not prevail in this pamphlet attack. Owen did not respond to this treatise, but in a short work entitled *Two Questions concerning the Power of the Supreme Magistrate*, published in 1659, argued against magisterial and human imposition in divine worship, which Owen deemed antithetical to gospel liberty:

> Although the magistrate is bound to encourage, promote, and protect the professors and profession of the gospel [...] yet in such differences about the doctrines of the gospel or ways of the worship of God as may befall men exercising a good conscience, manifesting it in their conversation, and holding the foundation, not disturbing others in their ways or worship that differ from

27   Owen, *Vindiciae Evangelicae*, in *Works*, 12: 577–9.
28   Calvin, *Institutes*, III. 20: 34, cited in Thomas Long, *An Exercitation Concerning the Frequent Use of Our Lords Prayer in the Publick Worship of God* (London, 1658), 50, 58 (where Calvin's letter to Somerset, dated 22 October 1548, is quoted to support Long's position).
29   Beza, *Annotation on the New Testament*, on Luke 11, cited ibid.
30   Martin Chemnitz, *Harmony of the Gospels*, 175, cited ibid.
31   David Paraeus on Matthew 6, cited ibid. 52.
32   Ibid. 53, 56.

them, there is no warrant for the magistrate under the gospel to abridge them of their liberty.[33]

III

Adiaphora had become a shibboleth during the early years of the English Reformation. Those who identified with the reformed theology, particularly that of Huldrych Zwingli of Zurich, were the most vociferous critics of the magisterial imposition of ceremonies in the Tudor Church of England.[34] The Vestiarian Controversy during Elizabeth's reign, John Hooper's dispute with Nicholas Ridley over the usefulness of the *adiaphora* in the Church, and the fall-out among Marian exiles in Frankfurt over the use of the Prayer Book, were just three notable examples demonstrating the explosive potential of the imposition of what many had regarded as 'matters indifferent' (i.e. neither prescribed nor proscribed in the Bible).[35]

Recently, Gordon Schochet pointed out that while the *adiaphora* became a hotly debated issue during the Restoration religious settlement, it failed to generate much historiographical interest.[36] In the context of discussing Samuel Parker's *adiaphorist* argument, Schochet included the exchange between Owen and Parker. This was

33   *Works*, 13:513. See also sermon notes on Owen's Parliamentary sermon delivered on 31 January 1649, Cambridge University Library, MS Add. 4876, fo. 622.

34   See G. W. Bromiley's 'Introduction' to *Zwingli and Bullinger* (London, 1953), 29: 'For Zwingli there were, strictly speaking, no *adiaphora*'.

35   For the theological context of John Hooper's radical anti-*Adiaphorist* position, see John R. Franke, 'The Religious Thought of John Hooper', (unpubl. D.Phil diss. University of Oxford, 1998); Verkamp, *The Indifferent Mean,* 70–6, 150–1. The fall-out among the exiles in Frankfurt is described in Patrick Collinson, *The Elizabethan Puritan Movement* (1967), 33, 72, 153; (William Whittingham), *A Brief Discours off the Troubles begonne at Franckford* (1575).

36   Gordon Schochet, 'Samuel Parker, Religious Diversity, and the Ideology of Persecution', in Roger Lund (ed.), *The Margins of Orthodoxy: Heterodox Writing and Cultural Response, 1660–1750* (Cambridge, 1995), 145, n. 35.

a continuation of a debate which dated back, as mentioned earlier, to the days of the Henrician reformation, and had re-surfaced during the early 1660s. William Bradshaw, a leading light in Jacobean Puritanism, was a vocal critic of human imposition and addition to divine worship whose treatise on the *adiaphora* and worship – first published in 1605 – was reprinted in 1660, connoting the heightened intensity of the debate.[37] Bradshaw argued that since for anything to 'be a *Mean* between two *Extreams*', it must be 'enclining no more to the one than to the other', thus ought not incite 'passions [to be] wrought. Otherwise, the issue or ceremony considered cannot be truly *adiaphorous*'. Thus, unsurprisingly, Bradshaw concluded that 'there is no absolute *Indifferent* thing', hoping to dismantle the logic of the Jacobean conformists.[38]

Owen's critique of the re-established Church of England was based on its imposition of ceremonies and other *adiaphorous* matters: its neglect of pastoral discipline, and the difference between the Dissenters and the Churchmen with regard to edification and reformation. These three *desiderata* will remain consistent throughout Owen's Restoration theological career, including his debate with Samuel Parker and Edward Stillingfleet. First of all, Owen was convinced that imposition of the *adiaphora* and taking of oaths to uphold such newly subscribed matters was the direct cause of 'expel(ling) all peace and union among Protestants', citing the 'Et cetera' oath of 1640 and the 'late oath at Oxford' of 1665 as two examples.[39] In his *Discourse concerning Liturgies,* published anonymously in 1662, Owen argued, using scholastic categories, that there was no distinction between 'circumstantial or accidentary part of God's worship' and 'worship substantially taken, or the substantial parts of it', thus concluding that 'whatever is instituted of God in and

---

37   William Bradshaw, *A Treatise of the Nature & Use of Things Indifferent* (1660 repr.). This was part of a larger reprint work of Bradshaw's eight treatises – originally published between 1604 and 1605 – concerning conformity and the *adiaphora*. For a helpful discussion of the ideological context of Bradshaw and Jacobean Puritanism, see Peter Lake, 'William Bradshaw, Antichrist, and the Community of the Godly', *JEH*, 36 (1985), 570–89.

38   Bradshaw, *A Treatise of the Nature & Use of Things Indifferent*, 19, 22, 23–4.

39   *Works*, 14: 522.

about those circumstances is a substantial part of his worship'. This was designed to disprove the validity of human imposition of the 'circumstantial' parts of worship; for Owen, all of divine worship was to follow the divine blueprint which, by the way, was 'few and easy to be observed', especially as a result of Christ's ministry.[40]

Between Owen and the Restoration Anglican apologists, especially Samuel Parker, there was a consensus that magistrates ought to be involved in upholding public religion, ensuring that vice be stamped out, and encouraging godly ministers.[41] However, Owen was clear that the magistrate *qua* magistrate did not possess any intrinsic right to direct the specifics of the already infallibly ordained worship of God.[42] This was a radical curtailment of the power of the magistrate:

> That the will of God is the sole rule of his worship, and all the concernment of it, and that his authority is the sole principle and cause of the relation of any thing to his worship in a religious manner; and consequently, that he never did, nor ever will, allow that the will of his creatures should be the rule or measure of his honour or worship, nor that their authority should cause any thing to hold a new relation unto him, or any other but what it hath by the law of its creation. And this is the sum and substance of the second commandment.[43]

A Peace Offering, published anonymously in 1667, is representative among Owen's Restoration writings for its succinct and lucid defence of conscience against human imposition. As the persecution against the dissenters mounted, Owen took to writing for liberty of

40   Ibid. 15: 42. See also Owen, *An Answer to Dr. Stillingfleet's Book of the Unreasonableness of Separation* (1681), in *Works*, 15: 421 for a Zwinglian stance on the *adiaphora*.

41   De Krey argues that Owen was joined by Philip Nye and John Humfrey during the late 1660s and early 1670s in drawing 'a sharp distinction between the external sphere of public morality and religious order' and the 'internal sphere of spiritual belief and worship': the former was of magisterial prerogative and the latter of the individual. See De Krey, 'Rethinking the Restoration', 58.

42   *Works*, 15: 43. See also *Truth and Innocence Vindicated* (1669), in *Works*, 13: 381 where Nebuchadnezzar the Babylonian king, and Roman emperors Caligula and Domitian are proffered evidence of usurpation of the divine prerogative to institute terms of worship.

43   *Works*, 15: 38–9.

conscience and for the autonomy of congregational churches. One of the recurring themes of *Peace Offering* is the identification of the 'great concernment in [...] religion' as 'to commend our conscience unto God', especially 'in the things of his own worship'.[44] This idea is recapitulated throughout the treatise to show how guaranteeing the liberty of conscience ensured the security and longevity of the public face of religion and peace. Owen countered the Anglican claim that once religiously indifferent issues are made into law, then it became civic matter, requiring all subjects' obedience. For Owen, this was a slippery slope.[45] Providing the exemplary dilemma and subsequent resolution in St Paul while he was in Rome – in Acts 16:21 – since he was accused of violating the civic mandate of refusing to accept any unsanctioned religion, of which Christianity was one such example, Owen commends Paul's non-violent resistance, for otherwise 'the light and truth of Christianity [...] must have lain shut up in darkness to this day'.[46] That became the ideological bolster for Owen to argue similarly for the case of Restoration Dissent.

During the period of the prorogation of the second Exclusion Parliament, Edward Stillingfleet, then the Dean of St Paul's, London, preached a sermon in May 1680, at the Guildhall. The sermon, subsequently published as *The Mischief of Separation*, went through four printings in less than twelve months, provoking both praise and scorn from Anglicans and Dissenters. The third volume of Owen's *Exposition of the Epistle to the Hebrews* was published around this time, thus helping us to trace some of Owen's own ecclesiology *vis-à-vis* the Church of England. In the *Exposition,* Owen continued his criticism of the Restoration Church of England for its imposition of the *adiaphora* in worship. Worship, for Owen, had reached its 'consummation' in the work of Christ as the 'high priest'. For Owen this meant that while 'carnal minded persons' could 'perform' the outward duties of worship as well in the Old Testament era, in the

---

44   Ibid. 13: 544, 547, 550, 555.
45   Owen was countervailing the Restoration churchmen's claim: 'as though that were grown a civil difference, by the interposition of a law, which before was purely religious', ibid. 549.
46   Ibid. 549–50.

New Testament, God's design of making the 'church unto a more perfect state in point of worship' was fulfilled.

From his exegesis of Hebrews 7:11–12, Owen concluded that the 'Levitical priesthood' stood for ceremonies and temporary things necessary 'for a season', but that with Christ all was made more instructive and less ceremonial, less material and more spiritual, not difficult but easy, and above all giving access to 'the Holy place'. Thus, to add human impositions and ceremonies not specified in God's will was to deny the 'efficacy of ordinances or institutions of worship' revealed in Scripture and through Christ.[47] The right to worship was of such paramount importance in Owen's thought that he even went as far as to argue that if 'a church should impose the observation of *Judaical ceremonies*,[48] and make their observation necessary, though not to salvation, yet unto the order and decency of worship', he would endorse and encourage separation from such churches.[49] 'Order and decency of worship' had been an Anglican slogan since the days of Archbishop Laud. If the Dissenters emphasised edification and individual pursuit of purity away from the mixture of unconverted mass, Anglicans – Laudians and Restoration churchmen alike – were concerned with the corporate and institutional nature of the church and the order, decency and beauty of holiness.[50] Thus Robert Grove bitterly complained that

> there is a *Liturgy,* or Set *Form* of Public Worship prescribed; That there are certain *Ceremonies* injoyned; That the use of these Controverted things gives great *Scandal* to the weak; That they cannot safely joyn in our mixt

47 Owen, *A Continuation of the Exposition of the Epistle to the Hebrews, III* (1680), in *Works*, 21:410, 415, 416–17, 430, 433.

48 This was an allusion to the ecclesiastical policies of imposition in the Restoration.

49 *Works*, 15: 426.

50 For a helpful discussion of the Laudian fascination with order and decency in worship, see Peter Lake, 'The Laudian Style: Order, Uniformity, and the Pursuit of the Beauty of Holiness in the 1630's', in Kenneth Fincham (ed.), *The Early Stuart Church, 1603–1642* (Basingstoke, 1993), 161–86.

Communion; That they leave our Assemblies for the sake of *greater Edification*, which they find elsewhere.[51]

IV

The early church – its faith and practice as well as the Fathers of the Church – were the most common and acknowledged source for theological justification and support. This patristic dependence was true of both the Anglicans and the Puritans.[52] For Owen, the practice of mutual charity and allowance of multiplicity of perspectives concerning issues secondary and tertiary was the lesson he drew from the early church. St Paul's epistle to the Philippians 3:16 is perhaps best known as the text Edward Stillingfleet had used in his famous sermon against the sin of separation and schism of the Dissenters. What has not been noted before was that actually Owen's exegesis of Philippians 3:15-16 was one of the controlling principles for his tolerationist position, as early as 1667.[53] The historical background for this text was the struggle that existed between the Jewish and Gentile believers. Owen argued that in most metropolitan centres, these two churches co-existed harmoniously, perhaps having taken Paul's apostolic exhortation given in Romans 14, yet 'differing as to some

51   Robert Grove, in *A Collection of Cases and other Discourses, Lately Written to Recover Dissenters to the Communion of the Church of England, By Some Divines of the City of London* (1694), 7.

52   For Anglican interest in Patristics, see, Jean-Louis Quantin, 'The Fathers in Seventeenth Century Anglican Theology', in Irena Backus, (ed.), *The Reception of the Fathers in the West: From the Carolingians to the Maurists* (2 vols, Leiden, 1997), 2: 987–1008; J. K. Luoma, 'Who owns the Fathers? Hooker and Cartwright on the Authority of the Primitive Church', *Sixteenth Century Journal*, 8 (1977), 45–59; John Spurr, *The Restoration Church of England* (New Haven, 1991), 107–9, 111, 158.

53   *Works*, 13: 561–2 where his exegesis of Philippians 3: 15–16 is linked thematically with the Pauline injunction in Romans 14 and 15. Not surprisingly Stillingfleet differed from Owen's interpretation of Philippians 3: 15–16 and the supposed link between that and Romans 14.

ceremonial observances'.[54] Taking the statement of Philippians 3:15-16 as acknowledging the diversity within the Christian communion, Owen intoned that '[c]oercion, restraints, corporal punishments, were far from their thoughts, yea, the very exercise of any ecclesiastical power against them who dissented' was an unthinkable course of action.[55]

After five years of state-sponsored persecution of religious dissent, the unexpected fall of Clarendon in 1667 presented itself as a potential reversal (at least modification) of fortune for the Dissenters.[56] However, while Dissenters with Presbyterian sensibilities such as John Humfrey and John Corbet were ardently pleading for comprehension at the heel of Clarendon's impeachment and subsequent fall, Owen was, to their chagrin, vying for toleration, not comprehension.[57]

His critique of the comprehension project and further espousal of the tolerationist rhetoric shows Owen's commitment to his congregationalist ecclesiology. Owen argued that to 'plant the kingdom's peace' on ecclesiastical uniformity was indubitably impolitic.[58] Not only was ecclesiastical uniformity unwise, but more importantly, at least for Owen, it was diametrically opposed to primitive ecclesiology, which clearly denied the co-extensive nature of church and state, a defining character of Christendom for over 1300 years since the days of Constantine:

> The true civil interest of this nation [...] *every Englishman is born unto;* he falls
> into it from the womb; it grows up with him, he is indispensably engaged into it

54   Ibid. 561. Owen also asserted: 'Differences in external rites of worship which were found amongst them, where the substance of faith was preserved, they looked upon as no breach of union at all'. Ibid. 563.

55   *Works*, 13: 561–2.

56   D. R. Lacey, *Dissent and Parliamentary Politics in England, 1661–1689* (New Brunswick, 1969), 55.

57   Ibid. 56.

58   Owen, *Indulgence and Toleration Considered* (1667), in *Works*, 13: 531. See also ibid. 573, 586, where Owen quotes Tacitus (*Annales,* xv. 44) to argue that the misery of Christians tended to strengthen, not weaken, their conviction, thus actually increasing the subversive potential of those long under persecuting hands of the regime.

[...] and is not at liberty to dissent from the community. But as for religion, it is the choice of men, and he that chooseth not his religion hath none.[59]

Recently Mark Goldie has convincingly demonstrated that the Restoration Anglican church was a persecuting institution. Apologists for this Augustinian just-persecution theory were quite numerous, and in addition to merely theological rationale, other factors such as political fear that the Dissenters were agents of the Jesuits, a hackneyed argument the erstwhile leaders in the Cromwellian Church had used against the Laudians, was brought to the fore of the national consciousness.[60]

Owen argued that the case with Protestant dissent in England was analogous to the case between Cain and Abel, a Puritan self-fashioning at the expense of the demonised Anglican prelatists.[61] Over against Stillingfleet's argument that if the Dissenters were willing to acknowledge in private that the Church of England was a true church, then it should lead to communion in public worship, Owen stressed that:

> This is one of the greatest evils that attend this controversy. Men are forced by their interest to lay more weight on a few outward rites and ceremonies, which the world and the church might well have spared, had they not come into the minds of some men [...] than upon the *most important graces and duties* of the gospel. Hence, communion in faith and love is scarce esteemed worth taking up in the streets, in comparison of uniformity in rites and ceremonies! Let men be as void of [...] true gospel faith [...] yet if they comply quietly with, and have a

59 *Works*, 13: 532.

60 Three of the most representative Augustinian henchmen during this period were: Richard Perrinchief, Thomas Long and Samuel Parker. Unsurprisingly, Owen comes to blows directly with Parker and Long. See Goldie, 'The Theory of Religious Intolerance in Restoration England', in O. P. Grell, J. Israel and N. Tyacke (eds), *From Persecution to Toleration* (Oxford, 1991), 331–68. See *Works*, 13: 556 where he speaks of the utter impossibility of cultural, epistemological and intellectual, let alone religious uniformity, thus critiquing the zeal of the Restoration church for their Sisyphean endeavour.

61 See especially Owen's commentary on Hebrews 11: 4 on the example of Abel whose faith was commended, above all, for right worship – externally and internally. For puritan self-fashioning see Margo Todd, 'Puritan self-fashioning: the Diary of Samuel Ward', *Journal of British Studies*, 31 (1992), 236–64.

little zeal for, those outward things, they are to be approved of as very orderly members of the church![62]

Thus, even though the Church of England did possess true marks of the church, since 'the generality of their members are openly wicked in their lives, and they have no lawful or sufficient ministry', Owen could not acknowledge it as a true church insofar as a church with which he was willing to communicate and join.[63]

Owen wondered out loud if 'we are some of the first who ever anywhere in the world, from the foundation of it, thought of ruining and destroying persons of THE SAME RELIGION with ourselves, merely upon the choice of some peculiar way of worship in that religion'.[64] Moreover, Owen provided a cogent critique of the Augustinian theology of *compelle intrare* (Luke 14:23), forcing of the human conscience in view of the future benefit of a broken yet conforming conscience:

> Now let others do what they will, conscience will still make this judgment, nor can it do otherwise. Whatever men can alter in the outward actings of men's lives, they can alter nothing in the inward constitution of the nature given it by God in its creation, which refers to its future end. How can this be forced?[65]

---

62   *Works*, 15: 395. Owen's position had much similarity with Edward Bagshaw's who stressed the counterintuitive nature of the Restoration ecclesiastical policies. Bagshaw argued that imposition of the indifferent things 'brings in the Essence, though not the Name of *Popery*' and that by imposing severe penalties for nonconformity, 'we seem to lay as much [...] stress upon these *Indifferent things*, as upon any the most material parts of our Religion'. Bagshaw, *The Great Question Concerning Things Indifferent* (London, 1660), 11, 12.

63   *Works*, 15: 396.

64   Ibid. 13: 526.

65   Ibid. 527. Elsewhere, Owen argues that religious coercion will often bring about the *opposite* of the desired effect: 'for no man, surely, is so vain as to imagine that compulsion and penalties are a means suited to persuade or convince the minds of men; nay, commonly it is known that they have a contrary effect, and do exceedingly confirm men in their own persuasions, and into an alienation from the things they are compelled unto'. Ibid. 533. Augustine's exegesis of Luke 14: 23 and its context of the Donatist controversy is in one of Augustine's letters: 'You are of opinion that no one should be compelled to follow righteous-ness; and yet you read that the householder said to his servants, "Whomsoever

However, Owen emphasised that the Church of England, as judged by the Thirty-Nine Articles, was doctrinally sound and based on its soteriological stance there were no real grounds for separation.[66] Consequently, this approbation of the Restoration Church as being in doctrinal agreement with the Dissenters then problematised the cause of Dissent, for as Anglican apologists such as Parker, Perrinchief, Thomas Long and Stillingfleet had bitterly argued, to separate over non-doctrinal issues was tantamount to schism and separation. And Anglican apologists buttressed their position by citing numerous magisterial reformers themselves. Bucer's approbation of the existence of liturgies, Melanchthon's specific endorsement of the *adiaphora*, and Calvin's twofold marks of the church – preaching and sacraments – were proffered as endorsing the Restoration Anglican polemic.[67] Therefore, it was incumbent upon Owen to base his plea for toleration on issues of worship and the virtually wholesale absence of pastoral discipline alone, projecting them to be of paramount signifi-cance. However, criticism of half-reformed Anglican worship and its

ye shall find, compel them to come in" [...] You are also of opinion that no coercion is to be used with any man in order to his deliverance from the fatal consequences of error; and yet you see that, in examples which cannot be disputed, this is done by God': *Letter* 93.2.5 (to Vincentius, A.D. 408); cf. *Letter*, 173.1 (to Donatus, A.D. 416).

66   Though on the whole Owen approved the doctrinal stance of the Anglican church, at other times he was an unambiguous critic of the Arminian innovation, which, to him, was prompted by the decline of Calvinist orthodoxy in the Jacobean and Caroline Church. For instances of approbation, see *Works*, 13: 354 where Owen argues: 'the chief glory of the English Reformation consisted in the purity of its doctrine, then first restored to the nation. This, as it is expressed in the articles of religion, and in the publicly-authorised writings of bishops and chief divines of the church of England, is, as was said, the glory of the English Reformation.' See also *Works*, 13: 182–206, 551–2, 554, 555; 2: 304. For instances of disapproval due to Arminian innovation, see *Works*, 14: 520–7; 2: 279–80.

67   See for example, Thomas Long's *Calvinus Redivivus; or, Conformity to the Church of England* [...] *Perswaded by Mr. Calvin* (1673); William Saywell, *Evangelical and Catholick Unity* (1682), 228–45 (Bucer); 246–55 (Luther); 256–61 (Melanchthon); 261–71 (Calvin); Francis Fullwood, *Humble Advice to the Conforming and non-Conforming Ministers and People* (1673), 86; idem, *Doctrine of Schism Fully Opened* (1672), 135–6.

attendant vices had been a consistent part of the Puritan polemic against the Church of England, thus it was not surprising to find Owen resorting to it as a way of legitimating the more radical Dissenters' wish for toleration. The fervour for true worship and the corresponding contempt of false worship had been a staple part of Owen's theological vocabulary. In his sermon delivered at the Commons on 31 January 1649, when the nation was still reeling from the shock of the unprecedented regicide of Charles I, Owen hammered away at the theme of false worship, especially how it precipitates the irreversible destruction of a nation when 'superstition and persecution, will-worship[68] and tyranny' rule; they become the 'procuring causes' and portents of sure disasters.[69] Thus it was a theological imperative for Owen – before and after the Restoration alike – to keep the purity of gospel worship intact.

This pursuit of the purity of worship required less than what was considered important for prayer book Anglicans: no Prayer Book, no ceremonies, and no altar. Owen had argued that one of the characteristics of the primitive church was not liturgical uniformity, but precisely the opposite: flexibility and freedom, mutuality and multiplicity of perspectives. Citing Origen for support, Owen argued that the early Christians recognised the intrinsic inevitability of flexibility over secondary and tertiary issues, one of which was over outward ceremonies and rites. So long as there was no compulsion to observe one tradition over another, there was *pax Christi* in the Church.[70] This 'variety of judgment and difference in practice', a mark of the new covenant worship, 'from the days of the apostles' was an

---

68   For the Puritan criticism of 'will-worship' of the Laudian church, see for example, Daniel Cawdrey, *Diatribe Triplex: or A Threefold Exercitation, Concerning* [...] *Will-worship* [...] *With the Reverend and Learned Dr Hammond* (1654); idem, *The Vindication of the Three-fold Diatribe* (1658; William Fenner's *Four Select Sermons* [...] *wherein the Idolatry and Will-worship of the Church of Rome is* [...] *Confuted, &c.* was published in 1668, indicating the depth of controversy the issue of liturgy and additions of worship had become.

69   *Works*, 8: 137–8, 143.

70   Ibid. 13: 563. Aside from Origen (*Adversus Celsus*, Bk. III), Owen also cited Justin Martyr's *Second Apology* and Ignatius' letter to the Philadelphians.

abiding quality of the visible church, thus to hold the Dissenters to be schismatics over the issues where no consensus had existed, was a betrayal of Christian charity.[71] In fact, the persecutory innovation in the church was in large measure attributable to the rancour caused by the Arian heresy. Arius had become a specially-targeted *persona non grata* during this period of intense polemic. Anglicans, including, yet not limited to Peter Heylyn[72], identified Arian's most dastardly error as his rejection of episcopal authority over him. The Dissenters, however, highlighted the violent persecution provoked by Arius as the main problem. Owen's emphasis of the primitive diversity of liturgical expression was designed to rectify the misdirected effort of the Churchmen in looking to the early church for *jure divino* episcopacy. Owen further charged the Anglican church with being duplicitous, for internecine doctrinal differences of greater import – for example, the Calvinist vs. Arminian divide – existed within the Church of England.[73]

Lastly, for Owen, the very point of dispute between Daniel Cawdrey and himself, the true nature of the gospel church, was re-hashed during the Restoration. The congregational nature of all the early churches was the lynchpin with which Owen attacked Parker and Stillingfleet and other Anglican apologists. Thus he argued that:

> there was no church before the end of the second century of any other species, nature, or kind, but a *particular congregational church* only, as hath been proved before. Let any one instance be produced of a church of one denomination, national, provincial, or diocesan, or of any other kind than that which is congregational, and I will give over this contest.[74]

---

71   Ibid. 553.
72   See Peter Heylyn, *Aerius Redivivus: or, The History of the Presbyterians* [...] *From the year 1536, to the year 1647* (1670).
73   *Works*, 13: 568: 'In the meantime, we know that the most of them who agreed together to press for severity against us for dissenting from them do differ among themselves in things of far greater importance in the doctrine of the gospel than those are wherein we differ from them'. For the Calvinist-Arminian theological divide in the Church of England up to the time of the Civil War, see Nicholas Tyacke, *Anti-Calvinists: the Rise of English Arminianism c. 1590–1640* (Oxford, 1987).
74   *Works*, 15: 441.

Instead of giving over the contest, Owen was certain that the English diocesan system was a positive impediment to a true reformation.

V

As one historian recently commented the 'dissenting agenda for reformation' during 1679-82, its emphasis on individual choice and liberty in religious matters was a call for 'the complete abandonment of the church settlement of 1662-65', striking 'at the heart the persecuting church championed by Restoration Anglicanism'.[75] However, when Owen's pre-Exclusion Crisis (1679–82) writings are examined, the rhetoric of returning to the purity of the early church is clearly discernible, providing the precedent for the renewed emphasis during the tumultuous years of the Popish Plot when both Anglicans and Dissenters were claiming themselves to be the true heirs of the reformation.

Religious persecution, in Owen's mind, was inconsistent with reformation. In a re-definitional exercise, Owen pushed the reformation back to the first Advent of Christ, thus giving two emphases. Firstly, positing a radical discontinuity between the Old and the New Testaments. We have already seen, in our discussion of the weakness and shadowy nature of the Old Testament worship, that Owen regarded the Old Testament as the preparatory stage before the beginning of true reformation and the climax of revelation in Christ. Secondly, he stressed the continuity between the apostolic and early church and the current dissenting churches. They were both anti-persecutorial and allowed for a multiplicity of liturgical perspectives without human imposition.[76] In that sense, Owen could extol the

---

75   Gary De Krey, 'Reformation in the Restoration Crisis, 1679–1682', in Donna Hamilton and Richard Strier (eds), *Religion, Literature, and Politics in Post-Reformation England, 1540–1688* (Cambridge, 1996), 234.
76   See especially his *A Discourse on Liturgies and their Imposition*, in *Works*, 15: 54–5. See also ibid. 13: 12 where Owen criticises the hermeneutical 'confusion'

suffering endured by the early church of the 'first reformation',[77] lament the treachery of the council of Constance and emperor Sigismund in reneging on the original safe conduct and in killing John Huss and Jerome of Prague,[78] offer both encomium for Cranmer and other framers of the Edwardian Prayer Book while reminding the readers that their reform was self-admittedly fragmentary and incomplete,[79] and finally encourage the members of numerous Interregnum Parliaments to get back to the zeal of the 'real reformation'.[80]

John Spurr has commented that for the Restoration churchmen to acknowledge the validity of the Dissenters' separation and to relax the terms of comprehension was 'tantamount to a recognition of the Dissenters' case for separation', and to betray the historical legacy and legitimacy of the anti-dissent ecclesiastical policies of the English church, and most significantly to admit that the Anglican pattern of reformation was not always licit and edifying.[81] Peter Heylyn, for instance, devoted his literary skills and energies to write the true history of the English Reformation. Following the examples of Cyprian and Augustine, the Restoration churchmen were careful to emphasise that a true reformation was always carried out in unity.[82]

among Anglicans, specifically referring to Herbert Thorndike's *Of Religious Assemblies and the Public Service of God* (1642) where Thorndike looks to the Old Testament examples and precepts to develop an Anglican blueprint for liturgy and worship.

77   *Works*, 13: 547.
78   Ibid. 565.
79   Ibid. 15: 29. See also ibid. 206–8.
80   Ibid. 8: 422–3, 424–5.
81   John Spurr, 'Schism and the Restoration Church', *JEH*, 41 (1990), 420–1; idem, 'The Church of England, comprehension and the Toleration Act of 1689', *EHR*, 104 (1989), 941–3.
82   (John Fell), *Of the Unity of the Church* [...] *written* [...] *by Cyprian Bishop of Carthage and Martyr* (Oxford, 1681). Augustine's anti-Donatist polemic was effectively utilised by the Restoration churchmen to persecute and stamp out dissent: see Mark Goldie's excellent essay, 'The Theory of Religious Intolerance in Restoration England', in *From Persecution to Toleration*, 331–68. *The Judgment of* [...] *St. Augustine, Concerning Penal Lawes Against Conventicles, and for Unity in Religion. Deliver'd in his 48th Epistle to Vincentius*

Owen, while commending the Edwardian reformers for their adherence to the word of God and for their zeal in pushing forward the reform, nevertheless pointed out the incomplete nature of their work, especially as regard the ceremonial issues. There were two reasons why liturgical imposition had to have been necessary before the time of the reformation: first, the 'disability of the present ministers of the churches to celebrate and administer the ordinances [...] to the honour of God and edification of the church', and secondly, the 'great importance of uniformity in the worship of God'. If such unreformed nature of the church necessitated liturgical impositions, as was the case in the Edwardian reformation (and Owen is not too critical of that), then they surely could not be made a fixture in the ecclesiastical life, for according to Owen, the church was to be reforming into the primitive pattern all the time, soon bringing about a 'timely expiration' of the Prayer Book liturgy.[83] To Owen, this was the legacy of the Edwardian reform which subsequent generations of reform-minded Protestants ought not to have owned; thus it was ludicrous to stay content with the imposition of the *adiaphora*.[84] Moreover, Owen's encomium of the episcopal reformers of the sixteenth century provided the requisite ammunition to critique the doctrinal deviation of the late seventeenth-century churchmen, especially Samuel Parker.[85]

(London, 1670) was reprinted to set forth Augustine as the apologist for the Anglican insistence on ecclesiastical unity and anti-separatism. Peter Heylyn left a rich historiographical legacy for the Church of England. Representative of his *apologia* for the Laudian and Restoration Church are: *Ecclesia Vindicata; or, The Church of England Justified* (London, 1657); *Ecclesia Restaurata; or, The History of the Reformation of the Church of England* (London, 1661); *Examen Historicum* (London, 1659); *Aerius Redivivus; or, The History of the Presbyterians* [...] *from* [...] *1536 to* [...] *1647* (London, 1670); *Cyprianus Anglicus: or, The History of the Life and Death of* [...] *William* [...] *Archbishop of Canterbury* (London, 1668).

83   *Works*, 15: 29–32.

84   Owen's view was also echoed in (Vincent Alsop), *Melius Inquirendum, or a Sober Inquiry* (London, 1681 edn), 31, 37; *A Proposal of Union Amongst Protestants* (London, 1679), 3.

85   *Works*, 13: 355.

Two different conceptions of edification also entailed two divergent views of reformation. Owen conceived the primary impetus of reformation to be individual believers and pastors in union with Christ, the aggregate sum of this individual union giving rise to a community of believers in a church. Neither reforming of the nation's 'faith by statute'[86] nor reformation by prelatical bishops could be envisaged, and that is why Owen's rhetoric of toleration was often couched in the language of a continuing reformation. For Owen, to complete effectively the work of reformation, no imposition of indifferent matters could be allowed. Such was precisely what Parker and Stillingfleet were calling for, and more crucially, the systematic fault within prelatical episcopacy was too great to be tolerated by anyone who seriously contemplated the work of reformation.

In fact Owen criticised the Restoration Church, turning the polemic of schism on its head, and argued that since the Church of England was not placing any more emphasis on conversion and edification, they were part of the *'fundamental causes of our divisions'*. Moreover, the virtual collapse of congregational discipline, Owen argued, robbed the established Church of one necessary tool for further reform. Consequently, he ruefully warned, '[n]either will things have any better success where the *discipline degenerates into an outward forcible jurisdiction and power*'.[87]

However, it was not until Owen's debate with Stillingfleet that the cause of the Reformation was brought to the fore of the polemic. Stillingfleet had charged the Dissenters with weakening 'the *Cause* of the *Reformation*' with their separatistic zeal. To bolster his claim, Stillingfleet quoted heavily from Calvin's *Institutes*. Moreover, Jean Daillé, Moise Amyraut, and Francis Turretin's anti-Roman writings were adduced as further proof of the damnable sin of unjustifiable separation.[88] Owen's answer to this charge was somewhat ambiguous,

---

86 See Norman Jones, *Faith by Statute: Parliament and Settlement of Religion, 1559* (London, 1982).

87 *Works*, 15: 115–16, 116–25, 121, 100; ibid. 433.

88 Stillingfleet, *The Unreasonableness of Separation* (London, 1681), 178–87. Calvin's *Institutes*, IV.i.9–19; IV.ii.1–6 were cited as proof of his anti-separatistic stance.

for herein Owen and his dissenting colleagues faced a dilemma. Could they justify their separation from the Church of England without having to hear from the Roman Catholics that such fissiparous and ever-dividing outcome is the richly deserved harvest of the first separation? Owen argued that the Church of England had right doctrine and possessed the two marks of the true church, but the main problem was the lack of desire for further reform:

> That though a church [...] do [*sic*] not profess any heinous error in doctrine [...] yet there may be sufficient reasons to refrain from its communion in church order and worship, and to join in or with other churches for edification; that is, that where such a church is not capable of reformation, or is obstinate in a resolution not to reform itself, under the utmost necessity thereof, it is lawful for all or any of its members to reform themselves, according to the mind of Christ and the commands of the gospel.[89]

Moreover, contrary to Stillingfleet's claim, Owen argued that 'the whole cause of the Protestant's separation from the church of Rome is strengthened and confirmed' by the Dissenters' refrain from communion with the Church of England. Principles of the Reformation which Owen owned for the cause of Dissent were: *sola scriptura,* the priesthood of all believers, absolute anti-popery. *Sola scriptura* was used by the Protestants to inveigh against the Catholic additions of traditions and the Apocrypha, among other things, as ways of having diluted the purity of the gospel. Much as the Dissenters agreed with the Thirty-Nine articles, they nonetheless dissented concerning the additional ceremonies that went beyond the principle of *sola scriptura*, as interpreted through the hermeneutics of the Puritans. The priesthood of all believers was an ambiguous principle for the magisterial reformers since this maxim was often taken to its extreme position of levelling all distinctions lay and clerical, and was associated – in their minds – with subversive anticlericalism.[90] However, for those who had embraced a Congregationalist ecclesiology, this was a welcome polemical tool to wield,

---

89   *Works*, 15: 397.
90   See Willem Balke, *Calvin and the Anabaptist Radicals* (Grand Rapids, 1981).

especially as the Anglicans were arguing that the laity had no power to choose its own pastors. Owen noted:

> This principle of the Reformation, in vindication of the rights, liberties, and privileges of the Christian people, to judge and choose for themselves in matters of religion, to join freely in those church-duties which are required of them, without which the work of it had never been carried on, we do abide by [...]. Yea, we meet with no opposition more fierce than upon the account of our asserting the liberties and rights of the people in reference unto church order and worship.[91]

In an oblique reference to the Laudian overtures made before the Civil War, prompted more recently by such events as the secret Treaty of Dover of 1670,[92] the Popish Plot of 1678–81,[93] and the further intensifying of persecution of the Dissenters,[94] Owen had enough confidence to claim that 'so far as there is a declension from this principle [of anti-Popery], so far the cause of the Reformation is weakened, and the principal reason of separation from the Roman church is rejected'.[95]

Finally, it must be remembered that for Owen true liberty of conscience, as secured by the reformation principle of the priesthood of all believers, would be a catalyst for further reformation in the church. The Church of England, though a real church, had no concrete plans for reformation, nor did its 'dalliances' with Popery and

---

91   *Works*, 15: 403–4.
92   Lacey, *Dissent and Parliamentary Politics*, 60, 63.
93   See Jonathan Scott, 'England's Troubles: Exhuming the Popish Plot', in Harris, Seaward, and Goldie (eds), *The Politics of Religion in Restoration England*, 108–31.
94   Richard Ashcraft commented that the period centring 1670 marked 'a significant intensification of the political persecution of religious dissidents', thus helping us to situate the historical context of Owen's tolerationist writings. See Richard Ashcraft, 'John Locke, Religious Dissent, and the Origins of Liberalism', in Gordon Schochet (ed.), *Restoration, Ideology, and Revolution* (Washington, 1990), 152. See also G. Lyon Turner, *Original Records of Early Nonconformity under Persecution and Indulgence* (3 vols, London, 1911), 3: 56; Victor Sutch, *Gilbert Sheldon: Architect of Anglican Survival, 1603–1688* (The Hague, 1973), 115.
95   *Works*, 15: 404.

damning of Dissent show any hope for ecclesiastical re-union, a hope
that was much dimmer than Owen was prepared to perhaps admit.

VI

Describing the rhetoric of toleration among the Dissenters, De Krey
explains that:

> Like the sectarians they embraced religious pluralism despite their attachment
> to a state church. They were utterly confident of the ability of individuals of
> different religious persuasions to 'live peaceably and quietly' under a regime
> devoted to liberty of conscience, an optimistic perspective that separated them
> from the conservative anthropology of traditionalist cases for uniformity.[96]

In terms of traditional theological anthropology it was actually the
Calvinists – of whom Owen was perhaps England's best known in his
life-time – not the Arminianising tendencies of the established Church
that had a less 'optimistic perspective'. Then, how does one account
for the claim of De Krey? The answer seems to lie in ecclesiological
differences. Since Owen and his Independent colleagues believed in
gathered churches of believers, since the Restoration Church of
England, though possessing of correct doctrine in the Thirty-Nine
Articles, was jeopardizing its purity and ecclesial validity due to a
woeful lack of discipline, and since the Dissenters' idea of reformation
held liturgies and impositions to be unnecessary if not positively
detrimental elements, it was inevitable that Owen, one who was so
committed to doctrinal orthodoxy, would be committed to religious
toleration as well.

The development of Restoration Anglican ecclesiology in a more
Roman Catholic direction, and its attendant view of the reform of the
church made dim the prospect of reconciliation between the Church
and Dissent.[97] Perhaps the political exigencies of the period called for

---

96   De Krey, 'Rethinking the Restoration', 80.
97   See John Spurr, 'Schism and the Restoration Church', 423. One of the earliest
     'warnings' to the 'defection' of the Laudians from the true legacy of the
     Reformation came from, not surprisingly, Richard Baxter, the leading Puritan

the granting of toleration in 1689. However, it is important that for Owen – and by extension other Independent Dissenters – a theology of religious toleration was based on his opposition to imposition of the *adiaphora*, congregationalist ecclesiology, and a vision of reforming the church which could only be allowed to practise outside the pale of a national church. The 'Protestant uniformity' pushed for during the Restoration soon gave way to the 'Protestant diversity' and pluriformity of the Glorious Revolution. Owen, albeit failing to anticipate the religious indifference that arose from a great multiplicity of religious perspectives, made a contribution to this diversity which, though incidental, was not insignificant.[98]

anti-papal polemicist. In his *Grotian Religion Discovered* (London, 1658), he divided the Episcopal men into two camps, the 'good old' episcopal men such as James Ussher, John Davenant, Joseph Hall, and Thomas Morton, among others, and the 'Grotian or Cassandrian Papists', who were theologically Arminian and allegedly aspiring an ecclesiastical re-union with Rome. On Baxter, see Lamont, 'False Witnesses? The English Civil War and English Ecumenism', in Bonney and Trim (eds), *The Development of Pluralism in Modern Britain and France.*

98   For the shift from a Protestant nation to a nation of Protestants, see C. John Sommerville, *The Secularization of Early Modern England: From Religious Culture to Religious Faith* (Oxford, 1992); De Krey, 'Reformation in the Restoration Crisis, 1679–1682', 248.

BRIAN E. STRAYER

The Edict of Fontainebleau (1685) and the Huguenots: Who's to Blame?

Much shorter in length than Henri IV's Edict of 1598, Louis XIV's Edict of 1685 repealed all acts of toleration granted the Huguenots over the past eighty-seven years. Its twelve articles ordered their remaining temples and schools destroyed and public worship prohibited. Provincial pastors were given two weeks to leave France or be sent to the galleys. Reformed infants must be baptised as Catholics and sent to Catholic schools; all children could be forcibly converted at seven. Calvinists caught attempting to escape faced life-time galley servitude for men and life imprisonment for women with state seizure of their goods; those who had already left France had four months to return and convert or their property would also be confiscated.[1] The bishops believed that without public places to meet, Reformed worship would soon degenerate into meaningless opinions. They failed to understand how Bible readings, psalm singing, and family prayers could be a viable way of passing on the faith to the next generation. Therefore, unlike the Holy Roman Empire, where *cujus regio ejus religio* forced Christians not sharing their ruler's faith to emigrate, Louis XIV's edict allowed the Calvinists to remain in France and worship privately.[2]

---

1   Daniel Ligou, *Le Protestantisme en France de 1598 à 1715* (Paris, 1968), 249; Eugen Bellon, *Scattered to All the Winds, 1685–1720: Migrations of the Dauphiné French Huguenots into Italy, Switzerland, and Germany* (West Lafayette, 1983), 23–4; William Carlos Martyn, *A History of the Huguenots* (American Tract Society, 1866), 510–12; Janine Garrisson, *L'Édit de Nantes et sa révocation: histoire d'une intolérance* (Paris, 1985), 12; Henry M. Baird, *The Huguenots & the Revocation of the Edict of Nantes* (New York, 1895), 28.

2   Daniel Ligou, 'La Peau de Chagrin (1598–1685)', in Philippe Wolf (ed.), *Histoire des Protestants en France* (Toulouse, 1977), 150; Margaret Maxwell,

Despite cancelling his grandfather's Edict of Nantes, Louis XIV never intended that the Revocation become a holocaust. The Huguenots, influential in commerce, government, and industry, were too important to the kingdom to risk their expulsion. For decades the French Calvinists had praised their monarch for his benevolent laws and tolerant attitudes toward them. Despite increasing pressure in the 1640s and 1650s by groups like the Company for the Propagation of the Faith and the Company of the Most Holy Sacrament to crush heresy, Louis XIV steadfastly resisted their demands for harsher laws against the Reformed. Why then, did he change his mind? In an absolute monarchy where the king ultimately determines religious policy, what person or group had sufficient influence to persuade Louis XIV to alter the course of the ship of state? An analysis of several power brokers, discussed below, leads to the conclusion that only the General Assembly of the Clergy, with its enormous *dons gratuits* in lieu of taxation, possessed the financial lobbying power to convince Louis XIV to crack down on the Huguenots.

Some have seen Louis XIV's midlife conversion after his secret marriage to Madame de Maintenon in 1684 as a search for respectability, a desire to regularise his private life while bringing order and stability to religious affairs and confessional unity between Catholics and Huguenots.[3] The Englishman Gilbert Burnet, travelling in France in 1685, specifically blamed the king's religion, but not the king himself, for the persecution of the Protestants:

> I do not see that the French King is to be so much blamed in this matter as his Religion is, which, without question, obligeth him to extirpate Heretics, and not to keep his Faith with them: so that instead of censuring him, I must only lament his being bred up in a Religion that doth certainly oblige him to divest

'The Division in the Ranks of the Protestants in 18th-Century France', *Church History*, 27 (1958), 108; Charles Gérin, 'Innocent XI et le révocation de l'Édit de Nantes', *Revue des Questions Historiques*, 24 (1878), 420–21; Geoffrey Adams, *The Huguenots and French Opinion* (Atlantic Highlands, 1991), 8.

3   John H. M. Salmon, 'The King and His Conscience: the Religious Problems of Louis XIV: Part I: The Gallican Church and the Huguenots', *History Today*, 15 (1965), 241; Georges Bordonove, *Les Rois qui ont fait la France: Les Bourbons. Louis XIV* (Paris, 1982), 199–200.

himself of Humanity, and to violate his Faith, whensoever the cause of his Church and Religion requireth.[4]

A century later, Calvinist historian Claude Rulhière agreed, portraying the Sun King as a naturally tolerant man who had been 'led astray' in his spiritual life by others. Who were these 'others,' and to what degree did they influence Louis XIV to abolish religious toleration in France?

Pope Innocent XI publicly expressed joy at the mass conversions in France but privately voiced reservations about the methods used to gain them. While he approved the use of bribes in conversions, he detested violence. He told Emperor Leopold I: '[I]f these conversions had been effected more by the holy and pious exhortations of the clergy than by the violence and fury of the soldiers', then the New Catholics would have become 'true converts'. But these half-hearted members brought 'profanations' to the Eucharist.[5] Far from having any influence on the Edict of 1685, however, the Pope was never even consulted.[6] Because the Holy See was at loggerheads with Versailles over the right of *régale*, the pontiff at first expressed indifference to the Edict of Fontainebleau. Innocent's coldness astonished the Gallican bishops and brought Louis 'diplomatic mortification' throughout Europe. But the Pope was caught in a trap. To endorse the edict would be recognizing that all hopes for reconciliation between French Catholicism and Calvinism were dead and tacitly acknowledging Louis XIV as the Catholic champion of Europe. To refuse to endorse it would increase Gallican bishops' suspicions that Innocent was a Jansenist. So the Pope delayed recognizing it.[7]

4   Gilbert Burnet, in E. S. De Beer, 'The Revocation of the Edict of Nantes and English Public Opinion', *Proceedings of the Huguenot Society of London*, 18 (1950), 308.

5   Innocent XI to Leopold I (c. 1685), in Pierre Blet, 'Les papes et la Révocation', in *La Révocation de l'édit de Nantes et le Protestantisme Français en 1685* (Paris, 1986), 271.

6   Louis O'Brien, *Innocent XI and the Revocation of the Edict of Nantes* (Berkeley, 1930), 56–8, 133–48.

7   Blet, 'Les Papes', 266–70; André Latreille, 'La Révocation de l'Édit de Nantes vue par les Nonces d'Innocent XI', *Bulletin de la Société de l'Histoire du Protestantisme Français*, 103 (1957): 229–30 (hereafter cited as *BSHPF*),

Much closer to the king's inner circle, Père François de La Chaize served as his confessor from 1675 to 1709. Louis sought his advice on a wide range of issues. Highly respected for his education, persuasiveness, and zeal, La Chaize garnered praise even from those – like Saint-Simon and Voltaire – who detested his Jesuit Order.[8] Although a firm defender of Catholic doctrine and morals, La Chaize showed remarkable tolerance toward individuals, welcoming Protestant savants and philosophes into his circle.[9] For three centuries, however, La Chaize has been blamed for the harsh policies of the Revocation. The Princess de Palatine blamed him for persuading the king 'to erase before God [...] the scandal resulting from his double adultery with Montespan' by eradicating the Calvinist heresy.[10] Ezechiel Spanheim, Brandenburg's ambassador to France, believed fear of losing his influence at Court forced La Chaize to advocate a harsh policy of persecution against the Reformed.[11] A century later, Minister of State Malesherbes and Chancellor D'Aguesseau held La Chaize responsible for the 'interests & passions & intrigues' which led to the Edict of 1685.[12]

Yet abundant evidence exists demonstrating La Chaize's indulgence toward the Huguenots. As early as 1677, the Holy See felt that his zeal for inspiring the king 'to extirpate the remaining heresy

Salmon, 'King', 246; A. Durrleman (Catherine Bergeal), *Eloge et condamnation de la Révocation de l'Edit de Nantes: Documents Rassemblés* (Carrières-sous-Poissy, 1935; repr. 1985), 18.

8   André Latreille, 'Preface', in Guitton, *La Chaize*, 1: vii; Georges Guitton, 'Le Père François de la Chaize au milieu des intrigues jansénistes', *Nouvelle Revue Théologique*, 74 (1952), 160; Warren Chandler Scoville, *The Persecution of Huguenots and French Economic Development, 1680–1720* (Berkeley, 1960), 31; Prince Michael of Greece, *Louis XIV: The Other Side of the Sun*, trans. Alan Sheridan (New York, 1983), 344.

9   Guitton, *La Chaize*, 1: 225–33.

10   Princess de Palatine, in Durrleman, *Révocation*, 53–4.

11   Ezechiel Spanheim, in Prince Michael, *Louis XIV*, 249–50.

12   Chrétien Guillaume Lamoignon de Malesherbes, *Mémoire sur le mariage des protestans fait en 1785 et 1786* (Paris, 1785), 45–6; Chancellor d'Aguesseau, *Oeuvres*, vol. 13, in Adolphe Michel, *Louvois et les protestants* (Paris, 1870), 22–3; Georges Minois, *Le confesseur du roi: Les directeurs de conscience sous la monarchie français* (Paris, 1988), 451–3.

from his realm' needed to be stimulated. In a 1681 letter to the Jesuit general of his order, La Chaize opposed the excess cruelties of the 'booted missionaries'. In 1684 he criticised the forcible baptisms of Protestant children, for which he was denounced to the General Assembly of the Clergy as being too indulgent toward heretics.[13] In 1686 he protested against the desecration of the bodies of relapsed Catholics whose corpses were being dragged behind carts (*la claie*) and tossed into ditches. He told the king that this 'odious and barbarous' practice must stop. Louis XIV made sure that it did.[14] His outspoken defence of religious rights led the Jesuits in 1689 to spread rumours that La Chaize advocated liberty of conscience for the Reformed![15]

But Louis XIV neither permitted his Jesuit confessor to give him political advice nor his ministers of state to offer him spiritual advice.[16] The historian Jean Orcibal succinctly concludes: 'I have found nothing to confirm [Chancellor] Daguesseau's conclusion that [...] Père de la Chaize inspired the Revocation.' Instead the evidence suggests that La Chaize advocated a policy of gradualism, employing missionaries, schools, and convents to re-educate Protestant children in the lifestyle of Catholic orthodoxy but without utilizing the methods of force and violence.[17]

Another leading figure was Michel Le Tellier, Chancellor of France. His desire to see the Huguenots converted allegedly made him the chief proponent of the harsh policy of destroying temples and sending Calvinists to prison or to the galleys.[18] The priest Soulier

---

13   Cardinal Cybo to Nuncio Varèse, 10 Mar 1677, in Minois, *Confesseur du roi*, 454–5; Guitton, *La Chaize*, 1: 231, 235, 254–5, 267.

14   La Chaize to Louis XIV, 1686, in Guitton, *La Chaize*, 1: 270–1.

15   *Gazette de Haarlem*, 17 June 1689, in A. J. Enschédé, 'Extraits de la *Gazette de Haarlem* sur les Persécutions Dirigées contre les Protestants Français (1679–1704)', *BSHPF*, 29 (1880), 407.

16   Minois, *Confesseur du roi*, 385–6; Guitton, *La Chaize*, 165.

17   Jean Orcibal, 'Louis XIV and the Edict of Nantes', in Ragnhild Hatton (ed.), *Louis XIV and Absolutism* (Columbus, 1976), 170 (see note 45); 'Préparatifs de la Révocation de l'Edit de Nantes', *BSHPF* 2 (1853), 340–2.

18   Anna Eliza Bray, *The Revolt of the Protestants of the Cevennes, with Some Account of the Huguenots in the 17th Century* (London, 1870), 50; William

praised Le Tellier in 1682 for his 'ardent desire to see Huguenotism destroyed in the Kingdom & all the King's subjects reunited under one Faith.'[19] Voltaire also viewed the Chancellor's role in shaping the Edict of Fontainebleau as decisive, citing his triumphant words, 'Now let thy servant die [...] for I have seen with my own eyes thy salvation', as indicative of his driving zeal.[20]

But a closer look at the facts shows that while Le Tellier had been an advocate of strict enforcement of the Edict of Nantes since 1661, his official correspondence reflects an attitude of moderate conciliation toward the Huguenots. Order and peace being his primary goals, he urged officials to avoid using excessive measures to annoy them. He punished contraventions to the religious laws calmly and without passion, sending the dragoons to Poitou in 1663, for example, only after Reformed rebels had attacked priests there. While he sought to curtail Protestant proselytizing, he did so with a spirit of compromise and negotiation. His actions from 1670 to 1685 demonstrate conciliation and moderation regarding the *Religion Prétendue Réformée* (RPR) seeking compromises and employing *douceur*, as he told Ministers Colbert and Seignelay, in order to avoid disorders. To his dying day, Le Tellier believed this edict reflected the king's piety and represented the triumph of his policies.[21]

More than the chancellor himself, it is his ambitious son, Minister of War Louvois, whom writers have blamed for the harsh reprisals of the dragoons during the Revocation. The *abbé* Choisy believed that Louvois' jealousy of La Chaize's influence at Court and his own lust for glory led Louvois to order his military officers not 'to suffer the insults of these *canailles*' who resisted the dragoons' efforts

Shipton Browning, *History of the Huguenots, from 1598 to 1838* (London, 1839), 193.

19 M. Soulier, *Histoire du Calvinisme Contenant sa Naissance, son Progrès, sa Décadence & sa Fin en France* (Paris, 1686), 614.

20 François-Marie-Arouet de Voltaire, 'Siècle de Louis XIV (1751)', in Emile de La Bédollière and Georges Avenel (eds), *Oeuvres complètes de Voltaire* (Paris, 1867), 2: 485.

21 Louis André, *Michel Le Tellier et Louvois*, 2nd edn (Paris, 1943), 458–71, 507–12.

to convert them.[22] For Anna Bray (1870), Louvois' 'passionate and malicious' nature, his 'falsehood and cruelty', predisposed him to treat the Huguenots with 'murderous and diabolical violence'.[23] But Louvois, neither a *dévot* nor a fanatic, did not hate the Reformed or any other religious group; what he despised was rebellion. He liked to quote Cardinal Richelieu's maxim that 'everything which causes trouble for religion also troubles the State'. For anyone stubbornly to 'profess a religion that displeases His Majesty' smacked not only of heresy but also of treason and revolt.[24]

Yet even in the 1680s, Louvois could be indulgent. Madame de Maintenon observed in 1684 that Louvois 'wishes for gentleness' in converting the Huguenots, 'which does not agree with his natural disposition, and his haste to conclude matters'.[25] At the height of the *dragonnades* in Poitou, when intendants Marillac and Foucault overstepped reasonable bounds in using troops against the Reformed, Louvois reprimanded them both and urged them to use more caution and moderation.[26] His correspondence demonstrates that he preferred using persuasion and bribes to effect conversions. Before 1681, the records reveal not a single instance in which he used rigorous measures against Protestants. When he did allow Marillac to quarter the dragoons in Calvinist homes, it was because 'His Majesty wishes to act violently against the Huguenots to convert them', not because he personally hated them. On many occasions, Louvois tried to moderate the conduct of the dragoons.[27]

While it is inconceivable that Louvois opposed the Revocation, he attempted to soften its impact whenever he could. In November 1685 he declared: 'It is essential to avoid falling into the disadvantage

22   *Abbé* Choisy, in Salmon, 'King', 246.
23   Bray, *Revolt*, 51.
24   André Corvisier, *Louvois* (Paris, 1983), 414; Louvois, in Jules Chavannes, 'Essai sur les abjurations parmi les réformés de France sous le règne de Louis XIV', *BSHPF*, 21 (1872), 9.
25   Madame de Maintenon to unknown, 13 Aug 1684, in Bray, *Revolt*, 50–1.
26   W. H. Lewis, *The Splendid Century: Life in the France of Louis XIV* (1954), 106.
27   Camille Rousset, *Histoire de Louvois et de son Administration Politique et Militaire jusqu'à la Paix de Nimègue* (Paris, 1861–3), 3: 439–48.

of thinking we wish to establish an inquisition in France, and it is far better to follow the pathway of kindness than any other'.[28] In effect, Louvois appears to have had no consistent programme. His policies changed from day to day, depending on the decisions of Louis XIV and his clergy, local circumstances, and the results gained. Before 1685, he exercised moderation, restraining both the troops and some over-eager intendants clamouring for longer lists of abjurations. After 1685 and especially during the War of the League of Augsburg (1689–97), he exercised considerable harshness toward stubborn Huguenots whom he saw as potential traitors in league with France's foreign enemies. The 'catechism of the sabre' then replaced the 'catechism of the missionary'.[29]

Among the alleged advocates of Revocation, no name appears more frequently than that of Françoise d'Aubigné, better known as Madame de Maintenon. Because of her descent from the famous Théodore Agrippa d'Aubigné, the sixteenth-century Huguenot poet and historian, biographers have assumed that Françoise was reared in that faith by her aunt until her mother sent her to the convent of the Ursulines at Niort.[30]

But certain 'inconvenient facts' obviate this thesis. First, her mother was a fervent Catholic who took her daughter to Mass, drilled her in the catechism, sent her to Catholic schools in Martinique, and enrolled her in the Ursuline convent in Paris, where she stayed for nearly five years until she married Paul Scarron in 1652. Second, despite having Calvinist relatives, Françoise never showed any willingness to adopt their beliefs; instead, she tried repeatedly to convert them to Catholicism. Third, a baptismal certificate dated 28 November 1635 proves that she was baptised as a baby in the Catholic faith at Niort. Fourth, despite rumours about her Protestant childhood, no records exist to prove that she was ever rebaptised into the

28   Louvois to Boufflers, 7 Nov. 1685, in Corvisier, 421–2.
29   Michel, *Louvois*, 309–12.
30   Bordonove, *Louis XIV*, 190; Chauvannes, 'Abjurations', 308; Guillaume-Adam de Félice, *Histoire des protestants de France*, 7th edn (Toulouse, 1880), 401; Alfred Rosset, *Madame de Maintenon et la Révocation de l'Edit de Nantes* (Audincourt, 1897), 1–5.

Reformed faith. Fifth, of the three letters (1672, 1680, 1685) often used to prove that Maintenon had once been or still was 'at heart' a Calvinist, one was falsified by an editor and the other two have been recognised as forgeries for over a century. Sixth, the myth of her 'conversion' to Catholicism in later life is based largely on a tradition established in the seventeenth century by the dames of Saint-Cyr (the school she founded near Versailles).[31]

So how did Madame de Maintenon treat the Huguenots? In 1681 she told Monsieur de Guignonville that the law enabling seven-year-olds to convert to Catholicism would be the means 'to save many more souls'.[32] To her cousin Madame de Villette, she wrote: '[If] God spares the King [from his serious illness], there will not be one Huguenot in twenty years'.[33] As her correspondence attests, she laboured unceasingly to turn this dream into a reality. 'I would feel great joy if we were able to convert [all] our Huguenots', she exclaimed to Guignonville.[34] Reports of Protestant conversions always brought her 'great joy' and 'grand pleasure'.[35] Because she herself frequently paid the pensions or found positions for converts that she knew, she considered them to be 'my little girls' and 'my pensioners'.[36]

Yet the woman who had grown up with poverty and debt was not above reaping unspiritual blessings from the Revocation as well. She informed her brother Charles that if he played his cards right, he might gain 800,000 *livres* from a tax farm auction of Huguenot lands in Poitou. 'Land in Poitou is going for almost nothing; the desolation of the Huguenots will help sell even more of it. [...] You can easily

31 H. Gelin, 'Madame de Maintenon Convertisseuse', *BSHPF*, 49 (1900), 169–76; Browning, *Huguenots*, 186–7; Acton, 'Louis XIV', 70.

32 Madame de Maintenon to Monsieur de Guignonville, 12 June 1681, in Marcel Langlois (ed.), *Lettres de Madame de Maintenon* (Paris, 1935–9), 2: 383–4.

33 Madame de Maintenon to Madame de Villette, 15 Apr 1681, in César Pascal, *La Révocation de l'Edit de Nantes et Mme. de Maintenon: sa vie, son charactère, son influence*, 2d edn (Paris, 1885), 50.

34 Madame de Maintenon to Monsieur de Guignonville, 7 Nov 1681, Langlois, *Lettres,* 2: 411.

35 Madame de Maintenon to *comte* d'Aubigny, 23 June 1682, ibid. 2: 435.

36 Madame de Maintenon to Madame de Brinon, 20 Feb 1683, in ibid. 2: 476–7; Langlois, *Madame de Maintenon* (Paris, 1932), 48, 58.

establish yourself grandly'.[37] Proselytizing could go hand in hand with profit-seeking. If Maintenon sometimes mixed mercenary motives with her spiritual zeal, however, she consistently opposed the use of violence to effect conversions. To a recent convert she wrote deploring the 'shameful methods' and 'cruel and inhumane' treatment many Huguenots had endured. She wished converters would 'win their hearts' by sweetness.[38]

Given her strong views concerning the importance of Protestant conversions, did Madame de Maintenon influence Louis XIV to pass laws forcing them to convert? That is unlikely for several reasons. First, the king began passing anti-Huguenot legislation in the 1650s and 1660s, long before he knew her and before she had become governess of his children at Versailles.[39] Second, despite the charges made by many writers that she was 'an unfaithful Esther' who betrayed her people, before 1685 there does not exist a single word in her authentic correspondence to show that she advised abolishing the Edict of Nantes.[40] Third, while recent biographers blame Maintenon for the Edict of Fontainebleau, her contemporaries did not. German envoy Ezechiel Spanheim, himself a Protestant, wrote in his *Relation*:

> I will add a few thoughts on the wicked role which some attribute to Madame de Maintenon in the unfortunate and cruel persecution endured by Protestants in

---

37 Madame de Maintenon to Charles d'Aubigné, 2 Sept 1681, in Eugène Bonnemère, *Les Dragonnades* (Paris, 1882), 28.
38 Rosset, *Madame de Maintenon*, 59–61; Jean Orcibal, *Louis XIV et les Protestants* (Paris, 1951), 91–2.
39 Daniel Robert, 'Louis XIV et les Protestants', *XVIIe siècle* (1967), 45.
40 A sampling of those who have blamed Maintenon for the Revocation include Jules Michelet, *De la Révocation de l'Edit de Nantes à la Guerre des Cévennes* (Paris, 1860; repr. Montpellier, 1985), 33–4; Bray, *Revolt*, 57; Pascal, *Révocation*, 61, 83, 86, 89, 100, 104; Albert Atger, *Les camisards et leurs adversaires* (Nîmes, 1905), 133; Baird, *Révocation*, 2: 20; Elisabeth Labrousse, *La révocation de l'Edit de Nantes. Une foi, une loi, un roi?* (Paris, 1990), 100; Etienne Gamonnet, *Au Bouschet de Pranles: Etienne Durand et les Siens: un siècle de Résistance Protestante Pacifique en Vivarais* (Montpellier, 1994), 29; Rosset, *Madame de Maintenon*, 39–44.

France. [...S]he has not had the power or the will to counteract [the King's plans], [...] but has fully resigned her will to support the King.[41]

In a 1753 letter to Monsieur Farney, Voltaire asserted: 'Why do you say that Madame de Maintenon played a large part in the Revocation? She had no part in it: that fact is certain. She never dared to contradict Louis XIV'.[42]

Instead, the sources show that Maintenon pleaded for kindness, gentleness and love in dealing with Calvinists. She saved one pastor from execution in 1670. In 1672, she counselled her brother: 'I beg of you, don't be inhumane with the Huguenots. It is essential to change people by kindness. Jesus Christ gives us the example of it'.[43] And if not all the conversions proved long-lasting or sincere, she contented herself with the hope that 'their children will be Catholics at least; even if the fathers are hypocrites; their external reunion will bring them closer to the truth as a sign of communion with the faithful'.[44] Madame de Maintenon played at best a passive role in discussions concerning the Edict of Fontainebleau and opposed the dragoon violence used to implement it. Furthermore, it would have been unthinkable for Louis XIV to allow his mistress to interfere directly in matters of state.

One Catholic prelate who praised Louis XIV's Revocation policies was Jacques-Bénigne Bossuet, 'the chief ecclesiastical opponent of Protestants in France'.[45] From his first polemic against Calvinism in 1655 to his death in 1704, Bossuet progressed from refutation to persuasion to rationalisation of forceful conversions. A priest in distant Metz in 1652, Bossuet became Bishop of Condom in 1671, a member of the Académie Française in 1672, then tutor to the Dauphin, and in 1681 was promoted to head the lucrative diocese of

---

41   Ezechiel Spanheim, *Relation* (1690, published 1882), in Rosset, ibid. 49–50.
42   Voltaire to Farney, 17 Jan 1753, in Rosset, ibid. 49.
43   Madame de Maintenon to Charles d'Aubigné, 1672, in Rosset, ibid. 45.
44   Madame de Maintenon to *comtesse* de Saint-Géron, 25 Oct 1685, in Langlois, *Lettres*, 3: 131.
45   James M. Moudy, 'Bossuet and the Protestants: A Chapter in the Seventeenth-Century Struggle for Religious Allegiance in France' (unpubl. Ph.D. diss. Duke University, 1953), iii.

Meaux. His numerous treatises attacking Protestantism and defending Catholic teachings earned him an international reputation.[46] In his *Exposition of the Doctrines of the Catholic Church* (1671), Bossuet urged the Reformed to give Catholicism a candid investigation. If they did so, they would come to appreciate its truth and gentle benevolence. Catholic principles, he asserted, condemned the use of force.[47]

Bossuet moved beyond using persuasive prose in the 1680s, however, to actively prosecuting Huguenots in his diocese. In 1683, for example, he ordered the sisters Marie and Magdeleine Mirot to be taken from their Protestant parents and sent to the Ursuline convent near Meaux for a Catholic education.[48] During the mid-1680s, documents show that he also participated in the demolition of temples and requested *lettres de cachet* to imprison Calvinists. Soon the Reformed began emigrating from Meaux.[49]

But participating in the persecution of Huguenots in one region does not prove that Bossuet caused the Revocation. For one thing, he did not become a member of the Council of State until 1697, long after the anti-Protestant policies were in place. For another, during the 1680s, he lived in Meaux, far from the power centres at Versailles and Paris. Finally, his writings show that before 1685, Bossuet preferred persuasion to force in dealing with the Huguenots.[50] Nonetheless, after the Edict of 1685 made the king's intent to abolish Protestantism perfectly clear, Bossuet became one of the most vocal apologists for the Revocation.[51] But sources show that he, like Madame de Maintenon, disapproved of the dragoons and did what he could to moderate their violence. Unlike other bishops, he did not favour

46   Ibid. 120; Elizabeth Israels Perry, *From Theology to History: French Religious Controversy and the Revocation of the Edict of Nantes* (The Hague, 1973), 209–10.
47   Jacques Bénigne Bossuet, *An Exposition of the Doctrines of the Catholic Church*, ed. and trans. John Fletcher (1671; Baltimore, 1829), xxii–xliv, lx, lxxxv–lxxxvii.
48   A. Peyrat, 'Bossuet et la Révocation de l'Edit de Nantes, Dépeches Ministerielles et autres Pièces Inédits (1683–1699)', *BSHPF*, 10 (1861), 52–66.
49   Ibid. 115–18.
50   Moudy, 'Bossuet', 273–4.
51   Scoville, *Persecution*, 31.

forcing the Reformed to attend Mass and confession, seeing this as 'idolatry' against the church. He adamantly opposed tossing their corpses into wayside ditches, believing that 'this causes more horror against Catholics than any good effects it has had on the reunited ones'.[52] To the end of his life, he continued to labour for Calvinists' conversion, sending them copies of his catechism and generous pensions. For, as he once remarked: 'There is nothing more necessary than French *livres* for the good success of the work'.[53]

Having discounted all of the usual suspects blamed for the Revocation, who is left? There was in France one powerful lobby that had for over a century consistently demanded the abolition of the Protestant heresy. From the lowest priest in his parish to the highest archbishop at Court, the Roman Catholic clergy viewed any law that tolerated heresy as a violation of the king's coronation oath. Since 1215, this royal 'oath of the sacrament' had included the following words: 'I will endeavour with all my authority in good faith to expel from my jurisdiction and the territories under my subjection all heretics so indicated by the Church'.[54] This oath was expanded during Henri III's reign to include a royal promise to keep the peace in France, to stop iniquity, to observe justice and mercy, and to preserve and defend the canonical privileges of the bishops and clerics.[55] Backed by the almost universal consensus of its prelates and the enormous wealth flowing from its benefices, the General Assembly of the Clergy was in a powerful position to remind the Bourbon kings of their oath and to influence their decisions on religious matters prior to granting them a generous *don gratuit*.[56] First convened under Charles IX in 1560, the General Assembly met every five years in Paris to settle church matters, defend Catholicism against attacks, and decide the amount of its tax gift to the Crown. The French kings naturally

52   Bossuet, in Langlois, *Lettres*, 5: 195; Moudy, 'Bossuet', 279–83.
53   'Bossuet et la Révocation de l'Edit de Nantes (1692–1699)', *BSHPF*, 4 (1855), 213–9.
54   Janine Garrisson, *L'Edit de Nantes: Chronique d'une paix attendue* (Paris, 1998), 99.
55   Bernard Barbiche, *Les institutions de la monarchie française à l'époque moderne, XVIe–XVIIIe siècle* (Paris, 1999), 24.
56   Bordonove, *Louis XIV*, 200.

depended on the Assembly as their 'cash cow' to help fund the monarchy in lean times. Every ten years when the Contract of Poissy came up for renewal, the Assembly wanted their privileges confirmed and their remonstrances acted upon, while the king hoped for a cash gift larger than the previous one.[57]

As might be expected, one of the issues on the Assembly's agenda involved what to do with the Protestant 'heretics'. At its first meeting in 1560, the Assembly told the King that 'the clergy are opposed to all toleration of sects, dissidents, and to all concessions in favour of heretics', and wished to see no doctrine contrary to Catholicism established in France.[58] In 1580 the Assembly called for the total destruction of all heresies for the 'conservation of the State.' In 1585, after thanking Henri III for revoking the Edicts of Pacification and abolishing 'liberty of conscience', they granted him increased subsidies to fight the Huguenots. The Bishop of Noyon reminded the king that 'the diversity of religion' ran contrary to his coronation oath and to 'the constitution of this realm'.[59]

Yet in a conciliatory speech to Henri IV in 1595, the Bishop of Mons said that the clergy would labour for the Huguenots' conversion by prayer, fasting, and tears, 'the true arms of ecclesiastics'.[60] Their mood changed dramatically, however, when Henri IV put his Great Seal to the Edict of Nantes in April 1598. Meeting in Paris a month

---

57   Norman Ravitch, *Sword and Mitre: Government and Episcopate in France and England in the Age of Aristocracy* (The Hague, 1966), 157–9; Guy Cabourdin and Georges Viard (eds), *Lexique historique de la France d'Ancien Régime*, 2nd edn. s.v. 'Assemblée du clergé' (Paris, 1990); Michel Perronet, 'Les assemblées du clergé et les Protestants', *Dix–huitième siècle*, 17 (1985), 141–2; Alfred Cauchie, 'Les assemblées du clergé sous l'ancien régime: Matériaux et origines', *Revue des sciences philosophiques et théologiques*, 2 (1908), 80, 89, 94; Bernard Dompnier, *Le venin de l'hérésie: Image du protestantisme et combat catholique au XVIIe siècle* (Paris, 1985), 115.

58   I. Bourlon, *Les assemblées du Clergé et le Protestantisme* (Paris, 1909), 8–9.

59   Michel Peronnet, 'Les assemblées du Clergé de France et la Révocation des édits de Religion, 1560–1685', *BSHPF*, 131 (1985), 457–8; Louis-Emile Serbat, *Les Assemblées du Clergé de France: Origines, Organisation, Développement, 1561–1615* (Paris, 1906), 323–4.

60   Claude d'Angennes de Rambouillet, Bishop of Mons (1596), in Yves de La Brière, *Comment fut Adopté et Accepté l'Edit de Nantes* (Paris, 1904), 12–13.

later, the General Assembly drew up remonstrances strenuously opposing the Edict. Among other things, they demanded that Protestants' preaching be limited or even stopped in dioceses where Catholics constituted a majority and that their burials in Catholic cemeteries cease. The assembly even instructed its general agents 'to stop as far as you can the publication, verification, and execution of the Edict'.[61] In 1605 the Assembly initiated two ominous procedures: introducing *cahiers* of complaints against the Reformed sent in by provincial bishops and urging the king to take a more restrictive view of the Edict of Nantes.[62]

Under Louis XIII, the clergy saw the Edict of Nantes as only a stop gap measure which they expected the king to abolish once he had defeated the Huguenots. The 1610 Assembly reminded Louis that as God was his father, the church was his mother, and she needed protection against the onslaughts of heresy.[63] At the Assembly of 1617, the Bishop of Macon told the king that the 'fields' of France had too many 'monsters and thorns, drunk with heresy spreading pell-mell with the wheat of holy doctrine'. In Béarn, the Calvinist 'brambles' thrived while the Catholic 'wheat' was smothered. The Assembly urged the king to reestablish Catholicism there, which he did.[64]

By the 1630s France's powerful bishops expressed an even more bellicose attitude toward the RPR. General Assemblies continually complained to Louis XIII and Louis XIV about Protestant infractions and disrespect for Catholic services. Bishops took Calvinists to court for these offences, sought to curtail their privileges, and even threatened to imprison them. At the 1635 Assembly, the Bishop of Orléans called the Calvinists 'enemies of your [the king's] State' and accused them of destroying altars and corrupting France. The king should extinguish their 'Monster Heresy' by burning their books, razing their temples, arresting and imprisoning them.[65]

61   Janine Garrisson, *L'Édit de Nantes: Chronique d'une paix attendue* (Paris, 1998), 318–19.
62   Perronet, 'Clergé', 461.
63   Ibid. 462; Dompnier, *Venin*, 117–18.
64   Bishop of Macon (1617), in Dompnier, *Venin*, 116; Garrisson, *Nantes*, 60.
65   Paul Fargues, *Histoire du Christianisme*. Vol. 5: *De l'Édit de Nantes à la Révolution* (Paris, 1938), 39; Bourlon, *Protestantisme*, 45–6; Alfred Rébelliau,

Partly in response to this crescendo of demands by the General Assembly, the Huguenots soon found themselves restricted by new laws governing their religious observance. Spies shadowed pastors, reporting those who used inflammatory words like 'martyr', 'persecution', or 'torment' in their sermons. Calvinist writers were forbidden to call the Pope 'Antichrist', to describe themselves as the 'true church', or to malign Catholicism as a 'deceit of Satan'. In some Catholic-dominated areas, bishops closed their temples.[66] In the 1640s, the Assembly lobbied for laws forcing the Calvinists to venerate the Holy Sacrament when they passed a cathedral and show respect for the Host in processions.[67]

When he came to the throne, the young Louis XIV was aware of the clergy's attitudes toward the Reformed. He daily encountered more ecclesiastics (75) at the Louvre than he did physicians (48), librarians (43), or musicians (28).[68] At the 1651 Assembly, the Bishop of Comminges told the thirteen-year-old king:

> We do not ask, Sire, that Your Majesty banish at present from his kingdom this unfortunate liberty of conscience which destroys the true liberty of God's children [...] but we wish at least that this evil thing not make progress and that [...] it can be made weaker, and bit by bit force the diminution of its forces.[69]

'Un épisode de l'histoire Religieuse au XVIIe siècle, III: La Compagnie du Saint-Sacrement et les Protestants', *Revue des Deux Mondes*, 17 (1903), 109–14; Bishop of Orléans, 17 Feb. 1636, in St. Bartoszewski, 'La remonstrance du clergé de France du 17 février 1636', *BSHPF*, 99 (1953), 36–43.

66   Garrisson, *Nantes*, 86–90.

67   Pierre Blet, *Le clergé de France et la Monarchie; Etude sur les Assemblées Générales du Clergé de 1615 à 1666* (Rome, 1959), 347; Garrisson, *Nantes*, 133.

68   Joseph Chambon, *Le protestantisme français jusqu'à la Révolution française* (Paris, 1958), 116.

69   Gilbert de Choiseul, Bishop of Comminges, 11 Apr 1651, in Dompnier, *Venin*, 124.

Comminges suggested that Louis XIV follow St Augustine's example with the Donatist heretics and wear the Reformed down with arguments and harassing tactics until they converted.[70]

This aggressive tone was reflected in the *doléances* of the Assemblies in the 1650s. In 1651 the bishops demanded that sixty temples built recently be torn down and no new temples erected.[71] Calling the Edict of Nantes 'a necessary evil', they asked that it be narrowly interpreted so that temples built since 1598 could be demolished, Calvinist colleges closed, and Reformed judges dismissed. In 1655 they wanted to abolish both Reformed synods and 'liberty of conscience'.[72] Behind this rigorous policy lay a shift in ecclesiastical attitudes. While the sixteenth-century clergy saw Protestants as heretics to be burned, the seventeenth-century *curés* saw them as schismatics, whose independence smacked of defiance against church and state.[73]

This argument persuaded the eighteen-year-old king to crack down on the Huguenots. As discussed elsewhere,[74] prior to 1656, Louis XIV had demonstrated remarkable tolerance toward the RPR. But when the Assembly of 1655 convinced him that these 'schismatics' threatened the State, the king issued the Declaration of 18 July 1656, which responded point by point to the bishops' demands. It prohibited Calvinists from worshiping in episcopal towns; Protestant seigneurs from choosing *curés* on their estates; Reformed judges from taking cases involving Catholic benefices; and pastors

---

70 Ibid. 118; Auguste-François Lièvre, *Du rôle que le clergé catholique de France à joué dans la révocation de l'édit de Nantes* (Strasbourg, 1853), 22; Georges d'Aubrisson, Archbishop of Embrun, in Urbain de Robert-Labarthe, *Histoire du protestantisme dans le Haut-Languedoc, le Bas-Quercy et le comté de Foix de 1685 à 1789* (Paris, 1896), 1: 78.

71 Blet, *Clergé*, 348–9.

72 Ibid. 351–2; Dompnier, *Venin*, 118; Bourlon, *Protestantisme*, 49–58.

73 Richard Golden, *The Huguenot Connection: The Edict of Nantes, Its Revocation, and Early French Migration to South Carolina* (Norwell, 1988), 20; Emmanuel Jahan, *La Confiscation des Biens des Religionnaires Fugitives de la Révocation de l'Edit de Nantes à la Révolution* (Paris, 1959), 1–2.

74 Brian E. Strayer, *Huguenots and Camisards as Aliens in France, 1589–1789* (Lewiston, 2001), ch.3.

from preaching outside their parishes.[75] The bishops also insisted that
Calvinists be prohibited from singing psalms in public and from
burying their dead in Catholic cemeteries. These points were incorporated into the *arrêt* of 11 January 1657.[76] Soon the Huguenots
felt a new wave of persecution. Mobs looted temples; officials prohibited their worship in episcopal towns and barred them from
hospitals, schools, and offices. One Calvinist predicted: 'In thirty
years [by 1687] it is possible to foresee the end of our Religion.'[77]

It was clearly the bishops' goal to persuade the king to revoke the
Edict of Nantes. The Assembly of 1660 attacked the edict as 'contrary
to Divine, Civil, & Canonical laws.'[78] The bishops asked the king to
exclude Calvinists from public office; close their schools, hospitals,
and temples; and stop their itinerant preaching and mixed marriages.[79]
To help magistrates interpret the Edict more casuistically, the bishops
issued the twenty-six *Maximes* in 1661. For example, for a Calvinist
temple to be 'legal', the building must have existed in 1596–7 with a
pastor, elders and deacons, holding frequent (not intermittent) public
(not clandestine) baptisms, weddings, and funerals – for which the
consistory must show written records. Believers must show a title for
their temple and prove that it stood on its original spot. Pastors must
be licensed and show proof of drawing a regular salary from the
church. Given the chaos during the Religious Wars (1562–98), this
was nearly impossible to do.[80]

That these *Maximes* influenced Louis XIV's thinking appears
evident in his *Mémoires* (1661) to the Dauphin. Calvinism, he stated,

---

75   Blet, *Clergé*, 358–60; Bourlon, *Protestantisme*, 67; Garrisson, *Nantes*, 120;
     Jean Vircoulon, 'Les premiers Réformés et leurs Cimetières en pays foyen',
     BSHPF, 143 (1997), 21–38.
76   Blet, *Clergé*, 360–1.
77   *Apologie des Eglises Réformées du Languedoc, où sont Continues les Justes
     Plaints sur le Sujet des Troubles qu'on leur Suscite, & des Maux qu'on leur fait
     souffrir, ou prejudice des Edicts de nos Rois* (N.p., 1657), 8–36, 39.
78   *Mémoires pour examiner les infractions faites aux édits et déclarations du roi,
     par ceux de la R.P.R.* (Paris, 1661), 22–3, 26.
79   Assembly of the Clergy, *Mémoires* (1661), 11–33.
80   Pierre Bernard, *Maximes à Observer au Jugement des Partages faits par
     Messieurs les Commissaires Exécuteurs de l'Edit de Nantes* (N.p., 1661), 1–15.

caused animosity, violence, and religious wars; therefore, he resolved to 'reduce gradually the number of Huguenots in my kingdom'. By interpreting previous edicts 'in the narrowest limits that justice and propriety would permit' and by rewarding all who converted with pensions and positions, he hoped over time to eradicate Protestantism.[81] But the bishops grew impatient with this policy of gradualism. When they met in 1665, they demanded the revocation of the Edict of 1598. Their twenty-one articles requested that Calvinist proselytizing be limited to their families, that Catholics not live with Protestants, and that the Reformed who disrespected Catholic rites be punished. Only 'severe and pitiless' measures could bring unity in France, they told him.[82]

The clergy's lobbying set the agenda for the laws that followed. Whereas the twenty-five years from 1631 to 1656 witnessed thirty-six new laws regarding the Reformed, the twenty-eight years from 1657 to 1685 saw 273 laws passed. Laws in the 1670s prevented seigneurs from hosting synods on their estates and pastors from preaching outside their parishes. More of their books were banned, more schools and temples closed, and more Protestant consuls, judges, and officers expelled.[83] The 1670 Assembly gave Louis XIV the formula for extinguishing the RPR:

> Your Majesty, in order to ruin Calvinism, you need only require [those] who profess it to exactly observe the Edict of Nantes, and to punish all contraventions of it by very severe penalties. Nothing more than this is necessary to

---

81   Louis XIV, *Mémoires* (1661), in Paul Sonnino (ed.), *Louis XIV: Mémoires for the Instruction of the Dauphin* (New York, 1970), 47, 55–7.

82   Bishop of Uzès, '21 Articles', in Blet, *Clergé*, 377–81; Bourlon, *Protestantisme*, 70–2.

83   Janine Garrisson, 'Le roi et les protestants en France, 1661–1685', in *Réformes et Révocation en Béarn, XVIIe–XXe siècles* (Pau, 1986), 256; *Edits, déclarations et arrêts concernant la religion p. réformée, 1662–1751* (Paris, 1885); Ariel Van Deursen, *Professions et métiers interdits* (Groningen, 1960), 363; *arrêts* of the Council of State, 9 Feb. 1674 and 6 Nov. 1674, Bibliothèque Nationale, Manuscrits Français 21617, ff. 51, 53.

reduce the heretics to such insignificant numbers that, the 1598 edict being no longer useful, it can then be revoked.[84]

The bishops persuaded the king in 1673 to require journeymen to be Catholics before being advanced to master craftsmen; this effectively eliminated non-Catholics from the highest positions in the guilds.[85] In 1680, one cleric told Louis XIV that too many illegal temples were still being built. He advised the king to tear them down, banish their pastors, confiscate Calvinist lands, and use the income to build Catholic seminaries.[86]

Flushed with success after defeating the Dutch, Louis XIV turned his attention once more to the Huguenots. His 10 July 1682 circular letter asserted that 'the reunion of the RPR into the folds of the church' was a 'holy enterprise [...] advantageous to the glory of God & the good of my State'. He encouraged the clergy to 'give me indications of your zeal for Religion' by taking 'any measures' to insure 'a happy end'.[87] The 1682 Assembly needed no second invitation. They sent a circular letter to all French prelates instructing them on how to convert Protestants to Catholicism in one generation. The bishops even used the term 'holy violence' to describe their new strategy.[88]

Fortified by the king's good will, they assembled in 1685, hoping to bring the *coup de grâce* to French Calvinism. Recognising that 'there is nothing so pernicious to salvation' as 'heretical books', the Archbishop of Paris identified 850 Protestant works whose publication would close a print shop forever. The king's edict of 23 August 1685

---

84   Bishop Varillas to Louis XIV (1670), in Puaux, 'Responsabilité de la Révocation', 267.

85   Jacques Wilhelm, *La Vie Quotidienne: Des Parisiens au temps du Roi-Soleil, 1660–1715* (Paris, 1977), 99.

86   'Fait l'an 1680. Huguenots. Pour faire que, dans six mois, ils viendront déclarer au greffe du Conseil leurs temples usurpéz & en consentir la démolition' (1680), 1–2.

87   *Actes de l'Assemblée générale du clergé de France de 1682, concernant la religion* (1683), 80–5; Louis XIV to commissioners, archbishops and bishops, 10 Jl. 1682, Bibliothèque Nationale, Collection Joly de Fleury, MS 1679, f. 133.

88   *Actes*, 6–11, 43–77; Blet, *Assemblées*, 433; Bourlon, *Protestantisme*, 80.

forbade anyone to preach or write against Catholicism.[89] Further legislation that summer mandated that temples where Catholics had married Protestants must be torn down. Reformed families could not hire Catholic servants, nor could judges hire Calvinist clerks. No Protestant could teach or practise law or medicine. Pastors could not live within six leagues of a place where worship had been forbidden; Calvinists residing in Paris for less than one year had to leave.[90] In a mood bordering on euphoria, the bishops voted the Crown a *don gratuit* of 3,000,000 *livres*, praising Louis XIV for 'ruining [...] the Exercises of those of the Pretended Reformed Religion', leading to the conversion of 'an innumerable multitude' of Calvinists.[91]

But they demanded more: demolishing all Reformed temples, prohibiting all Protestant worship, baptizing all Calvinist children as Catholics, and taxing all Protestants to rebuild Catholic churches, schools and seminaries. The clergy also discussed how to increase the number of missionaries working among the Reformed and how to raise 460,000 *livres* over the next eight years to provide pensions for pastors who abjured. On 22 October 1685, the Edict of Fontainebleau, whose terms are discussed at the beginning of this chapter, granted the bishops nearly all of their requests.[92]

The Jesuit historian Pierre Blet (1972) acknowledged that, in fact, 'Louis XIV and his Council examined the requests of the clergy and took from them new inspiration to enclose in increasingly tight

---

89   *Pleinte de l'Assemblée générale du clergé de France contre les calomnés, Injures, & Faussetez, que les Prétendus Réformés ont répandues & répandent tous les jours Preches, contre la Doctrine de l'Eglise* (Paris, 1685), 3–11; Archbishop of Paris, 'Mandement' (Aug 1685) and Edict of 23 Aug 1685, Bibliothèque Nationale, Manuscrit Français 7050, ff. 101–23; Walter C. Utt, *The Wrath of the King* (Mountain View, 1966), 16.

90   *Declarations du Roy* for 23 June, 26 Jl, 6 Aug, 14 Aug, 22 Aug 1685; *Edit du Roy* for 23 Aug 1685; *Ordre du Roy* for 17 Oct 1685, Bibliothèque Nationale, Manuscrits Français 21617, ff. 83, 85, 109, 113, 116–24, 136, 139.

91   'Contrat fait et passé entre le Roy & le clergé de France Assemblée par permission de Sa Majesté à Saint Germain en Laye pour le Don de la somme de trois millions de livres' (N.p. 21 Jl. 1685), 1–11.

92   Pierre Blet, *Les assemblées du clergé et Louis XIV de 1670 à 1693* (Rome, 1972), 444, 456–60, 470.

restrictions the worship of the R.P.R'.[93] Janine Garrisson (1998) agrees, stating that '[t]he Assemblies of the clergy, with the regularity of a metronome, solicited from the sovereign his eradication [of the Edict of Nantes] in exchange for the *don gratuit*'.[94] Bernard Barbiche (1999) emphasises that just as the General Assembly habitually 'intervened in the great doctrinal debates' of the era concerning Jansenism and Quietism, so it 'played an important role in the process that led to the revocation of the Edict of Nantes'. Of the three Estates, the clergy was the only one to be regularly assembled from the sixteenth to the end of the eighteenth century.[95]

It is worth repeating that in an absolute monarchy, 'the buck stops at the throne'. Until 1656, as Richard Bonney has shown, Louis XIV refused to follow the wishes of the bishops and issue restrictive laws against his Calvinist subjects. But with such enormous *dons gratuits* weighing in the balances and costly wars with Spain, Holland, and England on the horizon, one can understand how the high clergy's persistent campaign to undermine the Edict of Nantes gradually wore down the king's reluctance.[96] As the Bishop of Valence reminded the General Assembly in 1685, 'The destruction of heresy is solely *our affair*'.[97] Because the high clergy took the credit for influencing Louis XIV to launch the Revocation, they should be held accountable for its results.

93   Ibid. 470.
94   Garrisson, *Chronique d'un paix attendue*, 11.
95   Bernard Barbiche, *Les institutions de la monarchie française à l'époque moderne, XVIe–XVIIIe siècle* (Paris, 1999), 98.
96   Richard Bonney, *Political Change in France under Richelieu and Mazarin, 1624–1661* (Oxford, 1978), 398–9; idem, 'La France après la paix de Westphalie: absolutisme ou pluralisme confessionnel?', in L. Bély (ed.), *L'Europe des traités de Westphalie: Esprit de la diplomatie ou diplomatie de l'ésprit?* (Paris, 2000), 152–60.
97   Bishop Daniel de Cosnac, speech to the General Assembly of the Clergy, 2 July 1685, in Puaux and Sabatier, *Etudes*, 34.

DAVID L. WYKES

'So Bitterly Censur'd and Revil'd':[1] Religious Dissent and Relations with the Church of England after the Toleration Act

The 1689 Toleration Act, by suspending the penal laws against those who refused to conform to the Church of England and by allowing Protestant dissenters to gather their own congregations, has been widely regarded as one of the formative events in the development of modern religious dissent in England. The Toleration Act clearly marked a new phase in its development. Within a couple of years a considerable number of informal meetings had not only been gathered into congregations, but in many cases acquired meeting-places and endowments. During this period many new congregations were also formed. By removing the threat to dissenters worshipping in public who registered the buildings in which they met, the Act granted some measure of legal protection. Private meetings were therefore encouraged to acquire the permanent features of congregational organisation that are associated with modern dissent: the establishment of regular services and a system of church government, the appointment of a minister, the acquisition of a building to worship in and the endow-

1   John Hartley, *A vindication of Presbyterian ordination; from Scripture and antiquity, the judgment of the reformed churches, and particularly of the Church of England. With a brief reflection upon the arguments offer'd by Mr. Cantrell of Derby against it. By a lover of all hearty and charitable Protestants. To which is added, a Postscript relating to Mr Harris defence of his letter to Mr Cantrell* (Nottingham, 1714), 3, (iii). I am grateful to the Keeper of Western Manuscripts, Bodleian Library, Oxford, the Librarian of Lambeth Palace Library, London, the Managers of the Presbyterian Fund, and the County Archivists of Derbyshire, Hertfordshire and Oxfordshire for permission to use and quote from their records.

ments with which to support it.[2] Nevertheless, it is often overlooked that the Toleration Act was only one of two measures intended to establish the religious settlement of the Revolution, the other being concerned with comprehension. The Comprehension Bill offering generous terms by which moderate dissenters might be 'comprehended' (or accommodated) within the Church of England was however lost, largely due to the growing hostility after the Revolution of many Churchmen to the idea of concessions towards dissenters. Only the Toleration Bill therefore became law. As a result a great many ordinary and respectable dissenters were forced to obtain their freedom to worship in public from an act intended only to offer a qualified toleration to a despised minority.

Although the 1689 Toleration Act allowed Protestant dissenters freedom to worship in public, the Act did not remove but merely suspended the earlier penal laws against nonconformist meetings. It therefore fell far short of a full religious toleration and dissenters continued to be discriminated against in many important areas of everyday life. They were still subject to major political disabilities, and indeed restrictions in practising their religion in such matters as marriage, burial and the education of their children. Modestly titled 'An Act for Exempting their Majesties Protestant Subjects, Dissenting from the Church of England, from the Penalties of certain laws', it was really no more than an indulgence.[3] With the exception of the Test and Corporation Acts, which were intended to restrict office-holding to members of the Church of England, the involvement of dissenters in most areas of public life was not defined by the Toleration Act. As a result the extent of the protection offered by the Act was always in doubt. No mention was made of the right of dissenters to educate candidates for the ministry nor indeed their own children. It had never been the intention of the sponsors of the original bill in 1689 to offer a general toleration, but with the failure of the attempts to achieve comprehension, all dissenters, including the Presbyterians who had

2   D. L. Wykes, "'The Settling of Meetings and the Preaching of the Gospel": The Development of the Dissenting interest after toleration', *Journal of United Reformed Church History Society*, 5 (1993), 127–45.
3   1 Wm & Mary c. 18, *The Statutes of the Realm* (London, 1819) 6:74–6.

sought a fresh accommodation with the Church of England, were forced to seek their right to worship and their involvement in public life under the Toleration Act. Limited and ungenerous though the provisions of the Act appeared to dissenters, the breach of the Anglican monopoly was revolutionary for High Churchmen. Increasingly the choice was seen as being between a strict insistence upon allowing as lawful only that which was specifically permitted within the Act, and a more generous interpretation which permitted dissenters to take part in most areas of public life that were not actually proscribed.

The growth in High Church feeling by the end of William III's reign, and the resentment that many Churchmen felt at the increasing involvement of dissenters in public life led to a more rigorous enforcement of the existing statutes against dissenters, as well as the enactment of new legislation. Opponents of dissent concentrated their efforts on attacking what they saw as the two main abuses of the Toleration Act: the practice of occasional conformity (whereby dissenters evaded the sacramental tests of the Corporation and Test Acts in order to hold office), and the growth of nonconformist academies and schools. The setting up by dissenters of their own places of education was perceived by churchmen as helping to perpetuate dissent, not only by training up the next generation ministers and children, but by inculcating values hostile to the Church. High Church opposition culminated in the passing of the Occasional Conformity Act in 1711 and the Schism Act in 1714.[4] Both Acts were intended to reduce severely the freedom that dissenters had succeeded in exploiting under the Toleration Act.

There were also many areas of discrimination and persecution. Dissenters locally were subject to verbal abuse, frequent petty acts of harassment, intimidation and even violence. A Tory mob celebrated the death of William III in 1702 by attacking the dissenting meeting-

4   10 Anne c. 6, 'An Act for preserving the Protestant Religion by better securing the Church of England as by Law established' (1711); 13 Anne c. 7, 'An Act to prevent the Growth of Schism and for the further Security of the Churches of England and Ireland as by law established' (1714), *Statutes of the Realm*, 9: 551–3, 915–17.

house at Newcastle-under-Lyme. Mobs plundered and burnt meeting-houses in London, Bristol and the Midlands following Sacheverell's acquittal for sedition in 1710. Further riots against dissenters followed the accession of George I and the Jacobite rebellion in 1715. Most accounts, however, concentrate on these major outrages which took place largely in London and the West Midlands.[5] Certainly these areas experienced the full destructive force of the mobs, but if the wider context of the riots is examined, then it is clear that disturbances against dissenters were to be found in many places outside these areas. Only the determined efforts of a number of gentlemen in York opposing the mob frustrated attempts to destroy the Presbyterian meeting in St Saviourgate in June 1715, but because they were successful the only account of the disturbance, or of its seriousness, is in a private letter.[6] Edward Elwall led a small party who successfully fought-off the high-church mob which was attempting to pull-down the Presbyterian meeting-house in Wolverhampton. Intimidation did not end with the rioting. Because of his vigorous public defence of the Hanoverian accession, Elwall was particularly odious to the mob. 'They often, yea, very often, threatened to kill me', and on one occasion as he was riding down Bilston Street someone fired at him

---

5   G. Holmes, 'The Sacheverell Riots: The Crowd and the Church in Early Eighteenth-Century London', *P&P*, no. 52 (1976), 61–4; idem, *The Trial of Doctor Sacheverell* (London, 1973); A. P. F. Sell, 'The Walsall Riots, The Rooker Family, and Eighteenth-Century Dissent' *Transactions of the South Staffordshire Archaeological and Historical Society*, 25 (1983–4), 50–3; J. H. Y. Briggs, 'The Burning of the Meeting House, July 1715: Dissent and Faction in Late Stuart Newcastle', *North Staffordshire Journal of Field Studies*, 14 (1974), 70–1; N. Rogers, 'Riot and Popular Jacobitism in Early Hanoverian England', in E. Cruickshanks (ed.), *Ideology and Conspiracy: Aspects of Jacobitism, 1689–1759*, (Edinburgh, 1982), 70–88; P. K. Monod, *Jacobitism and the English People, 1688–1788* (Cambridge, 1989); D. L. Wykes, 'Old Meeting and James II's Religious Indulgence of 1687: The building of the first nonconformist meeting-house in Birmingham', *Midland History*, 16 (1991), 86–102, J. D. Oates, 'Jacobitism and popular disturbances in northern England, 1714–1719', 41 (2004), 113, 115–16, 128.

6   Leeds RO, Sheepscar, Vyner Collection, VR 6006 (13193), Mary Robinson to her son Metcalf Robinson, 9 Jun. [1715]. Cf. VR 6006 (13229), Mary Robinson to her fourth son, Thomas, at Trinity College, Cambridge, 9 Jun. [1715].

from a window, 'whether with a Ball or not, I can't say'. On another occasion about 'three-score of 'em' threatened his house, and 'continued roaring, *Down with the House*, a long time', eventually, 'by the Intreaties of some Neighbours, and throwing some Money to 'em out at the Windows, they march'd away to drink the Money', but before they went 'some of 'em to spite me and my Wife', knelt at his doorstep and drank the Pretender's health.[7] The Presbyterian minister in Crediton, Devon, published the sermon he had delivered on 5 November 1714, a major red-letter day in the dissenting calendar, 'when a Riot happen'd there in the Evening', to clear himself from misrepresentation. He was, however, sufficiently intimidated to refuse to comment directly on the riot for fear of antagonising his enemies.[8] There were also cruder, individual acts of arson against meetinghouses. An attempt was made to burn down Matthew Henry's meeting-place in Chester in October 1692:

> Four Pew doors, two on one side the Ile and two on t'other (one of them my wives seat) were thrown open to meet, and the fire kindled under them, it had gone no further than the burning of those doors when they discover'd it, but the light and roring of it was more terrible than one could imagin.
>
> Had it been undiscover'd one half hour (and who could have thought that it should have been so discover'd in the dead of the night) in all probability it would have been too strong to bee master'd.

7   E. Elwall, *A declaration against George, King of Great Britain and Ireland, and all his nobles and senators, Lewis King of France, and Philip King of Spain; against Charles Emperor of Germany and Mahmut Emperor of Turkey; and all other kings and states whatsoever under Heaven* (1732), 46; idem, *The supernatural incarnation of Jesus Christ proved to be false; having no foundation in the prophet, [...] And that our Lord Jesus Christ was the real son of Joseph and Mary* (1742), 28–9.

8   Josiah Eveleigh, *The Dissenters Joy in the Preservation of the Church of England. A Sermon, Preach'd in Crediton in Devon, From Psalm 122, 8. 9. On Nov. 5. 1714. when a Riot happen'd there in the Evening; and now publish'd upon Occasion of a late Trial of the said Riot, &c. With a Preface, containing an Argument against the Divine Right of an Uninterrupted Lineal Succession* (Exeter, n.d.), Preface (unpaginated). The Fifth of November marked both the Gunpowder Plot and William of Orange's successful landing at Torbay in 1688; both were seen as remarkable providential escapes from the threat of popish despotism.

Richard Lee, 'tho' an enemy to the Chapel', was very helpful in quenching the fire, because his own hay-loft adjoined it.[9] In September 1699, there was an arson attack on the Presbyterian meeting-house in Brentford. The fire was not discovered before it had done about £50 of damage. An earlier attack the previous February had caused near £30 of damage. It was reported that the two attacks had 'both sufficiently confirmed the Threats that were given out, when it was building, *viz. That it should certainly be burnt down in a short time*'.[10]

In addition to major acts of mob violence, many dissenters experienced verbal abuse and even physical intimidation in their everyday lives. Henry Newcome, the first minister of the wealthy Presbyterian Meeting at Cross Street, Manchester, in May 1690 met a poor miller at Knotmill, as he was coming home. He 'cursed me, and bade the devil go with all Presbyterians', though it was perhaps with some satisfaction Newcome noted that as the miller came into town, he was 'strucken off his horse and almost killed'. Earlier, in January, he had been 'much disturbed at the rabble throwing snowballs'.[11] In Chester Matthew Henry was told that Alderman Peter Bennet, keeping company in a tavern, 'rail'd bitterly at me, and swore by his maker three times if the Queen would give him leave he would cut my throat & the throats of my Congregation'.[12] Elections were times of particular risk for dissenters, not only during the poll, but because of the consequences arising from the result itself. During the poll for the parliamentary election at Chester in October 1710, Matthew Henry found it impossible to venture out to attend the funeral of one of his members: 'I durst not go to the fun[eral] nor preach the fun[eral] serm[on] to night as was intended'. With reports of a comprehensive Tory victory, he wrote 'Things look very threatening Lord fit us for suffering'. Attacks on dissenters were only too frequent during electioneering in the slogans and symbols used. During the Chester

9   Bod. Lib., MS Eng. Lett. e.29, fo. 103r, M[atthew] H[enry, Chester], to Philip Henry, Broad Oak, 21 Oct 1692.
10   *Flying Post*, 5–7 Sept 1699.
11   R. Parkinson (ed.), *The Autobiography of Henry Newcome, M.A.* (Chetham Society 27, 1852), 2: 271 (19 Jan 1689/90; 1 May 1690).
12   Bod. Lib., MS Eng. Misc. e. 330, Diary of Matthew Henry, 1 Jan 1704/5–31 Dec. 1713, fo. 33r (7 Feb 1706/7).

election it was reported that the cry of the mob was 'No more Rump-Parliaments', and 'Up with the Tackers, and Down with the Presby-terians and Tub-Preachers'. To ridicule the 'Anti-Loyal Churchmen', the populace had been provided with tubs of all sizes 'which they beat about the Streets'. Matthew Henry recorded that the losing candidates were rudely insulted at Northwich 'by one that mimick'd a preacher in a Tub, 'tis Strange how the clergy can be pleas'd with making a mock at preaching'.[13]

On the other hand, dissenters who were unwise enough to slander the Church of England found themselves in serious trouble. John Sparry, the Presbyterian minister at Burton on Trent, was convicted at the Assizes in 1710 for 'profane and impious words' made at a funeral against the Book of Common Prayer. He was alleged to have told his audience that 'there is no more Sense in it than in a Dog, and it is sinful'.[14] The following year another Presbyterian minister admitted at the Quarter Sessions in Ormskirk that he had written and published a book maintaining 'the practices of the Church of England were the practices of the Devill'. He was fined £200 and ordered to stand in the pillory for his scandalous libel.[15] Joseph Hussey, the Congregational minister at Cambridge, was also tried at the Assizes for comments about the Common Prayer Book, but under more favourable political circumstances in 1699 he was acquitted.[16]

In addition to the abuse of the street or the alehouse, dissenters were subject to an almost continuous barrage of high-flying sentiment from the pulpit and the press. John Hartley, the Presbyterian minister at Ashby-de-la-Zouch, complained that

> the Non-Conforming Ministers are, both from Press and Pulpit throughout the Land, so bitterly censur'd and revil'd, as Usurpers upon the Priesthood; [...]

---

13 Bod. Lib., MS Eng. Misc. e. 330, fos 88v, 89r (19, 21, 26 Oct., 2 Nov. 1710); *Post Boy*, 2–4 Nov 1710.

14 *Post Boy*, 23–6 Sept 1710; Bod. Lib., MS Eng. Misc. e. 330, fos 52r, 84r (16 June 1708, 5 June 1710).

15 BL, Stowe MS 750, fo. 33r, London Newsletter to the Mayor of Newcastle upon Tyne, 26 Jul 1711.

16 A. G. Matthews, *Diary of a Cambridge Minister* [Joseph Hussey] (Cambridge, 1937), 6.

> And challeng'd from Time to Time to shew their Commission, and prove their
> Authority for what they do.

The younger High Church clergy

> if almost any of them preach in a strange Place, (especially where there is a
> Dissenting Congregation) let the Subject be what it will, its Odds, they shall
> hale [haul] in by Head and Shoulders the Controversy about Orders, and take a
> Run at the Dissenting Teachers'.[17]

High Churchmen, Hartley maintained, sought to prove the Presbyterian ordination to be invalid, that they were no ministers, but 'most
bold Intruders upon the Sacred Function', who 'presume to do the
Work of the Priesthood, without being called or sent of God, and so
seduce and destroy the Souls of Men'.[18] Higgins Harris, the High
Church curate of St Peter's Derby, answering the accusation that we
'make our Pulpits ring with Hell and Damnation against the
Dissenters. That we tell the People [...] That they are no Christians,
and ought not to have Christian Burial', replied, 'To all of which I
readily plead Guilty'.

> For don't they causelessly and without Reason separate themselves from the
> Communion of our Established Church? Don't they withdraw their Allegiance
> from their Spiritual Governours [...] And are not they therefore Directly guilty
> of that Heinous Sin of Schism?[19]

---

17   [Hartley], *Vindication*, 3 (iii).
18   Ibid. iv.
19   Higgins Harris, *Un-Episcopal Ordination and Baptism Null and Void. Together
     With the Reasonableness and Necessity of the Clergy's refusing Burial, and
     denying the Eucharist to un-episcopally baptiz'd persons, Adult Dissenters.
     Prov'd from the Articles, Canons, and Rubricks of the Church of England.
     Being a Defence of a Letter to the Reverend Mr Cantrell, against the Remarks
     made upon it in a Late Book, Entitul'd, The Validity of Baptism administred by
     Dissenting Ministers, and the unreasonableness of refusing Burial to Children
     so Baptiz'd, farther argued from the Judgment and Practice of the Church of
     England. By Ferdinando Shaw, M.A. (as he stiles himself) a Dissenting Teacher
     in Derby* (Nottingham: printed by William Ayscough and sold by J. Hodges in
     Derby, 1714), 36.

Presbyterians were charged with keeping up a needless separation, thus destroying the union of the Church. In the words of Lord Weymouth, they disturbed the peace of the nation 'meerly for humour'.[20]

Individual dissenters were badgered to conform, and threatened with the consequences if they failed. Mrs Wittar, a member of Matthew Henry's congregation in Chester, during her final illness was visited by her local Anglican curate, who pressed her to take communion with the Church of England and so conform. 'She told him she resolved to adhere to the Diss[ente]rs if she receav'd, yet he prest her to it', telling her that 'she might dy in extremity'. As Matthew Henry recorded, after visiting her subsequently, 'his pressingness much disturb'd her'. She died a few days later.[21] Edward Wells, Rector of Cottesbach in Leicestershire, drew up a letter to send to those of his parish who 'are so Unhappy as to be Seduced from the Communion of our Church', trying to convince them of 'the Great Sin they lie under by such a Separation, and of the Weakness and Insufficiency of the Arguments made use of to Justifie their Practice'.[22] From the mid-1690s, the Society of Friends also had to endure a sustained attack on their teaching led by two apostates, George Keith and Francis Bugg, and the non-juror Charles Leslie.[23] In 1699, Bugg organised a major anti-Quaker campaign against Friends in Norfolk and Suffolk, with a petition to Parliament signed by 500 laymen and clergy complaining of the growth of Quakerism in those parts. In Derby Friends found themselves intimidated by Lady Shore

---

20   Bod. Lib. MS Ballard 10, fo. 65r, Lord Weymouth, London, to Arthur Charlett, Master of University College, Oxford, 18 Apr 1707.

21   Bod. Lib. MS Eng. Misc. e. 330, fo. 48r (4 Feb 1707/8).

22   [Edward Wells], *A letter from a minister of the Church of England to Mr. Peter Dowley, a dissenting teacher of the Presbyterian or else independent perswasion* (Oxford, fourth edn. 1706), 5.

23   R. Clark, '"The Gangreen of Quakerism": An Anti-Quaker Anglican Offensive in England after the Glorious Revolution', *Journal of Religious History*, 11 (1981), 404–29.

who threatened to petition Parliament about their meeting-house, though it was duly registered under the Toleration Act.[24]

It is clear that by Anne's reign, attacks on dissent from the pulpit were widespread, and to be found in most parts of the country. Almost any public occasion was used by the High Church clergy to condemn dissenters. John Potter, Vicar of Cloford in Somerset, in the Assizes Sermon preached at Taunton in March 1712, reminded his audience that the Act of Indulgence, as he termed it, was, in the words of the preamble to the Act itself, intended only to ease the scrupulous consciences of those who could not conform to the Establish Church for fear of sin.

> It is plain, I say, that They especially do take more Liberty than either the Law intends, or the Gospel allows, and use it for a Cloak (tho' a very Scandalous One, too thin as well as too short) to cover their shameful Schism and Hypocrisy.

He went on to castigate occasional conformists, 'who *can* communicate with us in the most Solemn Parts of our Worship, and yet, for the most Part, divide from us', but excuse themselves either 'by blaming us, as the Authors of the Separation Or by endeavouring to shelter themselves under the Pretence of Liberty indulg'd them by the Laws'. In common with all opponents of dissent he also denounced the nonconformist academies which trained dissenting ministers, 'where the most violent Doctrines against the Constitution are propagated'.[25]

The Toleration Act only gave ease from the recusancy laws to those who attended a registered meeting, but faced with reality the church authorities and the parish clergy gave up trying to enforce conformity. Nevertheless they bitterly resented the loss of the Anglican monopoly and the decline in their congregations, and blamed the growth of irreligion and atheism on the breach caused by the

---

24   See D. L. Wykes, 'The Norfolk Controversy: Quakers, Parliament and the Church of England in the 1690s', in Stephen Taylor and D. L. Wykes (eds), *Parliament and Dissent* (Edinburgh, 2005).

25   John Potter, *A Sermon Preach'd at the Assizes held at Taunton, March the 25th 1712. Before Mr Baron Bury, and Mr Justice Eyre* (London, 1712), 21–2, 23–5.

Toleration Act. John Potter in his Assizes sermon complained that the Act indulged 'the wanton Humour of Them, who are only troubled with itching Ears'. In November 1694, Philip Henry, father of Matthew, found himself forced to defend a member of his congregation from the Vicar of Marbury. 'As to his trotting hither to hear the Word of God, [...] I thought you had better understand the Terms of our present liberty, which require us, not to Shut our Doores against any': a somewhat disingenuous reply.[26] In the Archdeaconry of St Albans as early as 1689, William Jole, Vicar of Sarrat no longer presented those who seldom came to church, as 'they are excused by the late liberty granted and may goe whither they please, therefore here we must be silent'. By 1695 he was in despair, and told the Archdeacon, 'I sit still and let my neibours write here as they will concerning Parishioners. What if we should make our moane and say too many forsake the Church'.[27] Edward Bowerman, Vicar of Caddington, told his bishop that not one in a thousand understood the true meaning of schism, or would believe they were guilty of it:

> & they that continually stay at home, & never go to Church or meeting, do plead the Tolleration in their defence; & many have no other notion of the Indulgence, but that it is a libertie to do what they please, & go where they please, & stay at home when the please.[28]

It was a common complaint by parish clergy of the loss of parish discipline as a result of the destruction of the Church of England's religious monopoly, but attempts to enforce any sort of discipline risked creating nonconformists out of indifferent conformists. In 1699, the Bishop of London held a conference of his clergy in St Paul's to consider whether it was expedient in the current circumstances to

---

26 Bod. Lib., MS Eng. Lett e.29, fo. 113, Philip Henry, Broad Oak, to Mr David Jenks, minister at Marbury, 3 Nov 1694.

27 Hertfordshire RO, ASA 17/2, Archdeaconry of St Albans, Churchwardens' presentments, 1680–9, *s.v.* Sarrat (1689); ASA 17/3, *s.v.* Sarrat (1689), cf. Rickmansworth (1693), Bushey (1694). Cf. Worcestershire RO, St Helens, 807/2289/21 (ix).

28 Lambeth Palace Library, London, MS 933, Gibson Papers, vol. 5, no. 9, Edward Bowerman, Vicar of Caddington, to Thomas, Bishop of Lincoln, 5 Aug 1692.

adopt a unanimous resolution not to christen children at home in private. They were well aware that should they refuse, then the 'Fanatick Ministers would be called in to christen'.[29] Katherine Jackson told the Presbyterian minister of the Great Meeting congergation in Leicester, that she

> has heretofore partaked of this ordinance several times but Mr Dudley the Minister of her Parish would not admit her any more except she would promise to be confirmed by the Bishop, the next Opportunity, which she does not see any Rule for in Scriptures, & therefore desires to joyn with us.[30]

One of the most serious High Church attacks upon the dissenting ministry took place in Derby, where the town's clergy led by the Vicar of St Alkmund's, Henry Cantrell, refused to bury the children of dissenters. This represented a serious threat since it formed part of a wider attack by High Churchmen on the validity of the Presbyterian ordination. Cantrell was ordained at Lichfield in 1709, and after serving as curate of Brailsford near Ashbourne, was in March 1712 presented by the Corporation of Derby to the Vicarage of St Alkmund's, newly created from a perpetual curacy following its endowment by Samuel Goodwin, gentleman. Cantrell immediately attacked dissenters, preaching that 'Dissenting teachers have no authority to baptise, and consequently that children [...] sprinkled by 'em, ought to baptiz'd by an Episcopal minister'. In November 1712 he baptised Elizabeth and Honeylove, two of the daughters of John Key. At the time Elizabeth was about 3 years' old, but the father was so convinced by Cantrell's sermon that dissenting ministers had no authority to baptise, that he asked for the older daughter to be rebaptised.[31] Cantrell had earlier, whilst Curate of Brailsford, re-

---

29   Bod. Lib. MS Ballard 5, fo. 158r, Edmund Gibson, Lambeth Palace, to Arthur Charlett, University College, Oxford, 23 May 1699.

30   Leicestershire RO, Great Meeting Unitarian Chapel Records, Leicester, N/U/179/50, 'Declaration of Communicants', 1711–32/3, Katherine Jackson (29 Apr 1722) [contractions and abbreviations have been silently extended]. I am grateful to the Chairman and Vestry of the Great Meeting Unitarian Chapel for permission to use and quote from the volume.

31   Derbyshire RO, D916A/PI 1/1, St Alkmunds' Parish Register, Derby, 1538–1751, *s.v.* 5 Nov 1712.

baptised a 16-year-old boy, who had received 'only before, when an Infant, the Mock-Baptism of Presbyterians'.[32]

It was the decision of the High Church clergy in the town to enter into a resolution not to bury the children baptised by dissenting ministers, and to argue that 'no persons were Christians, but such who had received Baptism from Ministers episcopally ordain'd', thus striking at the roots of Presbyterian ordination, which provoked the major controversy. In the dispute that followed over 20 pamphlets were published locally.[33] In February 1712/3, Samuel Pegg of Normanton by Derby applied to Higgins Harris, curate both of St Peter's Derby and Normanton, to bury his child. Harris, at first agreed, but then the following day wrote to Pegg that he had forgotten that the child had not been properly baptised. He would therefore only agree to bury the child if Pegg would sign a declaration promising that he would never again allow any child of his 'to Receive the Mock Baptism of Dissenting Teachers or Other Lay-Persons'. Pegg was also to promise to ensure that every child of his already born not previously baptised according to the rites of the Church of England 'shall Receive Baptism from the Hands of a Regular Minister of the Establish'd Church of England'.[34] Pegg refused 'these unreasonable conditions', and so Harris would not agree to bury the child, and sent the Parish Clerk of St Peter's Derby, to prevent

> any Grave to be made in the Church or Church-Yard, and if any should happen to be made, to fill it up, and not suffer the Child to be Intern'd in either: And in his Master's Name to forbid any Clergy-Man from reading the Service of the Church over it.

32   Ferdinando Shaw, *The Validity of Baptism Administred by Dissenting Ministers, and the Unreasonableness of Refusing Burial to children so baptiz'd. To which is added, A Vindication of it, in Reply to the pretended Answers of a layman, and Mr. Cantrell, Vicar of St Alkmund's. With Some Remarks on a Letter to him by Mr Harris, Curate of St Peter's Church. Both Argued from the Judgment and Practice of the Church of England; and now published for the Conviction of Unprejudic'd Churchmen, and the Satisfaction of Protestant Dissenter* [...] *With a Preface By the Reverend Mr W. Tong, Mr B. Robinson, and Dr Oldfield.* (London, 1716), 83.

33   Ibid. 35.

34   Harris, *Un-Episcopal Ordination*, 25–6.

Pegg, who was at the time churchwarden, had a grave made in the chancel (which did not belong to the curate), and attending with his friends and neighbours, buried the child there himself, saying, 'the Lord gave, and the Lord hath taken away, blessed be the Name of the Lord; to which the Clerk said Amen'.[35]

It was the refusal of Cantrell to bury a child of Daniel Ward of Little Chester in February 1713/4, on the grounds that the child had not been baptised, which forced the Presbyterians to establish their own burial ground at their meeting in Friar Gate, Derby. Yet after the burial Cantrell still 'had the impudance to send for His "fees"' for the burial in his parish, 'which were not paid Him'.[36] Four years later, Cantrell demanded fees from John Hieron of Little Eaton, a chapelry of St Alkmund's Derby, for the churching of Hieron's wife and for registering the baptisms of their children. Hieron answered that he was willing to pay all the dues that Cantrell 'can lawfully demand Always & provided that he will enter or Register all the said children and the time of the Birth or christening of them in the usual Register book belonging to the said parish'. Cantrell replied that he was not bound to register the children in the parish register 'because they were not baptised by a lawful minister as the Rubrick before the office of baptism requires', though he still intended to claim the fees.[37] Cantrell was not alone in making such claims. Peter Walkden, nonconformist minister at Thornley near Chipping in Lancashire from 1711, paid the vicar 6*d*. for each child he baptised at his meeting, though the Bishop of Chester told Matthew Henry in April 1693 that in his opinion the clergy 'ought not to register the children we baptise, nor to demand

35   Shaw, *Validity*, 125.

36   PRO, RG4/5, 'A Register of children which I have baptiz'd since 16 Sept: 1698. F. Shaw', Register of Friar Gate, Derby, baptisms, 1698–1743, 79; Derbyshire RO, 1312D/A1, Account and Minute Book for Friar Gate Unitarian Chapel, Derby, 1697–1819, *s.v.* note on back cover of volume.

37   Derbyshire RO, D1293/PI/13, Little Eaton, Papers relating to a case between the Rev. Henry Cantrell and John Hieron, concerning the payment of fees for churching Hieron's wife and registering the baptisms of his children. Endorsed with legal opinion of J. Chauncey, 24 Mar 1717/8.

the fees'.[38] Although the controversy over the refusal to bury the children of dissenters was especially heated in Derby, Cantrell and Harris were not alone in their refusal. Cantrell himself claimed that neither the Rev. John Lord, Vicar of Ashby-de-la-Zouch from 1693 until his death in 1711, nor Mr Walters, late Vicar of Leek in Staffordshire, would read 'the Office over any, who had not been Baptised by an Episcopal Lawful Minister'.[39]

Dissenters, in particular dissenting ministers, even suffered indignities in death. Matthew Henry noted that when 'good Mr Bryan' minister at Newcastle-under-Lyme was buried at Stoke-on-Trent in September 1711, the curate that read over the Grave, 'a drunken sot', would not read any more than 'in sure and certain hope of a Resurrection – not, to eternal Life, and made several other alterations', because William Brian was a dissenting minister.[40] The *Observator* reported in 1707 that a curate at a church in Aldgate in London 'curtailed the office for the burial of the dead, leaving out the Words "Dear Brother, and the sure and certain Hopes of the Resurrection to eternal Life", when a dissenting Minister was bury'd in the churchyard'.[41] Before his death in August 1725, Isaac Gilling, minister of Newton Abbot, had asked to be buried in the church at Newton Abbot, but the parish being a peculiar, the ordinary, Sir William Courtenay, refused, saying 'they might bury him in one of the marshes'. He was therefore buried in his meeting-house.[42] James Pierce, whose reputation was blasted by the 1719 Exeter Controversy and the disclosure of his Arian principles, was buried in the churchyard of St Leonard's,

38 James Bromley, 'The rural life of a Lancashire minister 150 years ago', *Transactions of the Historic Society of Lancashire and Cheshire*, 32 (1880), 125; Bod. Lib. MS Eng. Lett. e.29, fo. 107r, Matthew Henry, Chester, to his father, Philip Henry, Broad Oak, 27 April 1693.

39 Henry Cantrell, *The invalidity of the lay-baptisms of dissenting teachers* (1714), 114.

40 Bod. Lib. MS Eng. Misc. e. 330, fo. 104r (12 Sept 1711).

41 *The Observator*, 4, No. 65, 11–15 Oct 1707.

42 'Memoirs of Himself, by Mr John Fox, of Plymouth: with Biographical Sketches of some of his Contemporaries; and some unpublished Letters from Archbishop Secker and Dr Samuel Chandler' *Monthly Repository*, 16 (1821), 328.

Exeter. Benjamin Avery prepared a long Latin inscription for Peirce's tombstone. The cutting of it was nearly finished when the rector, Richard Gay, intervened with a prohibition. Gay also objected to an alternative, 'Here lies the reverend, learned and pious Mr James Peirce': Peirce could not be reverend since he was not lawfully ordained, nor pious because he taught errors. The eventual inscription was 'Mr James Peirce's Tomb, 1726'. A marble tablet was erected to the memory of Philip Henry, the father of Matthew, in Whitchurch Parish Church where he was buried in 1696. In 1712, when the church was rebuilt, the opportunity was taken to remove his corpse to the churchyard and the monument to the porch.[43]

In addition to the individual acts of hostility and vindictiveness from local adversaries, a more concerted effort to suppress dissent using the penal laws not covered by the terms of the Toleration Act is evident. A number of dissenters who failed to register their buildings for worship under the Act were prosecuted during Anne's reign for holding illegal conventicles. The threat of prosecution has generally been disregarded by historians, presumably because it is considered to have been remote. Nevertheless, dissenters who failed to register their meeting-places, either on principle or by default, lost the protection of the Act and exposed themselves to the threat of prosecution from the laws against religious nonconformity, in particular the Conventicle Act. The antiquarian, Ralph Thoresby, registered his house in Leeds in July 1689 for worship. He endorsed the certificate with the words, 'This was to avoid danger from informers of private meetings for Repetition &c'. There are examples of individual dissenters being prosecuted for holding illegal conventicles, and of nonconformist preachers being prosecuted for failing to subscribe to the Thirty-Nine Articles or take the necessary oaths as required under the Toleration Act, particularly during the first few years after the passing of the Act, and again in Queen Anne's reign following a resurgence in the fortunes of the high-church party.[44] John Buckler was committed to

43   *DNB, s.v.* Philip Henry.
44   Yorkshire Archaeological Society, Leeds, DD241/5, Volume of miscellaneous
     manuscripts of Ralph Thoresby, fo. 111r; D. L. Wykes, 'Parliament, Friends
     and the Toleration Act', *JEH*, 45 (1994), 59–60.

Salisbury gaol in 1690 for preaching at the Presbyterian meeting in Warminster without making the necessary declarations. William Bray applied to register his house in Shiplake at the Oxfordshire Quarter Sessions in Michaelmas 1691, but he had already been presented 'for preaching at a Conventicle not being qualified'. In 1694 John Normanton, whom the Society of Friends in Southampton had disowned twelve months before, was presented for not attending church. The authorities had noted that Normanton was no longer attending a nonconformist place of worship, as a strict interpretation of the Toleration Act required if the recusancy laws were to be suspended. In Essex in 1690 a nonconformist minister, Mr Rogers, was prosecuted by the incumbent at Chelmsford 'for baptising a child in a private house', which had presumably not been registered under the Act. For some months after the passing of the Toleration Act, Philip Henry found himself unable to preach in public because there had been no quarter sessions held for Flintshire: and as 'the Act so positively requiring that the Oaths bee taken there, I am forced stil to remayn incapacitated, which I believe, some of my Observers are awareof [*sic*]'. He feared that any attempt to preach before he was qualified would result in prosecution. Indeed, a nonconformist minister was prosecuted for preaching in Essex in 1690 on the pretence that he had not taken the necessary oaths under the Toleration Act at the Quarter Sessions in that county.[45] Admittedly, dislike of subscription to the Articles of the Church of England, as required of ministers and preachers, led some at least to evade the requirement. Nevertheless, they ran the risk of prosecution. Edmund Calamy in confidence told John Fox, a ministerial student in Devon, that he himself had never

45   J. Murch, *A History of the Presbyterian and General Baptist Churches in the West of England; with Memoirs of some of their Pastors* (London, 1835), 87; Oxfordshire County RO, QSM/I/1/i, Quarter Sessions Minute Book, Easter 1688–Trinity 1693, 35; 'Calendar of the Sessions Books, 1689 to 1709', in W. J. Hardy (ed.), *Middlesex County Records* (1905) 100; *Southampton Friends to 1700* (Southampton, 1980) 12–13; C. Blackmore, Worcester, to Robert Harley, 9 May 1690, in HMC, *Fourteenth Report, Appendix, Part II. The Manuscripts of His Grace the Duke of Portland preserved at Welbeck*, 3: 447; Bod. Lib. MS Eng. Lett e.29, fo. 96r, [Philip Henry, Broad Oak] to [Mr Hunt], no date, but after May 1689.

subscribed, and that if Fox 'kept himself to himself' the omission would never be suspected. But Fox was aware of the danger. 'My father', who was anxious for him to become a minister, 'was overjoyed at it, and did not seem to value any risque of a prosecution, and some there certainly was'.[46]

There are rather more examples of prosecutions dating from Queen Anne's reign, when the political reaction against dissenters had intensified significantly. In 1705 the Presbyterian Fund Board sought a meeting with the Managers of the Congregational Fund to discuss 'the affair of Southwell & Yorkshire that have been both prosecuted on account of their Meetings'. Jeremiah Lepper, a labourer from Bicester, was presented at the Michaelmas Sessions for Oxfordshire in 1708, 'for having suffered an illegal conventicle to be held in his house'. He was convicted at the following Epiphany sessions and fined £20. The preacher was William Giles of Winslow in Buckinghamshire, almost certainly a member of Ketch's Baptist meeting. In July 1710, the Grand Jury of Caernarvonshire presented 17 individuals for being at and hearing of 'divine worship in a dissenting meeting at the dwelling house of William Lloyd of Caernarvon [...] without being qualified according to law [...] and Contrary to the Laws and statu[te]s in that case made and provided'.[47] A number of Quakers were also prosecuted under the Conventicle Act for holding meetings in an unregistered place. Nevertheless, they had either tried to register the places they were using for worship, or in the case of a burial or an occasional service were ignorant of the need to do so.[48]

46   'Memoirs [...] John Fox, of Plymouth', 135.
47   Dr Williams's Library, London, Minutes of the Presbyterian Fund Board, 5 Feb 1694/5–4 June 1722, 136 (5 Mar 1704/5); Oxfordshire County RO, QSR, Quarter Sessions Rolls, Michelmas 1708 & Epiphany 1709, s.v. Jeremiah Lepper jun. of Bicester and William Giles of Winslow, Buckinghamshire; R. Owen, 'Some Details about the Independents in Caernarvonshire', Transactions of Caernarvonshire Historical Society, 6 (1945), 44. Cf Wiltshire RO, D1/54/14, Bishop of Salisbury's Peculiar, Churchwardens' Presentments, 1692–9: Jonathan Rashly for keeping a conventicle at Avebury 'unlicensed', 1698.
48   Wykes, 'Parliament', 59–60.

Conclusions

Although the Toleration Act helped to define modern dissent, with the final loss of any realistic hope of moderate dissenters being accommodated within the Church of England, historians recognise the limited nature of the Act and how far its terms fell short of a toleration in modern terms. Historians have also given increasing weight to the importance of religious issues in the period after the Glorious Revolution. It is clear that dissent and relations with dissent were often a defining factor in the politics of the period. Even if the High Church cry of the 'Church in danger' during Anne's reign can be dismissed, there is little doubt of the concern of the Church and it supporters at the growth and development of dissent and the loss of Anglican authority or of the bitterness and fury it provoked. What has been less readily appreciated is the depth and extent of the hostility towards dissenters. It is clear that in addition to the major acts of mob violence, and the attempts in Parliament to pass legislation to suppress dissent, many dissenters experienced verbal abuse and even physical intimidation in their everyday lives. Matthew Henry was one of the most prominent and widely respected dissenting ministers of his generation, whose funeral in Trinity Church, Chester, was attended by eight of the City's clergy, who had a major congregation in a part of the country where support for Presbyterianism was strong. Yet he was subjected to an extraordinary amount of abuse and even threats of violence. How much worse the experience for dissenters in a rural parish, or parts of the country where dissent had comparatively little support? We are aware in the modern world of the destructive nature of racism and religious intolerance on its victims. Historians perhaps need to recognise the consequences for dissent in the period following the Toleration Act of the abuse, bigotry and intolerance dissenters faced.

Index

STUDIES IN THE HISTORY OF RELIGIOUS AND POLITICAL PLURALISM
Edited by Richard Bonney

This series addresses a new need. The constitution of many contemporary communities is radically diverse, and the need is to think anew about them. Through a mixture of edited collections and single-authored volumes, the series aims both to examine how radical diversity has arisen in the religious and political constitution of society and to analyse the implications for the future so as to help ensure the harmonious relations between communities and the best practice of government. Studies in the History of Religious and Political Pluralism will evaluate new trends and theories and make available the findings of empirical research which demonstrates the nature of the pluralistic world in which we live.

The series editor, Professor Richard Bonney, is Emeritus Professor at the University of Leicester and Chairman of the Europe-Islamic World Organization.